H DAKOTA

MINNESOTA

INS

DAKOTA

MICH.

CENTRAL

WISCONSIN

ACK HILLS

MICHIGAN

PRAIRIE

IOWA

SKA

LOWLANDS

ILLINOIS

INDIANA   OHIO

GREAT LAKES

MISSOURI

PLAINS

KANSAS

KENTUCKY

OZARK

AHOMA

ARKANSAS

TENNESSEE

AS

PLATEAU

EAT PLAINS

GEORGI

MISSISSIPPI   ALABAMA

GULF |PLAINS

LOUISIANA

SOUTHERN

LOWLANDS

TALES OF THE FRONTIER

Also by Everett Dick

THE SOD-HOUSE FRONTIER, 1854–1890
VANGUARDS OF THE FRONTIER
THE DIXIE FRONTIER
LIFE IN THE WEST

Tales of the Frontier

From Lewis and Clark to the Last Roundup

Selected and Retold

by Everett Dick

UNIVERSITY OF NEBRASKA PRESS · LINCOLN

"Rollingstone" and "Fasten Down the Safety Valve" are condensed from *A-Rafting on the Mississip'* by Charles Edward Russell, by permission of Appleton-Century. Copyright 1928 by Charles Edward Russell. Story #1 in "The Long Drive" is condensed from *A Vaquero of the Brush Country* by J. Frank Dobie, by permission of Little, Brown & Co. Copyright 1929 by J. Frank Dobie. "The Iron Horse to the Rescue" is reprinted with permission of the publisher from *Holy Old Mackinaw* by Stewart Holbrook. Copyright 1938, 1956 by The Macmillan Company.

Publishers on the Plains

UNP

Manufactured in the United States of America

To Lorle

Acknowledgments

THE AUTHOR AND THE UNIVERSITY OF NEBRASKA PRESS wish to thank the following institutions and their staffs for their generous help during the preparation of this book: Bancroft Library, University of California at Berkeley; Bennett Martin Public Library, Lincoln, Nebraska; Indiana State Library, Indianapolis; Kansas State Historical Society, Topeka; Minnesota Historical Society, Minneapolis; Nebraska State Historical Society, Lincoln; Union College Library, Lincoln; and the University of Nebraska Libraries.

We are grateful to R. R. Donnelley and Company for permission to condense and quote from primary materials appearing in the Lakeside Classics, edited by Milo M. Quaife. Thanks also are due the authors and editors of the following books published by the University of Nebraska Press from which material has been drawn for the commentary and some of the tales: *History of Steamboating on the Upper Missouri* by William E. Lass; *History of Nebraska* by James C. Olson; *History of South Dakota* by Herbert E. Schell; *Mollie: The Journal of Mollie Dorsey Sanford in Nebraska and Colorado Territories, 1857–1866,* edited by Donald F. Danker; *South Pass, 1868: James Chisholm's Journal of the Wyoming Gold Rush,* edited by Lola M. Homsher; *Man of the Plains: Recollections of Luther North, 1856–1882,* edited by Donald F. Danker; *The Family Band: From the Missouri to the Black Hills, 1881–1900* by Laura Bower Van Nuys; *Westward the Briton* by Robert G. Athearn; *The Hunting of the Buffalo* by E. Douglas Branch, with an introduction by J. Frank Dobie; *The Look of the West, 1860* by Sir Richard Burton, with a foreword by Robert G. Athearn; *Them Was the Days* by Martha Ferguson McKeown; *The Story of the Western Railroads: From 1852 to the Reign of the Giants* by Robert Edgar Riegel; *Our Landed Heritage: The Public Domain, 1776–1936* by Roy M. Robbins; *Joe Meek: The Merry Mountain Man* and *The Missouri* by Stanley Vestal; and *The Indian War of 1864* by Eugene F. Ware, with an introduction and notes by Clyde C. Walton.

Foreword

DURING THE past thirty years while gathering data for my books on the social history of the frontier, I have now and then found a story which appealed to me and have jotted down the source for future reference, thinking that it was good enough to share with others. When the idea of issuing these stories in book form took root and I saw that certain activities on the frontier were unrepresented, I began to hunt for specific stories which would help to round out the picture of conditions on the frontier during the century covered.

Naturally a story is often unique or exceptional rather than typical; that is what makes it worth the telling. The reader then should not necessarily think of the happenings recounted here as routine. To do so would be to gain a misconception of typical daily frontier life. The stories are specimens of what could and did happen on occasion as a result of conditions which normally obtain on the frontier.

Some of the stories are condensations of much longer accounts. Some are told practically in the words of the source. In no case has any fictional material been added or revision made which has changed the spirit contrary to the facts. The names used are those of the actual persons.

The stories are all true or at least have been told as true. No attempt has been made to go behind the scenes to discover whether the narrator was telling the truth, but obviously erroneous details have been brought into accord with historical fact. Some of these tales are old classics. Some are comparatively unknown, having been gleaned from original sources such as old journals or reminiscences written by historically obscure persons.

As far as possible almost every type of occupation or activity on the frontier is represented. These stories have been tried out on my students for the past three decades in an attempt to make the frontier live in the classroom. It is my hope that this volume may not only bring enjoyment to the reader but may at the same time help him to better appreciate our American heritage.

EVERETT DICK

Contents

III. / OVERLAND TRAILS

IV. / THE TRANS-MISSOURI FRONTIER

V. / THE LAST FRONTIERS

List of Maps

I. Opening Up the Way West

See the maps on pages 189, 190, 191, and 192.

WHILE IT IS POSSIBLE to show on a map the American frontier at various stages of its advance, the frontier should not be thought of as a fixed line, like the boundary of a country. Exploration and settlement are not static processes, and the frontier was constantly pushing into the interior. On the trans-Mississippi frontier at the beginning of the nineteenth century, the rivers were the highways admitting the advance forces of civilization—explorers, trappers, hunters, fur traders, the military, missionaries—and it was along the rivers that settlement began.

The Schoolmaster Sees the Devil

DANIEL BOONE is remembered primarily for his feats as a hunter and explorer in Kentucky and Virginia, but he spent the last twenty-five years of his life on the trans-Mississippi frontier. In the year 1795, when he was living at Point Pleasant in what is now West Virginia, he had the bad luck to lose his land because he had failed to make a proper entry of his claims. Just at this time he had word from a son, also named Daniel, of the beauty and richness of the land out west around St. Louis. When he heard that officials of the territory would be honored to have him make his home there, that was enough for the old pioneer. He loaded his family and a few belongings on pack horses, and set out on the long journey across the present states of Ohio, Indiana, and Illinois. Although he was then sixty-one years old, Daniel Boone led the way on foot, his rifle on his shoulder.

The land he picked for his new home was on the north bank of the Missouri River, about twenty miles from St. Louis, near present-day St. Charles, Missouri. A spring of sweet water was the inducement that led Boone to settle in this particular location. Pioneers valued such a spring more than the land surrounding it, not only for its supply of pure, icy water but because it was a meeting place for game—deer, elk, antelope, bear, and buffalo. Boone built his cabin about fifty feet to the east of this spring. It was said that he could (and did) take his gun and sit at the door and lay in a winter's supply of meat without leaving his chair.

During his first decade in Missouri, however, old Daniel was by no means chairbound. He still enjoyed hunting and tramping in the woods and usually went out in the company of one of his relatives, a hunter and trapper named Jim Davis. Boone and Davis frequently made trips of more than a hundred and fifty

3

miles out west to Howard County, where there were salt licks.
After the salt had been boiled down, they would fetch it home to
supply the Boone community. But as the seasons rolled by and
Boone approached his eightieth year, he felt less inclined to
endure the hardships of a winter hunt. Like an old hunting dog,
he stayed by the fireplace during the cold months, and Davis
went out alone on his treks to the western forests. He would often
be away for several months on trapping expeditions.

The western part of Missouri was occupied at this time by the
Oto Indians, who, according to tradition, originally were part of
the Winnebago tribe. Along with the bands later known to the
white man as the Iowa and the Missouri, they had separated from
the mother tribe at Green Bay, Wisconsin, and migrated to the
southwest in search of buffalo. Their permanent villages, located
in the country south of the Platte, consisted of large earthern
lodges, but they lived in skin tipis while traveling and on hunts.
Though not especially savage or warlike, the Oto resented the
white man's encroachment on their hunting grounds, and could
make it very uncomfortable for any trespasser unlucky enough
to fall into their hands.

On a hunting trip in 1813, Jim Davis found this out the hard
way. He was captured by a party of Oto who expressed their
objection to his presence by relieving him of his collection of
pelts, tinderbox, gun and ammunition, and every stitch of his
clothes. In that bitter weather, with the nearest settlement more
than a hundred miles away, it seemed obvious to them that he
would freeze to death, and taking his clothes not only appealed
to the Oto sense of humor but also would expedite the freezing
process. As a final gesture of disdain and mockery, one of the
braves thrust into Davis's hands an old British musket, loaded
with a single charge. Then the party went its way, leaving him to
his fate.

Poor Jim cut a sorry spectacle, standing there in the blowing
snow, naked as a jaybird, clutching his rusty musket, the mocking
laughter of the Indians echoing in his ears. But he'd be hanged if
he was going to turn into an icicle just to oblige some pesky redskins. He had to admit it was a mite drafty there in the woods,

but he still had a gun and one shot, and if he could just survive till morning, he reckoned he might make out somehow.

The first order of business was to look for a shelter where he could spend the night. There was a stream nearby, and while exploring under the shelving rocks along its banks, he spotted a hibernating bear holed up for the winter. Here was his opportunity! Not giving himself time to think of the consequences should he miss or if the gun should flash in the pan, he crawled up until the old smoothbore was almost against the bear's head. Then he fired. The bear tumbled over, and Jim's outfit was now augmented by one dead bear.

To the hunter, the bear represented a potential supply of food and clothing. The problem was how to get at it. Removing his gun flint, Jim used it for a crude knife to take the hide off the animal, splitting down the inside of the hind legs and pulling the pelt over the bear's body as he skinned. Once the hide was free, he drew the furry covering over his own body, inserting his arms where the bear's front legs had been, and forcing the head well down over his own head and face. Next he contrived to rig moccasins from the bear's hind feet. Then, warm and snug at last, he lay down beside the former occupant of the hide and had a good night's sleep.

As soon as it was light, Jim cut off as many bear steaks as he would need on the homeward journey, and started off. For three days he struggled doggedly eastward through the snowy wilderness. Without steel and tinderbox he could not make a fire, but the bear skin kept the cold out; and the meat, though eaten raw, sustained him. On the evening of the third day he arrived at the outskirts of the settlement, and turned in at the first house he came to, the home of Jonathan Bryan.

Bryan's house was actually two cabins connected by a breezeway. In one of the cabins there lived a boarder, an elderly itinerant Scotchman who, in the absence of a regular school, had established an "academy" and assumed the title of professor. When Jim trudged wearily up the pathway it was not yet candlelighting time, and the old gentleman was sitting alone half-dozing by the fire.

The latchstring was always out on the frontier. Not thinking of the sensation his appearance might create, Jim did not stand on ceremony; he pushed the door open and started in. Hearing the door creak, the old professor came to with a start. There was enough light so that he could plainly see the outline of an animal-like figure in the open doorway. For a moment he just sat there, possibly hoping that this evil apparition was a bad dream. But when it started toward him, the man of learning shot to his feet and tore out of the room crying "The Devil has come! The Devil has come!" at the top of his voice.

In the passageway between the cabins he collided with Jonathan Bryan, who went in to confront the monster and recognized him as Davis. After Bryan succeeded in calming the old Scotchman, the two of them went to the aid of their guest. During the three-day trek the bear skin had begun to dry up and shrink, shaping itself to Davis's body. It took considerable effort on the part of both men to extract the valiant hunter from his furry suit and restore him to human shape.

Jim Davis's remarkable adventure and his ingenious method of saving his life—to say nothing of the scare he had given the schoolmaster—made him forever famous in that part of Missouri. His exploit was not unworthy of Daniel Boone himself, and we can be sure that during the seven remaining years of his life Boone heard and told this unique "bear story" on many and many an occasion.

In mid-May of 1804 forty-five men left St. Louis on the most important expedition in the history of the trans-Mississippi frontier. The year before, with a stroke of the pen, President Thomas Jefferson had doubled the area of the United States: the Louisiana Purchase added to the nation some 820,000 square miles of wilderness lying between the Mississippi and the Rocky Mountains. In January Congress had voted funds for a western expedition, and the President had named as its leader a twenty-nine-year-old Virginian, Captain Meriwether Lewis, who had chosen as his co-captain a red-headed artillery officer, Lieutenant William Clark. Their instructions were "to explore the Missouri River, and such principal streams on it, as, by its course and communication with the waters of the Pacific Ocean . . . may offer the most direct and practicable water-communication across the continent, for the purposes of commerce." They were also to make geographic and scientific observations; to ascertain the routes of Canadian traders in their traffic with the Indians; to determine the feasibility of collecting furs at the source of the Missouri and transporting them downstream; and to cultivate friendship and trade with the natives.

The over-all design of the Lewis and Clark expedition has been aptly summed up by Bernard De Voto: "It was to fill in a space in the map of the world that had been blank white paper up to now, and to add to the heritage of the Republic and of mankind as much knowledge as might prove possible."

Northwest to Empire

"I Set out at four o'clock P.M., in the presence of many of the neighboring inhabitants, and proceeded on under a jentle brease up the Missouri. . . ." So in part reads the first entry in a classic American document, the *Journals of the Lewis and Clark Expedition.** Dated Monday, May 14, 1804, this entry was written by Clark, for Captain Lewis was detained in St. Louis by business.

*Some of the original spelling and capitalization has been retained in the quotations from the *Journals,* but they are not exact transcriptions.

Traveling overland, Lewis caught up with the expedition at St. Charles, Missouri—Daniel Boone's settlement—and on May 21, the three boats, now with their full complement of forty-five men, put out from St. Charles "at half passed three o'clock under three Cheers from the gentlemen on the bank."

River men had assured Lewis and Clark that early summer was a beautiful time for traveling on the Missouri, but almost at once they ran into "a hard wind from the W.S.W. accompanied with a hard rain, which lasted with Short intervales all night"— and, indeed, for most of the five weeks it took them to reach the mouth of the Kansas, where the great westering river changes its direction and swings northward. Time and again, hot, windless days were punctuated by violent rainstorms which whipped the usually placid river into foamy waves; and the men early made the acquaintance of the navigational hazards peculiar to the Missouri—snags, mats of driftwood, sandbars, treacherous, powerful currents—to say nothing of such minor nuisances as snakes and "noumerous & bad Ticks & Mosquiturs."

The flagship of the little flotilla was a keelboat, fifty-five feet long, drawing three feet of water, carrying one large squaresail and twenty-two oars. The other two boats—one painted white, the other red—were pirogues of six and seven oars respectively. They were about twice the length and depth of ordinary canoes, and were equipped with sails. Food, arms, ammunition, extra clothing, scientific instruments, and presents for the Indians made up the cargo. Except when they were favored with wind for sailing, it was the brute strength of the crews that kept the boats moving —men sweating at the oars and push poles, men floundering in the riverbank mud as they hauled at the tow ropes, men chest-deep in water struggling to shove a boat off a sandbar.

Both Lewis and Clark were experienced river men, but Clark was the more seasoned and skilled of the two, and it was usually he who served as pilot. Although Lewis was actually in command of the expedition and outranked Clark, he regarded him as a co-leader and always referred to him in speech and correspondence as "Captain Clark." The two men made an admirably balanced team—Lewis introspective, reserved, meditative, with a cultivated and inquiring mind; Clark outgoing, outspoken, genial, a natural-born frontiersman, with an intuitive understanding of the Indian mentality.

The rank and file of the "corps of discoverie" consisted of fourteen volunteers from the United States Army, three of whom were appointed to serve as sergeants; nine young men from Kentucky; two French watermen; another Frenchman, George Drewyer (Drouillard), engaged to serve as interpreter and hunter; and York, Clark's Negro servant. There were, in addition, seven soldiers and nine watermen who were to accompany the expedition as far as the Mandan villages (near present-day Bismarck, North Dakota) where Lewis and Clark expected to winter. Completing the roster were two horses to be used in hunting, and Scammon, Lewis's big Newfoundland dog.

On July 21, six hundred-odd miles from St. Louis, the party passed "the equator of the Missouri"—the point at which the Platte discharges its flood into Old Muddy—and on the next day, having found "a good Situation" on the Missouri's west bank a few miles above the mouth of the Platte, "we Concluded to delay at this place a few days and Send for Some of the Chiefs of the Oto nation, to let them know of the Change of Government [i.e., that the United States now held sovereignty over the area through the Louisiana Purchase], the wishes of our government to Cultivate friendship with them, the Objects of our journey, and to present them with a flag and Some Small presents."

The parley—the first ever held between the United States government and Indians west of the Missouri—took place on August 3 on a beautiful wooded bluff looking out over open prairie on the west and skirted on the east by the Missouri. The chiefs were received under an awning contrived from the main sail; there was a parade, speeches (which included "advice to them and Directions how they were to conduct themselves"), presentation of medals and gifts (breech cloths, paint, a canister of gunpowder, a bottle of whiskey), speeches of acknowledgment by the Indians (they promised to "pursue the advice and Derections given them . . . wer happy to find that they had fathers which might be depended on &c."), and as a grand wind-up Captain

Lewis fired "the air gun a few Shots (which astonished those nativs)." The site of this parley was christened the Council Bluff —the present city of Council Bluffs is about twenty-five miles downstream, but on the opposite (Iowa) side of the river—and subsequently the name came to designate the whole region near the mouth of the Platte.

Before leaving St. Louis the captains had been carefully briefed on the relations of the upper Missouri Indians with the French and Spanish traders who had been operating on the river since the 1780's. They knew that while the Omaha, Oto, and Arikara levied tribute for the privilege of trading on the river, their demands were mere flea-bites compared to those of the Sioux—in particular, the Teton Sioux. Called the "pirates of the Missouri," the Tetons shared with the Cheyennes the distinction of being the boldest and most formidable warriors on the Northern Plains. Usually they refused passage to upriver trading parties, compelling them to dispose of their goods at ridiculously low prices which the Tetons themselves set; and if they did allow a party to go on, it was only after exacting ruinous tribute. Up until the end of August the expedition had been passing through a region whose tribes were held in close fealty by St. Louis trading interests. When they reached the mouth of the James River, which marked the beginning of Sioux country, they were entering into a British sphere of influence, and it was crucial to both the foreign and domestic policy of the United States that American sovereignty be firmly asserted.

After twice setting the prairie on fire to signal their approach, the expedition made camp near present-day Yankton, South Dakota. Here on August 30 Lewis and Clark held a parley with five chiefs and seventy warriors of the Yankton Sioux. This meeting passed off amicably enough, but the Yanktons were a comparatively peaceful branch of the tribe. The real test did not come until September 25, when the little party met with the dreaded Tetons at the mouth of the Bad River. The ensuing four-day parley was conducted in an atmosphere of such great tension that Captain Clark did not sleep throughout the whole time.

On the first day, after the chiefs had been invited aboard the keelboat and given "1/4 a glass of whiskey which they appeared to be verry fond of," Clark went ashore with them "with a view of reconsileing those men to us." As he landed, three of the war-riors seized the rope of his pirogue, and "the 2d chief was verry insolent both in words and gestures, declaring I should not go on, stating he had not received presents sufficient from us. His ges-tures were of Such a personal nature I felt My self Compeled to draw my Sword"—at the same time signaling to the keelboat crew to prepare for action. "At this Motion Capt. Lewis ordered all under arms in the boat. Those with me also Showed a Disposition to defend themselves and me. The grand Chief then took hold of the rope & ordered the young Warriors away. I felt myself warm & Spoke in verry positive terms. Most of the Warriors ap-peared to have their Bows strung and took out their arrows from the quiver. As I [being surrounded] was not permitted to return, I sent all the men except 2 Interpreters back to the boat. The pirogue Soon returned with about 12 of our determined men ready for any event. This movement caused a number of the Indians to withdraw to a distance. . . . I offered my hand to the 1 and 2 Chiefs who refusd to receive it. I turned off & went with my men aboard the pirogue."

This episode set the pattern. Although the Indian band num-bered several hundred, whenever it came to a showdown it was the red man's nerve that failed. On the final day of the parley, as the boats were about to cast off, a number of Tetons grabbed hold of the moorings and "did not incline to let us go on. They sayed we might return back with what we had or remain with them, but we could not go up the Missouri any further. About 200 Indians were then on the bank. Some had firearms. Some had Spears. Some had a kind of cutlashes, and all the rest had Bows and steel or iron point arrows." Far from being intimidated, "Captain Lewis was near giving orders to cut the rope and to fire on them" and Clark, taking over from the gunner, aimed a small swivel cannon pointblank at the crowd on the bank. Black Buf-falo, the Sioux head chief, suddenly decided that he didn't want trouble—just another carrot of tobacco. And that was that.

The moral of this meeting, as Bernard DeVoto has written,

was that "a new breed of white man had come to the Upper
Missouri, one that could not be scared or bullied. The moral was
flashed along the Indian underground faster than the expedition
traveled." Less than two weeks later when Lewis and Clark met
with the Arikara, the grand chief "informed us the road was
open & no one dare Shut it, & we might Departe at pleasure." On
October 25 they reached the Mandan villages, and after staging
an impressive council for the Mandans and the Minnetarees—
tribes friendly to the whites—the party began building Fort Mandan, their winter quarters.

During the long winter months the captains held many parleys
with the Indians, with the double objective of promoting intertribal peace in order to guarantee the peaceful passage of the
Missouri for the fur trade and of gathering information about
the water route to the Pacific. Two recruits were attached to their
party: a veteran French frontiersman, Toussaint Charbonneau,
and his sixteen-year-old wife, Sacagawea—in English, Birdwoman.
A member of the Shoshoni, or Snake, tribe, she had been captured two years before by the Minnetarees and later sold to
Charbonneau. Because she would be able to act as interpreter
when they reached the land of the Shoshoni and because she
might be able to recognize the landmarks, the captains felt that
Sacagawea was a valuable acquisition.

On April 7, 1805, the same day that the keelboat started downriver for St. Louis, two pirogues and six canoes embarked on the
voyage up the river, their destination the western sea.

Now in the high plateau region of the Missouri watershed,
never before seen by white men, the expedition moved slowly
upstream, plagued by the cold rain and occasional snow, the
towropes often out. But game was abundant and the men marveled at the landscape—at the fissure the river had carved on the
face of the continent, here a broad plain where the stream had
widened to a mile, there cutting through a narrow, steep-walled
canyon. They passed and surveyed the Milk, Yellowstone, Mussel-
shell, and Marias rivers, and on June 12 Lewis, scouting ahead,
heard "the agreeable sound of a fall of water and . . . saw the
spray arrise above the plain like a collumn of smoke." As he

advanced farther, the water "began to make a roaring too tremendious to be mistaken for any cause short of the great falls of the Missouri."

Heartening as it was to reach this fabled landmark, the falls were a formidable obstacle. The larger pirogue had been left at the fork of the Marias; now the second also had to be abandoned. For twenty-five days the men toiled to transport the canoes and goods around the falls—an eighteen-mile uphill portage, one lap of which was overgrown with cactus that pierced even moccasins double-soled with buffalo hide. The heat was so great that the men worked naked, and when a storm arose "the hail & wind being so large and violent in the Plains, they were much bruised and some nearly killed, and others without hats or anything on their heads bloody. . . ." But on July 15 they were on their way again.

The river was narrower and swifter now, and it was constant gruelling work to keep the canoes moving forward. By the time the party reached the three forks of the Missouri's headwater, all were near exhaustion and they rested for several days. "We begin to feel considerable anxiety with rispect to the Snake Indians," Captain Lewis wrote on July 27. "If we do not find them or some other nation who have horses the successful issue of our voyage will be very doubtful or at all events much more difficult in its accomplishment. We are now several hundred miles within the bosom of this wild and mountainous country where game may rationally be expected shortly to become scarce and subsistence precarious without any knowledge with rispect to the country— not knowing how far these mountains continue, or where to direct our course to pass them to advantage, or intercept a navigable branch of the Columbia." But, as he noted the next day, one member of the party *did* have some knowledge of the country, for "our present camp is precisely on the spot that the Snake Indians were encamped" when the Minnetarees made the raid in which they took Sacagawea prisoner.

After exploring the south (Gallatin) and middle (Madison) forks, Lewis and Clark concluded that the third fork, which they named the Jefferson, must be the upstream extension of the Mis-

souri. They proceeded up the Jefferson, and on August 8 Sacagawea "recognized the point of a high plain . . . which she informed us was not very distant from the summer retreat of her
nation on a river beyond the mountains which runs to the west.
This hill she says her nation calls the beaver's head from a conceived re[se]mblance of its figure to the head of that animal. She
assures us that we shall either find her people on this river or on
the river immediately west of its source." The next day Lewis
went in quest of the Shoshonis, taking with him George Drewyer
and two enlisted men, Shields and MacNeal.

The Lewis party easily found the Indian trail which would
lead them to the Lemhi Pass over the Beaverhead Mountains.
Lewis left a note for Captain Clark at the forks of the Beaverhead
River, informing him of the route he planned to take, and on the
third day Lewis and MacNeal caught sight of an Indian on horseback approaching them from some two miles distance. When only
a mile separated them, Lewis "made him the signal of friendship
known to the Indians of the Rocky mountains and those of the
Missouri, which is by holding the mantle or robe in your hands at
two corners and then throwing it up in the air higher than the
head [and] bringing it to the earth as if in the act of spreading
it . . . ." Then Lewis displayed some trinkets—a looking-glass and
beads—and leaving his gun with MacNeal went forward alone
and unarmed. The Indian turned his horse and began to move
slowly away, at which Lewis "called to him in as loud a voice
as I could command, repeating the word tab-ba-bone [white
man]." The Indian halted again, but unfortunately he was made
suspicious by the approach of Drewyer and Shields, who had been
deployed to the left and right, and when Lewis was about a hundred paces away the Indian "suddenly turned his horse about,
gave him the whip, leaped the creek, and disappeared in the
willow brush in an instant."

The next morning they set out again on the trail of the
Indian, MacNeal now carrying a pole to which Lewis had affixed
a small American flag. Soon they came upon "a large and plain
Indian road" which, after about fifteen miles, took them "to the
most distant fountain of the waters of the Mighty Missouri in

surch of which we have spent so many toilsome days and wristless nights. . . . I had accomplished one of those great objects on which my mind has been unalterably fixed for many years. . . . After refreshing ourselves we proceeded on to the top of the dividing ridge from which I discovered immence ranges of high mountains still to the West of us, with their tops partially covered with snow. I now decended the mountain about ¾ of a mile which I found much steeper than on the opposite side, to a handsome bold running Creek of clear Cold water. Here I first tasted the water of the great Columbia river."* Thus Lewis and his three companions became the first Americans to cross the Continental Divide. They had, moreover, crossed the boundary of Louisiana Territory; beyond lay no man's land—a vast region unowned by any nation.

On their second encounter with the shy Shoshonis, which occurred the next day, the Lewis party had better luck. Although the first group that they met—a man, two women, and some dogs—ran away, very shortly Lewis and his men came upon three women. "The short and steep ravines which we passed concealed us from each other until we arrived within 30 paces. A young woman immediately took to flight; an Elderly woman and a girl of about 12 years old remained." Lewis instantly put down his gun, and although the "female savages" appeared much alarmed they saw the white men were too near for them to escape and "seated themselves on the ground, holding down their heads as if reconciled to die which they expected no doubt would be their fate." Instead Lewis "took the elderly woman by the hand and raised her up; repeated the word *tab-ba-bone* and stripped up my shirt sleeve to show her my skin"—for his face and hands were tanned as dark as their own; and presented her with trinkets.

Shortly after they had started toward camp about sixty mounted warriors came charging up at the gallop, but the women saved the situation by hastening to show the chief their presents. "These men then advanced and embraced [Lewis] very

*Lewis drank from the headwaters of the small Lemhi River, a tributary of the Columbia.

affectionately in their way which is by putting their left arm over your wright shoulder clasping your back, while they apply their left cheek to yours and frequently vociferate the word *âh-hi-e, âh-hi-e,* that is, I am much pleased, I am much rejoiced. Both parties now advanced and we were all caressed and be-smeared with their grease and paint till [we were] heartily tired of the national hug." With Drewyer as interpreter, Lewis told the chief that his visit was a friendly one, the peace pipe was smoked, gifts were distributed, and all returned to camp where a lodge had been prepared for the white men. Here, at a formal council, Lewis explained fully the object of the expedition and his need for horses and information to pass through the mountains.

In order to give Captain Clark time to reach the forks of the Jefferson, Lewis spent two days at the Shoshoni camp before asking Chief Cameahwait if some of his people would accompany the white party to the rendezvous with Clark. At once, the atmosphere of cordiality changed to one of suspicion. The warriors, the chief explained, considered this a plot to lead them into a Minnetaree ambush. In the end, however, it appeared to Lewis that "we had all of the men of the village and a number of women with us . . . now very cheerfull and gay."

On August 16 when they reached the rendezvous Lewis was disconcerted to find that Clark had not arrived. The Indians became uneasy, and to restore their confidence Lewis offered Chief Cameahwait his gun, telling him that "if I deceived him he might make what use of the gun he thought proper, or in other words he might shoot me." Then Lewis asked Drewyer to retrieve the notes he had left for Clark, and pretended that they were a message from Clark saying the progress of the rest of the expedition had been slowed but to wait for him.

When Captain Clark finally arrived on the morning of August 17, there occurred an almost incredibly melodramatic scene. As Nicholas Biddle has reconstructed it from the *Journals,* Sacagawea, who was walking with her husband a hundred yards ahead of Clark, began "to dance and show every mark of the most extravagant joy, turning round him and pointing to several Indians, whom [Clark] now saw advancing on horseback, sucking her fingers at the same time to indicate that they were of her native tribe. As they advanced, Captain Clark discovered among them Drewyer dressed like an Indian, from whom he learnt the situation of the party." On reaching the camp, Captain Clark "was received by Captain Lewis and the chief, who after the first embraces and salutations were over, conducted him to a sort of circular tent or shade of willows. Here he was seated on a white robe; and the chief immediately tied in his hair six small shells resembling pearls . . . . The moccasins of the whole party were then taken off, and after much ceremony the smoking began. After this the conference was to be opened, and Sacagawea was sent for; she came into the tent, sat down, and was beginning to interpret, when in the person of Cameahwait she recognized her brother. She instantly jumped up, and ran and embraced him, throwing over him her blanket and weeping profusely."

Just as the encounter with the Teton Sioux had climaxed the first phase of the expedition, this meeting with Sacagawea's tribe was the turning point in the infinitely more difficult lunge westward to the Pacific. The Shoshonis pledged allegiance to the United States; they provided horses, and help in freighting the expedition through the pass, and information about the country west and south. There were weeks of hardship and peril and frustration ahead of them, but on November 7, while the rain pelted down, Captain Clark could at last write in his journal: "Great joy in camp. We are in *view* of the *Ocian* . . . ."

Captain Lewis considered the promotion of the American fur trade the major means of holding Upper Louisiana under control. According to Lewis, "The Indians were friendly to the British merchants and unfriendly to the Spanish for the plain reason that the former sold them goods at a lower rate." Unless the American traders were able to supply the Indians, the government would lose its influence over the tribes, and the Northwest frontier would be in jeopardy.

> *The whole problem of frontier defense was inti-*
> *mately bound up with the fur trade and Indian policy.*
> *Lewis and Clark had made a good beginning in estab-*
> *lishing cordial relations with the upper tribes; the*
> *main exceptions were the Teton Sioux. As a means of*
> *further strengthening the new ties of allegiance, repre-*
> *sentative chiefs of the western tribes were sent to the*
> *States so that they might be properly impressed with*
> *the greatness and might of the United States.*
>
> Condensed from Herbert S. Schell's
> *History of South Dakota*

Doranto

EN ROUTE to the Pacific on their famous expedition, Lewis and Clark spent the winter of 1804–1805 with the Mandan Indians, not far from the present site of Bismarck, North Dakota. Homeward bound in August of 1806 they again visited at the Mandan villages, holding several councils and renewing pledges of friendship. On this occasion, Captain Lewis urged a celebrated Mandan chief, Shahaka, or Big White, to accompany him back to Washington to meet the President and see for himself the power of the people who lived in the country far to the east. But Big White, although flattered, declined the invitation.

"Father," he said, "we wish to go down with you to see our Great Father, but we are afraid of the Sioux who will be on the river and will kill us on our return here. The Sioux have stolen our horses and killed eight of our men, and the Arikara have also struck us."

Captain Lewis assured Big White that the Great Father would send a special guard of armed men to protect him on his return journey, and the chief finally was persuaded to make the trip, taking along as well his wife Yellow Corn, his son White Painted

House, and his squaw-man interpreter. On the way downriver the expedition stopped with the Arikara two days, and Lewis managed to affect a reconciliation between Big White and the Arikara chiefs.

In Washington, Big White met the Great Father, President Jefferson, and later visited the President at Monticello. Then, in the spring of 1807, the chief and his entourage started for home under the protection of a small military escort commanded by Ensign Nathaniel Pryor, a veteran of the Lewis and Clark expedition. Traveling with them under a separate escort were twenty-four Teton Sioux who had been visiting in St. Louis, and also a trading party and twenty trappers led by Captain Ezekiel Williams. The latter group intended to hunt beaver and other fur-bearing animals in the unexplored region beyond the Missouri, and each man was equipped to stay in the wilderness for two years.

When the party reached the Grand River, Big White's earlier forebodings proved to be prophetic, for the Arikara, despite their pledges of peace, were again at war with the Mandan nation. They refused to allow the party to proceed upriver, and a clash ensued which resulted in several casualties. Big White, refusing to risk the lives of his wife and son, returned to St. Louis with his escort, but Captain Williams' men were not to be deterred by intertribal warfare, and decided to carry on overland.

It was a brave though foolhardy decision. Of the twenty men who comprised the party, only Williams and two others survived the months of privation and hardship to return to civilization. However, although the original project of crossing the Rockies and trapping at the headwaters of the Columbia had to be abandoned, Williams did bring back considerable information about the hitherto little-known valley of the Platte, to say nothing of a fund of stories about happenings on the expedition.

One of the most unusual of his tales had as its setting the country to the south and east of the junction of the forks of the Platte in Nebraska. At the time the group reached his region— early June of 1808—they had lost only one man, William Hamilton, who had taken sick and died; and the morale of the party was still good. They had been warned that they were traveling through hostile country, but their only recent contact had been with a band of Pawnee who had met with Captain Lewis, had exchanged presents with him, and were inclined to regard the whites as friendly people.

One evening after Williams and his men had made camp for the night, two young Indians, a man and a woman, rode up and dismounted by the campfire, apparently exhausted by hard riding. Their sudden unheralded appearance at first caused general alarm, for it was supposed that the man might be a spy for some band readying an attack. But Big White had told Captain Williams that war parties were never accompanied by women, and also it was evident that the two had made a long and difficult journey. Questioning them through his Mandan interpreter, Williams was able to learn the story behind this strange visit.

The man—or rather boy, for he was only sixteen—was named Doranto and was the son of the grand chief of the Skidi (Wolf) branch of the Pawnee, which lived on the Loup Fork of the Platte. The year before, while he was out swimming with some other youths of the tribe, a band of Teton Sioux had swooped down in a lightning raid and had carried away the young prince. Bound to a horse, he had been convoyed to their main village at the bend of the Missouri in present-day South Dakota.

As the son of a chief, Doranto was an important prisoner, but as a captive he was compelled to serve as a slave, according to Indian custom. It fell to him to perform the household chores ordinarily assigned only to squaws—carrying wood and water, scraping hides, and similar menial tasks; he was never allowed to go on a hunt or a war raid, and was looked down on as one of an inferior caste. Naturally this was very galling to Doranto's proud spirit, but there was one important compensation. Since he was doing women's work, he was frequently thrown in the company of a beautiful girl named Niargua, the daughter of a chief in the village. Doranto made the most of his opportunities, and before long had completely won Niargua's heart.

The growing familiarity between the two was noticed by Niargua's mother, who dutifully reported the matter to her husband. It would have been a flagrant breach of Indian etiquette for a chief's daughter to become the wife of a slave, and moreover one who belonged to a tribe which the Sioux regarded as hereditary enemies. Shocked and angry, the chief not only reprimanded Niargua severely, but beat her with a lodge pole. Then, haling in Doranto, he threatened to shoot an arrow through his heart for his impudence in aspiring to a maiden so much above him.

Like other lovers before and since, Doranto and Niargua were drawn even closer together by parental opposition. The only difference was that now they were careful to conceal their feelings and no longer talked together where others could observe them. Realizing that Niargua could never be his bride so long as he remained a prisoner, Doranto proposed that she elope with him as soon as he could devise a plan of escape. Without hesitation, Niargua declared that she was ready to go wherever he went, and to share his fortunes even unto death.

Now it happened that Niargua's parents were not the only ones keeping a watchful eye on the lovers. A certain young warrior who had unsuccessfully sought Niargua's hand exhibited his jealous hatred of Doranto at every opportunity; he lorded it over the Pawnee, and constantly made him the butt of contemptuous remarks and actions. As an alien and a slave, Doranto had no choice but to endure the jeers and swallow the insults; any attempt at retaliation would, he knew, ruin their chances for escape. But still there were bounds beyond which honor forbade him to allow his enemy to go. This point was reached when the Sioux offered Doranto the insult which, in the eyes of a Plains Indian, was the greatest possible. According to tribal law, a person insulted in this way had the right to murder the offender if he could, although it was considered more honorable to settle such a difficulty by single combat, using weapons mutually agreed on. Public sentiment demanded that the offended party take action. A man who did not demand satisfaction was labeled a dog and a coward, and forever despised by all. Needless to say, Doranto forthwith challenged the young Sioux, who was no less eager for the fight, certain he could thus eliminate his rival permanently, raise himself in the tribe's estimation, and gain favor in

Niargua's eyes. War clubs and knives were the weapons chosen, and a place and date selected.

At the appointed time the whole village gathered to see the spectacle. The two youths, stark naked and armed for combat, took their positions about thirty yards apart. Waiting for the signal, Doranto glanced over at Niargua, standing in the crowd. The look in her eyes gave him courage. He told his arm to be big and his heart strong. When the signal came, the Sioux charged in impetuously, anxious to sweep his enemy off his feet. His momentum carried him past Doranto who, being cooler and more deliberate, timed his actions better, and swung with his war club just at the right moment to land a stunning blow on the back of his enemy's neck as he passed. The blow brought the Sioux to the ground, and Doranto sprang upon him, quickly dispatching him with his knife. A loud lament went up from the relatives of the dead warrior, but no hand was raised against Doranto, for he had won his victory in fair combat.

As a result of this trial of valor, Doranto's position in the village was entirely different. He was now regarded as an adopted son—a man, not a woman; a warrior, not a slave—and he was free to go to war, and to hunt the buffalo, the elk, and the antelope. Unfortunately, Niargua's father did not share the sentiment of the other members of the tribe. Having made up his mind that Doranto was unworthy, the old chief was not about to revise his judgment. Niargua was his favorite daughter, and she must become the wife of some distinguished warrior whom he himself would choose.

But like many another father he was no match for a daughter in love. Niargua bided her time until the chief was absent from the village, attending a council with a neighboring tribe of Sioux. She alerted Doranto who, while the village slept, picked out two of the chief's best horses and led them to a sequestered place. He was soon joined by Niargua, bringing a supply of provisions. In a moment they were mounted and away like fleeting shadows into the June night.

The Pawnee village was at least three sleeps distant, and the lovers knew that they could expect relentless pursuit. Their elopement would not be discovered until morning, and they hoped by then to have enough of a head start so that, barring mishaps, they could not be overtaken. But taking no chances they had traveled night and day ever since leaving the Sioux village, stopping only when it was absolutely necessary for their horses to rest and graze.

Having heard their story, Captain Williams tried to prevail upon the young couple to camp under the protection of his party, and rest overnight. But Doranto replied that they had not slept since they had begun their flight, nor did they dare to think of closing their eyes until they had reached the village of his tribe. They knew only too well what Doranto's fate would be if he again fell into the hands of the Sioux.

After an hour's rest and a hot meal, Doranto and Niargua appeared to be much refreshed and ready to resume their journey. The Williams' party was particularly impressed by the courage and cheerfulness of the Teton girl. As the time came to start off, she leaped unaided from the ground to her Indian saddle, reined up her horse, and took her place beside the youth for whose sake she had borne so much hardship and danger.

When they rode away into the night, Doranto and Niargua also rode out of the pages of white man's history. Captain Williams never succeeded in learning whether they reached their destination, and no other report exists of this incident. But there is every reason to suppose that the brave young lovers rejoined Doranto's tribe and lived happily ever after among the Pawnee on the Great Plains.

As for Big White and his family, they too reached home, but to get them safely there required the mounting of a 150-man expedition and the expenditure of more than four thousand dollars. On this second try they left St. Louis in mid-May, 1809. Although the Sioux—as usual—showed a disposition to be troublesome, the Arikara were friendly and Big White's party reached the Mandan villages in September, more than three years after the chief's departure with Lewis and Clark to visit the Great Father.

*The War of 1812 with England temporarily checked
westward expansion, but the years after 1815 saw the
resumption of large-scale settlement of the Lake Plains
and the Mississippi Valley frontier. In 1817 the steamboat* Washington *initiated successful steam navigation
on the Ohio-Mississippi route, and already military
installations were completed or under construction on
the river above St. Louis—Fort Armstrong (near present-day Rock Island, Illinois), Fort Crawford at Prairie
du Chien, and Fort Snelling (near present-day St. Paul,
Minnesota). There was constant pressure on Congress
for the extinguishment of Indian titles to lands in the
so-called Northwest Territory, comprising the present
states of Ohio, Indiana, Illinois, Michigan, Wisconsin,
and part of Minnesota. In his message to Congress in
1825, President Monroe urged removal of the Indian
tribes to the land west of the Mississippi River (although existing treaties with some of the tribes guaranteed them possession* forever *of the land they were
occupying), and for all practical purposes the removal
policy was adopted at this time, finally becoming law
in 1830.*

*There was peace between the United States and
tribes of the Northwest Territory from 1816 to 1827,
but it was a period of incessant fierce intertribal wars,
and finally in 1825 the government intervened, calling
a council of the belligerents at Prairie du Chien. The
purpose of the council was set forth in the preamble to
the treaty which resulted from it: "The United States
of America have seen with much regret that wars have
for many years been carried on between the Sioux and
the Chippewas, and more recently between the confederated tribes of Sauk and Foxes and the Sioux, and
also between the Iowas and the Sioux. . . . In order to
promote peace among these tribes and to establish
boundaries among them and the other tribes who live
in this vicinity . . . the United States have invited the*

Chippewa, the Sauk and Fox, Menominee, Iowa, Sioux, Winnebago, and a portion of the Ottawa, Chippewa, and Potawatomie . . . to assemble together in a spirit of mutual conciliation to accomplish these objects. . . ."

Appointed commissioners to represent the United States were General William Clark, of expedition fame, and General Lewis Cass, Governor of Michigan Territory. Clark and Cass labored day after day with the chiefs, making themselves familiar with Indian bark maps and drawings, striving to set up boundaries which were just and would be respected by the tribes concerned. The Indians saw clearly that it was a benevolent effort for their good, and the treaty was signed in a friendly atmosphere on August 19, 1825.

The Race of Death

DURING the summer of 1828 a Sioux Indian, while hunting on the Iowa shore near the mouth of Paint Creek, shot and scalped a Winnebago, mistakenly believing him to be the slayer of his brother. As a result of this tragic mistake, there occurred one of the strangest athletic contests on record.

The brother of the slain man was Big Wave, a Winnebago chief, and his whole band rose up in wrath at the murder. Together with more than a thousand of their fellow tribesmen they assembled at Fort Snelling, clamoring for the arrest of the Sioux. The commanding officer, recently transferred from duty in New Orleans, was Lieutenant Colonel Zachary Taylor, later to be the twelfth President of the United States.

It seemed to Taylor the better part of wisdom to accede to the demand of the Winnebago chieftain. There were fewer than a hundred men in the garrison; moreover, Taylor knew that the

Winnebago were spoiling for a fight. Following the discovery in 1822 of lead and other mineral deposits around Galena, Illinois, there had been an influx of whites into their hunting grounds, and war clouds had been gathering ever since. The previous summer they had fired on a steamboat at Prairie du Chien, and only prompt action on the part of General Cass, who brought troops up from St. Louis, had prevented a full-scale uprising.

Taylor told Big Wave he would see what could be done, and dispatched an arresting officer to the Sioux camp. The Sioux made no objections to turning over the guilty man, who was brought back to Fort Snelling and placed in confinement. As soon as they learned he was in custody, Big Wave and his band again assembled at the fort, and demanded that the Sioux be given to them for punishment. However, Taylor after consulting with his officers, decided against surrendering the prisoner. Instead he sent Lieutenant Reynolds and Dr. Elwise, the surgeon of the garrison, to offer a payment in horses as an indemnity. Such an offer was by no means unusual and normally would have been acceptable; but Big Wave talked in a threatening and insolent manner, declaring that nothing would satisfy his people but to kill the Sioux themselves in their own way.

Lieutenant Reynolds argued that since the man was virtually a prisoner of war it would be dishonorable to kill him in cold blood. Seeing that his words seemed to impress Big Wave, he suggested a compromise. He proposed that three weeks from that day the Winnebago bring twelve of their most expert runners to the prairie outside the fort, each man to be armed with a toma-hawk and a scalping knife. The prisoner would be produced and at a signal would start running for the camp of his tribe. The Winnebagoes, who would be posted seven paces behind him, would be free to give chase and capture and scalp him if they could.

This seemed a fine idea to the aggrieved tribe, and they readily accepted. They looked forward to a day of great sport, feeling certain that even if the Sioux happened to be a good runner three weeks of confinement would sap his strength. They at once summoned the best runners of their nation, and had them train daily in full view of the fort. Before long the chosen twelve became so accurate at throwing the tomahawk that they could hit a tin can swinging from a tree limb at a distance of twenty-five feet.

However, Lieutenant Reynolds, who was determined that the Sioux should have a sporting chance to save his life, had a few tricks up his sleeve. To begin with, he put the Sioux in strict training. Dr. Elwise prescribed his diet and directed that his muscles be massaged, and morning and evening he was sent out to the parade ground, out of sight of the Winnebagoes, where he ran lap after lap. Three days before the appointed race the prisoner was timed, and performed the almost incredible feat of running a mile in three minutes and nine seconds!

Speed and endurance were not the only elements involved in Reynolds' strategy. A drumbeat was to signal the start of the race for life, and Reynolds arranged for the drummer to be stationed behind a screen some twenty paces out in front of the Sioux. Thus the sound of the drumbeat would reach him a fraction of a second sooner than it would his enemies. Also, the Sioux was told that after the Lieutenant raised his hat in the "get set" signal, he would wait two minutes before he lowered it for the drummer to sound "go." Finally, and most important, to enable the Sioux to dodge the deadly tomahawks which would be hurled the instant the starting signal was given, Reynolds taught him to bound to one side as he started off, instead of dashing straight ahead.

Word of the impending death race spread far and wide through the wilderness, arousing the same interest and excitement as would news of a circus among the whites in after years. When the day came, a crowd of about three thousand—Indians, French traders, soldiers, and American frontiersmen—had gathered to watch the novel execution. It was a grand holiday for everyone but the prisoner.

Reynolds, on behalf of the Sioux, and Chiefs Pine Top and Warkonshuterkee, representing the Winnebago, made the final arrangements. The course, marked out by white flags, lay along the prairie which ran for some miles beside the river. At the

appointed time, the Sioux was escorted to the starting point by a
squad of soldiers. He had painted his face black with a figure of
a horse in white on his forehead, indicating that he was con-
demned to die but had a chance to save his life by his fleetness.
Following came his twelve executioners, marching in single file
and intoning a low monotonous chant. Except for their breech-
cloths, they were naked, their ribs painted white and their breasts
adorned with hieroglyphic signs. From chin to forehead their
faces were striped in black and white, and their hair was plaited
in a number of small braids and further adorned with red or
white feathers and a fringe of small bells. Each man carried a
tomahawk in his right hand and a scalping knife in his left.

Observing that his protégé appeared restless and uneasy, Lieutenant Reynolds took him aside and asked him if he was afraid to
run. "I can outrun all the Winnebagoes," the Sioux replied, "but
I am afraid that I cannot outrun all the horses that are mounted
by armed Indians." The Lieutenant assured him that they would
not be allowed to interfere; he himself would be riding the fleetest
horse on the field and would make it his business to see that no
hostile horseman approached the Sioux.

All being in order, the chiefs and Reynolds mounted their
horses and moved into position at one side of the starting point.
Now Reynolds took one last look around the field, saw that it
was clear, and raised his hat high above his head. The twelve
Winnebagoes tensed themselves for the start, tomahawks poised,
and held their positions, muscles straining, as interminable seconds ticked away. The Sioux remained limp and relaxed until he
saw Reynolds' arm start to descend. When the drum thump came,
the crouching Sioux, just as rehearsed, bounded to the right and
sped forward while a dozen tomahawks swished through the air
far to his left.

Three of the Winnebagoes ran with great fleetness for a mile,
keeping within twenty yards of the Sioux, but Reynolds soon saw
that his man had entire command of the race. Coaching from
on horseback, he had a hard time preventing him from running
all out and using up reserves of speed that might have to be
called on in case of treachery. When all but a few of the pursuers

had dropped out of the race, Reynolds called to the Sioux to step up the pace. Now the disciplined training given him by his white friends proved its value, for he quickly pulled even farther ahead of his bloodthirsty pursuers. At the end of two miles the last of the Winnebagoes faltered and gave up. By the end of the fourth mile even Reynolds' horse was showing signs of wearying, and since the field was clear, Reynolds reined up. The Indian did not look back, but streaked straight ahead and was soon out of sight.

Some years later when Governor Doty of Wisconsin was meeting with the Sioux nation to sign a treaty, the Sioux racer, now a chief, appeared at the council. He inquired for his friends Reynolds and Elwise, and was told that they had been transferred to Florida, where both had died. The Sioux immediately left the council, painted his face black, and took to the gloom of the forest to lament his saviors. Nor could he be persuaded to return and take part in the treaty-signing until he had gone through the Indian ceremony for mourning the dead.

Mother Love

BEGINNING in 1802 Indian agents were appointed to go and live among the tribes to regulate trade and commerce, to license traders, to protect Indian rights, and to teach the red man the white man's ways. The agents were subordinate to superintendents who, in turn, were responsible to the War Department, which managed Indian affairs from 1789 until 1849. But even with the best will in the world these government officials were frequently helpless to prevent tragic injustices. For example, the marriages which traders and soldiers on the frontier contracted with Indians were all too often matters of temporary convenience for the white man which brought grief to the Indian girl.

A particularly dramatic and moving case in point concerns Pe-we-ne, a pretty Chippewa maiden of the upper Mississippi country, who became the wife of an American trader named James Campbell. About the year 1819 a son, to whom the father gave his own name, was born to them, and Campbell was anxious that the child be raised and educated in civilized society. When the boy was still a tiny baby, Campbell, with Pe-we-ne's consent, took him to Florissant, Missouri, near St. Louis, and placed him in the care of a respectable American family. Young James remained with this family till about 1828; then he was returned up the river and entrusted to Mocrice Blondeau, the government interpreter to the Sauk and Fox tribes. Blondeau had a farm on the west bank of the Mississippi about six miles above the present city of Keokuk, Iowa.

According to Dr. Isaac Galland, who was called in once when James was ill, the boy was very shrewd and sprightly, remarkably fair-skinned for a half-breed, and bore a marked resemblance to his father. The doctor was surprised at his easy, fluent, and correct pronunciation of English for in the Blondeau household French was the language spoken. The doctor thought that James was then about nine or ten years old.

In August, 1829, Mr. Blondeau died, and Pe-we-ne came to reclaim her son as soon as she heard the news. James was being looked after by Mr. Blondeau's brother-in-law, Andrew St. Amont, and Dr. Galland urged Pe-we-ne to permit her son to remain among the whites so that he might receive the benefits of an education. Pe-we-ne's answer was that James's father had gone to Santa Fe and perhaps never would return, and since Mr. Blondeau was now dead it meant that the boy was alone among strangers who would take little or no interest in his welfare. She could not bear to see him thus forsaken. She would take him back to the wilderness and keep him with her until he was old enough to look after himself.

Accompanied by her brother La-mas, two sisters, and a few other Chippewa families, Pe-we-ne and her son moved to a white settlement in Illinois near the Mississippi River. Almost daily, while the Indian men were hunting ducks and geese along the river, the women visited the homes of the white people to exchange dressed skins and feathers for melons and pumpkins and corn and other garden produce. On these bartering excursions young James always served as interpreter.

Now it happened that five or six years previously an American family living in this settlement had lost a little boy, an only son, about the same age as Pe-we-ne's son. Several Indian families encamped in the vicinity had left for the interior wilderness at about the same time he disappeared, and there was a strong suspicion that they had made off with the little white boy. The bereaved parents had organized a pursuit and had done everything in their power to recover the child, but no trace of him had ever been found.

The tragedy had not been forgotten when Pe-we-ne arrived in the settlement with her light-skinned, English-speaking son, and soon it began to be noised about that there was a white child among the Indians who very much resembled the lost boy. When this news reached the bereaved family it created a great stir. A meeting was called and a group appointed to investigate the matter.

White men came to the lodge of La-mas, and despite Pe-we-ne's cries and entreaties James was taken away by force. Pe-we-ne followed after them in great distress, not having the least idea what lay behind such extraordinary conduct. At length they arrived at a house where a crowd of white people was gathered, and James was taken to stand before a strange white woman. For a moment she looked at him, as Pe-we-ne said, "em-tesh-e-tak"— with all her heart—then clasped him in her arms, seemingly beside herself with grief or joy, for her tears flowed in streams, and she shrieked and exclaimed even while hugging and kissing the boy.

All during this scene, which lasted some time, Pe-we-ne stood silently by, wondering what on earth it could mean. The mystery was at last explained to her by her son. He said that the white woman who had displayed so much affection for him claimed to be his real mother, and that Pe-we-ne was accused of having stolen him away five years before. His parents had mourned him as dead, but now by an act of the Great Good Spirit Pe-we-ne had been impelled to bring him back. He had been identified indisputably as the lost child by a scar on his forehead under his hair. The white woman had described it to him, James said, before she looked to see if the scar was there.

To Pe-we-ne all this was perfectly astounding and utterly inexplicable. At first she had been alarmed for her son's safety, and had followed his captors in an agony of suspense, but on witnessing the scene of maternal love her fears gave way to amazement.

With her son still acting as interpreter, Pe-we-ne was further informed that for the better security of James's "parents," she and all the other Indians in the settlement were ordered to decamp immediately and leave the area without delay. And she was sternly warned that any attempt to carry James off again would mean certain death for herself and all who tried to help her.

Thus robbed of her child, Pe-we-ne hastened to make the long and difficult trip to St. Louis to lay her case before the "Red-Headed Father," William Clark, who had been governor of Missouri until its admission to the Union in 1821 and was now Superintendent of Indian Affairs. Pe-we-ne begged him to intercede in her behalf, and Clark wrote a note to Dr. Galland, asking him to investigate and if possible to restore the boy to his mother.

Galland at once set out to make inquiries. He interviewed a number of people and learned that everyone in the settlement believed beyond a doubt that James was the long lost child. He was told that any attempt to restore the boy to Pe-we-ne would be resisted by the whole community. Even supposing James *were* Pe-we-ne's child, it would be to his best interests to be left with the adopted white parents; they were well enough off to see that he had a good education and to give him a good start in life when he reached manhood. The situation seemed so hopeless to Galland that he left the neighborhood without attempting to undeceive the parents who believed James to be their son.

Having lost all hope of recovering her captive child through official channels, Pe-we-ne set off all alone to visit him. On her arrival, far from being granted the privilege of seeing James, she was severely beaten and driven off the premises. Disobeying orders to leave the neighborhood at once, she concealed herself in the thickets and brushwood which surrounded the house, on the chance that she might get a glimpse of her beloved boy. One day she succeeded in attracting his attention, and mother and son enjoyed a brief reunion in her place of concealment. But these meetings were not repeated often before they were discovered, and Pe-we-ne again was beaten and driven off. Yet she persisted in returning and was caught in the act of throwing a pair of beautifully ornamented moccasins over the fence to James. She was again cruelly beaten, but no punishment was too great to endure for the sake of the sight of her son.

Several months went by and winter came on, but still Pe-we-ne lingered in the adjacent woods. Despite the harshness of the weather, repeated brutal punishment, and gnawing hunger, she refused to be driven away. At last, death came to end Pe-we-ne's vigil and relieve her sufferings. Several days after she died her body was found near the fence. It had been partly devoured by the domestic animals belonging to the family.

❦

Fur trade was the only business carried on in the trans-Mississippi country beyond the few scattering settlements along the lower Missouri. Large parties of hunters and trappers remained constantly in the wilderness, wandering all over those vast regions in quest of beaver and other fur. Each spring expeditions set out for various points in the Far West from Santa Fe to the British boundary, carrying supplies and recruits and bringing back the furs collected during the previous year. The great bulk of this business was done along the Missouri River, where trading posts were established throughout the entire valley. . . . From its very nature this business was one of adventure and excitement, and particularly attractive to those who were fond of an independent and out-of-door life. . . . In those days a trip to the mountains meant adventure of the genuine sort—absence from civilization, ever-present danger from the Indians, game of all kinds in abundance, and the

*grandeur and beauty of nature still unknown except
to a very few.*

—Chittenden, *History of Early Steamboat
Navigation on the Missouri River*

Adventures of an Engagé

A ST. LOUIS boy named Joseph LaBarge heard the tales of adventure related by the traders who came back every year from the distant mountains, and made up his mind that this was the life for him. In 1831, when he reached the age of sixteen, he told his father that he was determined to join one of the fur-trading expeditions and see something of the Indian country. LaBarge senior sympathized with his son's feelings and agreed to let him go, stipulating only that he must also secure his mother's consent. As might be expected, her objections were not easy to overcome, but she finally gave in; and in 1832 Joseph signed a contract binding himself to serve for three years with the American Fur Company.

Founded in 1808 by John Jacob Astor, this organization had grown to be the largest fur-trading company in the United States. Its Northern Department, operating from a base at Mackinaw, soon won control of the trade in the Great Lakes and upper Mississippi region, and in 1822 the firm opened its Western Department, with headquarters at St. Louis. Under the leadership of the enterprising head of the Western Department, Pierre Chouteau, Jr., the company became the first to use steamboats instead of the hand-hauled keelboats in the upper Missouri trade. In 1819 a government-built boat, the *Western Engineer,* had managed to steam as far as the Council Bluff in Nebraska, but the venture was regarded as a failure. The boat had run aground countless times, its boilers repeatedly clogged with mud and sand, and the abrasive action of the sandy water damaged the engine valves.

Obtaining fuel was also a problem: the boat often had to halt
while the crew went ashore to cut wood. Although steamers were
used in increasing numbers on the lower river, no other attempt
was made to send a steamboat beyond Independence, Missouri,
until 1831. On April 20 of that year the *Yellowstone*—a side-
wheeler of new design, specially built for the American Fur Company—embarked on a voyage which took her as far upriver as
present-day Pierre, South Dakota. By midsummer the vessel was
back in St. Louis laden with buffalo robes, furs and peltries, and
ten thousand pounds of buffalo tongues. Now persuaded of the
feasibility of the project, Chouteau scheduled a second trip for
the following spring, and this time the *Yellowstone* made it clear
up to Fort Union, the fur-trading capital of the upper Missouri,
a distance of eighteen hundred miles.

One of those aboard the *Yellowstone* as she puffed and pad-
dled her way up "Old Muddy" on her historic 1832 voyage was
young Joseph LaBarge, but he went only as far as the Council
Bluff. He had signed on to work as an *engagé*, or clerk, and was
bound for Cabanne's trading post. Situated near the mouth of the
Platte a few miles north of present-day Omaha, the post had been
established for the company about 1824 by Jean Pierre Cabanne,
the present *bourgeois* (fur-trader's lingo for boss: usually pronounced "booshway"). The company employees were quartered
in a row of low wooden buildings near the river, but Cabanne's
house was two stories high and boasted a balcony. Here Cabanne
entertained such distinguished visitors as the artist George Catlin,
who was aboard the *Yellowstone* in 1832, and scientist and explorer Prince Maximilian von Wied-Neuwied, who made the
upriver trip the following year.

During the summer Cabanne's was a lively spot, and Joseph
was surprised—and perhaps a bit disappointed—to find so many
reminders of civilization in what he had pictured as untamed
wilderness. But when the cold weather came and river traffic
ended he realized that he was indeed on the far frontier. That
first winter he became well acquainted with the Skidi Pawnee,
one of the four bands of the Grand Pawnee nation, who lived
about a hundred miles west of the Missouri on the Loup fork of

the Platte. Unlike nomadic Indians, such as the Sioux, the Pawnee lived in permanent villages. In the spring and fall they would go out on extended hunts, roaming far to the south and west, but during the winter months they stayed in their villages, going out chiefly to hunt for furs. Pelts were salable only if the animals were taken in the winter when their coats were thick and strong. The women of the village prepared the skins for trading, scraping them down and rubbing them with fat until they were soft and flexible.

To procure the furs, Cabanne would send out a clerk and a few men with the merchandise to be bartered, and the party would stay with the Indians until the trade was over. On his first trip to the Pawnee village, Joseph lived in the lodge of Chief Big Axe, and pleased his host by working hard to learn the Pawnee language. By the time the snow melted and the high water of spring came, he had become tolerably proficient.

As soon as the river was open, the furs were loaded on bull-boats and shipped down to the mouth of the Platte, where they were reloaded into mackinaws and sent on down to St. Louis. Mackinaws, used only for downstream navigation, were flat-bottomed boats, about fifty feet long with a twelve-foot beam. They normally carried a five-man crew, the steersman occupying an elevated perch in the stern overlooking the cargo and the four oarsmen in the bow. Bullboats were light craft, devised for use on extremely shallow streams like the Platte, Cheyenne, and Nio-brara. Their willow-pole frames were covered with rawhide, and they were poled along by a two-man crew.

In May of 1833 Joseph went back to St. Louis for a visit to his family; and on his return to the post he found that Cabanne had been replaced as *bourgeois* by Major Joshua Pilcher. A vet-eran trader and frontiersman, Pilcher took a great liking to the young *engagé*, giving him increased responsibilities and putting special opportunities for winning distinction in his way. This was most signally demonstrated in the winter of 1833–1834 when it was time to choose a man to carry the express to Fort Pierre.

The express, which went to all the posts, was of vital impor-tance in the early fur trade. It was the means by which the main office in St. Louis kept the traders informed of developments in the States, and by which the partners in the field sent down orders for supplies, information about the condition of snow in the mountains, and forecasts for the coming summer's trade. Usually an express started downstream from Fort Union before the arrival of the northbound express originating in St. Louis, and the two would meet and exchange dispatches at Fort Pierre. Since the express was carried in the dead of winter, it was a task fraught with peril and hardship, even though there was little danger from the Indians at this time of year.

When the express from St. Louis arrived at Cabanne's, Major Pilcher called Joseph aside and asked him to take it on to Fort Pierre. "There are old *voyageurs* here I could send," he said, "but I can't trust them. I want you to go. What do you say to it?" Joseph had never been so far above the post in his life, but he replied that if the *bourgeois* had confidence in him he was ready to go.

The journey, which he made on horseback, took him along the Nebraska shore to a point opposite present-day Vermillion. There he crossed to the Dakota side, and struck out on a northwesterly course roughly parallel to the river. Next to Fort Union, Fort Pierre was the most important of the upper-river posts. It was the hub of a number of smaller posts which served chiefly as gathering stations where pelts and robes were collected from the neighboring Indians, and was something of a metropolis of the wilderness, for about six hundred Indian lodges were located in the vicinity.

Joseph arrived in good time to meet the Fort Union express, which came in the next day, and since his upriver trip had gone off without a hitch, he was feeling his oats when he started back to Cabanne's. He felt that now he had proved himself as good a man as any of the seasoned *voyageurs*, and the wilderness had few secrets from him. One little episode sufficed to put him in a somewhat humbler frame of mind. In camp one night he was roasting a chicken when he had the curious sensation that he was being watched. Looking up, he saw four gray wolves ranged on the opposite side of the fire, staring at him. Joseph later confessed that he almost panicked and ran, but somehow he managed to control himself and stay put. Getting his gun and pistols ready for action, he sat quietly and stared back. Apparently the wolves decided he was not what they wanted for dinner, and after a few minutes they slipped away as silently as they had come.

Major Pilcher was succeeded as *bourgeois* at Cabanne's by the formidable Peter A. Sarpy, the most famous of the traders along that stretch of the Missouri.* Late in the fall of 1834 Sarpy sent Joseph down the river a few miles to the post at Bellevue to take charge of a herd of about one hundred and fifty horses which the company was wintering there. They would be used to bring furs in from the mountains the next summer. The herd was kept on the east side of the river, where there were protected bottomlands and young cottonwood trees, on whose bark the animals thrived.

Preparing the browse, as this forage was called, was a time-consuming job. First, the trees had to be felled and cut into three- and four-foot lengths. Next the logs were stood on end around a fire, and turned occasionally until the frozen bark was warmed through. Then the thawed bark was peeled off with a drawknife, and when it had been cut into short pieces it was ready to be consumed. As for the stripped logs, they were split and piled on the river bank to season. The next summer this "horse wood" would be picked up by the company's steamboats and used for fuel.

The winter of 1834 was extremely severe, and the river froze from bank to bank. Joseph was lodging with some of his fellows at Bellevue, and had to cross the ice to reach the horse corral. The pathway ran between two air holes in the ice, one just above the path, the other some hundred yards downstream. Late one afternoon when it came time to feed the horses, all signs indicated that a blizzard was in the making. Already it was snowing quite hard and the wind was coming up. But Joseph had his job to do, and he set out across the river wrapped in his blanket coat, which was held tight to his body by a belt, and armed with tomahawk, rifle, and knife.

*See page 41.

With the northwest wind at his back, he had no difficulty in crossing to the Iowa shore, but by the time his chores were finished the blizzard was on full blast. The wind had risen to a gale and was driving obliquely across the expanse of the river, completely obliterating the narrow trace that led to warmth and shelter. Nonetheless Joseph was confident he could find the way back to the post; he had crossed so many times that he felt he could make the trip blindfolded. Ducking his head, he started back across the river at a slow run. At what he judged was about midstream he paused momentarily to get his bearings, but he was surrounded by a whirling curtain of white. Visibility was nil. There was nothing for it but to keep going, and he ran on. The next thing he knew he had plunged feet first into the icy waters of the Missouri.

Joseph realized instantly that he had dropped through one of the air holes. But which one? If it was the lower one then he was finished, for the swift current had carried him under the ice. If it was the upper hole, then he still had a chance—he might bob to the surface through the downstream exit. But perhaps the current did not flow directly from one hole to the other; or perhaps he would not be near the surface when he reached the escape hatch. . . .

In spite of his perilous situation Joseph kept his wits about him. Fortunately he was an expert swimmer. Even though hampered by his heavy clothes he soon rose to the surface, bumping his head against the overlaying ice sheet. Sinking and rising he hurtled downstream, continually smacking his head against the icy ceiling. His lungs were bursting and he had all but reached the limit of his endurance when suddenly his head shot out of the slushy water into the open air. Grabbing for the edge of the ice, he clamped himself to it and hung on until he was able to draw his knife. He plunged this into the ice far enough to give him some leverage, and by dint of superhuman exertion finally managed to pull himself out of the water. He was amazed to discover that throughout the whole ordeal he had hung on to his rifle.

He had escaped the river, but he was soaked to the skin, and if he did not get quickly to a fire he would perish of exposure. Although the air was warmer than the water, in the driving wind his clothing was soon frozen as hard as a suit of mail. Orienting himself by the direction of the wind, Joseph struggled on against the storm until at last he could make out a blurred grayish shape looming ahead—the post! Only a few more yards and he was safe. Not until he was warming himself by the fireplace did he fully appreciate what he had been through and the miracle of his survival. Then the reaction set in; and he thought he would never stop shivering.

The other men found it hard to believe his story, even with the evidence of the frozen clothing. "Your time hasn't come yet, LaBarge," one of them said. "Your work remains to be done." And in fact Joseph LaBarge was destined to live well beyond the allotted three score and ten and to become the most famous steamboat pilot on the Missouri—the river that had so nearly claimed him that winter afternoon at Bellevue.

Nicomi

As RIVER traffic increased between St. Louis and the northern posts, the settlement at Bellevue grew into a flourishing little town. The site was said to have been given its name in 1807 by Manuel Lisa, the founder of the Missouri Fur Company and the first of the large-scale operators to penetrate the upper river. However, there is no mention of Bellevue in fur-trading records until after 1823, when both a trading post and the Council Bluff Indian Agency were located there. The agency, which served the Omaha, Oto, Missouri, and Pawnee tribes, formerly had been located a few miles upriver at Fort Atkinson. At the time of its founding in 1819, this fort was the westernmost military installation in the United States.

A man prominently identified with Bellevue from 1824 on was Peter A. Sarpy, a St. Louisan related to the Chouteaus of the American Fur Company. When Sarpy went to work for the company, one of his first assignments was to deal with a group of independent fur traders who were encroaching on the company's territory. His method of handling them, which amounted to a small-scale "shooting war," was effective, but it almost cost the company its federal charter and necessitated the payment of a huge indemnity to the traders whose outfits Sarpy had seized. No man to be trifled with, Sarpy was forthright, scrupulously honest, and absolutely fearless, and though he sometimes played up to influential persons, he did so simply as a matter of expediency, as the quickest means of achieving his ends. He was respected by the Indians, who gave him the name of Na-ka-gah-he, or Big Chief, and he went out of his way both to praise their good traits and to condemn the treatment they had received from the whites.

A famous and characteristic story about him concerns the time he was holding forth to a group at the Bellevue trading post on the virtues of the red man. A stranger present took issue with Sarpy, saying that the Indians were a lying, thieving, treacherous lot, and that the sooner they were exterminated the better it would be for the country. Sarpy bounced to his feet and thrust his face so close to the stranger's that their chins almost touched. "I am Peter A. Sarpy, sir!" he snapped. "If you want to fight, sir, I am your man, sir!" With that, he whipped out his pistol and shot out the only light in the room—a candle on a table a few paces away. Another candle was hurriedly produced and lit, but there was no fight. The stranger had evaporated.

Quite as remarkable in her way was another post inhabitant, Nicomi, a very beautiful Indian woman of Omaha and Iowa descent. She had been born about 1808, and as a young girl had been married to an Englishman, Dr. John Gale. In those days it was the army's custom to hire civilian physicians. Gale, who had come to America in search of adventure, contracted to serve with the Sixth Infantry and came with the troops to Fort Atkinson.

According to one story, Gale sought Nicomi's hand after she had saved his life by guiding him to shelter through a blizzard.

He built his bride a comfortable log cabin near the fort and lived there with her when his duties permitted. Nicomi was a faithful and loving wife. She made buckskin suits for her husband, and often would go into the timber along the Missouri to gather plants, herbs, and the barks of roots to be used in concocting his medicines. As the wife of a white medicine man, Nicomi's lot was far happier than that of the average Indian wife who had to carry wood and water and endure without complaint blows and beatings from her Indian lord and master. Dr. Gale was considerate of her and her relatives, and devoted to their two babies, especially the first-born, little Mary.

Their idyllic life together came to an end in 1827. Fort Atkinson had been established for the protection of the fur trade, but during the years since its founding seventeen treaties had been signed with the tribes in the region, and the government decided it was no longer necessary to maintain a military post at this point. Orders were received by the commanding officers that the fort was to be abandoned and the troops transferred downriver.

As was the case with many another white man on the frontier, Dr. Gale balked at the idea of taking his wilderness wife to live with him in civilized society. But he deeply loved little Mary, and he had no intention of leaving the child behind. Certain that Nicomi would never consent to his taking Mary away, he said nothing to her of his impending departure, but went to the fur-trading post to lay his problem before Peter Sarpy and to discuss with him the plan he had made for outwitting the Indian mother. Sarpy, however, was not at all encouraging. He knew Indians, and he told Gale flatly that he would never succeed in making off with Mary, no matter what trickery he employed.

Their entire discussion was overheard by Nicomi's brother, who was standing just outside the room where the two men were talking. Nicomi had heard the rumors that the fort was to be deactivated and the white soldiers sent away, and she sensed that her husband might have plans which did not include her. Enlisting the help of her Indian kinsfolk, she had arranged to have the doctor shadowed until she could find out his intentions.

In spite of Sarpy's counsel, Gale decided to carry out the

scheme he had laid before his friend. At the post he bought a supply of food and clothing which the little girl would need on the long trip to St. Louis, ordering that the items be held until called for. Then he bided his time until he had arranged passage on a boat going downriver.

The afternoon before the scheduled departure of the boat, Gale went to the cabin and told Nicomi that he had been called away temporarily on business and would be leaving a few days hence. He asked her to pack his belongings in readiness for the trip, and further requested that she go into the woods the next day to gather a quantity of a certain type of medicinal herb—a task which he knew would occupy her until nightfall. By that time he expected to be well on his way downriver with little Mary. Assuring Nicomi that he would return on the morrow to look after the children while she was in the woods, he returned to the fort to conclude his arrangements.

Although she concealed her feelings, Nicomi was not deceived by Gale's story or by his ruse for getting her out of the way. She had learned from her brother of the conversation between Gale and Sarpy. Further, her brother had seen the purchases Gale made at the trading post, and this confirmed her suspicions that he planned to rob her of little Mary. During the night she whisked the two children to a hiding place she already had pre-pared—a cave in the woods known only to the Indians. Here she and the little ones would remain until her brother hung a cloth on a tree within view of the cave as a signal that all was well.

When Gale came to the cabin not long after sunrise, he found his valise dutifully packed just as he had requested, but no sign of Nicomi or the children. Although he searched for a time, he knew in his heart that it was useless, that he had been outwitted. Returning to the trading post, he entrusted a sum of money to Sarpy, and asked him to look out for his family. As soon as Gale's boat was out of sight Nicomi's brother ran to give the "all clear" signal, and Nicomi returned to the cabin with Mary and the baby. She never expected to see her husband again.

But Gale found that he could not forget his little daughter. When Mary was eight or nine, he returned from Cantonment

Leavenworth in Kansas, where he had been stationed, meaning
to assert his parental rights and take Mary to St. Louis to be educated. When he learned that during the intervening years the
younger child had died, Dr. Gale, to his credit, did not have the
heart to deprive Nicomi of her surviving daughter.

Two or three years later, in 1834, Dr. Gale returned to Bellevue for the last time. He had contracted a mortal illness and
knew that he had only a few months to live. Despite his condition, he made the hard journey upriver, feeling that he would
die easier if he had seen to it that the little daughter he so deeply
loved was situated with a white family. He arranged with an
Indian friend to have Mary at the boat landing when the steamboat was about to embark. But at the last moment the Indian
betrayed the plan to Nicomi, and again she hid in the woods
until the boat was gone. A few months later Dr. Gale died, and
was buried at Fort Armstrong in Illinois.

Four years after Gale's death—the mourning period stipulated
by Indian custom—Peter Sarpy and Nicomi were married. Perhaps
he recognized in her a fiery spirit akin to his own, and certainly
the Indian woman was one of the few people not afraid to stand
up to him. In 1839 he persuaded her to come and live with him
in St. Louis, promising that she could return once a year to visit
her tribe. But although they had a fine house in St. Louis and, as
befitted a man of Sarpy's wealth, lived in some style, Nicomi
never got used to her new surroundings. At first Sarpy thought
her unhappiness would pass, but when he saw how miserable she
was, he allowed her to return to her wilderness home for good.
He continued to be a devoted husband until his death, and provided generously for her and her daughter in his will.

Nicomi lived to a great age—she died in 1888—admired by
her Indian compatriots and respected by the whites. Accounts of
her courtship by Dr. Gale were widely circulated during the first
half of the nineteenth century. Perhaps because her name means
"Voice of the Waters," it was said that the character of Minnehaha
(Laughing Water) in Longfellow's poem *Hiawatha* was suggested
in part by the story of Nicomi. In 1850 her daughter Mary became the wife of Joseph LaFlesche, a head chief of the Omaha,

of mixed French and Indian blood, and their eldest child Susette, known as Bright Eyes, became well known for her efforts to secure more equitable and humane treatment of the red man.

Fort Atkinson, the scene of Nicomi's courtship, fell rapidly into decay. When Prince Maximilian von Wied-Neuwied visited the site in 1833 he reported that everything of value had been carried away by the Indians, and that the only inhabitants of the ruins were rattlesnakes. But Bellevue was to thrive until well past the middle of the century, and Peter Sarpy's post continued to be a rendezvous for Indians, traders, and travelers.

In 1822 Major Andrew Henry and General William R. Ashley founded what in time came to be known as the Rocky Mountain Fur Company. Their early experiences convinced the partners that the system of fixed trading posts would never pay, and they reorganized their operation on a plan of their own. They employed no traders, hired no Indian trappers. Instead they recruited daring young white men who knew the rifle and the steel trap as they knew their own hands, men who could ride and shoot, self-reliant, lusty fellows who would harvest the fur wherever and whenever it could be found in spite of hell or high water, in spite of rival trappers, hostile Indians or the Devil himself.

Instead of building permanent forts, Ashley and Henry held an annual rendezvous, or fur fair, in some convenient, previously appointed valley in the mountains. Supplies were brought to rendezvous by pack trains, which also carried the furs back to market in St. Louis. Under this system the beaver trappers had no occasion to return to the settlements or sleep under a roof.

The hardships and constant danger faced by American trappers toughened those who survived to a high degree of courage, address, skill, and physical fitness.

*And the discipline maintained by their employers
(both military men) was strict. Thus overnight Ashley
and Henry created a new career, a new way of life—in
fact a new breed of men, that hardy race of explorers,
daring fighters, skilled hunters and trappers, known
then and thereafter, because they lived the year 'round
in the Rockies, as the "Mountain Men."*

—Condensed from Stanley Vestal's
Joe Meek, the Merry Mountain Man

The Mountain Men

THE NAMES of the Mountain Men—among them Jim Bridger,
Thomas Fitzpatrick, the Sublette brothers, Jedediah Smith, Joe
Meek, and Kit Carson—crop up again and again on the most
stirring pages in the early history of the Far West. The vast and
rugged region north from Santa Fe to Canada was their theater
of action, and their heyday dates from March of 1824 when Fitzpatrick and Smith, following directions given them by the Crow
Indians, located the great South Pass through the Rockies and
entered the beaver-rich Green River Valley.

Assured that there was a practicable route across the Continental Divide, Ashley and Henry immediately moved their company's base of operations westward from the mouth of the
Yellowstone, and in 1825 the first rendezvous was held at Henry's
Fork of the Green River, near the present Wyoming-Colorado
line. In 1826 the original proprietors sold out their interest, and
in 1830, when the name of Rocky Mountain Fur Company was
adopted, a group which included Fitzpatrick, Bridger, and Milton
Sublette became the owners.

Every summer for sixteen years, from 1825 to 1840, a pre-
determined spot in central or western Wyoming was the scene of
that wild and wonderful carnival of the wilderness known as

rendezvous. Bands of trappers made their way from every point of the compass to meet the company's *bourgeois* with his load of supplies from St. Louis, trade their furs, refit for the coming year, and blow off steam as only the mountain men could.

The chosen meeting place would always be in a river valley where there was plenty of good clear water, timber for fuel, and grass for the stock. By the time the St. Louis pack train pulled in the valley would be swarming with trappers, Indian bucks and squaws, dogs, ponies, and mules. The grand lodge for the *bourgeois*, which served as company headquarters, was at the center of the encampment. Around it were the tipis belonging to the Indian wives of the free trappers—those lords of creation who owned their own outfits, and were free to trade their furs with any of the competing companies. Scattered about everywhere were improvised camps—wickiups, huts, even unsheltered bedrolls on the ground—belonging to lesser mortals: the hired trappers, who were paid wages by the company, and the so-called skin trappers—those who were in debt for their equipment and were pledged to sell all their furs to the company at company prices.

The most conspicuous men on the scene were the free trappers. Most of them had adopted the wilderness as their permanent home, and they aped the manners, habits, and dress of the Indians. Their long hair came down over the collars of their hunting shirts or was plaited into braids and bound with colored ribbons. They wore bright-colored ruffled calico shirts and hunting coats of buckskin with fringed sleeves, fancy brass buttons, and fur collars; their leggings and moccasins were adorned with beadwork; and some wore parti-colored sashes in which were tucked a pistol, a knife, and the stem of an Indian pipe. But an even more brilliant spectacle than a free trapper duded up for rendezvous was his favorite saddle horse. In addition to the finest of silver-mounted horse hardware—Spanish bridle, tooled leather saddle, beaded saddlebags—the animal would be decked out with eagle feathers tied to its mane and tail, and painted with vermilion or white clay or whatever hue best contrasted with its natural color.

First order of the day after the arrival of the *bourgeois* was the distribution of mail; after that the packs of goods were opened and trading began. As each trapper's name was called he came forward with his beaver skins and other pelts which a clerk checked in and credited to him on the company's books. Against this credit was charged what he took in the way of trade goods: flour, sugar, coffee and tobacco, ammunition, clothing, perhaps a new gun, blankets, and gewgaws which would appeal to the Indian women.

After these transactions had been taken care of, the *bourgeois* ordered kegs of diluted raw alcohol rolled out, and the trappers, armed with kettles and cups, came running to "wet their dry." Now there would be feasts at every mess fire, tall tales told, tight fixes recalled, and—as the liquor went down and the bragging went up—all kinds of contests and show-off activities—races and shooting matches and wrestling and feats of horsemanship. Competition invariably led to fights: there would be black eyes and bloody noses galore around camp, and sometimes more serious damage. But it was all part of rendezvous and usually the combatants would end up peacefully playing cards together or devising practical jokes to spring on the greenhorns out from St. Louis for their first season in the wilderness.

From mid-June to September was vacation time for the mountain men. During the summer the trapping was unprofitable and they took it easy. The rest of the year was another story: months of cruelly hard work under conditions in which survival was problematic. Starvation, dying of thirst, drowning, death from exposure were routine occupational hazards for trappers in the Rockies. The kick of a pony's hoof, the claws of a grizzly, an arrow from an Indian bow might cut short their lives at any moment. When rendezvous-time rolled around they felt entitled to cut loose with a little celebrating. After all, before rendezvous came again their bones might be whitening in the mountains.

1

Each band of trappers, called a brigade, was led by a captain who planned their route, saw to it that a green hand always hunted with an old-timer, and decided whether the brigade should fight or run when, as frequently happened, they encountered hostile Indians. During a hunt the brigade would split up in groups of two and three men who would drop out of the main line of march to work on their own, rejoining the party with their catch at a camp farther on.

In the early spring of 1832 the brigade Jim Bridger was captaining spent a few days encamped with a band of Rockaway Indians—friendlies—on Bear River. Trouble started when one of the trappers was impertinent to the chief's daughter, and in the ensuing fracas Bridger's partner, Milton Sublette, was so badly cut up that it was feared he would not live. Joe Meek, a twenty-two-year-old Virginian, was left with the veteran trader—as Sublette said, "to take care of him if he lived and to bury him if he died"—while the brigade carried on with the spring hunt.

It was forty days before Sublette had healed up enough to move on; by then, once Joe helped him on his horse, he was able to stay in the saddle. During their enforced stay in their lonely camp, old Milt had complained about the lack of excitement; however, when they reached the headwaters of the Green River they ran into plenty of it—in the form of a band of Shoshoni warriors. Usually the Shoshoni, also known as the Snakes, got along pretty well with the mountain men, but for some reason this band came at them screaming war whoops. Since Joe and Milt were armed only with single-shot rifles, there was nothing to do but make a run for it.

Farther down the stream they saw the Shoshoni camp, and Milt shouted that their best chance was to make for the large medicine lodge in the center of the camp. Such a lodge was a holy place and anyone who took refuge in it was temporarily safe from violence. Accordingly, Joe and Sublette tore into the village on the dead run; jerking up their mounts at the big lodge, they flung themselves from their saddles, rushed into the sanctuary, and immediately sat down side by side facing the fireplace.

Moments later their pursuers and others of the tribe came crowding in, brandishing their weapons menacingly and howling threats. But the two white men knew that a council must be held before any action was taken against them, and they sat impassively, taking care to show no signs of fear.

Presently the lodge was filled and the council began. Most of the warriors seemed to be in favor of killing the trappers, but one old man argued that they should be allowed to go free. This was Chief Bad Left Hand, known to the whites as "Goche" or "Gothia" (from the French translation of his name, *Mauvais Gauche*). The council went on throughout the day, the old chief continuing to maintain that there was no merit in slaughtering two harmless travelers, the others insisting that they must die. Just at sunset, while their fate still hung in the balance, there was a great commotion and everyone ran outside to see what had caused the excitement—everyone, that is, but the two white men and Chief Gothia. (Milt and Joe later figured that he must have arranged the diversion as the only way to save their lives.) Beckoning them to follow, the chief led the two into the brush at the opposite end of the village. There they found an Indian girl holding their horses, already saddled. Both Milt and Joe had time to notice that the girl was unusually attractive, but they were in a little too much of a hurry just then to tell her so.

"Ride if you wish to live," the chief said. "Ride without stopping all night, and tomorrow linger not." Following this excellent advice, Joe and Sublette were soon out of reach of the Shoshoni, and eventually succeeded in rejoining their brigade.

After rendezvous that year the brigades were reorganized, Joe being assigned to accompany Jim Bridger and Thomas Fitzpatrick while Sublette went out with another band. The Sublette group chanced to fall in with Chief Gothia's village. Milt lost no time in cultivating the chief's friendship and that of his comely daughter, who was none other than the girl who had helped him and Joe to escape. Her name—in the Shoshoni tongue Umentucken Tukutsey Undewatsey—was Lamb of the Mountains. Sublette was happy to turn over a generous number of ponies to Chief Gothia in return for the privilege of making the beautiful Mountain Lamb his wife.

2

While Sublette was courting the Mountain Lamb, the brigade which Joe Meek had joined was engaged in a game of hide-and-seek with a rival brigade belonging to the American Fur Company. The latter outfit had been dogging the Rocky Mountain party, led by Jim Bridger and Thomas Fitzpatrick, hoping to be guided to good hunting ground. Naturally the veteran mountain men were not about to do their competitors any such favor. Instead, they led them on a wild-goose chase across the mountains to the Missouri, avoiding the beaver streams and killing all the game found along the way. Their destination was the Blackfoot country, where game was scarce and the red man hostile, the idea being to starve out—or scare out—the less experienced men of the American Fur Company, and then proceed to the hunting grounds. The maneuver succeeded—the rival brigade was attacked by the Blackfeet and sustained such heavy losses that it all but ended their company's operations for that season—but it was not without cost to the Bridger brigade, who had their troubles with the Blackfeet, too.

Among the rocky hillsides at the headwaters of the Missouri they made contact with a numerous band of Blackfeet. Seeing the size of Bridger's party (eighty trappers and camp keepers), the Indians apparently decided not to risk an engagement, and sent one of their chiefs out into the open carrying a peace pipe. He was accompanied by seven unarmed warriors. Bridger, however, was fearful of treachery. While he and Fitzpatrick were mulling the situation, one of the free trappers, a young Mexican named Loretto, came up and asked to speak with them.

It happened that two years before, when Loretto was doing some hunting with the friendly Crows, he had fallen in love with a Blackfoot girl whom the Crows had captured in a raid. He had bought her from her captor for two or three ponies, and since then she had borne him a baby and followed him as his wife and camp keeper, facing every danger and suffering every privation of the trapper brigade. Now Loretto told Bridger that he recognized the Blackfoot band as relatives of his wife, and there was nothing to worry about. Accordingly, Thomas Fitzpatrick and seven trappers went to meet the Indian group, leaving their guns behind. After shaking hands all around, they sat down and began to parley in sign language.

As this was going on, Loretto's wife cried out and began to signal—she had recognized her brother among the Blackfeet on the hillside. One of the Indians parleying with Fitzpatrick got up to see what was going on, and a young warrior rode out to explain. This meant there was now an unequal number at the parley; moreover, the young warrior had forgotten to leave his bow and quiver behind. To equalize matters, Jim Bridger took his rifle and rode out, accompanied by Loretto's wife to act as interpreter. Just as they reached the group Jim saw that the young warrior's bow was strung, and he cocked his gun. The Blackfoot chief, alarmed by the hostile click, instantly grasped the gun barrel, forcing the muzzle downward and causing the gun to discharge. The Indian then jerked the gun out of Bridger's hands and clubbed him on the head with it, knocking him to the ground—a feat which would have been more difficult to accomplish but for the fact that by this time Jim had two arrows in his back. In the confusion Loretto's wife was thrown from her horse and seized by the Blackfeet, who ran with her back to the hillside.

A wild scene followed, with members of both parties scrambling for cover behind trees and rocks and firing at long range. During lulls the white party could hear the distracted cries of Loretto's wife, calling out for her husband and child, and finally Loretto could endure it no longer. Heedless of the danger, he mounted and galloped over to the Blackfoot band, carrying the baby, which he gave into its mother's arms. This bold and noble act impressed the Blackfoot chief, who said that he was free to go back to the trappers unharmed. Loretto pleaded that his wife and baby be permitted to return with him, but the chief sternly refused, saying that she belonged with her people. Finally, at his wife's insistence, Loretto went back alone to the brigade.

There were no further hostilities. The Blackfeet lost nine warriors; the trappers three men killed and six horses. Although Jim Bridger recovered from his wounds, he continued to carry one of the arrowheads in his back as a souvenir. But there was an unexpectedly happy sequel to this unfortunate incident. In the summer of 1835 the Rocky Mountain Fur Company and the American Fur Company ended their rivalry by joining forces, and Loretto hired out as interpreter at a fort which they built in the Blackfoot country. Subsequently he was able to find and reclaim his wife and child, and brought them back in safety to make their home at the fort.

3

After the Blackfoot fight the Bridger-Fitzpatrick brigade proceeded with "business as usual," trapping in the Beaverhead Valley. They spent Christmas in winter quarters at the forks of the Snake, and it was then Joe Meek first learned that the Mountain Lamb had become the wife of Milton Sublette. Joe had thought about the beautiful Indian girl plenty during the long days in the wilderness and the lonely nights around the campfire. But old Milt had got the jump on him, and he had to be content with admiring Isabel—as Milt had renamed her—from far off.

One day, though, Joe had a chance to show his feelings. Toward the end of January the main camp was moved to a new locale where game was more plentiful. Joe had been left behind to round up some stray animals; when he finally caught up with the rear of the train he found himself riding beside the Mountain Lamb. It was a bitter day, the air thick with frozen ice particles, and she was trying to shield the new-born babe she carried from the piercing wind. Cold as he was, Joe instantly divested himself of his blanket coat and wrapped it around the Lamb and her lambkin, telling her to hurry onto camp.

The blanket coat, called a capote, was Jim's only upper garment, and this gesture left him naked to the waist except for his fur cap. With the strays to herd he could make only slow progress, and he rode all afternoon exposed to the biting wind and sleet. When he finally arrived in camp he was so near frozen that after he was lifted off his horse, he had to be rolled in the snow to restore his circulation before he could safely go near the fire.

After rendezvous in 1833 Milt Sublette returned to St. Louis with a pack train: an old wound in his leg refused to heal and he had decided to seek medical aid in the States. He planned to return to the mountains, but the leg had to be amputated; and old Milt, knowing he would never see the beaver country again, confided the Mountain Lamb to Joe Meek's care. At the 1835 rendezvous Joe was swapping his beaver for presents for her, and soon moved his belongings into her lodge.

Many years later, Joe told his biographer, Mrs. Frances Victor, that Umentucken was the most beautiful woman he had ever seen. "When she was mounted on a horse," he said, "she made a fine show. She wore a skirt of beautiful blue broadcloth, and a bodice and leggins of scarlet cloth, of the very finest make. Her hair was braided and fell over her shoulders; a scarlet silk handkerchief, tied on hood fashion, covered her head, and the finest embroidered moccasins her feet. She rode astride like all the Indian women, and carried on one side of her saddle the tomahawk for war, and on the other the pipe of peace." Her horse, a dapple gray named All Fours, cost Joe three hundred dollars, and the saddle and bridle another two hundred.

Small wonder that the Indian woman's highest ambition was to win a trapper, and by Joe Meek's own account the Mountain Lamb made him very happy. He was proud not only of her beauty but of her courage. Once when the brigade was in camp on the Yellowstone she and some of the other women went out to pick cherries. (The dried fruit, pounded up with meat and tallow, was used to make pemmican, a staple of the trappers' diet during the winter months.) While they were thus peacefully engaged, the group was attacked by a war party of Blackfeet. A number of the women were captured, but Umentucken dived into the Yellowstone and swam to safety across the swiftly running stream, bullets slapping the water all around her. Another time, when Joe was on a hunt, an Irish trapper named O'Fallen accused her of assisting in the escape of two Indian captives he had bought from the Shoshonis, intending to use them as slaves. Warned that O'Fallen was coming to give her a whipping, Umentucken was ready with Joe's pistol. In sight of the whole camp, she forced the bully to throw down his whip and beg for mercy.

Umentucken was destined to share Joe's life only two years. One June afternoon in 1837 thirty Bannock warriors came to the camp of the Bridger brigade to demand the return of some horses they claimed were stolen. A Bannock hothead tried to yank a bridle from Jim Bridger's hand and one of the trappers fired. In instant retaliation the Bannocks let fly with their arrows. One of these struck the Mountain Lamb, piercing her valiant heart.

Until about 1843 the fur trade remained the most important activity in the trans-Missouri country. As James C. Olson has written in his History of Nebraska: *"The traders and trappers roamed everywhere, involving themselves and their government with the Indians and even with foreign powers, drinking, gambling, squawing and carousing, making huge fortunes almost overnight and losing them even more rapidly. Through it all, however, they were exploring this vast, wild country—both plain and mountain—seeking the sources of its rivers and finding new roads to the West. The map of the West was indeed first drawn on a beaver skin."*

In the years to come, precious metals rather than peltries would be the magnet drawing adventurous men into the western wilderness. But as early as 1827, long before the fur trade was played out, an advance guard of prospectors already had tried their luck in the Rockies.

Fat Man's Misery

IN THE summer of 1827, a party of twenty-four men led by James Cockrell set out from Independence, Missouri, on a quest that they hoped and believed would make their fortunes. Four years previously Cockrell had discovered a vein of silver-bearing ore while beaver-trapping in the Rockies. Upon his return to Missouri he had told friends of his discovery, and finally had succeeded in organizing an expedition to search out and develop the mine. As the only man in the party who had ever made the trip to the mountains, Cockrell was elected captain; and all looked to him to guide them on the long journey across the plains and through the mountain maze.

Every man took one horse, a scant amount of bedding, a good gun, and a quantity of powder and lead. These last items were particularly important, not only because they would be traveling through an area occupied by hostile Indians but because they would be dependent on the game they could kill for food. Cooking utensils were a luxury they dispensed with: meat was roasted or broiled over a fire, trapper-fashion. They had no means of carrying supplies to last more than a week and game was scarce, so they were soon on short rations; and the little band looked forward eagerly to reaching the "buffalo belt." In this region, which began at the Great Bend of the Arkansas River about two hundred miles west of Independence, grew the short, nutritious grama grass, called buffalo grass, on which the big beasts grew sleek and vigorous. Once the prospecting party made it to the Great Bend, the meat supply problem was solved. For days together they were never out of sight of great buffalo herds.

Continuing westward along the Arkansas River, the party reached the Raton Mountains, not far from present-day Trinidad, Colorado, and turned northward. Cockrell announced that they were now in the vicinity of his silver find, and spirits were consequently high, but after a week of fruitless searching for the site, the men became distrustful and threatening. They questioned whether he had ever found any ore; or, if he had, they suspected that he was unwilling to share his secret with his comrades. By the time Cockrell finally did locate the mine it was literally a life-and-death matter, for the men had become very menacing, swearing that they were not going to be led out on this long, dangerous trip only to be duped.

Even when they actually had arrived at their goal, there was a good deal of grumbling. Never having seen crude ore, the adventurers assumed that the silver would look as it does in its refined form. They had visions of cutting it out of the rocks with their tomahawks, loading up their horses, and leading them triumphantly home, much as Cockrell had done when he returned to Independence, his saddle bags clanking with the silver dollars he had secured in exchange for his beaver skins. Now, instead of glittering bars of bullion, they were confronted with dirty-looking rocks with shiny specks in them. Let down and disappointed, the prospectors selected some of the best-looking stones, loaded them on their horses, and started glumly on the six-hundred-mile trek home.

As they proceeded down the Arkansas through country swarming with hostile Indians, the little party knew many uneasy moments but encountered no real trouble until they camped one night on the river bank about where Dodge City now stands. After a hearty supper of buffalo meat, they set their guard around the horses—the prime target of any Indian raid—and lay down to sleep.

Two men at a time stood guard, and they were relieved every three hours, but on that night their vigilance was to no avail. Silently the lurking redskins closed in on the camp, crawling on their bellies through the tall grass which grew along the river until they had reached a position between the guards and the horses. Then suddenly they rose up firing their guns, shaking their buffalo robes, yelling and warwhooping like mad men to frighten the horses. While a reserve squadron of Indians ran the horses off, the original attackers fired upon the whites bivouacked along the river. Caught completely unawares, the prospectors had no recourse but to jump into the stream and head for a point where they were protected from bullets and arrows by the slope of the bank. There they huddled, up to their knees in water, throughout the rest of that cold October night.

The next morning a dismal council was held, and it was decided that their only chance was to try to reach the Missouri on foot. Walking, the men knew, they could cover barely half the distance each day that they had made on horseback; and winter

would soon be on them. And even more serious was the problem
of food. After they had left the buffalo belt there was small like-
lihood that they could kill enough game to subsist on. No one
was so optimistic as to suppose that all would make it back to
Independence. In the ordeal that lay ahead it would be a question
of survival of the fittest; and the least fit, it was unanimously—
and sadly—agreed, was Clark Davis, perhaps the best-liked member of the party. Davis weighed some three hundred pounds, and
since he was a short, small-boned man, his weight—twice that of
most of his comrades—consisted largely of fat. Whatever each man
thought of his own chances, it was a foregone conclusion that
Davis could never stand to walk four hundred miles carrying his
rifle and ammunition.

Before leaving the scene of the raid, the forlorn group made a
bonfire of their saddles and bridles and any other belongings they
could not carry, so that the Indians would realize no further advantage from their victory. Then turning their faces grimly
toward the Missouri they set out on the long march. Impeded in
many places by tall grass and drifting sand, they could make only
twenty or twenty-five miles a day.

True to his comrades' prediction, Davis was unable to keep
up. During the first week his feet blistered terribly and his fat
thighs were chafed raw from rubbing together. Every morning
after going a little way he would begin to puff and pant and
falter; gradually he would lag farther and farther behind; and
finally it became necessary to depute five or six men to remain
with him to protect him from the Indians. The party would halt
for the night, and three or four hours later Davis and his escort
would plod into camp. In the interval before they turned up, the
men would gather in little groups to express their concern, and
to brood over the prospect of having to leave the lovable Davis
to be devoured by the prairie wolves. When they pictured themselves breaking the news to his family, the men actually wept.

Nightly the band expected the rearguard to bring the sad
news that Davis had collapsed and given up. But after the first
few days his feet hardened, his general powers of endurance began

to improve, and to the surprise and relief of all, each night he
reached camp a little sooner.

After the party left the buffalo range they traveled through
a desolate country where game of any kind was scarce. Within a
few days the men had eaten what meat they could carry on their
backs, and the gaunt hikers were reduced to a famishing condition. Now, ironically enough, Davis's fat proved a blessing, giving
him extra reserves of energy. Instead of trailing the party he took
the lead, and it began to appear that he would be the only one
to reach home. At Council Grove, with a hundred and thirty
miles still to go, the party went into a dismal camp near a patch
of timber, and it seemed to many of them that they were doomed
to die there. Worn out by weary days of tramping, the starving
men huddled on the ground, with neither the strength nor the
spirit to make another move. All, that is, but Davis. He was as
pert and frisky as a mustang who had never known the saddle.

"Boys," he said, surveying the demoralized group, "I will go
and kill a deer." To men perishing from hunger, who had seen
no game for days, his words sounded like a cruel and tantalizing
joke. But although Davis received no encouragement, he was determined to go on his hunt. Off he went, and he had traveled no
more than a few hundred yards when he spied two fine deer
standing in the open timber. His comrades heard a shot and, as
soon as he could reload, another. Silence—and then a shout:
"Come here, boys! There is meat in plenty."

In a trice the beaten men had forgotten their weakness. Rushing pell mell to the scene, they found Davis standing triumphantly over his kill. No one paused to congratulate him; time for
that later. Butchering the animals like savages, the men drank
every drop of blood that was in the two deer, devoured the raw
livers, sucked the marrow out of the leg bones. Not a scrap or
particle went to waste.

Davis's deer hunt was the turning point. The supply of meat
sustained the party until they reached the settlements and safety.
The specimens of silver which they brought back were sent to
St. Louis, but they did not assay very high. However, even if it
had turned out that the mine was a rich one, it would have been

of no practical value. The Cockrell expedition was the first prospecting party that ever left the western borders of Missouri for the Rocky Mountains, and they were more than thirty years ahead of the time when silver mining would be successfully carried on in the Rockies. But the venture is noteworthy if only because perhaps never in the history of the frontier had one hundred and fifty pounds of excess fat proved of such value. To the twenty-four brave men whose lives it saved, it was worth more than all the gold and silver in the Rockies.

The fur trade was at its height at a time when the Santa Fe trade was just beginning to assume proportions worthy of notice. The way to Santa Fe originally had been opened by the Mallet brothers, French explorers, in 1739, and though the Spanish tried to prohibit the French from trading with their New Mexican settlements, numerous pack trains crossed the wilderness during the 1740's and 1750's. But the French were gradually losing their hold on North America, and by the terms of a treaty signed in 1763 all the land west of the Mississippi became Spanish.

Following the Louisiana Purchase, the new American nation moved quickly to exploit the lands in the Southwest. In the years 1806 and 1807 an expedition led by Captain Zebulon M. Pike traveled through what is now Colorado and New Mexico, exploring the headwaters of the Arkansas and Red rivers. Pike was arrested by the Spaniards in Santa Fe, but soon set free, and his report, published in 1810, focused interest on the region. Two years later a Missouri trader named Thomas Becknell conceived and carried out the idea of striking directly across country to Santa Fe instead of going by the circuitous mountain route—an expedition which defined the Santa Fe Trail for future trade caravans. The War of 1812 and Mexico's revolt against

*Spain temporarily curtailed trading activity, but in
1821, after the proclamation of Mexican independence, the embargo on foreign trade was lifted, and the
Santa Fe Trail was opened to the commerce of the
Southwest.*

*The importance of the trade with Mexico was first
officially recognized in 1824 when Missouri's Senator
Thomas Hart Benton introduced a bill to secure a survey from the Missouri River to the Mexican boundary.
But as yet there were few treaties with the Indians,
and the Comanches, the Kiowa, and other hostiles
harassed the trading caravans. Indeed, the Indian menace grew to such proportions that in 1829 three companies of infantry escorted the annual caravan to
Chouteau's Island, a trading post established by August P. Chouteau in the valley of the upper Arkansas.
It was at about this time that bands of the southern
branch of the Cheyenne and the Arapaho, migratory
Plains Indians of the Algonquinian family, drifted
down into the region from the north, and began to be
seen along the Santa Fe Trail.*

Friday, the Indian White Boy

NEAR THE end of May, 1831, a sizable village of Arapaho Indians
established a temporary encampment close to where the southern
branch of the Santa Fe Trail reached the north fork of the Cimarron River. One fine sunshiny afternoon when the village children
were out playing, a group of the more venturesome boys wandered far afield trying to catch prairie dogs. It was late in the
day by the time they tired of their sport and started back to camp.
Their elders, meanwhile, had completed preparations to break

camp, and when the boys reached the top of a little hill a mile or so from where home had been, the whole village was on the move, part going east and part west.

Seeing that the westward-moving band would pass quite close to them, the tired youngsters sat down on the hill to await its approach. As it drew nearer and a boy would recognize the ponies and dogs and camp equipment of his family's lodge, he would run and join the caravan. One by one they became part of the moving throng, until finally only a little chap about nine years old was left. There he sat patiently until the last of the lodges had passed, and the procession came to an end with a wrinkled old man, hobbling along in an effort to keep up. The old man noticed the boy and beckoned him down from his post on the hillside. What was the child doing here all by himself, he wanted to know.

"I await my father's tipi," the boy replied.

The old man said: "Your parents have gone toward the rising sun. Make haste and join them before nightfall."

Obeying the old warrior's instructions, the boy started on a run to catch up with his family in the eastbound band. His path took him over dry, sandy country to the northeast of the Cimarron. Shortly after he crossed the river a high wind came up, as is often the case on the plains in spring; it obscured the trail left by the band and his own as well. The exertion of running and the hot, dry wind made him unbearably thirsty; and when night came he turned back to the Cimarron, exhausted and thoroughly frightened. The next day he could discover no trace of a trail in any direction. Casting about aimlessly, at last he found himself on the site of the deserted camp. Here he picked up some scraps and refuse on which he fed ravenously, and he decided to stay where he was and wait for his family to come back for him. He could not know it, but they supposed that he was with his friends in the westbound band.

The long day passed, and another, and another. After the first day there was no more food, and the boy became too weak to move from the shelter he had made for himself in the brush and tall grass by the river. His mind wandered; he imagined himself at a village feast, surrounded by great caldrons of soup and mounds of boiled and roasted meats. On the seventh day he fancied that he had been transported to the spirit world and was galloping along in the happy hunting ground. When he heard voices and saw men and animals approaching, it seemed to him all part of his delirious vision.

"It must truly be the happy hunting ground," he thought, "for here are horses for me to ride and the buffalo to chase. But what queer buffalo! How long their horns are, and how white! And there is a red one—and a yellow one—and a black one! And who are the men?"

As two of the men started walking toward him, the little fellow finally realized that they were palefaces. Although he had never seen any whites before, he had been taught by his people that they were cruel and hateful. But he was too feeble to try to run, too feeble even to struggle when the taller of the two men picked him up and carried him back to their camp. He was terribly frightened, supposing he would be killed immediately; instead the men gave him food and drink. He was treated so kindly and everything about him was so strange that he could scarcely believe he was not in the happy spirit world.

The boy's rescuers were two famous mountain men, Thomas Fitzpatrick and William Sublette, on their way from Missouri to Santa Fe with a trading caravan.* The "queer buffalo" were oxen which the traders used to pull their wagons. Up until about 1824 goods for Santa Fe had been packed on mules. But, as the trade grew to vast proportions, wagons were used; and oxen were substituted for the mules, because they were able to draw heavier loads, especially through muddy or sandy places. When the caravan stopped for noon hour—nooning, as it was called—Fitzpatrick

*Captain William Sublette was an older brother of Milton G. Sublette (see page 49). Fitzpatrick, who was then head of the Rocky Mountain Fur Company, was traveling to Santa Fe as the guest of the trading firm of Smith, Jackson, and Sublette. The caravan left Independence, Missouri, on May 4, 1831. It stayed several days at the spot where the Indian boy was found, searching for Jedediah Smith who had mysteriously disappeared. On reaching Santa Fe, his friends learned that Smith had been killed by Comanches.

had spotted a strange object in the underbrush, and he and Sublette had gone to investigate. The date was Friday, June 3, and Friday was the name they gave to the little Indian boy.

From that day, a new life opened for Friday. With the good care given him, he recovered quickly and was well and strong long before the caravan reached Santa Fe. Fitzpatrick, who took a special interest in him, treated the boy as if he were his own son. As soon as he finished his business in Santa Fe—which included engaging Kit Carson to work for the Rocky Mountain Fur Company—Fitzpatrick took Friday back to St. Louis and put him in school. Usually Indian boys fretted at classroom discipline, but Friday was an apt student and liked going to school. Soon he forgot the language and ways of his people, and adopted the language and customs of the whites.

News of the finding of the lost boy no doubt was relayed to the Arapahoes from Bent's Fort, the main trading rendezvous of the Cheyenne and the Arapahoes on the upper Arkansas River, and eventually Friday's parents heard that their boy had been saved by the mountain men and was living among the whites. However, no steps were taken to reclaim him until the late 1830's, when the United States Government was drawing up a treaty with the tribe. During the parley the Indians mentioned that an Arapaho boy, lost on the Cimarron some years before, was supposed to have been found by a company of traders, and they were offering a large number of horses to anyone who would return the lad. Being anxious to consolidate friendly relations with the tribe, the government requested Thomas Fitzpatrick to bring Friday to Bent's Fort, where he would be restored to his parents.

When the situation was explained to the boy, he would hardly listen. The whites were now his people, he said, and he would live and die among them. But finally he was persuaded to accompany his foster father back to the plains, with the understanding that he would soon return to St. Louis.

Friday's demeanor at the reunion was in strange contrast to the joy shown by his family. Seven years' absence had so weaned him away that he refused to own them. Parents and friends were

alien to him, and he had completely forgotten the language and
ways of his childhood. His father and brothers pressed their
mouths in astonishment and his mother wept at his repudiation
of them. It was only after much urging by the fur traders and
mountain men that Friday consented to leave the fort and go
among his people.

At the village he was received with honor and made welcome
by the whole band. His fellow tribesmen vied with one another
to pay him respect. Feast after feast and council after council
celebrated the return of the boy who had triumphantly survived
a miserable death alone on the prairie. Now he was famous
throughout the tribe, hailed as "the little chief" and "the Arapaho American." Flattered and touched by the honors and the
attention, Friday made an effort to accommodate himself to
Indian ways and eventually become reconciled to the life. He
strove unceasingly to teach his fellows a better way of life, and
was respected by red men and white alike for his sobriety, hon-
esty, and sense of justice. He was a chief by birth, but he refused
to claim that dignity until he had earned it by his own deeds.

Friday never lost his deep affection for his benefactor, Thomas
Fitzpatrick, whose kindness he repaid by a lifetime of loyalty to
the whites. He returned several times to St. Louis to visit his
friends there, and on at least one occasion his path and Fitzpatrick's crossed again. This occurred in July, 1854, when Fitzpatrick
and a group of traders encountered a band of Arapahoes in the
wilderness. An Easterner traveling with the traders never forgot
his surprise when one of the savages rushed up to Fitzpatrick,
grabbed him by the hand, and greeted him warmly in English.
In 1864, when the Overland Stage station was at Latham, Colorado, Friday came every now and then to spend the day at the
station, where he was always hospitably entertained and given
tobacco. Frank Root, who was in charge of the mail transfer at
this point, considered him to be one of the best and most trustworthy Indians he ever knew.

Though a warrior chief, Friday never became the head chieftain of the Arapaho. Among a people bred in a tradition of
hostility to the whites, his friendship for them was almost cer-

tainly an insurmountable barrier to his attainment of the supreme headship. He was believed to be about sixty years old
when he died in 1881.

*

Bent's Fort

BENT'S FORT, located in the upper valley of the Arkansas River
in what is now eastern Colorado, was an important fur-trading
post from about 1828 to 1852. In this isolated stronghold, six
hundred and fifty miles west of Fort Leavenworth and five hundred miles from the nearest settlement, William Bent reigned
like a feudal lord of medieval times. Scores of employees lived
within the spacious fort. Its herds grazed on the surrounding
prairies, and an irrigated garden furnished vegetables for summer
and root crops for winter use. Meat was preserved in an ice
house, which also supplied cool drinks for summer. Among other
amenities were a billiard table and a small telescope with a range
of seven miles. During trading fairs there were jolly parties
graced by Indian beauties. Small wonder that this citadel of the
plains loomed large in the thoughts of lonely trappers in the
Rockies and weary traders and travelers on the Santa Fe Trail.

The Bent family originally haled from Massachusetts, and
William, born in 1809, was one of five brothers who became noted
frontiersmen. In 1826, after three years spent working for the
American Fur Company, he and the two elder Bent brothers
formed a partnership with a French-Canadian, Ceran St. Vrain,
and settled on the upper Arkansas, where they put up a stockade.
Two years later they moved down the valley, closer to the hunting grounds, and began building what became known as Bent's
Old Fort, near the mouth of the Picketwire (originally Purga-
toire) River.

After the fort was completed in 1832, William was placed in
charge of it and of the trading activities which centered there.

His fearless conduct and love of justice won him the respect and confidence of the Indians, and among the trappers he had a reputation for courage remarkable even among that daring breed of men. In 1835, he took as his wife Owl Woman, daughter of White Thunder, Keeper of the Cheyenne Medicine Arrows, the sacred symbol of the tribe.* Since the keepers of the medicine-arrow and Sun-Dance rites stood first in priestly dignity among the Cheyenne, William Bent gained much prestige among the Indians from this union. Moreover, his association with the tribal elders and wise men taught him to value Indian learning, including their knowledge of the healing arts.

1

Most whites thought of the Indian medicine man as a quack who relied solely on incantations, magic, and the help of the spirits to drive disease from the one who was ill. And it was true that Indians did look upon sickness as a visitation of an evil spirit, to be treated in part by certain magic potions and elaborate religious rituals which often called for drumbeating and dancing. Before commencing his work, the medicine man offered up many weird incantations, and if the disease was one of long standing, he fasted and spent time by himself in some lonely place. But prayers and ceremonies were by no means all that Indian practitioners had to offer. Many of them were very skilled in treating ordinary ailments, and their knowledge of herbal medicine, handed down from father to son, was greater than that of the white layman, although not equal to that of a well-trained physician. For example, they knew particular weeds which could

---

*"The set of four medicine arrows, each of a different color, constitutes the tribal palladium [object upon which the safety of the tribe was dependent] which they claim to have had from the beginning of the world, and is exposed with appropriate rites once a year . . . , and on those rare occasions when a Cheyenne has been killed by one of his own tribe, the purpose of the ceremony being to wipe away from the murderer the stain of a brother's blood. . . . No woman, white man, or even mixed blood of the tribe has ever been allowed to come near the sacred arrows." *Handbook of American Indians*, I, 253–254.

be applied to rattlesnake bites and insect stings. But when it came to contagious diseases, like measles, smallpox, and diphtheria, neither magic nor their forest medicines were efficacious.

As there was no physician at the fort, William Bent did his own doctoring. He had a number of medical books, and on his trips to take furs to Independence he replenished his medicine chest. By consulting his books and using standard remedies, he was able to look after the health of his family and the personnel of the fort.

Then one day Bent himself became ill with a cold and severe sore throat. As the infection progressed, his throat filled with pus and became so swollen that he could scarcely breathe and could neither eat nor talk. His Cheyenne wife had to feed him broth through a quill which she passed down his throat. When a friend of Bent's, a guest at the fort, went to his lodge to inquire about him, Bent wrote on a slate that he was certain to die if he did not get relief very soon, and that he had sent for a medicine man of his wife's tribe.

The Indian, whose name was Lawyer, was a plain-looking person, with nothing in his garb or manner to denote his dependence on the magic or the supernatural. He called for a spoon and, using it for a tongue depressor, carefully examined Bent's throat. Then, shaking his head, he went outside, and returned shortly with a handful of sand burs. The burs were about the size of small garden peas, radiating stiff barbs as sharp as fish hooks. The wily medical man of the mountains next asked for a piece of sinew, a lump of marrow grease, and an awl. After making five or six threads of the sinew and tying a knot in one end of each, he took the awl and pierced each bur, ran the sinew through it down to the knot, then rolled it in marrow grease to coat the barbs. These preparations completed, he took a small flat stick, something like a Chinese chopstick, notched one end, pushed the greased bur down the patient's throat and pulled it out, bringing out on the barbs a quantity of the sloughing flesh which was choking the patient. He repeated this process with each sand bur, and soon Bent was able to breathe much more freely. Shortly thereafter he began to swallow soup, and in a day or two was well enough to take solid food.

Bent told his friend he would certainly have died if the Indian had not been there to attend him. No medicine known at that time would have reduced the swelling, and the nearest surgeon was many weeks' travel away. All who knew Lawyer considered him the shrewdest doctor among the Cheyenne. Certainly his treatment of Bent's case was striking demonstration of how Indian ingenuity could solve a problem that would have defeated a white man unused to operating without elaborate equipment.

2

One of the most familiar figures at Bent's Fort was John S. Smith, known as "Uncle John" to every trader, trapper, and hunter from the Yellowstone to the Mexican border. He was married to a Cheyenne, a sister of Chief Yellow Horse, and at one time was Thomas Fitzpatrick's interpreter. Uncle John had an expert eye for the value of frontier merchandise, and during the trading fairs, when pelts and buffalo robes were bartered for scarlet cloth, looking glasses, beads, guns, and ammunition, he was always ready to appraise everything from a beaver skin to a burro. Indeed, for an Indian or a Mexican to attempt to effect a trade without Uncle John Smith having something to say about it was almost illegal.

Like many old-timers he was a notable storyteller, with a vast stock of yarns based on his adventures in the wilderness. Perhaps his favorite tale, and one that he was frequently called on to relate, had its beginning in the year 1845. For more than three years he and his friends Bill Comstock, Dick Curtis, and Al Thorpe had been trapping on the Medicine Bow Range, and had accumulated a great quantity of beaver, otter, mink, and other skins which were cached in the hills. In April they raised the cache and started on foot on the long trek back to Independence, driving their five pack mules ahead of them. Four of the mules were laden with the precious pelts; the fifth carried their blankets, frying pan, extra ammunition, and personal belongings. By mid-June they had covered six hundred miles and reached the Arkansas River.

About four in the afternoon the first day after reaching the river, they went into camp at Point of Rocks—a rocky bluff rising abruptly from the prairie to the west of present-day Dodge City. They tethered their mules on good grazing ground on an elevation which could easily be defended, and had just settled down to rest when the mules became uneasy. In Uncle John's words, "Them critters can tell when Injins is around. They was pricking their ears and snorting, so we didn't waste no time grabbing our guns."

Reconnoitering over the ledge, the mountain men saw a Mexican bull train under attack on the trail below. The train was attempting to corral but sixty painted Pawnee were circling around it, howling and showering arrows into the oxen, and the wagons were in confusion. As the Smith party scrambled down the scarp to the aid of the train, the last wagon was cut out by part of the band. A man, a woman, and a little boy jumped out of it and began running, pursued by two Indians. One of them caught and killed the man, pausing to scalp him; the other overtook the woman, pulled her up on his horse, and dashed away into the hills. The Indian who had killed the man now took out after the child, who was running toward the Smith party as fast as his little legs would carry him. Just as the redskin reached down for the boy, Al Thorpe sent a bullet which toppled him from his horse. Dick Curtis scooped up the boy, and the mountain men raced for the wagon train, which by now had completed circling and formed into a corral. There the boy was gently tossed in a wagon where he'd be out of the way while they beat off the attack.

By the time they had stood off another charge it was getting dark, and the Indians withdrew into the sandhills on the other side of the river. When a half hour passed and they did not return, the Mexicans yoked up, the mountain men secured their mules, and the two parties pushed on cautiously up the road. As they traveled through the night, the little boy slept comfortably on some blankets provided by his rescuers.

By daylight they had made fourteen miles. During a three-hour halt to graze the stock, John Smith took the boy some coffee and fried meat. When the little fellow put his arms around Smith's neck and asked, "Where's Mama?" the old trapper was scarcely able to keep back the tears. Instead of replying, he questioned the boy and learned that his name was Paul Dale and that he was seven years old. His father and mother were missionaries who had been sent out to Mexico by a society in the East. They had been living in Santa Fe since Paul was a baby, and were on their way back to his grandmother's in Pennsylvania. They had arranged to travel as far as Missouri with this empty wagon train, which was picking up a sawmill in Independence.

When Paul had finished his breakfast once again came the forlorn inquiry, "Where's Mama?" and again Smith diverted him, this time by suggesting that he ride one of the mules when they pulled out. This prospect took Paul's mind off his troubles, and he was "shore tickled" when Smith rigged him a saddle out of blankets and hoisted him aboard. During the days that followed the old trapper became very attached to the boy—"purtiest little fellow you ever seen"—and Paul was never very far from his Uncle John, as he now called him. When he was tired of riding the mule, Paul picked flowers and chased prairie owls, or tagged along at the trapper's side.

When they reached the Great Bend, near the mouth of the Walnut, the Indians attacked again. One Mexican was killed and Al Thorpe got an arrow in his arm, but the Indians lost sixteen or eighteen warriors before they finally galloped off for good. During the fight Paul delighted the mountain men by his spirit. Every time a redskin fell, his piping voice could be heard from the wagon—"There goes another one, Uncle John!"

Ten days later the train reached Independence, where the trappers got a good price for their furs; each man had a shot bag full of gold and silver coins. They decided to invest the lion's share of the money in a six-mule wagon, harness, and trading goods, and join the first big train back to Santa Fe. Meanwhile Smith and the boy would stay with an elderly aunt of Smith's, who lived in Independence.

Everybody in the settlement heard about Paul's tragedy and had suggestions for his future. Some thought he should be put in an orphan asylum in St. Louis; others offered to adopt him. But Smith allowed that if any adopting was done, it would be by him. He bought Paul a coal-black pony, and had a suit of buckskin made for him out of the pelt of a blacktail deer he had shot on Powder River. Dressed in his buckskins and wearing a white sombrero, the lad was the very picture of a Spanish Don, and became the pet of the whole community.

Toward the end of August, Smith and the other trappers got their new outfit together and joined a caravan belonging to Ceran St. Vrain, which was headed for Mora, New Mexico, where Colonel St. Vrain had a big store. They reached Bent's Fort about the last of September and camped near the fort. Knowing that William Bent kept cows, Smith thought he would try to get some milk for his coffee, and at supper-time strolled over to the fort accompanied by Paul. On Smith's previous stopovers there had always been squaws doing the cooking, but this time there was a white woman leaning over the adobe hearth. Hearing them enter, she looked up and saw Paul. For a moment she stared unbelievingly, then gave a scream and rushed to throw her arms around him, crying, "My boy! My boy!" While Paul clung to her, she told how she had prayed that she might find her son again, and Paul assured her earnestly that he knew all the time his mama would come back.

All choked up, the old mountain man walked outside, sorry to lose the boy yet happy he had found his mother. When he had collected himself he went to get the other trappers, and they returned to the fort, to hear how Mrs. Dale had escaped from the Indians. The mother looked ten years younger than when Smith had seen her a few minutes before. While the trappers told how they had rescued her boy and fought off the Pawnees, she sat hugging Paul as if she still couldn't believe he was really there. Then, in turn, she told her story.

The night of the raid the Indians took her to their camp on the Saw Log, a little creek to the north of where the attack had occurred. The next day they continued north, and as they rode along she observed the ponies to see which was the fleetest, and noted the position of the sun to check the course they were taking. Mrs. Dale was a woman of grit and education, and she was determined to escape. If she could get free of the Indians, she planned to ride back to the Santa Fe Trail in hopes she would be picked up by a caravan.

The night of the fourth day after leaving the Saw Log, Mrs. Dale determined to make a break for freedom. By this time her captors had relaxed their vigilance and, having ridden hard all day, they were tired. When all was quiet she crawled out of the lodge where she had been put with some old squaws, and slipped through the camp to where the horses were picketed. Locating the speedy iron-gray pony she had decided on, she loosened him and mounted, using the lariat for a bridle. She kept the horse to a walk until they were four miles out of camp; then taking a bearing from the North Star, she urged him southward at an easy lope.

By daybreak Mrs. Dale figured she had covered forty miles. Since there were no pursuers in sight she paused at a little stream to water her horse and slake her own thirst. Then she continued on at as fast a pace as she thought the gray could sustain. The pony, a cayuse as tough as buckskin, carried her through most of the day without faltering. But in the late afternoon he began to tire and by sunset he was so played out she feared he would drop dead beneath her. She herself was too exhausted even to nibble on the piece of dried-out buffalo meat she had been hoarding, and blacked out the moment she lay down.

When Mrs. Dale awoke she was amazed to see the sun near the western horizon; her sleep had lasted nearly twenty-four hours. Although much refreshed, she was so stiff and sore that she could scarcely mount, but the gray was as fresh as a daisy and carried her southward through the night at a brisk clip. Just at daybreak the Raton Mountains loomed up to the west, and by noon she had reached the Santa Fe Trail. There, a little distance to the east, a large caravan was moving toward her.

It was an American train bound for Taos, and the master was prompt to succor the heroic woman, giving her food and a bed in one of the wagons. When he had heard her story, he bought her Indian pony for thirty dollars and took her on to Bent's Fort. There the womenfolk had cared for her until she was well enough to hire out to William Bent to help with the cooking. Bereft of her husband and child, she intended to earn enough to pay her way back to her mother's home in Pennsylvania.

After hearing the account of this miraculous escape, the trappers made up a pot for Mrs. Dale, collecting about eight hundred dollars; and a trainmaster offered to take her and her son to Independence free of charge. As a parting present, Smith gave Paul two hundred dollars for himself. In later years, whenever he told the story, Uncle John invariably concluded it with these words: "I never felt so miserable before nor since as I did parting with the kid that morning. I hain't never seen him since; and he must be a grown man now. But I hain't never forgot him."

A Connecticut Yankee in the Santa Fe Trade

UNLIKE the fur trade, which was in the hands of immensely wealthy companies, the trade to Santa Fe was carried on by individuals with limited capital. It was always precarious in that it involved transporting goods across hundreds of miles of Indian country; moreover, the Mexican government placed galling restrictions upon the import of goods and the export of gold. But a generous profit could be realized on a comparatively modest investment, and an enterprising trader usually could find ways of getting around the various regulations and avoiding payment of at least part of the tariff.

In 1841, at the age of twenty-three, Josiah Webb left Litchfield, Connecticut, with a thousand-dollar stake from his father and an urge to make his mark in the mercantile world. His first two ventures—clothing stores in Savannah and St. Louis—failed, and in mid-July of 1844 he arrived in Independence, Missouri, to try his luck on a trading trip to Santa Fe. Though not a financial success, this first expedition taught him considerable about the "commerce of the plains" and he decided to try again. While in St. Louis purchasing goods for his second trip, he made the acquaintance of George P. Doane, with whom he formed a partnership.

Returning to Independence, Webb and Doane commenced buying their outfit: two large wagons and a kitchen wagon, fifteen yoke of oxen (two teams of six oxen each and a three-yoke for the kitchen wagon) and sufficient goods to make two good wagon loads. The merchandise—in which they invested $6,300—consisted of dress goods, cotton flags, bandanas, shawls, ties, suspenders, beads, necklaces, fancy hairpins, pearl shirt buttons, gilded vest buttons and coat buttons, needles, scissors, razors, coffee mills, shovels, spades, hoes, axes, percussion caps, inkstands, shaving soap, and candlewick. The two large wagons each carried 5,500 pounds of goods and the small one 1,500 in addition to provisions.

At this time wagonmakers were experimenting with iron axles —a new departure for freight wagons, and considered risky. If an iron axle should break or get badly sprung out on the plains, a trader would be in a bad fix: a wooden axle could not be fitted to the box for an iron one, nor could an iron axle be straightened if it was badly bent. Nonetheless, Webb bought a wagon with the new axles, and became the first trader to take a vehicle so equipped to Santa Fe.

The start, made in mid-June, 1845, was inauspicious. Because of heavy rains the trail was almost impassable, and it took thirty days instead of the usual fifteen to reach Council Grove, where the wagon trains formed. As soon as a sufficient number of trading outfits had gathered there, the caravan was organized and from then on all went well. On the eighty-third day out from Independence the wagons entered Santa Fe.

Webb and several other traders had parted company with the train at the crossing of the Arkansas, riding on ahead to get information from the authorities at Santa Fe about the amount of tariff the ever-changing rules provided for that year. They learned that it would be the same as the year before: $600 per wagon. Since the charge was by the wagon rather than by weight, the traders' practice was to halt just before reaching Santa Fe and repack the wagons, emptying as many as possible. Then, leaving the empties, they would proceed to the customs house with a few heavily loaded wagons.

Even before the caravan arrived, Webb had negotiated the sale of his goods to an old-time American trader living in Santa Fe, who, because he was a resident, was permitted to retail merchandise. In this deal Webb and George Doane cleared $2,800 over and above the cost of the goods and their expenses. A sum covering the cost of the venture was paid over at once to Doane, who was leaving right away for Independence with the wagons; the $2,800 profit was to be paid to Webb in gold dust.

The Mexicans charged a six per cent export tax on cash, and prohibited altogether the exportation of silver bullion, ore, or gold dust. Consequently, when Webb received the gold dust, he was also given, as a cover, what purported to be a draft on a St. Louis bank for $2,800. He was to produce this if he was questioned when he went through customs. The gold dust itself would be smuggled out of Santa Fe by a trader named Nick Gentry. The latter, not having sold any goods, was not under suspicion. He was to meet Webb and turn over the gold at Las Vegas, a little settlement a few miles to the east.

The afternoon before Webb intended to start he learned that the customs officers were after him. Deciding to take the bull by the horns, he got a Spanish-speaking friend to act as translator and went to see Don Agostin Doran, a customs official who was friendly to the Americans in the sense that he could be bribed to look the other way when they brought their wagons in. Don Agostin told Webb that he had concocted a very clever scheme, and that ordinarily it would work; but the trader to whom he had sold his goods had told the whole story, and it was known that he had received the gold dust. However, no attempt would be made to confiscate the contraband gold dust if Webb paid over $168, the export duty on $2,800 cash.

Webb protested that he had neither cash nor gold dust, but Don Agostin merely smiled and shrugged. "The gold dust is but a small package," he said, "and probably we could not find it. But the young man is a very much larger package, and we shall be very careful that he does not leave town until he pays the $168. And even if he should leave Santa Fe, it would be the worse for him as we should denounce him. All the people would be on the lookout, and he could not get out of the country without being arrested." To avoid all this trouble Webb need only hand Don Agostin the $168, and he would be given a receipt to show when he passed through customs. It was so simple—"Pay the money, take the paper, and go in peace." Seeing that there was no way out of it, Webb paid up.

The next morning he went through customs without a hitch, and that afternoon arrived at Las Vegas. There he met Gentry and received instructions about locating the gold dust, which had been cached in a clump of bushes near where the trail crossed Sapello Creek. Webb found the gold without difficulty, but by the time he had retrieved it and returned to Las Vegas the wagon train he had planned to join already had pulled out for "the States." It was then November 2, and it would be another week or ten days before enough Americans assembled to make up another train. Since he was still on Mexican territory, Webb did not dare to keep the contraband gold with his gear. He was lodging with a Mexican family who accommodated travelers, and in the room where the harness and baggage were kept there was a pile of shelled corn. Not knowing what else to do, he thrust the sack into the pile as far as he could reach.

A day or two later Webb's host had company from Santa Fe— a young man named Ortiz whom he had frequently seen with government officials. Webb could understand little Spanish, but he heard the word "contrabandista," and he thought that at the same time Ortiz cast a peculiar look at him. This was enough to convince Webb that he must find a safer hiding place. The next morning, under the pretext of going out hunting, he started out very early with the gold, which was sewed up in a double bag of buckskin. He "planted" it in a water-ditch bordering a cornfield, and then—after killing a wild goose to substantiate the story that he was out hunting—returned to his quarters somewhat easier in his mind. But after the bag had lain in the ditch for more than a week, Webb began to fear that the water might soak through the buckskin. Again he went on a "hunt," and this time moved the gold to a cache in some rocks.

Finally, toward the middle of November, a wagon train started back to Independence. There were six Americans in the party, including a trader named Pruett who was carrying about $4,000 in gold dust, two Mexicans, twenty mules, and two horses. As the wagon train passed near Webb's cache, he recovered his gold and hid it among his belongings.

After taking on more provisions at Rio Moro, the caravan moved out for the States on November 16. Webb's original plan had called for him to leave at least a month earlier in order to avoid the hazards and hardships of a trip across the plains in winter, but by the time the party reached the Arkansas the weather was bitter. It was apparent that the crossing was going to be difficult. The river was frozen over from bank to bank, and where the current was rapid and the water deep the ice was too thin to bear the mules. In any case, they were unshod and would be unable to stand on the ice.

There ensued an argument between Pruett and Webb about whether or not they should attempt to go on. Pruett pointed out that a storm was coming up, and even if they did succeed in getting across there was no shelter on the north shore for some distance. He proposed that they make for a cottonwood grove two or three miles upriver on the south bank, and go into camp until there was a better prospect for fair weather. When Webb insisted that they proceed, Pruett said he felt a sick headache coming on—"I can do nothing to help, but if you can get across without me, go ahead." Webb and one of the other men tried for awhile to cut a path through the ice for a ford, but when it began to snow they gave up and followed the others upriver.

The party encamped on what would have been an island in high water. It was covered with willows, a luxuriant undergrowth of grass, and a good many old cottonwoods. About two P.M. the cook had got the last of the meat in the kettle and was preparing coffee when Pruett, who had climbed onto a wagon wheel to see how things looked outside, called that a large herd of buffalo was coming into the valley for shelter. This was a great relief as it assured them of a meat supply.

After two days the weather abated, and on the morning of the third day about ten o'clock they determined to attempt the crossing. First, the wagons were run across the slick ice by hand. Then, with one of the party riding ahead on the bell mare, the others drove the mules a few at a time across the open channel. Often, when a mule was part way across he would try to scramble onto the ice to get out of the Arctic water, and his forefeet, lashing the ice, would break off large chunks. As a result, the channel on the far side became clogged with ice and the mules could not get through; they had to be roped and slid ashore. By this time the poor beasts would be three-quarters frozen, and the men would run them through the willow brush and slough grass, which whipped their legs and warmed them up. It was nearly sunset before they were all across.

Another storm was imminent, and the men worked against time, handicapped by frozen clothes and fingers, until at last they had the train hitched up and could move upriver in search of shelter. Two miles along they found a cottonwood grove which provided protection for the mules and fuel for a campfire. Here they stayed for two days while the snowstorm raged. Then, after slaughtering several buffalo, they loaded up and started northeast.

The weather continued excessively cold all the way from the Arkansas to the Missouri. They were compelled to break ice and wade all the larger streams. But they knew the country, and by making shorter or longer drives could be sure of arriving at a good camping spot each night. This was the key to their survival, for camping on the open prairie in a winter storm could mean the loss of stock or even of the whole party.

Meanwhile back in Independence there was much concern about Webb. Other returning traders had told of his intention of returning by the end of November, and with the passing days, his friends began to fear the worst. In fact, George Doane had

begun preparations to take a party out to look for his partner
when Webb arrived with the bag of gold dust. Appropriately
enough, he was just in time for Christmas.

II. Pioneering on the Middle Border

See the map on page 193.

WHILE TRADERS AND TRAPPERS and explorers were opening the way West from the Missouri, profound changes were taking place on the Old Northwest frontier—the interior wilderness westward from Ohio to the Mississippi. Theoretically, after the defeat of the confederated Indian tribes at the Battle of Fallen Timbers, the United States boundaries extended to the Mississippi. But in actual fact the white settlements were isolated outposts in a region over which the Indians still had dominion. The Treaty of Greenville (1795) set up five travel routes over which "the said Indian tribes will allow to the people of the United States a free passage by land and water," and for many years white movement was restricted to these routes, which linked together the scattered Northwest settlements and united them to the old communities in the East. All the while the United States Government, by negotiation, purchase, and force of arms, was steadily carrying forward its policy of pushing the Indian tribes across the Mississippi, and this process was substantially complete by 1832—the year of the brief and bloody Blackhawk War, the last major clash between red men and white east of the Mississippi.

During the years between 1810 and 1840, as Seymour Dunbar writes in *A History of Travel in America,* "the people of the interior beheld a revolution in their surroundings, methods, and material affairs . . . . The young men who penetrated to the interior on foot or by pack-train at the rate of ten or twenty miles a day were soon travelling in stage-coaches at a speed of seventy-five or a hundred miles a day. Families who floated down the rivers in flatboats, consuming weeks in their journeys, could in a few years embark on steamboats and be carried from Cincinnati to New Orleans in a week. Pioneers who once staggered through swamps to fight the Indians found themselves assembling, not long afterward, to discuss the building of a local railroad. These incongruous conditions and situations, furthermore, often existed at the same time. The ark and steamboat lay side by side along the river banks; the east-bound stages still passed the west-bound pack-trains and Conestoga wagons; the last Indian fighting and the first railroad planning went on together."

In the Potter's Field

DURING THE FIRST THIRD of the nineteenth century the frontier house of entertainment was commonly known as a tavern, although by the 1830's the term "hotel" was coming into use. No matter what the name, the accommodations were crude and unpretentious. A typical tavern was built of logs and consisted of four rooms—a kitchen, a combination dining room and bar, a sleeping room for the guests, and a room which served as quarters for the landlord and his family.

Usually a traveler arrived on horseback. After turning his mount over to the care of a stable boy he went to the well where he washed his face and hands in a basin—or perhaps a servant poured water over his hands from a gourd—and dried himself on a towel that already had done duty for a half-dozen travelers before him. The underbrush, some distance from the house, served as a rest room.

Supper was served family-style, with all the guests seated around a table heaped with smoking hot dishes common to the back country. Afterward, when the table had been cleared, some of the men might start a card game; others would gather by the fire. There they sat with their chairs tilted back against the wall, their feet cocked as high as their heads against the side of the fireplace, and amused themselves by spitting in the fire. To one side of the room was a bar upon which stood a bucket of water and a dipper. If anyone wanted something stronger he called for spirits. The proprietor then produced a decanter and a small glass, and the guest would pour his own drink, washing it down with a swig of water from the community dipper. The landlord kept count of the number of times each guest served himself, and the score was settled the next morning before the travelers departed.

The sleeping room, filled with double beds, was commonly called the "potter's field" because no one had a bed of his own. The first guests to retire could choose where they wished to lay their heads; later comers were assigned to the vacant places. Needless to say, a man often awoke in the morning to find a complete stranger snoring beside him. That useful garment known as the nightshirt, although gaining in popularity in the East, was never seen on the frontier. A man traveling in the interior simply slipped off his trousers and boots and slept in the shirt he had worn during the day. As for bedclothes, one sheet per bed was the rule and since it was changed only once a week the guest who arrived the latter part of the week found the pillow slip greasy and the sheet something less than immaculate. Fortunately for the traveler's peace of mind, sheets often were made of checked blue cotton and did not show the signs of use so much as if they had been the bleached muslin of today's hotels.

Just as today, of course, some hostelries were much better kept than others, and there were landlords like Captain John Berry of Andersontown, Indiana, who prided themselves on the cleanliness of their establishments. Berry's tavern was located on one of the first two wagon roads in Indiana, the Berry Trace, so named because Captain Berry had marked it out. Up until about 1826 incoming white settlers from the East moved first along the Whetzel Trace which began at the eastern boundary of the state near the present town of Laurel and ran in a generally westward direction to the White River. Here, just south of Indianapolis, it joined Berry's road which led northward.

Of all the wayfarers—settlers, government officials, land speculators, soldiers—who sought accommodation at Berry's tavern, the most rollicking, roistering group was comprised of the circuit judge and lawyers who traveled from one seat of justice to the next as the court was convened in the various counties. Indeed, it seemed that they stayed awake nights thinking up practical jokes to play on one another.

One of Hoosierdom's most famous stories concerns an occasion on which James Whitcomb, soon to be governor of Indiana, stayed at Berry's with several other prominent lawyers. Whitcomb owned a nightshirt, and what is more he carried it about the country with him and used it. His companions naturally knew of this eccentricity and they also knew of Captain Berry's inordinate pride in the cleanliness of his tavern. In these two seemingly unrelated factors they saw the makings of a fine practical joke.

Taking Berry aside, two of the lawyers informed him that on an earlier visit Whitcomb had formed a very poor impression of the cleanliness of the sheets. In fact, he found their condition so objectionable that he had brought with him a special shirt to wear in bed so that he might not soil his regular shirt. At first Berry refused to credit a word they said; he could not believe that his distinguished guest would ever be guilty of such boorish conduct. But the jokers persisted and in the end prevailed on Berry to watch through a crack in the door when Whitcomb retired for the night.

Sure enough, just as his informants had claimed, he saw Whitcomb remove his shirt and put on another one even longer than the ordinary shirt, as though to protect himself from the bed. Mortally insulted, Berry burst open the door, rushed in, sprang upon Whitcomb, and bore him to the floor, preparatory to inflicting dire punishment on a man who dared to cast such undeserved aspersions on his cherished tavern. The jokers, hearing the struggle, hurried to pluck the enraged innkeeper off the astonished and indignant Whitcomb, and confessed the hoax. They had quite a time convincing Berry that people in other parts of the country really wore such things as nightshirts, but finally peace was restored and all was quiet in the potter's field.

At the time of the signing of the Declaration of Independence, seven of the original thirteen states claimed title to various portions of the vacant lands west of the Appalachian Mountains. New York tendered her western lands to Congress in 1780, and in 1784 Virginia relinquished her claims to the country northwest of the Ohio, reserving certain areas. Between 1784 and

*1802 the other five states also ceded their western hold-
ings—cessions which, as Roy M. Robbins writes in* Our
Landed Heritage, *"conveyed to the government of
these united states the title to a body of land known as
the* public domain. . . . *The government of the United
States thereupon assumed toward the immense bodies
of western lands the position of a trustee of society,
holding not only the right of eminent domain but also
the right of individual ownership. Realizing that this
relation should continue no longer than was absolutely
necessary, it became the anxious desire of the . . . government to transfer the title into private hands."*

The Settlers' Stratagem

IN 1796, during the second administration of President George
Washington, Congress passed a law establishing a national land
policy. According to its terms, public land was not to be occupied
until the Indian title had been cleared and the land surveyed and
marked off into plots. It was then to be sold to the highest bidder
at a public auction. The law also fixed the minimum price at
$2.00 per acre (lowered to $1.25 in 1820). If no one bid that high
at the auction, anyone interested could go to the land office and
buy the desired plot at the minimum price.

More often than not the land-hungry frontiersmen paid no
attention to these provisions. As they saw it, the land belonged
to the people, so why not operate on a help-yourself basis? They
moved on to the best acreage they could find, built their cabins,
and planted their crops. Further, they argued that when the land
on which they lived had been surveyed and came up for sale, they
should have the right to buy it in at the minimum price. After
all, they had opened up the new country and made it habitable;
and if the land had appreciated in value, it was owing to their

enterprise and efforts. But the hard fact was that their occupancy was illegal, and at the land sales they were obliged to bid against the so-called land sharks—speculators who made a business of buying up choice property, holding it until the price rose, and then selling it for a profit. Naturally, these speculators were cordially hated by the settlers, and many were the schemes they devised to keep the profiteers from grabbing the land on which they had labored and built their homes.

One of the most elaborate of the schemes to outwit the speculators was that devised by a group of settlers in Hancock County, Indiana, in 1821. In January of that year a site in adjacent Marion County had been named as the location of the capital of the state; the future city of Indianapolis had been platted and the lots put up for sale. There ensued a rush of settlers and speculators to the area, and large eastern land syndicates sent out their agents, known as landlookers, to locate and report on potentially valuable land not only in the city itself but in the surrounding countryside.

Their advent dismayed the Hancock County settlers, for they feared that when the land on which they had built their homes came up for public auction they would never be able to compete with the bids of the wealthy syndicates. Realizing that concerted action was called for if they were to defeat the land sharks, the men of the county formed themselves into a secret organization known as the "Home Defenders." Its members were pledged to drive out the speculators even if it meant killing them.

Before resorting to such desperate measures, however, they decided to try a ruse suggested to them by an incident which had happened not long before. A group of agents looking over some land ten or fifteen miles southeast of Indianapolis had been fired on by settlers concealed in the woods, and the agents had mistakenly concluded that this particular section was still occupied by Indians and would be a good place to stay away from. It occurred to the Hancock County settlers that if word got around their own area was a hotbed of hostiles, they might be able to scare off speculators until the land sale was over.

Accordingly, plans were laid to stage an "Indian uprising" the

minute any speculators showed their faces in the county. Thirty
of the Home Defenders were assigned to play the part of Indians.
They were dressed in regular Indian costumes and when the signal for action came they were to put on warpaint and other
Indian trappings to make themselves look as fearsome and menacing as possible. Twenty-five others wore the usual homespun
garb of the pioneer, hunting shirts and coonskin caps. Three of
the most resolute men were selected to keep a lookout for the
speculators, who they knew would be coming by way of the White
Water valley from Cincinnati or over the Whetzel Trace from
the east, and would be easy to identify because of their dandified
city clothes—broadcloth suits and stove-pipe hats. Finally, it was
arranged that mounted men would be in touch at all times with
the lookouts, in readiness to carry the word the instant that the
speculators put in an appearance.

The Home Defenders had laid their plans none too soon.
Only a few days after they had set up their organization, the
couriers on duty rode through the settlement summoning the
citizens to mobilize at a previous selected meeting place and alerting them to be ready for action. No sooner was the main body
of the Defenders assembled than one of the lookouts came galloping in to report that a group of fifteen or twenty land sharks
from Cincinnati would be in the neighborhood within two or
three hours. It was customary for the speculators to travel in a
band for self-protection and for each man to supplement his city
wardrobe with a pair of pistols.

Anticipating their probable route, the Home Defenders sent a
couple of men to meet the landlookers. The two represented
themselves as guides who would be pleased to conduct them on a
tour of the best land in the county. This amiable offer was grate-
fully accepted, and the party jogged along in high good humor,
having a jolly sociable time. All at once they heard several shots,
and a moment later a number of backwoodsmen rode at breakneck speed across their front, stopping every now and then to fire
back in the direction from which they had come. Dismounting at
a little distance from the alarmed speculators, they took up positions from which to defend themselves from the still unseen foe.

Soon a large body of Indians came warwhooping over the hill, but their advance was checked by a fusillade of shots and the redskins withdrew behind the brow of the hill.

The embattled backwoodsmen took advantage of this lull to remount their horses and gallop over to the speculators. They said that they had been attacked by a strong Indian war party, that two of their men had been killed, and that since the savages outnumbered them two to one they would no longer be able to hold their ground unless the city men came to their aid. But before they could finish their moving appeal for help in defending their homes, the redskins burst over the hill, riding like the wind, firing and uttering hideous warwhoops as they bore down on the whites.

After one look the landlookers looked no more. Wrenching around their horses they took the back trail at top speed followed by the settlers shouting adjurations for them to be men, to stand and fight. Hard on their heels came the bloodthirsty savages, yelling like fiends and sending bullets whining past the stove-pipe hats. For a little way the men in homespun kept up with the speculators in their mad retreat; then cursing them as a pack of cowardly villains they stopped and fought a rousing sham battle with the Indian detachment of the Home Defenders—just in case any of the speculators should chance to look back. None did; indeed it was said that these gentry did not draw rein until they reached Cincinnati.

The "Indian uprising" accomplished its purpose. No speculators appeared at the land sale, and the settlers were able to buy in their land at the minimum price of $1.25 an acre. Moreover, although the "redskins" had collected no scalps they could fairly claim to have topped off the palefaces, for the woods of western Hancock County were found to be plentifully strewn with stove-pipe hats.

Traders on the Mississippi

BECAUSE OF the scarcity of money on the frontier, payment for merchandise usually was made in the form of produce. When the pioneer went to the store to trade, he brought beeswax to exchange for gunpowder, a keg of lard for dry goods or window glass, pork for tools. The merchant had to maintain a feeding pen for the cattle and hogs which were bartered for various articles of his stock in trade, and his bins were bulging with the wheat and corn and potatoes he had to accept in lieu of cash if he was to do any business.

But while barter was convenient for his customers, it left the merchant with the problem of converting the produce he received into the cash he would need to buy merchandise. Wheat could be ground and turned into flour, cattle could be slaughtered, the meat salted and the hides tanned, but still he had to market these commodities to get the wherewithal to restock his store. This meant a trip to some large town or trading post where he could receive payment in cash.

1

It was common practice for a merchant who lived in a community on the Mississippi to float his produce downriver in a flatboat to New Orleans, where both the cargo and the boat could be sold for cash. The flatboat, which was usually built on the riverbank, resembled a big box about three times as long as it was wide; its square ends were slanted upward from the bottom to enable it to glide through the water better, and it was steered by an oar at the stern. It had to be constructed upside down so that the carpenters could fasten the planks on the bottom. The cracks were then caulked with pitch and flax or hemp to make the hull watertight. Next the boat was eased into the water on rollers made of small logs, and then came the "flatboat turning"—an operation in which the whole community took part.

A rope was run to the top of a tree on the riverbank and down to one side of the boat. Rocks and earth were piled on the other side until it sank even with the surface of the water. Then the crowd pulled on the rope and flipped the big box right side up. After a bucket brigade had bailed out the water, the job was completed by nailing planking over the hull to form a deck. As soon as the boat had dried out, it was loaded with grain, flour, pork, and other articles of trade. If any livestock and poultry were carried, they were placed in pens on the deck. Once the merchant had engaged a crew of two or three boatmen and a pilot to do the navigating, he was ready to go to market.

On the face of it, floating down the Mississippi in a flatboat sounds like an ideal vacation project for adventurous young men, but the account of a trip made by Daniel M. Brush makes it clear that travel by flatboat was far from being a picnic. Brush and his crew embarked from Jenkins Landing in southern Illinois on December 22, 1834, bound for New Orleans with a cargo of cattle, corn, and other produce. In those days it was quite an event when anyone went on such a long journey, and many of the townspeople turned out to witness their departure and bid them godspeed.

For the first three days of the voyage everything went well. Christmas morning was especially beautiful; there was not a ripple on the water and the skies were bright and clear. Except for the steersman, the men were lounging about the deck, taking their ease in the sunshine, and the boat was gliding along nicely. Then without any warning there was a dull thud, and a shiver ran throughout the length of the craft. The bow began to rise out of the water as if it were being pushed up by a giant hand. After a moment the boat slowly began to settle, and the men saw that a hole had been punched in its bottom by the top branch of a sunken tree whose roots were fastened in the riverbed. The big box had struck a hidden snag, and remained hung up on it, the rough timber protruding through the planking. The water was pouring in, and it seemed certain that the boat was about to sink, so the cattle were released from the pen and allowed to swim ashore, some making for an island, others for the Missouri bank.

The crew then set to work to salvage the other cargo, conveying it ashore in a borrowed rowboat.

This operation took several days, but fortunately the weather was fair. If a storm had come up, the boat would have been battered to pieces. When the cargo had been unloaded, Brush borrowed a cable, rigged a windlass on shore, and succeeded in pulling the boat off the snag and towing it to the bank. Here the damaged plank was removed and replaced, and after the bottom had been caulked the cargo was reloaded. They had lost fifteen head of cattle, and considerable corn was ruined owing to spoilage.

Brush had planned to resume his journey on January 4, but in the meantime a cold wave had come on and the ice was so thick that they dared not put out. All night long as they lay tied up at the bank the men could hear the ominous grating of ice against the hull. Although the weather had not abated by morning, Brush feared that conditions would get worse and ordered the crew to cast off. The battering of large ice chunks floating downstream made the boat unmanageable, and there was constant danger of its being crushed against a bank or an island. The weather grew so cold that it seemed the river would freeze over solid, but after about a week they were through the worst of the ice.

At Natchez, Mississippi, Brush sold the cattle, and they proceeded south with the rest of the cargo, running nights as well as days. About midnight on January 29 a violent storm broke, with gale winds and torrential rains. The waves were so high that there was danger of swamping, but by dint of hard labor they reached a sand bar protected by a bluff. The men came back on board after tying up the boat, assuring Brush that all was well. Nonetheless, he was unable to rid himself of an uneasy feeling and finally went to check the moorings. It was a good thing he did so, for the stake to which the rope was tied had worked loose in the sand and the boat was starting to drift away.

As was not uncommon, scores of traders arrived at New Orleans at about the same time Brush did, and the markets were glutted with produce, cutting prices to a low figure. After bargain-

ing for five days, he managed to sell his cargo and also the flatboat, which would be cut up and used for timber or fuel. His
business done, on February 5 he boarded a steamboat for the
return trip to Illinois. At Cairo, which was reached on February
14, the steamboat was held up by ice, and Brush and the pilot,
unwilling to wait for the river to thaw, walked through the snow
the rest of the way to Jenkins Landing, arriving three days later.

Although Brush had not received as much for his produce as
it had cost him, he knew he must be prepared to undertake
equally long and hard journeys in the future. There was no other
way he could secure cash to buy goods from wholesale houses in
the East and keep in business as a frontier merchant—but he
could always hope for better luck next time.

2

In the spring of 1841, J. H. Burrows, a pioneer merchant at
Davenport, Iowa, found that all his money was invested in produce, leaving him no funds to replenish the goods at his store.
Consequently, he loaded his salable commodities on the steamboat *Smelter* and accompanied it upriver, stopping off at Snake
Hollow (present-day Potosi, Wisconsin), where he made a profitable sale. His luck was even better at Prairie du Chien. The
American Fur Company, which had a post there, had received no
spring supplies, and purchased his entire remaining stock. The
great part of the fur company funds paid out in those days was
in Spanish dollars, and Burrows received his payment in gold and
silver coins.

Burrows was anxious to get his gold and silver safely home,
but the *Smelter* was going on upriver and would not be returning
for at least a week. However, he learned that the next afternoon
a stage would pass through the village of Grove, some twelve
miles from Prairie du Chien, and he made up his mind to catch
it. The next morning before starting out he wrapped each of the
coins he had received in brown paper; then taking a few at a
time he wrapped them in small rolls and loaded his pockets with
all they would hold. He tied the rest in a strong handkerchief.

Taking a lunch, he left about eleven o'clock and walked three miles down the Wisconsin River to the ferry. The river was bank deep and racing along in its angriest mood. The ferryman was nowhere to be seen, nor did he ever appear though Burrows rang the bell off and on for half an hour. Finally, he began to fear that he would miss his stage. The ferryman's canoe was drawn up on the bank, and though Burrows had never ridden in a canoe and did not know how to handle one, he launched the unstable craft and started across the river.

A swift stream at flood tide was a poor place to learn canoeing. In Burrow's own words, "I soon found that I had to sit very still, flat in the bottom. The canoe kept going round and round, and every few minutes would dip some water. Meanwhile the current was conveying me swiftly down to the Mississippi. I thought I was lost. I would have given all my money to be safe on either shore, and why I was not drowned was always a mystery to me. . . . I noticed that as the canoe whirled around, each time brought me nearer to the shore. I also began to manage the paddles to better advantage, and soon struck the willows, which I caught, and pulled the canoe as near the shore as I could; then jumped overboard, and got on dry land as soon as possible."

After he had wrung out his sopping clothes, he set out again for the stage line, but about a mile farther on came to a creek at the flood stage. There was neither ferry nor bridge, and it could not be forded as the banks were straight up and down. "After examining up and down the stream," Burrows later recalled, "I saw there was no way but to jump it. I chose the narrowest place I could find, pitched my bundle of money across, and then took a run and jumped. Just made it, and that was all. As I struck the edge of bank, one of my coat pockets gave way and fell, with its heavy contents, in four feet of water. I hunted up a forked stick, and luckily, the lining having gone with the pocket, soon fished it out and made for the stage house, which I reached without further trouble, only to find that the stage had gone! I then determined to make my way to Dubuque on foot, where I hoped to get a boat."

At dusk he approached a lonely cabin and decided to ask if he might stay there overnight. The knowledge that he was carrying a small fortune made Burrows extremely uneasy; he thought of hiding the money in a nearby pile of brush but was afraid that he might be observed. When he requested lodging from the woman at the cabin, she referred him to her husband who was at the barn. He was a man of singularly uncouth appearance, and though he made Burrows welcome, the merchant's worry increased. After the chores were done, they went to the cabin together. In a few minutes supper was ready, and Burrows went to the table carrying his bundle with him. As they sat down, they were joined by two of the hardest-looking men he had ever seen. Eyeing him sharply, they took their places on either side of him, and Burrows felt sure that he had fallen into a robbers' den. But when the head of the house bowed his head and asked a blessing on the meal, all his fears for his money and his life evaporated. He was among Christians and could relax his vigilance.

At break of day Burrows was on the road again determined to reach Dubuque some time that night. At noon it began to rain, and all afternoon he slogged on through a cold downpour. By sunset he had reached Parsons' Ferry on the Mississippi, fifteen miles above Dubuque, and after yelling for nearly an hour got the ferryman to come over to the Wisconsin side and ferry him back to the Iowa shore.

At eleven o'clock that night, after hours of plodding in inky darkness over miry roads through pelting rain, Burrows reached Dubuque, having walked seventy-five miles in thirty-six hours. He was not familiar with the town, but after wandering about for some time met a man who was kind enough to escort him to a good tavern. Describing the end of his adventure, Burrows wrote: "I did not waken until noon the next day, when my landlord knocked at the door and said there was a boat at the landing, going downriver. I was so sore and stiff I could scarcely dress myself, and could only get downstairs by sliding down the banister. . . . We started toward night, and reached home the next forenoon. I was so lame and crippled for ten days that I had as much as I could do to attend to my business.

"Such were the trials and labors of a pioneer merchant of those early days."

The initial penetration of a region was commonly followed by three waves of migration. In the first wave were the traders, hunters, and trappers, who were more concerned with exploiting the country than improving it. Similarly, the "squatters" who followed them, although they usually made some slight improvements on the land they occupied, depended mostly on hunting and the natural products of the forest for their support. But with the arrival of the settlers frontier life entered on a new, basically different phase. Unlike those who had preceded them, the settlers were not transients; as their name suggests, they had come to stay—to domesticate the wilderness and make it into the abiding place of an organized society. Preachers and teachers were in their front ranks, and the church and the schoolhouse early became focal points of community activity. The rural post office, often set up in a private home, was another center for settlers who might be scattered over half a county. Frequently the postmaster maintained a small general store, and from such beginnings a village would be born.

If the conditions of existence, even in this later stage of pioneering, today seem almost incredibly primitive, they could be endured because of the settlers' confidence that better times were coming. Their vision of the future, as Herbert S. Schell has written, gave them the fortitude and patience to stand up under grinding toil and privation, such setbacks as crop failures, and the continual threat of sickness and accidents. Also, great as its hardships were, "life on the frontier was, nevertheless, not much different from that which prevailed in rural communities in the older sections of the country, and its drab and dull features can be easily exaggerated when measured by the present-day mode of living with all its comforts, gadgets, and diversions."

The Circuit Rider and the Sinners

As SETTLERS pushed out into the wilderness, occupying widely scattered holdings, the Methodist church appointed traveling ministers, called circuit riders, to serve those areas where there were not enough church members in any one place to support a resident minister. The circuit rider made his rounds on horseback, stopping long enough with each little group of believers to preach, perform marriage services, and conduct the funerals of settlers who had died and been buried since his last visit. The circuit rider had to be a vigorous man, wise in the ways of the frontier, for it was often necessary for him to travel through blizzards and rainstorms, to cross flooded streams or ice-choked rivers, if he was to be at the appointed meeting place at a certain hour on a certain day. Once every three months there was a quarterly meeting at which the presiding elder would preach, and once a year all the people of several circuits would meet at a designated spot and camp out together for a week or ten days to worship and hear many preachers besides their own itinerant minister.

These camp meetings attracted both devout church members and those who were less interested in worshipping the Lord than in the opportunity for a little social life. Catering to this less godly element, an enterprising peddler would set up a stand near the camp ground and sell pies, candy, cakes, cigars, tobacco, whiskey, and other alcoholic drinks. Rowdies from the surrounding area would gather here to "liquor up" and engage in devilment with kindred spirits among the crowd that hung around the whiskey seller. After imbibing, it often happened that the rowdies—sometimes referred to as "Cainites"—would be moved to invade the camp grounds and create a disturbance. In these wars between "the saints" and "the sinners," the camp superintendent was charged with the duty of protecting the camp from the Cainites.

1

One of the most revered figures on the Middle Border in the early days was Peter Cartwright, a circuit rider who feared neither the elements on his lonely rounds nor the devil in the form of drunken rowdies at camp meetings. In the year 1832 Cartwright was camp superintendent of a meeting held in Fulton County, Illinois. The camp was well laid out, adequate preparations had been made, and the prospects were good for an excellent meeting. But merchants from the adjacent town of Canton had sent a peddler to set up a whiskey stand. Since the Methodist people were opposed to the use of tobacco and spirits, and since they did not wish to risk having the meeting disrupted by drinkers, they asked the huckster to leave camp. He refused to budge and defied Cartwright to put him out. Cartwright countered by having him hauled into court, where he was convicted by the jury and fined ten dollars—a big sum in those days. The peddler said that he had no money to pay the fine. The judge thereupon ordered an officer to take him to the lock-up, which was in the county seat about ten miles away.

The officer appeared reluctant to do his duty, and Cartwright learned that the peddler's friends had sworn they not only would rescue the prisoner but would give a sound drubbing to anyone attempting to take him to jail. Consequently, Cartwright arranged that he himself and four stout Methodist brethren be deputized to act as escort. Armed with clubs, they set out on horseback, the prisoner in their midst, and arrived at the outskirts of the county seat without seeing hide or hair of any rescuers. At this point, with jail in the immediate offing, the prisoner hauled his wallet out of his pocket and paid the ten-dollar fine.

On returning to camp, Cartwright found "the sinners" in a towering rage because "the saints" had taken legal steps to seize and impound all the peddler's supply of spirituous liquors. Informed that the rowdies would break up the camp meeting if the drink was not released forthwith, Peter Cartwright refused to put an end to the drought. The campers, he said, could "whip the whole regiment."

After the usual service at candlelighting time, Cartwright set up a strong guard and ordered fires to be kept burning to illuminate the grounds. Before long the troublemakers began their assault, heralding it with a sort of wilderness serenade. From a distance they began to howl like wolves; drawing nearer they barked like dogs and hooted like owls; and finally they poured into the camp grounds, crowing like roosters. Again and again they attacked only to be beaten off by the guards. In his autobiography, Cartwright has described the climax of the melee, which lasted nearly all night:

> One ringleader among them came right before the preachers' tent, slapped his hands, and crowed and passed on. I stepped to a fire close by, and gathered a chunk of fire, and threw it, striking him right between the shoulders, and the fire flew all over him. He sprang and bounded like a buck. I cried out, "Take him! take him!" but I assure you it would have taken a fleet man to have taken him, for he ran as though the very devil was in him and after him. When I returned to the tent, one of the guard came and told me that they were taking wheels off the wagons and carriages; and looking through an opening in the tent, I saw one of them busy in loosening my carriage behind the tent, where I had tied it to a sapling for fear they would run it off. I slipped round, gathered a stick in my way, and came up close behind him and struck at him, not with much intent to hurt, but to scare him. However, the stroke set his hat on one side of his head; he dashed off in a mighty fright, and his hat not being adjusted right, it blinded him, and fleeing with all speed he struck against a tree and knocked himself down, bruised his face very much, and lay senseless for several minutes; but when he came to himself he was as tame as a lamb, and his dispensation of mischief was over. This put an end to the trouble of the rowdies, and afterward all was peace and quiet.
>
> We had a very singular and remarkable man among us, a traveling preacher in the Illinois Conference; his name was Wilson Pitner. . . . He was uneducated, and it seemed impossible for him to learn; but notwithstanding his want of learning, and in common he was an ordinary preacher, yet at times, as we say in the backwoods, when he swung clear there were

very few that could excel him in the pulpit; and perhaps he was one of the most powerful exhorters that was in the land.

On Monday he came to me, and desired me to let him preach at eleven o'clock, saying, "I have faith to believe that God will this day convert many of these rowdies and persecutors." I consented; and he preached with great liberty and power. Nearly the whole congregation were powerfully moved, as he closed by calling for every rowdy and persecutor to meet him at the altar. . . . There was a general rush for the altar, and many of those who had interrupted and disturbed us in the forepart of the meeting came and fell on their knees and cried aloud for mercy; and it is beyond my power to describe the scene. But more than fifty souls were converted to God that day and night . . . and great good was accomplished, although we waded through tribulation to accomplish it.

2

Methodist preachers on the frontier enjoyed their religion and encouraged their flock to shout and sing. At camp meetings it was customary to have a penitents' pen down in front of the assembly. When the preacher appealed for sinners to come forward and be saved, those who responded entered the pen and knelt in prayer. Sometimes a man or woman would fall prostrate in the pen, perhaps to rise with a shout of victory—"Glory to God" or "Hallelujah." The minister would add his voice to the shouts of praise, crying "Another sinner's down! Glory to God!"

Smart alecks and rowdies sometimes mimicked these old-time preachers, much to their righteous indignation. In his autobiography, Peter Cartwright tells of an experience of this kind which befell him in Springfield, Illinois. One day when he had ridden in to do some trading he noticed a party of three young people whose city clothes made them conspicuous in a frontier town. All three were complete strangers to him.

After finishing his trading, Cartwright mounted his horse and started for home. About two miles from town, he overtook a light wagon drawn by two excellent horses. The wagon cover was rolled back and he saw that the occupants were the two dudes and the fashionable young lady he had noticed earlier. According to the old circuit rider:

> As I drew near them, they began to sing one of our camp meeting songs, and they appeared to sing with great animation. Presently the young lady began to shout, and said, "Glory to God! Glory to God!" The driver cried out, "Amen! Glory to God!"
>
> My first impressions were that they had been across the Sangamon River to a camp meeting that I knew was in progress there, and had obtained religion, and were happy. As I drew nearer, the lady began to sing and shout again. The young man who was not driving fell down and cried aloud for mercy; the other two shouting at the top of their voices cried out, "Glory to God! Another sinner's down!" Then they fell to exhorting the young man that was down, saying, "Pray on, brother; pray on, brother; you will soon get religion." Presently up jumped the young man that was down, and shouted aloud, saying, "God has blessed my soul. Halleluiah! Halleluiah! Glory to God!"
>
> Thinking all was right, I felt like riding up and joining in the songs of triumph and shouts of joy that rose from these three happy persons; but as I neared the wagon, I saw some glances of their eyes at each other, and at me, that created a suspicion in my mind that all was not right; and the thought occurred to me that they suspected or knew me to be a preacher, and that they were carrying on in this way to make a mock of sacred things, and to fool me. I checked my horse, and fell back, and rode slowly, hoping they would pass on, and that I should not be annoyed by them anymore; but when I checked my horse and went slow, they checked up and went slow too, and the driver changed with the other young man; then they began again to sing and shout at a mighty rate, and down fell the first driver, and up went a new shout of "Glory to God! another sinner's down. Pray on, brother; pray on, brother; the Lord will bless you." Presently up sprang the driver and said, "Another sinner's converted, another sinner's converted. Halleluiah! glory to God!" A rush of indignant feeling came all over me, and I thought I would ride up and horse whip both of these young men; if the woman had not

been in company, I think I should have done so; but I fore-bore. It was a vexatious encounter; if my horse had been fleet, as in former days, I could have rode right off, and left them in their glory but he was stiff, and when I would fall back and go slow, they would check up; and when I would spur my stiff pony, and try to get ahead of them, they would crack the whip and keep ahead of me; and thus they tormented me . . . till I thought it was more than any good preacher ought to bear.

Wondering how long he would have to put up with this crude heckling, the backwoods preacher recalled that about a mile ahead was a very deep, treacherous mud hole. Many wagons got stuck there, and had to be pried out with rails. On the right-hand side of the road at this point stood a stump about two feet high. To avoid getting stuck it was necessary to drive as close to this stump as possible. There was a bridle path skirting this dis-agreeable spot, and Cartwright determined to ride at top speed along it and thus pass by his tormentors, who would not be able to go very fast through the muddy stretch.

Cartwright's account continues:

When we came to the commencement of the mud, I took the bridle path, and put spurs and whip to my horse. Seeing I was rapidly leaving them in the rear, the driver cracked his whip and put his horses almost at full speed, and such was their anxiety to keep up with me, to carry out their sport, that when they came to this bad place they never saw the stump on the right. The forewheel of the wagon struck centrally on the stump, and as the wheel mounted the stump, over went the wagon. Fearing it would turn entirely over and catch them under, the two young men took a leap into the mud, and when they lighted they sunk up to the middle. The young lady was dressed in white, and as the wagon went over, she sprang as far as she could, and lighted on all-fours; her hands sunk into the mud up to her armpits, her mouth and the whole of her face immersed in the muddy water, and she cer-tainly would have strangled if the young men had not relieved her. As they helped her up and out, I had wheeled my horse to see the fun. I rode up to the edge of the mud, stopped my horse, reared in my stirrups, and shouted at the top of my voice, "Glory to God! glory to God! Halleluiah! another sinner's down! glory to God! halleluiah! glory! halleluiah!"

The famous circuit rider then delivered a stiff lecture on the consequences of sacrilegious conduct. Since they had just experienced some of these consequences, the mud-besmeared sinners were in the mood to listen.

It turned out that the three were from Ohio on a visit. Before they returned to their home they attended a camp meeting, wound up in the penitents' pen, and really did "obtain religion." After Peter Cartwright had baptized them and taken them into the Methodist Church, he could truly shout "Glory to God."

Barring Out the Teacher

IN SOUTHERN INDIANA during pioneer days it was traditional for the male pupils at country schools to force a test of artfulness and endurance between themselves and the teacher at Christmas time. According to custom, a week or so before Christmas the big boys prompted the little youngsters to ask the teacher whether or not he was going to treat the school. If he meekly agreed to do so, everyone would have been bitterly disappointed. The excitement of matching wits and muscle with the schoolmaster far outweighed the pleasures of the treat. Hence when the question was put to him, the popular pedagogue would refuse to make any promises. It was then up to the boys to seize possession of the schoolhouse and bar out the schoolmaster until he surrendered and promised to treat.

The treat demanded might consist of striped store candy, or perhaps an apple or an orange for each pupil. Oranges were regarded as a particular luxury because prior to the Civil War they had to be imported from Spain. Sometimes cider—which by Christmas time was quite hard—would be added to the treat.

With the passage of time, "Barring Out the Teacher" evolved its own set of rules and regulations and its own code of sportsmanlike conduct. For example, according to frontier social usage, inside the schoolhouse the teacher's word was law and his person inviolate, but outside the building he was a mere mortal, shorn of his regal powers. Parents and friends of the children—indeed, the whole neighborhood—watched the annual battle with deep interest. At the larger schools there usually were many older boys, some of whom were bigger and stronger than the teacher, so the contest was by no means one-sided.

In the late 1850's Benjamin Kennedy was teaching an Indiana school which had many adult pupils on its roster. One December day a group of little girls approached him and asked whether he was going to treat. Kennedy responded that he might treat the little folks but that he would never think of supplying Christmas goodies to grown men and women because they might resent being treated like children. Kennedy's reply was taken seriously by the opposition.

Shortly before Christmas another emissary, a ten-year-old boy, asked, "Teacher, are you going to treat?" Kennedy, acting as if this was such a trivial matter that he had never given it a moment's thought, replied offhandedly that he didn't think he would do so. The lad warned him that if he refused the big boys were going to lock him out of the schoolhouse. Still pretending indifference, Kennedy asked when they would do that. When the boy said that they were planning to come early the next morning, Kennedy guessed that he was not, after all, a messenger from the enemy camp, but was trying to curry favor with the teacher by reporting on plans he had overheard.

That night when Kennedy got home to his boarding place, he first swore his hostess to secrecy. Then he told her that he wouldn't be there for breakfast and asked her to put up a double lunch for the next day. About midnight he took his lunch and books and went back to the schoolhouse. There he built up a nice fire and made himself comfortable to await the dawn invasion.

When the fire burned low and the first streaks of daylight appeared, the wily schoolmaster hid himself under a seat in a dark corner. Before long there was the sound of voices and in came a half-dozen of the older boys. They stirred up the fire, threw on wood, and stood around for a while warming themselves. Then one squad went to lower the bar which locked the door from the inside, while a second group jammed the windows tightly with wooden wedges. These measures taken, they sat down to talk over their plans to outguess the old fox. They tried to foresee just how the teacher would meet their tactics, but it was observed that Ben Kennedy was as tricky as the devil himself.

At length one boy, who had been a bit nervous all along, remarked that when they had arrived there was a lot of fire in the stove and the room was unusually warm for having been empty all night. He ventured a guess that Kennedy might be there already, perhaps hidden up in the loft. This suggestion momentarily shocked the group into silence. Finally, one boy said that if Kennedy *was* there, he had heard enough about himself to last for a long time. Another boy proposed that they search the loft as soon as it was full daylight.

The master could contain himself no longer. Rising up in his corner, he greeted the boys suavely, complimenting them on their eagerness for learning as demonstrated by their arriving at the schoolhouse before daybreak in order to be at their books. Any teacher, he said, would be proud of such pupils. The startled boys, who had jumped to their feet when he announced his presence, stood about glumly, not looking at him or at each other. Because he was in his sanctuary, Kennedy had no fear that they would attack him. He invited the boys to sit down and talk things over, but they were in no mood to parley. One declared that they might just as well go home for breakfast, and they took themselves off. Watching from a window as they crossed the clearing, Kennedy deduced from their earnest conversation and their scowling, over-the-shoulder glances at the seat of learning, that although they had suffered a defeat, they were by no means willing to concede the loss of the campaign.

Once they were out of sight of the schoolhouse, the boys lay in ambush beside the road, ready to capture the teacher when he went home for breakfast. But of course Kennedy had provided himself with extra rations, and he was not to be starved out. Noon came and still there was no sign of the teacher. Finally hunger conquered their zeal and the disappointed boys dispersed.

Next morning was another story. This time most of the pupils, young and old, were in the schoolhouse before Kennedy arrived and had him barred out. Although they announced their intention to stay there until spring rather than admit him, Kennedy refused to surrender. At a peace talk held through the window he proposed a race to settle the question, promising that he would treat if any of them could catch him before noon. After some discussion the challenge was accepted, and Kennedy withdrew to a spot fifty yards away.

Presently the door was flung open and out dashed six of the fleetest runners in the school. Kennedy sped eastward to the main road and headed for the town of Franklin eight miles away. The boys had youth on their side, but he had the stamina for an endurance race and knew how fast to set the pace. Travelers on the Franklin road pulled up to gawk at the spectacle of the long-legged teacher galloping along, reeling off the miles, followed by a string of boys pelting after him several hundred yards in the rear. Just outside the town limits Kennedy slowed down to a walk. When the leaders caught up with him, he said they would wait for the others and all go into town together. Why? To get the treat, of course.

Redfaced and sweating as though it were the Fourth of July instead of Christmas, teacher and students went merrily into the general store and got baskets of treats which they carried back to the waiting small fry. Thanks to the schoolmaster's sporting gesture, honor was satisfied all around. The treat was distributed in an atmosphere of peace and good will wholly appropriate to the season, and for many years thereafter the tale of the teacher's marathon was a favorite Christmas story in that part of Indiana.

Pioneer Horse Play

BECAUSE OF their essential role in early-day land transportation and communication, horses figure prominently in most accounts of frontier days. Time and again, a good horse might mean the difference between life and death; on the less serious side, horses played an important part in pioneer social life and pastimes. To borrow present-day terminology, a horse was something of a status symbol. When a young man was courting the village belle, for example, it certainly did his cause no harm if he could call for the young lady driving a highstepping trotter or a spanking team. And of course frontier history is replete with true tales of the money won (and sometimes the lives lost) as the result of a proud owner "bragging on" the speed or intelligence of a favorite mount.

1

In 1831, some hospitable families in the little settlement of Hickory Creek, Illinois, were moved to give a neighborhood dance to which they also invited three young men from nearby Chicago. The prospective attendance of these city blades set the maidens of Hickory Creek all of a-twitter; by comparison with the local swains, the Chicagoans were smart and dashing men of the world whom it would be very difficult to impress.

On the appointed day, according to a contemporary account, the three Chicagoans "set off in high spirits. They took care to be in good season, for the dancing was to commence at two o'clock in the afternoon. They were well mounted, each priding himself upon the animal he rode, and they wore their best suits, as became city gallants who were bent on cutting out their less fashionable neighbors and breaking the hearts of the admiring country damsels." When they arrived at Hickory Creek, "they were received with great politeness—their steeds were taken care of—a dinner provided them, after which they were ushered into the dancing-hall."

Here were assembled all the neighborhood beauties—most of them white, "or what passed for such, with an occasional dash of copper color"—in their best gowns, their 'kerchiefs redolent of oil of cinnamon. When the gentlemen joined the ladies and all the guests took their places in long rows on the puncheon floor, they were a merry and happy company. But as the afternoon wore on there began to be seen black looks and scowls on the faces of the country boys. "In vain they pigeon-winged and double-shuffled—in vain they nearly dislocated their hips and shoulders at 'hoe corn and dig potatoes'—they had the mortification to perceive that the smart young sprigs from Chicago had their pick and choice among their sweethearts, and that they themselves were fairly danced off the ground."

The party lasted until dawn of the following morning, but when it came time for the conquering heroes to take their leave, no one among the local youths politely offered to bring their horses from the stable. In fact, none of the country contingent was to be seen.

"Poor fellows!" said one of the city party. "They couldn't stand it. They've gone home to bed."

"Serves them right," said another. "They'd better not ask us down among their girls again!"

They walked back to the stable and groped their way around in its dark interior. The only animals they could find were a trio of queer-looking nags tied to the manger. Had some rogues been trying to cheat them by making off with their own mounts and substituting these strange nondescripts? Taking the beasts out into the gray light of morning for a closer inspection, the Chicago dandies got the shock of their lives.

For these were their horses all right—at least, the original bodies—but where were their manes and tails? "A scrubby, pick-etty ridge along the neck and a bare stump projecting behind were all that remained of the flowing honors with which they had come gallivanting down to 'bear away the bell' at Hickory

Creek, or, in the emphatic language of the country, 'to take the rag off the bush.' "

One Beau Brummell sat down on a log and burst into tears; the second took the matter more philosophically—his horse was a borrowed one; and the third, breathing threats of vengeance, checked the premises, hoping to find the culprits. But he and his mates soon realized that undoubtedly the country bumpkins were in some safe nook, laughing up their sleeves; and they would only make even bigger fools of themselves by continuing to hang around.

Mounting their clownish-looking steeds, the woebegone gallants started homeward. Unfortunately, there was no back way into Chicago. They had to ride across the prairies and approach the little settlement in full view of the whole community. Moreover, in those days when so little out of the ordinary happened, it was the custom of all the settlers to turn out and welcome any newcomer. And so it befell on this day. Received by the shouts, the jeers, and the condolences of their acquaintances, the three cavaliers ducked out of sight as soon as possible, and "it is on the record that they were in no hurry to accept, at any future time, an invitation to partake of the festivities at Hickory Creek."

2

The earliest settlement of Wisconsin was around the lead mines in the southwest corner of the state.* A majority of the early settlers were Southerners who came up the Mississippi River from Missouri, Kentucky, or the neighboring states. They came to mine for lead, and many, having made their fortunes, bought land in the area and settled down to enjoy their comfortable circumstances. The flow of wealth from the rich lead mines was freely spent on entertainment and on such luxuries as fine horses. The Kentuckians in particular, being bred in a state deservedly famous for its horseflesh, made a point of importing blooded stock.

*See page 26.

One of the pioneers in this prosperous region was Jacob Hoosier, who arrived in 1828 and located on a piece of land near Plattesville, about sixty miles southeast of Prairie du Chien. In time he built a stone house on his place and developed a good farm on which he lived like a gentleman. He was known far and wide as a crack rifle shot and as a lover of race horses. On the neighboring property lived a Kentuckian, Mr. James Vineyard, who also was a sportsman and an excellent judge of race horses. Not surprisingly, there was a difference of opinion between the two about which had the fastest horse in his string, and in a match race Hoosier's nominee was thoroughly beaten.

Seeking revenge for his loss, Mr. Hoosier went down to Edwardsville, Illinois, where he purchased a fleet sorrel mare which he called Big Ann. He engaged a jockey to care for and train the mare, and when he judged her to be in top condition challenged Vineyard to a race against the new contender. Accepting the challenge, the Kentuckian too began to make preparations for the big event, which soon was the talk of the whole neighborhood.

At first, Vineyard was confident of another victory, but Hoosier seemed so calmly certain of the contrary that Vineyard began to have misgivings. Wanting to know exactly what he was up against, he and some friends bribed Hoosier's jockey to look the other way one night while they took the sorrel out and tested her speed. Finding that she had the legs of their horse, they gave Big Ann's jockey an additional bribe to hold his mount back and allow Vineyard's horse to win. Positive that they now had a sure thing, the conspirators went looking for men who had money to wager on Big Ann.

Somehow Hoosier discovered that his jockey had been bribed to throw the race; but he kept this knowledge to himself. He continued to accept all the bets that came his way, and on the morning of the race not only wagered an additional five hundred dollars which a friend had secured for him, but drove up all his cattle and horses and bet them against cash stakes eagerly offered by the Vineyard crowd.

The race, which was witnessed by every lover of racing in

southwestern Wisconsin, was run in the autumn of 1848. The course was a mile straightaway, and the stakes were held by the judge of the local court who also supervised the running. As the hour approached, the dishonest jockey brought out Big Ann and began leading her back and forth. Soon the rival Vineyard entry appeared, and at once Mr. Hoosier stuck two fingers in his mouth and whistled sharply. In response to this signal a young man dressed as a jockey emerged from a thicket of hazel brush and came running up to Big Ann. Mr. Hoosier then whipped out a brace of pistols and ordered the dishonest jockey to surrender the big sorrel's reins to the new rider.

This unforeseen turn of events threw the Vineyard crowd into an uproar. They insisted that all bets were off and tried to withdraw their money. But welshing on bets was not tolerated on the frontier. It was an unwritten law that bets fairly made must stand, and there was nothing in the terms of any of the wagers which specified that a particular man was to ride Big Ann. Determined to see that fair play ruled, Judge Paine held onto the stakes and ordered the horses to the starting line.

When the new jockey climbed on Big Ann's back, the instructions given him were simply to win the race or have his head blown off. With this threat ringing in his ears, he gave the sorrel an exemplary ride and brought her in an easy winner. The victory meant about $10,000 to her owner, but even before he collected from the judge, Mr. Hoosier went over to Ann and praised and patted her. With his arms around her lathered neck, he assured his champion mare that she would never have to race again—that, in fact, it was the last race for both of them as he was quitting the racing game.

As soon as they returned home, Big Ann was turned out to pasture, there to take her ease for the rest of her life. As for Vineyard and his cronies, while history is silent on the point, it seems pretty certain that never again were they so misguided as to bet money, marbles, or chalk on a "sure thing."

*The settlers' right to pre-empt the land on which they
lived was recognized by Congress in a series of laws
enacted between 1830 and 1841.* In general, these
laws provided that a U. S. citizen (or a person who had
filed a declaration of intention to become a citizen)
who migrated to the public domain, built a dwelling,
and made certain improvements on the land should be
allowed to purchase up to 160 acres at the minimum
price per acre. There were also provisions specifying
that to be eligible for pre-emption the individual must
be the head of a family, a widow, or a single man over
twenty-one; that he must not be the proprietor of 320
acres of land in any state or territory; and that he must
not quit or abandon his residence on his land to reside
on the public land in the same state or territory.*

*By enacting these laws, Congress intended to make
sure that the public domain should not fall into the
hands of those who already had enough land; that the
domain should be settled in small farms so as to extend
the blessing of cheap land to the largest number of
citizens; to protect the settlers from intrusion and allow them a reasonable time to earn sufficient money
to buy the land; and to place the settler on an equal
basis with the speculator in competition for land.*

The Settlers Hold Their Own

WHILE THE PRE-EMPTION LAWS were a victory for the settlers, they
also benefited a less deserving segment of the citizenry—the squatters who took up land with no intention of buying it. In such
cases, the squatter would file on a choice tract, put up some kind

*See page 86.

of a dwelling, clear the required acreage, and farm the land until the government sale was announced; he would then sell out his claim, receiving cash for land he had never paid a red cent for. On the frontier in the 1830's and 1840's much of the best land was held and disposed of by men who did not own one foot of ground, and this traffic in pre-emption claims frequently was attended by flagrant dishonesty and injustice.

1

In 1831 John and Rebecca Burlend and their five youngest children emigrated to the United States from Yorkshire, England. Traveling steerage in the vessel *Home* they made the long voyage from Liverpool to New Orleans, and then continued by steamboat up the Mississippi to Philips Ferry, Illinois. Here they had the good fortune to meet a squatter named Oakes who was willing to sell his claim on an eighty-acre tract in Pike County. During his occupancy of the land, Oakes had improved it by building a cabin and breaking up about twelve acres, three of which were sown with wheat while the remaining nine were ready to be planted with corn and oats the following spring. There were also about four hundred sugar maples on the land, which Oakes had tapped the preceding year. The Burlends paid Oakes the sum of sixty dollars for his house, improvement right, and sugar-making utensils. As he had lived on the land less than four years—the duration of a pre-emption right—he had not yet bought it from the government; and the Burlends acquired legal title by paying one hundred dollars—the minimum price of $1.25 per acre—at the land office at Quincy, Illinois.

During their first three years of pioneering John and Rebecca experienced the customary vicissitudes of frontier life. They put more land into cultivation and built up a little dairy herd; and although buying livestock and farm implements had exhausted their small cash reserve, they counted on replenishing it by making and selling maple sugar.

In the autumn of 1834 their nearest neighbor, an old hunter named Paddock, offered to sell them his adjoining eighty-acre claim, of which fourteen or fifteen acres were broken up, and on which he had built a stout log cabin. Having been on the land more than three years, he would lose all right to it unless he paid the government one hundred dollars before his pre-emption claim expired in the spring. As it happened, he had the money to do so, but Paddock was one of those sons of the wilderness who became restless and moved along as soon as a region began to get settled up. Since he was asking only fifty dollars and was willing to take payment in cattle and produce, the Burlends finally decided to accept his offer, gambling on raising a hundred dollars from their maple sugar to buy in the land at the government sale. In return for a good cow, a heifer, and seventy bushels of wheat, they received the pre-emption certificate which Paddock had obtained from the land office.

In a few days the old hunter had headed into the western wilderness and the Burlends were free to move onto his land. According to law, it was mandatory for anyone taking up a pre-emption claim, or holding a claim purchased from another party, actually to live on the land. But settlers were often careless in such matters and in the Burlends' case it would have been inconvenient to move because of the cattle and dairy. So they stayed on the home place and Paddock's cabin stood unoccupied.

One day John Burlend happened to be on the new claim repairing a fence when he saw a man named Carr, of very disreputable character, snooping around the premises. When Carr realized that he had been observed, he came up to John and asked a number of extremely pointed questions about pre-emption rights. This led John to suspect that Carr might attempt to take possession of the vacant claim. Much disturbed, he talked the situation over with Rebecca that night. They considered burning down the hunter's cabin as one way of keeping out unwelcome tenants, but at last concluded that they should occupy it, even though it mean dividing the family.

Since John was needed at home to tend the livestock and run the dairy, it became Rebecca's unpleasant duty to hold the fort on the adjacent claim. The next day she moved to the cabin, taking with her the two youngest children and a small stock of provisions. Although she saw the other members of the family frequently during the day, the nights were long and anxious and she dreaded the appearance of an unprincipled intruder.

One afternoon after she had been living in the cabin about a week, a man whom she later learned was Carr, a woman, and two children drove up in a clumsy wagon containing a few pieces of furniture. Rebecca shut the door and tried to fasten the latch, but there was no lock and Carr quickly forced it open. Taking no notice of Rebecca, he bade his wife walk in, saying to her, "Well, my dear, this is our house. How do you like it?" Not until he had carried in the furniture did he address a word to Rebecca, and then it was to tell her that they could do without her company, and that they wished her to be a good neighbor and go home. Rebecca's answer was to take her bed and belongings into the second of the cabin's two rooms.

That evening when John strolled over to visit her, he was confronted by Carr holding up a paper, which he said was a certificate from the land office giving him title to the claim. Although Carr slammed the door on him and held it, John soon succeeded in forcing his way in. Seeing the Burlends engaged in whispered conversation, Carr declared that if they intended to spend the night in his house, he would go and make use of theirs; and forthwith departed.

After talking the situation over, John and Rebecca decided that John should ride the fifty miles to the land office at Quincy, taking with him the pre-emption certificate endorsed by Paddock, and find out whether Carr had purchased the claim by perjury or fraud. John then went home to prepare for the trip, and—in Rebecca's words—"on his arrival found Mr. Carr, whom, as I afterwards learnt, he quickly made scamper."

The next morning, after taking provisions to Rebecca, John left on his secret mission, which would take him three days. Meanwhile Rebecca had to stick it out at the cabin. Describing her plight, she later wrote:

> It was most uncomfortable for me to be thus left with only two little children under the same roof with a family whose sentiments were the most unfriendly imaginable, and whose character stood assuredly not very high for probity. In the

fullest and worst sense of the word, I was a prisoner, not
daring to leave the room, and exposed to the jeers and taunts
of a malicious man who left no means untried, short of personal violence, to expel me from the house; telling me my
husband had sent me there to get rid of me, with a thousand
other fabricated and tantalizing remarks.

The third day, which was the Sabbath, having sent for my
Bible, I endeavoured to solace myself by perusing its sacred
pages. This made him more furious than ever; uttering the
most blasphemous imprecations, he vowed 'he would be both
rid of me and my cursed religion before long.' About ten in
the forenoon, two or three of his friends came to see him . . .
[and] assisted him in his attempts to deride me. I really
thought I now must surrender, and had it not been for the
man's wife, I am apt to think I should have been obliged to
withdraw. After dinner my situation took a favourable turn.
By some means or other many of our neighbors having learnt
where I was and on what account, came to the house to see
me. For a while my keeper refused admittance to all, till by
and by there was quite a crowd at the door. I conversed with
some females whom I knew through an aperture in the wall,
which served as a window; and [finally] a number of men
favourable to our interests told my disappointed persecutor
if he did not allow the females to visit me, they would convince him he was no master. Awed by this declaration, he
opened the door and the house was immediately filled, Mr.
Carr and his party appearing completely nonplused. And, so
strangely had matters changed, that religious worship was
held in the place that evening. . . .

This was too much for Mr. Carr; he entirely left the premises during the service. Towards nightfall my husband was
announced, who was much surprised to find me so well attended. He told Mr. Carr, in the presence of the persons
congregated, where he had been, and how his perjury had
been detected. The sum of the particulars is that Mr. Carr
had paid for the land, having previously sworn there was no
improvement on it, although a pre-emption certificate had
been obtained at the recording office. Of course the purchase
was illegal, and Carr liable to a heavy penalty. But the most
agreeable part of the intelligence to me was that there was no

necessity for me to remain any longer in the house. I therefore very willingly left it and accompanied my husband to our own habitation, having first thanked my friends for their kind interference and regard.

The next morning Carr's wife was waiting at the Burlends' doorstep to say that her husband was willing to compromise, and would either buy their pre-emption right or sell them his certificate. Since they did not have cash in hand to buy out Carr, John and Rebecca sold their claim for eighty dollars—a thirty-dollar profit—and peace again reigned in the neighborhood.

2

Under the federal system of land surveys, as soon as title to Indian lands had been cleared, they were surveyed and marked off into sections of 640 acres, which could then be subdivided and sold in smaller parcels. However, the eagerness of the pioneers to claim the land and the lack of sufficient appropriations to carry on the surveys resulted in the occupancy of much unsurveyed land. When a pioneer came to a tract that suited him, he would measure off the land he desired to claim—perhaps using a length of grapevine—put up a house, and start in farming. He knew that eventually the government surveyors would catch up with him, and he would find out just how efficient his measuring job had been. Sometimes when the survey lines were run, a man's house would turn out to be on his neighbor's claim and his barn on his own. In such situations there was bound to be trouble, and the practice of settling on unsurveyed lands was the cause of many disputes.

In the 1840's a New York State man by the name of Landt found some land to his liking in Adams County, Wisconsin, near what is now Big Spring. After estimating as accurately as possible where the boundary lines of his claim would be, he went into the forest, felled some trees, called in his neighbors for a house-raising, and soon had built a log house at what he thought was approximately the center of his claim. Nearby he set out some apple trees which he had brought from New York, with the idea of starting the first orchard in that region.

About the time he was getting his home started, a Mr. Winchell claimed the land lying next to Landt's. Winchell had found a good site for a sawmill, and was setting one up in anticipation of an influx of settlers and the consequent demand for lumber to build houses and barns.

During breakfast one morning the Landt family saw their neighbor and his son walking around the cabin, looking over the orchard and yard, and generally making themselves right at home. As soon as he had finished breakfast, Landt went outside to learn what they wanted. It turned out that Winchell had in mind to do him a favor—he was generously offering Landt the privilege of moving his apple orchard to a tract on the other side of the house. It so happened, said Winchell, that the trees were on *his* claim, and when he came over next morning to break the land, they would be in the way.

Taken aback by his neighbor's officious manner almost as much as by his assumption of proprietorship, Mr. Landt finally managed to reply that he had done the best he could to locate his claim, and that since no official survey had been made, he, by occupancy custom, had more right to the land than his important neighbor. Furthermore, said Landt, he had brought those choice trees from New York, they were valuable property, and if any were damaged or destroyed he would hold Winchell responsible.

The next morning Winchell appeared with plow and oxen, and broke a forty-acre tract running up to within a short distance of the house. But apparently Landt's warning did have some effect, for he stopped short of destroying the orchard. It was as well for him that he did so. During the next year the surveyors came through the area, and when the official line was drawn the arrogant mill owner's pretensions were cut down to size. The boundary ran a quarter of a mile to the north of Landt's house and so close to the sawmill that Winchell's lumberyard was on Landt's claim. Not only was the apple orchard on Landt's land, but so also was the forty-acre tract that Landt had plowed. Unwittingly he had made Landt a gift of his labor.

As a result of this shock, Mr. Winchell lost his cocksureness and became a much more accommodating man to deal with.

Landt, who harbored no ill will, deeded him the land on which
the lumberyard stood in return for a tract of the same size elsewhere, and henceforth the "good neighbor" policy was practiced
on both sides of the boundary line.

> *Even before the middle of the nineteenth century,*
> *the extensive promotional activities of land companies,*
> *railroad and steamship corporations, and townsite*
> *boosters were a significant factor in accelerating settle-*
> *ment. In pamphlets, brochures, and planted newspaper*
> *stories, the various interests—legitimate and illegiti-*
> *mate—propagandized the rich endowments and nat-*
> *ural advantages of the particular localities to which*
> *they wished to attract settlers. Only too often, how-*
> *ever, the glowing pictures they painted were more*
> *closely akin to pipe dreams than to sober fact, and in*
> *some cases promotional schemes amounted to outright*
> *fraud.*

Rollingstone

THE DECADE beginning in the year 1849, when Minnesota became
a territory, was a boom period which saw a tremendous influx of
settlers into the region. New towns were founded about every five
miles along the Mississippi, and the great river hummed with
traffic. During these years the steamboat *Dr. Franklin,* skippered
by Captain Russell Blakely, ran regularly between Galena, Illinois, and St. Paul, loaded to her utmost capacity on her upriver
trips with emigrants and their household goods, farm implements,
and livestock.

One spring afternoon in 1852, just after the vessel pulled out
of Galena, a portly, prosperous-looking passenger, obviously a
city man and just as obviously impressed with his own importance, came to the clerk's office, produced a wallet, and said, "I
want a ticket to Rollingstone."

"It gathers no moss," said the clerk, who knew of no settlement by that name on the river, and was not going to let any
fat city feller make a fool of him. "Where would you like to
go to?"

"I said Rollingstone."

The clerk considered. "You ain't thinking of Prairie du Chien,
by any chance?"

"No, my good man, I am *not* thinking of Prairie du Chien.
Not being crazy, I am not thinking of any place except the place
I want to go, which is Rollingstone."

"Well, mister, I'm not crazy either; and there isn't any such
place."

"Oh, isn't there?" said the traveler. "Cast your eye over that."
And he drew from his pocket an impressive map, with elaborate
illustrations all around the border. A boldly printed legend declared it to be a map of the city of Rollingstone, and to judge
by this documentary evidence Rollingstone was quite a place.
Tied to its wharf was the very steamboat they were aboard, with
crowds of people on its decks and vast quantities of cargo being
unloaded. Leading away from the riverfront, which teemed with
warehouses, were broad, tree-lined streets, laid out in artistic
curves and lined with imposing buildings—a public library, a post
office, an opera house, and a spacious lecture hall, to say nothing
of numerous schools and churches. As additional proof that the
city founders were men of rare refinement, there were parks plentifully ornamented with flowerbeds—even a large greenhouse
where flowers were grown at public expense. The clerk's jaw
dropped a foot. For seven years he had been sailing up and down
the river, never dreaming that its banks harbored a metropolis of
such magnificence.

Satisfied by the clerk's expression that he had made his point,
the traveler reaffirmed that Rollingstone was where he wanted to

go, and reiterated his request for a ticket. The bemused clerk appealed to the captain, who called into consultation the ship's officers. The map was passed from hand to hand and admired by all, but no one had ever heard of Rollingstone. After further study of the map, Captain Blakely, who knew the Mississippi as he knew the palm of his hand, surmised that from the shape of the river bend the "city" was on land belonging to the Mdewakanton Sioux, and not far from the headquarters of their great chief Wabasha. There was only one white settler within ten miles of the place, and if other palefaces should appear the Sioux would likely "lift their hair" without ceremony.

Although it was carefully explained that the streets and flowerbeds, the elegant opera house and monumental library existed only in the imagination of a rascally town promoter, the traveler remained unconvinced. He said that the previous fall a crew of artisans had been sent from New York to Rollingstone to construct the public buildings and houses shown on the map, and at that very moment a very large number of colonists were on their way to take up residence in the city. He himself was simply an early bird, eager to get in on the ground floor of such a promising proposition. No amount of argument could shake his belief in the reality of Rollingstone; he insisted on being put ashore at the site, wherever it might be. Finally the captain gave up, and before he retired to his cabin left orders that the *Franklin* should be stopped three miles above Wabasha's camp, which they would reach about midnight.

When he came on deck next morning, Captain Blakely was much surprised to see that the passenger for Rollingstone was still with them. The mate explained that the gentleman, after taking one good look at the desolate spot where they proposed to put him ashore, had announced firmly that this was *not* Rollingstone. He stayed on board until the boat reached St. Paul; there, he said, he would be able to learn about Rollingstone from someone who knew a little something—and he gave it as his considered opinion that the officers of the *Franklin* were a pack of numbskulls.

When the *Franklin* returned to Galena, there, sure enough,

were the Rollingstone colonists, nearly a hundred strong. Their
gear included wagons and farm implements, all had their furniture, and some had even brought pets—canaries, goldfish, dogs,
and cats. Although Captain Blakely told them bluntly what they
would find at Wabasha's prairie, they all took passage on the
Franklin, no more impressed by his remarks than the advance
courier had been.

The captain learned from his strange passengers that they
were mostly office workers—clerks, bookkeepers, salesmen—who
were weary of humdrum, constricting city life and longed for the
wide, open spaces of the bounteous West. They had read in the
newspapers of the rich, wonderful country in the West, and then
one day a man appeared who knew all about the western settlements and was willing to lead them to a glorious new life. This
accommodating personage was the founder of Rollingstone, responsible for the library, the opera house, and all its other
splendors.

The captain asked the colonists if any of them had ever done
any farming. No, they said, not exactly; but they knew all about
it from a series of lectures they had attended in New York the
previous winter. Farming was simply a matter of plowing the
soil, planting the seeds, and letting them grow until they had
become crops which a person could harvest. Nothing to it; it was
as easy as a, b, c. Noticing that they had neither tents nor lumber
in their equipment, Captain Blakely asked them what they
planned to use for shelter. It wasn't always fair weather, even in
the wonderful West, and when there was a storm a man could
get mighty wet and cold unless he had a roof over his head. But
as he might have known would be the case, the colonists referred
him to the famous map—surely it was obvious there were plenty
of houses for all. At this, Captain Blakely could contain himself
no longer. "Houses! *Houses!* Why, there are only two white men
within fifty miles of that place. There's nary a sign of a house;
it's all open prairie and bottomland—and no lumber to be had
this side of Black River Falls or the Chippewa River. You don't
have to take my word for it. Come on with me to St. Paul, where

you'll be sure of shelter and a piece of bread to eat, and let a committee go back and investigate."

But he might as well have been arguing with the wind. When the boat reached Wabasha Prairie, the whole colony disembarked with all their bags and baggage, wagons, what-nots, hair trunks, parlor clocks, and canary birds. The captain left them milling helplessly around on the riverbank, beyond them bleak prairie, with no sign of human habitation except the smoke rising from Chief Wabasha's campfire three miles to the south.

Whatever else could be said about it, Rollingstone soon did have one requisite for a city—namely, people. Succeeding steamers brought additional colonists until there were about four hundred engaged in a pitiful, hopelessly inept battle against the forces of nature and the wilderness. They managed to build a few lean-tos out of boards secured from passing lumber rafts. Some tried their hands at building sodhouses; others lived in caves dug into the riverbank. The knowledge of farming acquired in a New York lecture room did not prove of much use in making things grow. Bushels of seeds were planted; few matured. Some of the settlers learned to catch fish, and some tried to do a little hunting. A mysterious disease—possibly due to contaminated water—reached epidemic proportions and carried off many. There was no doctor among the colonists, and the nearest medical man was seventy-five miles away.

As summer turned into fall, the discouraged survivors began to leave the ill-fated spot and try to make their way back to New York. A few vowed they were going to stick it out through the winter, but a few weeks of subzero temperature, cutting wind and driving snow, was enough. When spring came, the only traces of the magnificent city of Rollingstone were a scattering of rickety shacks and a long row of graves.

Fasten Down the Safety Valve

TRAVELING BY river steamboat was relatively comfortable compared to traveling by stagecoach or train, even during the boom years of the 1850's when cabins were jammed and decks nightly covered with sleeping third-class passengers. But what the steamboat contributed in comfort it lacked in safety, and steamboat wrecks were a regular occurrence, often costing scores of lives.

Three major causes accounted for most of these accidents. In flood time, trees would wash out, the root end settling in the riverbed and the upper branches becoming snags which could make a hole the size of a door in a vessel's hull. Explosions were a second danger. Boilers and engines were not as well made in those days, nor had safety devices yet been developed; moreover, the owners and crews were not as safety-conscious as they later became. The third hazard was fire. The western river boats had upper works like tinder and paper, and once a fire started in that flimsy structure it burned to the waterline with startling speed.

A good number of these accidents occurred during the course of steamboat races. It was the custom during a close race to burn lard, fat hams, or anything else in the cargo that would make a hot fire; frequently, too, the engineer would tie down the safety valve, which otherwise operated automatically to allow the boilers to blow off steam when the pressure rose to a dangerously high level. Although steamboat racing was widely denounced, the racing instinct was ineradicable in true rivermen. Nobody could keep out of it if the chance offered. Even the passengers would be carried away by the racing spirit, and when their vessel was overtaking or attempting to keep ahead of a rival, disregarding their safety they would call for the crew to give the boat all she could stand. As for the owners, they had to admit that it was only good business, when two boats were navigating the same stretch of river on about the same schedule, to try to beat the other boat to the next landing, for the first to arrive got the lion's share of the freight and passengers.

One of the most famous races on the upper Mississippi was that which took place in 1854 between the *Dr. Franklin,* then captained by Daniel Harris, and the *Nominee,* whose master was Orrin Smith. The *Nominee,* a recent comer on the run between St. Paul and Galena, began cutting in on the business which the *Franklin* had come to think of as rightfully hers. On the upriver trip the two vessels had been in sight of each other for a day, first one taking the lead, then the other; and they came to port with both crews eager for a downstream race that would resolve the rivalry between the two.

They left St. Paul in the evening, the *Nominee* getting away first and passing out of sight before the *Franklin* was ready to cast off. So that there might be no question of a fair race, the *Nominee* stopped at a point about eighty-five miles downriver and waited for the other boat. At the wheel of the *Franklin* was Stephen Hanks, a cousin of Abraham Lincoln and one of the most skilled and courageous pilots on the river. When he saw the *Nominee* lying still, he slacked up to give her the chance to go first. But Captain Smith waved him on; and as soon as the *Franklin* had steamed by, he took out after her.

From then on it was nip and tuck. For mile after mile the boats were almost side by side. The passengers who crowded their decks preferred to miss meals rather than a moment of the contest. The rivals were close enough so that the passengers could shout back and forth, and there was a constant interchange of jeers and taunts. Since the two boats were very nearly matched as to build and power, the piloting would make the difference.

The first major test of the pilots' skill came a few miles below La Crosse. Here, at a point called Crooked Slough, the river was full of islands and short cuts. Painted Rock Slough, one of these cut-offs, could be readily run at certain stages of water, saving about a mile and a half over the long channel. If the water was too low it could not be run at all, but there was an intermediate stage at which, though the boat would scrape bottom, it was possible to bump through. From certain old marks of his, Hanks

knew that the water was at the bumping stage, so he kept to the
regular channel. The *Nominee,* however, elected to run Point
Rock, and by the time she had scraped and ground her way to
the lower end, the *Franklin* was two miles ahead.

At Guttenberg, the *Franklin* had to stop and take on wood.
The passengers feared that the enforced halt would allow their
rival to pass them, but Captain Smith left them no time to stand
around and worry. The wood was on a flatboat, which he hitched
alongside, almost without stopping. "Now you fellows come and
do a little honest work," the mate yelled to the passengers, and
the words were scarcely out of his mouth before the air was full
of flying cordwood. The pick-up was made in record time, and
the flatboat was cast loose to get back as best it could.

Since both boats were carrying United States mail, they had
to make stops, race or no race. When the *Franklin* stopped for
the mail sacks to be slung on or off, the *Nominee* shot ahead;
when the *Nominee* had to stop, it was the *Franklin's* turn. To
provide light in making landings at night, steamers used great
torches, which were iron baskets filled with pine chips and resin;
these were suspended over the water at the bow. The *Franklin*
was carrying a plentiful supply of resin in barrels, and this was
now fed into the furnaces with pitch, oil, and anything else that
would make a hot fire. Long since, the engineer had fixed a piece
of timber between the safety valve and the deck above. By the
time the *Franklin* reached Dubuque the boiler breechings and
smoke stacks were redhot, and crew members were standing by
with the fire hose.

At Dubuque, which ended the first lap of the race, the *Franklin* was ahead by nearly twenty minutes. There was a wild scene
on the levee while the freight was being put ashore and loaded
aboard, the mate exhorting the roustabouts with a rigamarole of
slashing sarcasm and hide-searing profanity that would have
made even a bullwhacker prick up his ears. The *Franklin* was
first away, and at half-past three that afternoon she steamed into
Galena, having made the run from St. Paul in a bit under twenty-
two hours. Except for the stop at Dubuque, never once during
this record run did Stephen Hanks take his hands from the wheel.

III. Overland Trails

See the maps on pages 194 and 196.

THE "MANIFEST DESTINY" of our country to extend from sea to shining sea was realized in the years between 1840 and 1860. It was during these decades that the outline of the continental United States was drawn on the map as we now see it. The Oregon Treaty of 1846 with Great Britain established our northern boundary at the forty-ninth parallel. In 1848 the Treaty of Guadalupe Hidalgo, ending two years of war with Mexico, brought New Mexico and California into the Union; and Mexico also relinquished her claims to the Republic of Texas, which had won its independence from her in 1836 and had been annexed to the United States in 1845. Finally, in 1853 the Gadsden Purchase, comprising some 30,000 square miles lying south of the Gila River, rounded out our possessions in the Far West and fully restored the Rio Grande as a natural border to the south.

But while treaties and battles make history, it is in the epic westward movement of the American people—men, women, and children on the march to claim half a continent—that we find the great central drama of the times. Never before in the world's history had so vast an area been occupied and settled so rapidly; never before had settlement been achieved on such a grand scale largely by the initiative of individuals and by private enterprise.

The "great migration" westward was not the result of an organized movement. The people who came to the banks of the wide Missouri in the 1840's and 1850's were the poor, the oppressed, the ambitious, the adventurous. Cheap land, gold and silver, the chance to start over in a new country, religious freedom—these were the objectives impelling tens of thousands to attempt the trek to the land of promise beyond the Rockies.

The Oregon Trail

Up until the 1840's the Missouri River was the way west to the Rockies, but as far back as 1813 a fur trader and explorer, Robert Stuart, had proposed an alternate route overland through the broad, level valley of the Platte. The feasibility of this proposal was demonstrated in three phases. In 1830 Jedediah Smith and his partners took ten wagons and two light carriages from St. Louis to the head of the Wind River in present-day Wyoming; in 1832 Captain Benjamin E. Bonneville led the first wagon train through South Pass; and in 1838 a missionary party, headed by Reverend W. H. Gray, succeeded in getting a two-wheeled cart all the way to the coast. Thus, the switch from keel to wheel already was an accomplished fact by the time the country east of the Missouri was settled up and Americans were beginning to look farther west for the lands on which they could stake out their claim on the future.

The glowing accounts of the land riches of the Northwest, publicized mainly by missionaries, excited national interest in Oregon, and in May, 1841, the first band of settlers set out from Independence, Missouri, on the road which was to become known as the Oregon Trail.

1

John Bidwell left his home in New York State with no particular destination in mind except "west." He stopped in Platte County, Missouri, in 1839 and took a job as a schoolteacher. Quite by chance he met a Frenchman, Joseph Robidoux, who operated a trading post at St. Joseph, Missouri, and who had just returned from California. Robidoux' stories of this bountiful and beautiful land excited young Bidwell, and he resolved to

organize an immigrant party. He talked up the project, and so
persuasive was he that within a few months he had secured five
hundred recruits. About half of those pledged intended to go to
California while the remainder were Oregon-bound. It was agreed
that they would form a wagon train and travel together across
the plains and the Rockies, then separate for the final leg of the
journey to their respective destinations.

The departure was scheduled for the spring of 1841, but
during the preceding fall, just when everything looked promising,
the roof started falling in on Bidwell's scheme. In addition to
reports of Plains Indian attacks on white travelers, the Missouri
newspapers carried stories about the hostility of the Spanish in
California, and as a result many families backed out.

When Bidwell reached the place of rendezvous at Saply
Grove, Missouri, on May 1, 1841, he found only one wagon had
arrived ahead of him. However, during the next few days wagons
trickled in at the rate of one or two a day, and eventually the
party totaled sixty-nine, including men, women, and children.
Oxen, mules, and horses made up the wagon teams. Unlike later
immigrants, this first party had no cows. Each family furnished
its own supplies. As Bidwell later wrote in his account of the
journey, "It was understood that every one should have not less
than a barrel of flour, with sugar and so forth to suit, but I laid
in one hundred pounds of flour—more than the usual quantity.
This I did because we were told that when we got into the mountains we probably would get out of bread and have to live on
meat alone, which I thought would kill me, even if it did not the
others."

As a first step to organizing the train, a captain was elected—
a man named John Bartleson from Jackson County, Missouri.
"He was not the best man for the position, but we were given to
understand that if he was not elected captain he would not go;
and he had seven or eight men with him, and we did not want
the party diminished, so he was chosen."

Bidwell's doubts about the abilities of the captain were soon
justified. "In five days after my arrival we were ready to start, but
no one knew where to go, not even the captain. Finally a man

came up and announced that a company of Catholic missionaries
were on their way from St. Louis to the Flathead nation of
Indians with an old Rocky Mountaineer for a guide, and that if
we would wait another day they would be up with us. At first we
were independent, and thought we could not afford to wait for a
slow missionary party. But when we found that no one knew
which way to go, we sobered down and waited."

It was probably the wisest decision they ever made: enthusiasm
and a few hundred pounds of provisions would hardly have
sufficed to keep the party alive, let alone to get them across the
plains. Moreover, the "old Rocky Mountaineer" turned out to be
none other than Thomas Fitzpatrick, the legendary Broken
Hand, who knew the region through which they were to travel
as well as any man in the world. Among the three Roman Catholic priests whom Fitzpatrick was guiding, there was another
figure of equal fame on the frontier. This was Father Pierre Jean
DeSmet, whose life as a missionary to the Indians had begun
some ten years before, and who was known and loved by red men
and white from the Council Bluff to the mouth of the Columbia.
The other members of Fitzpatrick's party were John Gray, an
old mountain man, a young Englishman named Romaine, and
ten or eleven French Canadians.

Because some of the Fitzpatrick party were pulling handcarts,
this necessarily slowed down the rate of travel, but, as Bidwell
wrote, the two groups were generally together "because there was
often work to be done to avoid delay. We had to make the road,
frequently digging down steep banks, filling gulches, removing
stones, etc." And of course there was the need for mutual protection from the Indians. "When we camped at night, we usually
drew the wagons and carts together in a hollow square and picketed our animals inside the corral. The wagons were common
ones of no special pattern, and some of them were covered. To
lessen danger from Indians we usually had no fires at night and
did our cooking in the daytime."

After crossing the Missouri at Independence, the band traveled across the northeast corner of Kansas and followed along
the Blue River to the Platte. It was just before they reached the

Platte, about two weeks out, that they had their first Indian scare. One of Bidwell's party, a man named Dawson, "who chanced to be out hunting some distance from the company and behind us, suddenly appeared without mule, gun, or pistol, and lacking most of his clothes, and in great excitement reported that he had been surrounded by thousands of Indians. The company, too, became excited, and Fitzpatrick tried, but with little effect, to control and pacify them. Every man started his team into a run, till the oxen, like the mules and horses, were in full gallop. Captain Fitzpatrick went ahead and directed them to follow, and as fast as they came to the bank of the river he put the wagons in the form of a hollow square, and had all the animals securely picketed within. After awhile the Indians came in sight. There were only forty of them, but they were well mounted on horses and were evidently a war party, for they had no women except one, a medicine women. They came up and camped within one hundred yards of us on the river below.

"Fitzpatrick told us that they would not have come in, if they were hostile. . . . When the Indians had put up their lodges, Fitzpatrick and John Gray, the old hunter mentioned, went out to them and by signs were made to understand that the Indians did not intend to hurt the man or take his mule and gun, but that he was so excited when he saw them that they had to disarm him to keep him from shooting them. They did not know what had become of his pistol or of his clothes, which they said he had thrown off. They surrendered the mule and gun, thus showing they were friendly. They proved to be Cheyenne Indians. Ever afterwards the man went by the name of 'Cheyenne' Dawson."

It may well be that convoying this excitable band of tenderfeet across the plains and over the Rockies was Thomas Fitzpatrick's most difficult exploit; certainly it is a tribute to his patience (and to his sense of humor) as well as to his frontier skills that he got the job done.

Near Soda Springs, in present-day Idaho, the company divided, about half of it continuing on to Oregon with Fitzpatrick, the other half leading west for California with Bartleson and Bidwell. Although they suffered great hardships, and were forced to abandon their wagons in the Sierras, the party finally arrived in the San Joaquin Valley in November, 1841. They were the first band of settlers to travel on one of the world's great natural highways—the Oregon Trail.

2

In 1842 Lieutenant John C. Fremont explored and reported favorably on the Platte Valley—South Pass wagon route, and the wide publicity given to his report greatly stimulated interest in Oregon. In 1843 more than a thousand persons traveled the two-thousand-mile trail, and the "great migration" was officially on. Independence was the jumping-off place, just as it was for the Santa Fe Trail; in fact, for the first forty miles immigrants followed the old trail to where a crude sign marked the "Road to Oregon." Here they turned northwest to the Platte, which they followed to its forks, then proceeded along the North Platte to the Sweetwater and South Pass. Across the Continental Divide the trail dropped southward to Fort Bridger; there it turned northwesterly to Soda Springs and continued along the Snake to Fort Hall. The final stretch was down the Columbia to Oregon's Willamette Valley.

The first large party of about a hundred wagons was organized at Independence in 1843, the wagons having converged there singly or in small groups. A compact was drawn and a captain elected; he was given much the same authority as a ship's captain. Assistant captains were appointed; also, leaders of units comprised of four or five wagons. The compact provided for jury trials for serious crimes, but its principal purpose was to organize a staff of men with adequate authority to keep the train moving at reasonable speed and with a minimum of confusion.

No day on the trail was the same. There were storms, buffalo stampedes, Indian scares, loss of animals, wagon breakdowns, births, weddings, and deaths. Yet the routine of life in a wagon train did have a prevailing pattern. A typical day has been described by Jesse Applegate, a member of this first large organized party. The following account (somewhat abridged) from his jour-

nal gives a good idea of what life was like for immigrants crossing
the plains in 1843:

> It is four o'clock A.M. The sentinels on duty have dis-
> charged their rifles—the signal that the hours of sleep are over;
> and every wagon and tent is pouring forth its night tenants,
> and slow-kindling smokes begin largely to rise and float away
> on the morning air.
>
> Sixty men start from the corral, spreading as they make
> through the vast herd of cattle and horses that form a semi-
> circle around the encampment, the most distant perhaps two
> miles away. By five o'clock the herders begin to contract the
> great moving circle and the well-trained animals move slowly
> toward camp, clipping here and there a thistle or tempting
> bunch of grass on the way.
>
> In about an hour five thousand animals are close up to
> the encampment, and the teamsters are busy selecting their
> teams and driving them inside the "corral" to be yoked. The
> corral is a circle one hundred yards deep, formed with wagons
> connected strongly with each other, the wagon in the rear
> being connected with the wagon in front by its tongue and
> ox chains. From six to seven o'clock is a busy time; breakfast
> is to be eaten, the tents struck, the wagons loaded, the teams
> yoked and brought in readiness to be attached to their respec-
> tive wagons. All know when at seven o'clock the signal to
> march sounds that those not ready to take their proper places
> in the line of march must fall into the dusty rear for the day.
>
> It is on the stroke of seven; the rushing to and fro, the
> cracking of the whips, the loud commands to oxen and what
> seems to be the inextricable confusion of the last ten minutes
> has ceased. Fortunately every one has been found and every
> teamster is at his post. The clear notes of the trumpet sound
> in the front; the pilot and his guards mount their horses, the
> leading division of wagons moves out of the encampment, and
> takes up the line of march, the rest fall into their places with
> the precision of clock work, until the spot so lately full of life
> sinks back into that solitude that seems to reign over the
> broad plain and rushing river as the caravan draws its lazy
> length toward the distant El Dorado.
>
> The wagons form a line three quarters of a mile in length;
> some of the teamsters ride upon the front of their wagons,

some walk beside their teams; scattered along the line companies of women and children are taking exercise on foot; they gather bouquets of rare and beautiful flowers that line the way; near them stalks a stately gray hound or an Irish wolf dog, apparently proud of keeping watch and ward over his master's wife and children.

Next comes a band of horses; two or three men or boys follow them, the docile and sagacious animals scarcely needing this attention, for they have learned to follow in the rear of the wagons. Not so with the large herd of horned beasts that bring up the rear; lazy, selfish and unsocial, it has been a task to get them in motion.

[After some five hours of traveling, the train makes the noon halt—or "nooning"—at a place chosen by the pilot.] As the teams are not unyoked, but simply turned loose from the wagons, a corral is not formed at noon, but the wagons are drawn up in columns, four abreast. [The noon halt lasts perhaps an hour.] It is now one o'clock; the bugle has sounded, and the caravan has resumed its westward journey. It is in the same order, but the evening is far less animated than the morning march; a drowsiness has fallen apparently on man and beast; teamsters drop asleep on their perches and even walking by their teams, and the words of command are now addressed to the slowly creeping oxen in the softened tenor of women or the piping treble of children.

The sun is now getting low in the west and at length the painstaking pilot is standing ready to conduct the train in the circle which he has previously measured and marked out, which is to form the invariable fortification for the night. Within ten minutes from the time the leading wagon halted, the barricade is formed, the teams unyoked and driven out to pasture.

Everyone is busy preparing fires of buffalo chips to cook the evening meal, pitching tents and otherwise preparing for the night. [In these preparations, of course, guarding against an Indian attack is the overriding consideration.] All able to bear arms in the party have been formed into three companies, and each of these into four watches. Every third night it is the duty of one of these companies to keep watch and ward over the camp, and it is so arranged that each watch takes its turn of guard duty through the different watches of the night.

It is not yet eight o'clock when the first watch is to be set; the evening meal is just over, and the corral now free from the intrusion of the cattle or horses, groups of children are scattered over it. Before a tent near the river a violin makes lively music, and some youths and maidens have improvised a dance upon the green; in another quarter a flute gives its mellow and melancholy notes to the still air, which as they float away over the quiet river seem a lament for the past rather than a hope for the future.

But time passes; the watch is set for the night, the council of old men has broken up and each has returned to his own quarters. The flute has whispered its last lament to the deepening night, the violin is silent and the dancers have dispersed. Enamored youths have whispered a tender "Good night" in the ears of blushing maidens, or stolen a kiss from the lips of some future bride—for Cupid here as elsewhere has been busy bringing together congenial hearts. All is hushed and repose from the fatigue of the day, save the vigilant guard, and the wakeful leader who still has cares upon his mind that forbid sleep.

He hears the ten o'clock relief taking post and the "All well" report of the returned guard; the night deepens, the last care of the day being removed, and the last duty performed, he too seeks the rest that will enable him to go through the same routine tomorrow.

When the Apple Orchard Moved

NO MATTER HOW EAGERLY emigrant families looked forward to going west, and no matter how high their hopes for the future, it was seldom indeed that they could leave their homes in the East without a pang. They were saying goodbye to family and friends and familiar surroundings; moreover, most of their household goods and personal possessions would have to be left behind, and it was difficult, even painful, to decide what to leave and what to load in the wagons.

The wagons weighed over a half ton when empty. The immigrant guides and, more importantly, those who had made the trip recommended about 2,500 pounds of cargo; a heavier load would wear out the mules or oxen when the going became harder in the mountains. Joseph Ware's *Guide to Immigrants,* which was considered reliable since he had made the trip himself, suggested the following for a family of four: 800 pounds of flour, 700 pounds of bacon, 75 pounds of coffee, 200 pounds of lard, 200 pounds of beans, 100 pounds of dried fruit, and 25 pounds of salt and pepper. Cooking utensils, tools, ammunition, extra axles, and "private baggage" were to make up the remaining 400 pounds. Nonetheless, in spite of all the warnings about overloading, the immigrants often insisted on taking along beds, bureaus, stoves, and chairs. Since the unessentials were the first to be jettisoned when the oxen started to play out, it was the exception indeed when these articles arrived in Oregon. The trail west of Laramie was littered with the beloved possessions of scores of immigrant families.

Perhaps the strangest cargo to travel along the Oregon Trail was that carried in one of three wagons belonging to Henderson Lewelling. Mr. Lewelling made a comfortable living in southwest Iowa growing and selling fruit trees, but the "Oregon fever" hit him in 1846 and he decided to pull stakes and go west with his family. He also decided to take his business with him in the form of a wagonload of apple-tree seedlings and graftings. To transport his future orchard he made two boxes twelve inches deep and wide enough and long enough to fit tightly in the wagonbox. When these were filled with earth and the seedlings transplanted, he had a portable nursery.

Lewelling bought three good yoke of oxen to pull this heavily laden wagon. Two other wagons—one for provisions and one for household goods—made up the rest of his outfit. On April 17, 1847, accompanied by three wagons of neighbors, the Lewellings left for St. Joseph to join a train commanded by Captain Whit-comb. Also traveling in the party was the Reverend Dr. Elijah White, veteran of several trips over the trail, who originally had gone to Oregon as a missionary and later was appointed an Indian agent.

Lewelling's "moving orchard" was a source of consternation and merriment to the other immigrants, and later of criticism. Once on the great road to the west, caring for the trees was no easy task. Every evening the plants had to be watered, an espe-cially arduous chore when it was impossible to draw the wagon up close to the banks of a stream and the buckets of water had to be carried some distance. Yet Lewelling remained steadfast in his purpose, provided, he said, that it did not endanger the health or life of his family.

On the North Platte he was urged by Dr. White to leave the trees, since the oxen were becoming footsore and worn out with the weight of the load. White predicted that if the cattle were not relieved they would die. But Lewelling was so emphatic in his refusal to abandon the seedlings that the other travelers ceased to remonstrate with him and left him to his own resources.

The nurseryman decided that it would be best for his little caravan to travel alone in order that they might proceed in a more leisurely fashion. Instead of standing guard at night, they belled the cattle, grazing them until they were ready to lie down, and grazing them again in the early morning hours. On the Sweetwater in Wyoming they lost two oxen, one by poison and one by inflammation of the feet. Fortunately, the other two wagons were now becoming lighter and their oxen could spell off the tree-wagon cattle. Thanks to this trading around and to judicious driving, the cattle improved, growing stronger day by day.

The Lewelling party crossed over the mountains at Pacific Springs and followed the usual route via Fort Bridger to Fort Hall. After a long pull across the sagebrush plains, through the valley and over the mountains, they arrived at the Umatilla River in the upper reaches of the Columbia watershed. They were met at this point by Marcus Whitman—the heroic missionary, who, as much as any one man, was instrumental in securing the Oregon country for the United States—who piloted the little procession to the Dalles, which they reached on October 1.

Here Lewelling constructed two flat boats to float their goods down the river. They now carefully wrapped the fruit trees in cloth to protect them in the various handlings and from the frosty night air. With the boats completed about November 1, they started down the river. At Wind River they unloaded the goods and trees and used the craft to ferry the animals across to the north side where there was a path for stock. Loading the goods and trees again, they floated to the upper Cascades where the boats were unloaded, released, and allowed to go bumping down the boiling, tossing stream to a point below the lower Cascades where they were captured and reloaded into the wagons which had hauled the precious trees and goods over the portage. From now on the going was good. On November 17 they tied up at a point opposite Fort Vancouver. Three days later Lewelling's son Lewis came driving in the cattle.

Lewelling had now reached the goal of his expedition—the mouth of the Willamette Valley—with his precious cargo of fruit trees. After carefully exploring the country, he purchased some land adjacent to the townsite of Milwaukee and began clearing off the dense fir trees. Soon he was able to plant the orchard and nursery.

He had now realized his ambition. He had brought a cargo of living trees across the plains, over the mountains, and down the Columbia—the first cultivated or grafted trees to reach the Pacific. About half the trees he had carried from Salem lived to become the progenitors of the great Oregon and Washington apple orchards. Within the next few years immigrants came pouring into the country and assured him of an unlimited market. His widely reported exploit in bringing trees across the plains advertised his nursery from one end of the country to the other. This, together with the superior varieties of apples he brought, established the reputation of Oregon and Washington fruits. Lewelling sold hundreds of thousands of fruit trees at a dollar each and became immensely wealthy.

*In 1838 more than twelve thousand members of the
Mormon Church (Church of Jesus Christ of Latter-
Day Saints), having been driven from Missouri, settled
at Nauvoo, Illinois, on the banks of the Mississippi.
Persecution had followed them since the founding of
their church in 1830, but the governor of Illinois had
granted them a favorable charter and they hoped that
at last they would be allowed to dwell in peace, with
freedom to worship according to the tenets of their
faith. Instead, their Illinois neighbors rose up against
them. In 1844 their founder, Joseph Smith, and his
brother Hyrum were killed by a mob while awaiting
trial for "treasonable design." There were further outbreaks of violence during the following year, and early
in 1846 the Mormons were ordered to leave the state.
On February 6, under the leadership of Brigham
Young, the first company of exiles crossed the Mississippi on the ice, determined to seek the site of a new
Zion somewhere in the West beyond the borders of
civilization.*

The Mormon Trail

THE MORMON MIGRATION contributed some of the saddest yet
most stirring pages to the history of the settlement of the West.
Its first phase ended in the spring of 1846 when the Mormons,
having crossed Iowa, reached the banks of the Missouri River.
Realizing that time-consuming preparations must be made before
they started across the plains to seek their temporary home, Brigham Young sought permission from the federal government to
stop for the winter in Indian country on the west bank of the

Missouri. The Mexican War was then in progress, and the government agreed to grant Young's request if the Mormons would furnish five hundred "volunteers" for the Army. The necessary men were found, and more than three thousand Mormons crossed the river to a site a few miles above Bellevue. Here during the summer and fall they built a temporary log and sod town which they called "Winter Quarters."

1   ¢

Winter Quarters put the fortitude of the Saints to a severe test. Before spring came, more than six hundred had died of malaria and scurvy, exposure and starvation. A sympathetic army officer, Colonel Thomas L. Kane, who visited the temporary town in July, 1846, has left a first-hand account of the building of Winter Quarters and the conditions of life there.

> After the sorrowful word was given out to halt and make preparation for winter, a chief labor became the making of hay; and with every day dawn brigades of mowers would take up the march to their position in chosen meadows, a prettier sight than a charge of cavalry, as they laid their swaths, whole companies of scythes abreast. . . . When they set about building their winter houses, too, the Mormons went into quite considerable timbering operations, and performed desperate feats of carpentry. They did not come ornamental gentlemen or raw apprentices, to extemporize new versions of Robinson Crusoe. It was a comfort to notice the readiness with which they turned their hands to woodcraft; some of them, though I believe these had generally been bred carpenters, wheelwrights, or more particularly boat-builders, quite outdoing the most notable *voyageurs* in the use of the axe. . . .
>
> Inside the camp, the chief labors were assigned to the women. From the moment when, after the halt, the lines had been laid, the spring wells dug out, and the ovens and fireplaces built . . . the Empire of the Tented Town was with the better sex. They were the chief comforters of the severest sufferers, the kind nurses who gave them in their sickness those attentions with which pauperism is hardly poor, and which the greatest wealth often fails to buy. And they were a nation of wonderful managers. . . .

Every day closed as every day began, with an invocation of the divine favor; without which, indeed, no Mormon seemed to dare to lay him down to rest. With the first shining of the stars, laughter and loud talking hushed, the neighbor went his way, you heard the last hymn sung, and then the thousand-voiced murmur of prayer was heard, like bubbling water falling down the hills. . . .

In the camp nearest us on the west . . . the number of its inhabitants being small enough to invite computation, I found as early as the 31st of July, that 37 per cent of its inhabitants were down with the fever, and a sort of strange scorbutic disease, frequently fatal, which they named the Black Canker. The camps to the east of us, which were all on the eastern side of the Missouri, were yet worse fated.

The climate of the entire upper "Misery Bottom," as they term it, is during a considerable part of summer and autumn, singularly pestiferous. The Mormons were scourged severely. The fever prevailed to such an extent that hardly any escaped it. They let their cows go unmilked. They wanted for voices to raise the psalm of Sundays. The few who were able to keep their feet, went about among the tents and wagons with food and water, like nurses through the wards of an infirmary. Here at one time the digging got behind hand; burials were slow; and you might see women sit in the open tents keeping flies off their dead children, some time after decomposing set in.

But I am excused sufficiently the attempt to get up for your entertainment here any circumstantial picture of horrors, by the fact that at the most interesting season I was incapacitated for nice observation by an attack of fever . . . [and for a month] had very small notion of what went on among my neighbors. I recollect hearing a lamentation over some dear baby, that its mother no doubt thought the destroying angel should have been specially instructed to spare.

I wish too, for my own sake, I could forget how imperfectly one day I mourned the decease of a poor Saint who, by clamor, rendered his vicinity troublesome. He, no doubt, endured great pain; for he groaned shockingly till death came to his relief. He interfered with my own hard-gained slumbers, and I was glad when death did relieve him.

2

Through all these tragic months Brigham Young worked tirelessly to organize his followers for the hegira to the New Zion, wherever that might prove to be. Elected head of the Mormon Church in 1847, Young was as able as he was zealous and indefatigable—in Bernard DeVoto's words, "a great leader, a great diplomat, a great administrator ... one of the makers and one of the finders of the West."

In the spring of 1847 he set out with an advance company of about a hundred and fifty to seek out the site for their future home. Although their route lay along the Platte, paralleling the Oregon Trail, Young directed that they travel on the north side of the river in order to keep as far away as possible from the Gentiles. All during the journey the leaders prayed for God's guidance to the proper location of the New Zion. After leaving Fort Bridger they struck out across the Wasatch Mountains, and on a July day reached an eminence overlooking the Salt Lake Valley. Young, who lay ill in his wagon, now arose and halted the little caravan. He gazed long and earnestly at the scene before them, then declared, "This is the place." On July 24, 1847, the Mormons entered the valley and almost immediately laid out the beautiful, spacious community which they named Salt Lake City.

By late fall more than four thousand Saints had followed the pioneer band, rejoicing at having left their persecutors a thousand miles behind. Nonetheless, that first winter and spring there was great suffering. They had arrived so late in the season that very little could be raised, and the whole colony was near starvation. In their hunger for bread they searched out old flour sacks and shook them to recover the pitiful sprinkling of flour which clung to their insides.

Recalling those days, Priddy Meeks, a physician from South Carolina, wrote in his journal: "My family went several months without a satisfying meal of victuals. I went sometimes a mile up the Jordan to a patch of wild roses to get the berries to eat which I would eat as rapidly as a hog, stems and all. I shot hawks and crows and they ate well. I would go and search the mire holes and find cattle dead and fleece off what meat I could and eat it. We used wolf meat which I thought was good. I made some wooden spades to dig seagoes* with, but we could not supply our wants. . . . I would take a grubbing-hoe and a sack and start by sunrise in the morning and go, I thought, six miles before coming to where thistle roots grew, and in time to get home I would have a basket and sometimes more of thistle roots, and we would eat them raw. I would dig until I grew weak and faint and sit down and eat a root and then begin again."

A fairly large acreage of winter wheat had been sown and gardens planted, but a series of frosts severely damaged the plantings, and as early as the end of May the Rocky Mountain crickets began ravaging the crops. On May 28 there was another heavy frost which killed beans, squash, cucumbers, and melons and damaged the corn. By June 4 the combination of frosts and the visitation of crickets had awakened general alarm. The wheat was heading out and the crickets seemed to be eating the heads off as fast as the plants developed. Many of the Saints were beginning to talk of hitching up and leaving the valley, but one old man, full of faith, steadied the settlers with his reminder that the Lord who brought them there was able to sustain them even if their crops failed, because the earth was the Lord's and the fullness thereof. As for Brigham Young, "Here we are and here we stay," he had said when they first arrived.

Finally the crickets came so thick and fast that it made the earth black in places. "It did look like they would take what little we had growing which looked nice and flourishing," wrote Dr. Meeks. "Now everything did look gloomy, our provisions giving out and the crickets eating up what little we had growing, and we a thousand miles away from supplies."

And then, in that darkest hour, came the never-to-be-forgotten Sunday of their salvation. A meeting was held out-of-doors at which one of their leaders, Apostle Rich, stood in an open wagon and preached. As the Apostle made reference to their need, he said (according to Meeks):

*The sego lily is the Utah state flower.

" 'Brethren, we do not want you to part with your wagons and teams for we might need them'—intimating that he did not know but we might have to leave. That increased my solemnity. At that instant I heard the voice of fowls flying overhead that I was not acquainted with. I looked up and saw a flock of seven gulls. In a few minutes there was another larger flock passed over. They came faster and more of them until the heavens were darkened with them and lit down in the valley till the earth was black with them; and they would eat crickets and throw them up again and fill themselves again and right away throw them up again. A little before sundown they left for Salt Lake, for they roosted on a sandbar; a little after sunrise in the morning they came back again and continued that course until they had devoured the crickets and then left *sine die* and never returned. I guess this circumstance changed our feeling considerably for the better."

The crops had been saved. In a report sent by messenger to Brigham Young, who was then leading a party of several hundred across the plains from Winter Quarters, the church authorities stated that while the crickets had done much damage earlier in the season, the seagulls had swept the hungry insects before them, and that the hand of the Lord had favored His people.

On August 10, after most of the wheat had been harvested, the Saints celebrated with a harvest feast and thanksgiving to God for His providence to them. There was dancing and the firing of a cannon, and from the valley there arose shouts of hosanna and songs of praise to God who had delivered them from the devourer.

By Handcart to Zion

IN THE FIFTIES, as the result of intensive missionary work, large numbers of converted Mormons from both the United States and Europe flocked to the New Zion at Salt Lake City. A per-

petual immigration fund had been established to assist the converts, most of whom were extremely poor, but the drain on the
church treasury was very heavy. Buying and equipping wagon
trains was a major source of expense, and at last in 1855 Brigham
Young decreed a less costly mode of travel.

"We cannot afford to purchase wagons and teams as in times
past," he wrote. "I am consequently thrown back on my old plan
—make handcarts, and let the emigration foot it. They can come
just as quick, if not quicker, and much cheaper. I can promise
them they will be met with provisions and friends far down on
the plains. . . ."

Five companies were organized, the first of which, numbering
about five hundred persons, set out on July 17, 1856, from
Florence—the town which had grown up on the site of old Winter
Quarters. According to a traveler who passed them on the trail,
"The carts were generally drawn by one man and three women
each, though some carts were drawn by women alone. There were
about three women to one man. . . . It was the most [mixed] crew
I ever beheld. Most of them were Danes, with a sprinkling of
Welsh, Swedes, and English, and were generally from the lower
classes of their countries. Most could not understand what we
said to them. The road was lined for a mile behind the train
with the lame, halt, sick, and needy."

Despite their forlorn appearance, however, their morale was
good, and as they trudged along they sang the handcart song:

> Some must push and some must pull
> As we go marching up the hill;
> As merrily on the way we go
> Until we reach the valley, oh.

When they reached Emigration Canyon on September 26, they
were met by Brigham Young and a delegation of Saints, including a brass band, and triumphantly escorted into Salt Lake City.
Possibly with a view toward popularizing the operation with
future converts, Young wrote to his missionaries in England that
"almost all of the sisters who have this season crossed the Plains

in the handcarts have got husbands; they are esteemed for their perseverance."

Although the first three companies made the crossing without unusual difficulties, the last two, which started late in the season, were caught by an early fall snowstorm in central Wyoming. Of 1,076 immigrants, more than two hundred perished—one of the major tragedies in the history of the overland trails.

John Chislett, a Saint from Liverpool, England, was a member of one of these ill-fated groups and has left a very graphic account of their experiences. His company, commanded by Captain Willie, was comprised of about five hundred Europeans. The company was divided into hundreds, each with a leader. The equipment for a hundred consisted of twenty handcarts, one wagon pulled by three yoke of oxen, and five round tents, each sleeping twenty. The tents and provisions were hauled in the wagon while personal belongings and baggage were carried in the handcarts, each person being allowed seventeen pounds—a total of eighty-five pounds per handcart. A rig of this kind was simply a box mounted upon an axle between two wheels, with a handle which could be used to pull or push it.

Handcarts in such large quantities as were required were in short supply. The Willie Company, which traveled up the Mississippi on steamboat, had to wait nearly three weeks for their carts, camping near Iowa City. It was mid-August by the time they arrived at the Missouri, and one experienced leader objected to their starting that late because of the risk of running into snow in the mountains. But he was overruled, and the Company left Florence on August 18.

It had been decided that each handcart should carry a hundred pound sack of flour, and this added weight caused the poorly made carts to break down. They had been constructed of unseasoned wood, and the axles would snap off at the shoulder. These frequent breakdowns slowed them down so much that they were unable to travel even at the snail pace of oxen. The flour sacks were transferred to the wagons, but near Wood River, in Nebraska, buffalo stampeded their cattle and they never did find them again; this necessitated yoking the cows to the wagons, and lightening the loads by once more carrying the flour sacks in the handcarts.

At Fort Laramie on September 1 the leaders calculated that they would run out of food about three hundred and fifty miles short of their destination. Captain Willie received a dispatch from Salt Lake City stating that relief would be forthcoming by the time they reached the South Pass, but even though rations were cut to meet the emergency it was apparent that they would be out of food before they got to that point. As they penetrated farther into the mountains, they found their clothing and bedding inadequate protection against the cold. Adding to their troubles, dysentery broke out, and Chislett said he did not have enough well men in his hundred to pitch a tent when they camped. His account continues:

> We traveled on in misery and sorrow day after day. Sometimes made pretty good distance, but other times were only able to make a few miles progress. Finally we were overtaken by a snowstorm which the shrill wind blew furiously around us. The snow fell several inches deep as we traveled along, but we dared not stop, for we had a sixteen-mile journey to make, and short of it we could not get wood and water.
>
> As we were resting for a short time at noon a light wagon was driven into our camp from the west. Its occupants were Joseph A. Young [the Prophet's eldest son] and Stephen Taylor. They informed us that a train of supplies was on the way, and we might expect to meet it in a day or two. More welcome messengers never came from the courts of glory than these two young men were to us. We pursued our journey with renewed hope and after untold toil and fatigue, doubling teams frequently, going back to fetch up the straggling carts, and encouraging those who had dropped by the way to a little more exertion in view of our soon-to-be-improved condition, we finally, late at night, got all to camp—the wind howling frightfully and the snow eddying around us in fitful gusts. . . .
>
> In the morning the snow was over a foot deep. Our cattle strayed widely during the storm, and some of them died. But what was worse to us than all this was the fact that five persons of both sexes lay in the cold embrace of death. . . . Being surrounded by snow a foot deep, out of provisions, many of

our people sick, and our cattle dying, it was decided that we should remain in our present camp until the supply-train reached us. It was also resolved in council that Captain Willie with one man should go in search of the supply-train and apprise its leader of our condition, and hasten him to our help. . . .

The storm which we encountered, our brethren from the Valley also met, and, not knowing that we were so utterly destitute, they encamped to await fine weather. But when Captain Willie found them and explained our real condition, they at once hitched up their teams and made all speed to come to our rescue. On the evening of the third day after Captain Willie's departure, just as the sun was sinking beautifully behind the distant hills, on an eminence immediately west of our camp several covered wagons, each drawn by four horses, were seen coming toward us. The news ran through the camp like wildfire, and all who were able to leave their beds turned out *en masse* to see them. A few minutes brought them sufficiently near to reveal our faithful captain slightly in advance of the train. Shouts of joy rent the air; strong men wept till tears ran freely down their furrowed and sunburnt cheeks, and little children partook of the joy which some of them hardly understood, and fairly danced with gladness. . . .

The first Americans to settle in the Mexican province of California were traders and sailors attracted by the climate (which "freed a man from ague"), but not until 1840 did American settlement become numerically significant. In late October, 1841, the first overland immigrants, thirty-seven landseekers led by John Bidwell,* moved into the San Joaquin Valley, and a few weeks later a party of twenty-five Americans and New Mexicans arrived from Santa Fe over the Spanish Trail. By 1846, the year which saw the outbreak of the war with Mexico, there were about five hundred American traders and settlers scattered from Sonoma to San Diego.

*See page 129.

The California Trail

BY FAR THE BEST-KNOWN and most influential of the early settlers
in California was Johann Augustus Sutter. Born in Germany of
Swiss parents in 1803, he emigrated to the United States in 1834,
after seeing service as an officer in the French army. During the
next few years he did some trading in Santa Fe, later farmed near
St. Charles, Missouri. In 1838 he visited the Oregon country and
Hawaii. In 1839 he landed in San Francisco, and in August of
that year settled on a site at the junction of the Sacramento and
American rivers. Here, in 1841, he built Sutter's Fort.

A shrewd and energetic man, Sutter prospered uncommonly.
He bought cattle and horses, sowed grain and planted vineyards,
built barns, granaries, warehouses, a tannery, a grist mill, and a
winery. Among the small army of laborers serving him were
Indians and a group of Hawaiian natives whom he had brought
with him from the Islands. His shipments of hides, grains, flour,
dried meat, cheese, butter, and smoked salmon went to Vancouver, Alaska, Hawaii, Mexico, and South America. In the same
year that he built his fort, Sutter renounced his American citizenship to become a Mexican subject. He was given the rank of
captain and named "Guardian of the Northern Frontier." More
importantly, he received from Governor Alvorado a grant of
141,000 acres of land in the Sacramento Valley.

With such a stake in the region, Sutter was anxious to bring
in settlers. Instead of sending agents to the States and Europe,
he decided to try to siphon off some of the flow of immigration
to Oregon. In 1845 he sent an old mountaineer, Caleb Greenwood, to Fort Hall at the juncture of the Oregon and California
Trails. Greenwood's mission was to divert Oregon-bound parties
to California by offering them free land and supplies on easy
credit.

1

Among the parties which arrived in Fort Hall in the summer of 1845 was a large wagon train headed by Presley Welch. Greenwood talked to the members of the party, stressing the advantages of Sutter's offer, the fertility of California's soil, and the superiority of its climate. He succeeded in persuading eight wagons to split off from the main party and follow him southwest over the mountains and deserts of the California Trail.

Traveling in this offshoot party was a Texan named Jim Kinney. He had a big wagon drawn by four yoke of oxen for his provisions and bedding, and a spring hack pulled by a span of fine mules. His wife drove the light rig and a hired man was in charge of the big wagon. Kinney himself always rode a mule. According to another member of the party, he was "a typical southerner. He had long black hair, long black mustache, heavy black eyebrows, and was tall, weighing about 225 pounds. He had a violent temper and was a good deal of a desperado. . . . He would not obey the train rules, but he was such a powerful man and apparently held life so lightly that no one wanted to cross him."

As the train was creeping west across the barren desert country, Kinney saw an Indian peeking out of the sagebrush and ordered his driver to stop. Since his wagon was in the lead, the whole train came to a standstill. Going to the wagon, he got out a pair of handcuffs and started back to the Indian. One of the members of the party, Jarvis Bonney, asked him what he was up to.

"Where I come from we have slaves," Kinney said. "I am going to capture that Indian and take him with me as a slave."

Bonney said, "The first thing you know, that Indian will escape and tell the other Indians and they will kill all of us."

"I generally have my way," Kinney said. "Any man that crosses me regrets it. I have had to kill two or three men already because they interfered with me. If you want any trouble you know how to get it."

He waited a moment, and when Bonney said nothing more

rode back to where the Indian was, jumped off his mule, and struck him over the head. The Indian put up a fight but was no match for the burly Texan. In a trice he had overpowered the red man, put the handcuffs on him, and dragged him back to the hack, tying him to it with rope looped around his neck. Then Kinney told his wife to hand him his blacksnake whip. She obeyed at once, being as afraid of him as the men were. Ordering his wife to drive on, Kinney slashed the Indian across his naked shoulders with the murderous whip as a hint not to pull back. The Indian threw himself on the ground and was dragged along by the neck, but Kinney kept slashing him until finally the captive got up and trotted along behind the hack.

What happened after that has been told by B. F. Bonney, the son of the man who remonstrated with the Texan. "For several days Kinney rode back of the Indian, slashing him across the back with the blacksnake to do what he called 'break his spirit.' After a week or ten days Kinney untied the Indian and turned him over to his ox driver, telling him to break the Indian in to drive the ox team.

"Kinney had a hound dog that was wonderfully smart. He had used him in Texas to trail runaway slaves. After two or three weeks Kinney did not tie the Indian any more at night, as he said if the Indian ran away the dog would pick up his trail and he could follow him and kill him to show the other Indians the superiority of the white man. He said he had killed plenty of Negroes and an Indian was no better than a Negro.

"After the Indian had been with Kinney for over three weeks, one dark windy night he disappeared. Kinney called the Indian his man Friday. In the morning when Kinney got up he found the Indian had taken a blanket as well as Kinney's favorite Kentucky rifle—a gun he had paid $100 for. He had also taken his powder horn, some lead, and three hams. Kinney was furious. I never saw a man in such a temper in all my life. Every one in the train rejoiced that the Indian had escaped but they all appeared to sympathize with Kinney for they were afraid of being killed if they showed any signs of satisfaction. Kinney saddled his mule, took his dog along, and started out to track the Indian. The wind had blown sand in ridges and hummocks, covering the Indian's trail. So after hunting for half a day in all directions and being unable to track him, Kinney returned to the wagon train and we started on."

It is pleasant to think that there must have been great rejoicing when the young brave returned to his parents' lodge bringing the prize of a lifetime—a white man's gun. And it is certainly not too much to suppose that the story of how he outwitted his captor must have been told many times around Indian campfires.

2

The early California landseekers generally were well prepared for the trip west. Few of them, however, fully comprehended how very great was the distance they would have to travel. Always there was the urge to take short cuts, try poorly defined trails— anything to get there in the shortest possible time. For most of these early immigrants, the main sources of information about the country they traversed were the immigrant guidebooks.

The inaccuracy of many of these guides resulted in hardships epitomized by the experiences of the Donner party of 1846.

Organized in central Illinois by two well-to-do brothers, Jacob and George Donner, and well supplied with both goods and money, the members from the first decided to follow the route described by Lansford Hastings in his *Emigrants' Guide*. At Fort Laramie other wagon-train captains urged them to stick to the well-known trails, but they refused to listen. "There is a higher route," one stoutly maintained, "and it is of no use to take so much of a roundabout course." A few of a cautious turn of mind left the main company at the Big Sandy to journey to Fort Hall and thence on to California over the usual trail, but the eighty-nine members of the Donner party hurried on to Fort Bridger. There they learned that Hastings already had gone on, leading a party westward, but had left word that he would mark the trail.

Thus assured, they started at once, only to meet their first setback at the head of Weber Canyon. Stuck into a forked stick was a note from Hastings asking them to wait until he could show them a better route through the Wasatch Mountains. For eight days they camped—the first of many delays that brought disaster—then sent a messenger to seek him. The messenger returned with instructions from Hastings to follow another trail. This proved almost impassable; for days the toiling emigrants pushed aside boulders, or guided their cattle along twisting paths with giddy depths below, before they emerged in the valley south of Great Salt Lake. Thirty days had been required for a journey that should have taken twelve. They hurried on, with food supplies running low, until they stood on the edge of the desert on September 9. For sixty-four hours they plodded across this grim expanse toward Pilot Peak; then at the far side they had to waste more precious days while men returned to search for lost draft animals.

When they paused to take council they realized for the first time the direness of their straits. Supplies were virtually exhausted with much of their journey remaining; just how much no one knew, for all had lost faith in everything Hastings told them. The season, too, was well advanced; September was passing rapidly, and with it the hope of crossing the Sierras before snow began to fall. Should they press on, or try to return to Fort Bridger? Memories of their recent suffering provided the answer: "feeble and dispirited . . . they slowly resumed their journey," after sending two mounted men ahead to bring back food from California. Hopes revived somewhat on October 19, when one of the men who had been sent ahead returned with five pack mules loaded with food and with two Indian guides. When, on the morning of October 23, the company walked the grassy meadows along the Truckee River and started into the Sierras, they believed they had nothing more to fear.

The climb up the narrow canyon of the Truckee was cruelly difficult, but five days later the first pioneers camped on the shores of a calm lake high in the mountains, where they could look ahead to the steep granite ridge of the summit two thousand feet above them. At Prosser Creek, six miles behind, the rest of the party had stopped to repair a broken wagon. Another day or two would see all safely across. But that night the first storm of the winter came whistling in from the north, a month early. By daylight six inches of snow covered the ground, while the passes ahead were blocked with drifts from three to five feet deep. In a flurry of panic they forgot all discipline and rushed blindly toward the rocky crest, but as reason returned discipline was reestablished. Now they packed their supplies on their animals' backs and started ahead, only to be driven back by sleet that coated the rocks with slippery ice. The next day, they planned, they would try again on foot, but that night a new storm roared in. When it subsided several days later their animals were gone, and all the mountains were buried under three feet of snow.

There was no question now; they were snowbound in the High Sierras. Frantically they turned to building crude shelters at both Donner Lake and Prosser Creek: tents from the canvas of their wagons, huts of brush and snow. In these the eighty-one survivors huddled day after day as the snow deepened and the numbing cold grew more intense. "No living thing without wings can get about," wrote one of the party on November 28. With each day the scant food supply dwindled, until by mid-December they were eating anything they could chew: hides boiled to the consistency of glue, bones crisped until powdery, twigs and bark of trees. Four men had died and one was insane by then; clearly something must be done or all would perish. So fifteen of the bravest—eight men, five women, and the two Indian guides from California—volunteered to scale the summit in the hope that one or two might get through to summon help. This little band—the "Forlorn Hope"—started on December 16, carrying starvation rations designed to last six days. Thirty-two days were to pass before they saw the first signs of civilization.

Few parties in history have endured such horrors as the Forlorn Hope—and lived to tell the tale. By December 25, when they had been without food for four days, they made the terrible decision that one must die that the others might live. Huddled together they drew lots, but when one held up the shortest stick none of the remainder had the heart to kill him. Nor was that necessary, for nature was a more ruthless executioner. That night a new storm blew in; for two days and nights the little group huddled under blankets as the snow piled deep upon them. When, at noon on December 27, the wind and snow ceased, four of the party were dead.

Now came perhaps the most terrible chapter in the history of the West. Driven past the point of human endurance, the survivors could think only of their overwhelming need. They resorted to cannibalism. For two more days they stayed in this "Camp of Death" gathering strength to go on. Then once again they struggled on toward civilization. The strings of their moccasins and snowshoes were boiled and consumed, and once they were fortunate enough to kill a stray deer. The two Indians collapsed on the trail and were shot. All this time the seven survivors were struggling through waist-deep snow as they moved down the west slope of the mountains. At last, on January 10, 1847, they reached an Indian village, so exhausted that they reeled and staggered like drunken men.

The first of several hurriedly organized relief parties reached the Donner Lake camp on February 19, and others followed until all survivors were brought down the mountains. For two months they had lived on nothing but boiled hides and charred bones; there, too, death had been a frequent visitor and cannibalism practiced as a last resort. Of the eighty-nine immigrants who had set out from Fort Bridger, only forty-five survived.

*

The Mexican War, which had begun in May of 1846, ended in September of 1847, with the capture of Mexico City. That same fall Johann Sutter (who had regained his American citizenship) and James W. Marshall, a millwright, formed a partnership to construct a sawmill forty miles north of Sutter's Fort on the Coloma, a fork of the American River. The mill was completed by the end of the year, but the tailrace needed deepening to speed the flow of the water. On January 24, 1848—just nine days before Mexico formally transferred the province of California to the

United States—Marshall, while inspecting the tailrace,
noticed the presence of numerous bright brass-colored
particles the size of wheat grains. Three or four days
later Sutter confirmed that the particles were gold.
Their efforts to suppress news of the discovery failed.

Gold! Gold!! Gold!!!

SAN FRANCISCO was the first town to learn of Marshall's discovery.
By the end of May, 1848, three-fourths of its male inhabitants
had left for the gold fields. Places of business closed, crews deserted vessels in the harbor, and both of San Francisco's newspapers were compelled to suspend publication. "The whole country," the editor of *The Californian* recorded in his last issue on
May 29, "from San Francisco to Los Angeles, and from the sea-
shore to the base of the Sierra Nevada resounds to the sordid cry
of gold! gold!! gold!!! while the field is left half planted, the
house half built, and everything neglected but the manufacture
of shovels and pickaxes."

The citizens of San Jose and Monterey quickly followed the
example of the San Franciscans. Henry Bee, keeper of the jail at
San Jose, had in his custody ten Indians, two of them charged
with murder. Not unmindful of his duty, but keen also to get to
the gold fields, he took his prisoners with him, and made profitable use of their labor until other miners put an end to what
they quite naturally regarded as an unfair arrangement.

There were some big strikes by these early birds, some running
as high as $100,000 in five months. But while these were the ex-
ceptions, few if any of the early miners returned empty-handed.
Many of them averaged $60 to $100 a day, and it was estimated
that in 1848 alone more than $10,000,000 worth of gold was
extracted from the river beds adjacent to Sutter's Fort.

1

The original resting place of gold is in the solid rock, but with the passage of time erosion or rotting, caused by freezing and thawing, releases some of the gold and it washes down into the sand and gravel in the beds of streams or along their banks. Such mineral deposits are known as placers, and placer mining consists of washing the gold ore free from the gravel and other materials. The first gold miners simply shoveled up the loose sand and gravel and washed it in a pan or a cradle-like device known as a rocker. The lighter dirt and sand was carried away, leaving the heavy sand and gold in the bottom of the pan or cradle. Every miner carried a jug of mercury for use in extracting fine gold from the sand. When the fluid metal was poured into the pan, the gold and quicksilver would stick together. The application of heat separated this amalgam; the gold could then be stored away and the mercury replaced in the jug ready to be used again.

After the loose gold had been reclaimed, the gold-seekers tackled the much more difficult job of removing the ore from its original resting place. Usually gold-bearing rock, known as quartz, was found in a vein or lode—an ore deposit running consistently through a mountainside or extending back under the soil many feet—although sometimes it lay in a pocket. In the latter case, what might at first appear to be a rich strike would quickly peter out.

If the gold-bearing rocks were well eroded, they could be pulverized after a fashion in a rude dragstone mill known as an arrastra. In this method of mining the gold ore was spread out thin in a shallow circular stone pit. A sweep, to which was attached a heavy stone, projected from a central rotating post, and a mule or other animal hitched to the outer end of the sweep circled the arrastra dragging the stone over the quartz, grinding it to particles. The pulverized ore could then be treated the same as pay dirt in placer mining.

The drawback to such crude methods was that much of the gold was not recovered, and eventually stamp mills were brought in. Operating on the principle of the pestle and mortar, these machines raised and let fall heavy steel weights, reducing the ore to a pulp from which the gold was extracted by amalgamation—the process depending on the principal that gold adheres to mercury. Stamp mills were much more efficient than the arrastra, but they were also much more expensive. Thus, when a lode was worked beyond the stage when it could be exploited with primitive equipment, the lone hands and "ten-day miners" disappeared from the scene with their pans and their rockers, and a mining company, financed by the sale of stock shares, would take over.

Sam Ward, a well-known figure on the California mining frontier, was a leading spirit in the formation of one of these companies. In 1849 considerable gold had been washed out of the area that later came to be known as Quartzburg, but by 1851 the easy gold had been removed and placer mining was no longer feasible. A lode known as the Washington Vein, discovered in 1850, had been profitably worked with an arrastra; however, the owners felt that a stamp mill was needed if the lode was to be exploited to its full advantage. To obtain capital for buying and installing the mill and for operating expenses, they were willing to sell a half interest in the mine, and the company in which Sam Ward became a stockholder was formed to acquire it.

In order to keep an eye on operations, Ward moved into the Quartzburg area and set up as an Indian trader on the River of Grace. There were a good many stockholders in the East as well as in California, and Sam, who held proxies from a number of them, attended meetings of the company and voted their stock. After the installation of the stamp mill in the autumn of 1851, all the stockholders in the vicinity turned out to see the results of the first week's operations.

To recover the gold, four workmen held the corners of a buckskin sheet into which was poured the rich amalgam of gold and quicksilver; then, lapping the corners over one another, the workmen squeezed the improvised bag into the shape of a ball. By this means the fluid mercury was forced through the pores of the buckskin, leaving the valuable dense matter inside the bag like a golden ball of butter from a churn. Since miners were happy if they retrieved a ball the size of a hickory nut, it was hard for the assembled stockholders to maintain their composure when the sheet was opened and seen to contain a lump the size of a large apple. All in all, the recovery operations that afternoon yielded five lumps as large as the first one, and a number of others the size of walnuts. When the gold was weighed out, it amounted to $5,064. This called for a drink all around.

While the drinks were being downed, Sam Ward heard the mining superintendent inquire at what hour the next day the stage left for San Francisco. Now what, wondered Sam, lay behind that question? Either the superintendent intended to make off with the gold, which was highly unlikely, or else he was planning to tip off friends in San Francisco to buy up Washington mine stock before the anticipated jump in its price when the richness of the mine became generally known.

This seemed such a sound idea to Sam that he decided to act on it himself. As soon as his drink was finished, he mounted his mule and started off—not toward San Francisco, but in the opposite direction. Had he ridden toward his home, which lay in the direction of San Francisco, it might have precipitated a race to that city. Instead, it was assumed that he was going to visit a friend whose cabin was on the road he had taken, and with whom he often stayed. Three miles down the road, Sam made a big circle and returned home on an Indian trail. Just after dusk, without anyone seeing him, he galloped away, leading a second horse as an alternate. The next evening, after a seventy-five mile ride, he arrived in Stockton, where there were several stockholders who had paid up their assessments and never received any dividends. Sam had little difficulty in buying 150 shares at $14 a share—the price they had originally paid. Then he boarded a Sacramento River steamer for San Francisco. Arriving at dawn the next day, he looked up a friend and commissioned him to buy up additional shares. For the next two days, in order to avoid rousing suspicion while these transactions were taking place, Sam himself lay low.

By the third day it was apparent that word must have arrived from the superintendent, for a series of discreet inquiries as to the availability of Washington mine shares caused something of a stir in San Francisco financial circles. Possibly the hush-hush atmosphere contributed to the feeling that inside information of an earth-shaking nature had come from Quartzburg; at any rate, the price of shares jumped from $14 to $35. When the price reached this figure, Ward had his friend sell his 200 newly acquired shares, netting him a profit of $4,000. He then came out of hiding and confirmed the superintendent's report to the parties who had purchased his stock.

As it happened, the tremendous yield of that first week turned out to be from a rich pocket, not a lode. Although the mill was worked for another eighteen months, it barely paid expenses. But a few years later, when Sam looked at the worthless stock he had retained "to take the chance," he said that to complain would have been ingratitude, since he had made a good thing of taking advantage of those who had attempted to take advantage of a tip. When a gold rush was on, it was conventional to head for the gold fields, but this episode proved—at least to Sam—that there was more money in rushing the other way.

2

Gold prospecting was one occupation in which it seemed that luck counted for more than a man's natural endowments and such qualities as industry and perseverance. Probably there was not a miner in the gold fields who could not cite a dozen instances in which some purely fortuitous circumstance determined whether a fortune would be gained or missed.

In his autobiography, *Forty Years on the Frontier,* Granville Stuart told of a time in 1853 when he was prospecting not far from Dog Town with his brother James and Abe Folk. As they passed through the mountains on their way to their cabin, they traveled up a gulch from which several thousand dollars worth of gold had been taken three years before. Then the paying gravel had given out and the miners had moved on.

Pausing to look over the abandoned diggings, Stuart noticed an old case knife. Almost idly he began to pick away at the bank at the edge of the diggings. A few minutes of scratching on the bedrock yielded four dollars worth of gold. It then dawned on them all that they had found the pay streak through the gravel, which the earlier miners had lost where it made a bend around a hill. To stake out a claim to their discovery they needed only to tack up a signed notice stating its size and boundaries. But they had neither pencil nor paper, and since they were certain that no one would bother to stick a shovel into those old worked-over diggings, they went serenely on to their cabin two miles away, planning to return and post the claim notice the next day.

It so happened, however, that the next day was Sunday, and James and Abe thought it would be a good time to wash out their clothes. Stuart, who was eager to secure their claim, argued that they ought not to wait to put up their notice, but the other two laughed at him. What was the big hurry? They pointed out that the whole area was as dry as powder and no prospectors would be heading that way until the winter rains set in, providing the water supply to wash the pay dirt. Since the rainy season was two months off, Stuart allowed himself to be convinced, and joined the others in their laundering operations.

When the three partners went back to their mine on Monday morning, they found claim notices up and several men digging industriously away. On Sunday afternoon Tom Neal, who had mined there in 1850, had happened along with several friends. They were on their way to some gulches up country and he stopped to show the others where he had mined in times past. Seeing the old case knife lying on the bank where Stuart had scratched out the gravel, he picked it up and began to dig. It did not take Neal long to reach the same conclusion as the earlier visitors; he too realized that he had found the lost pay streak. One of his friends produced paper and pencil, and they laid claim to the whole gulch.

A few weeks later, when the winter rains began, Tom and his companions set up their sluice boxes and took out coarse gold to the amount of $25,000. Some was in the form of nuggets weighing out at from $100 to $300 each. There is a saying that cleanliness is next to godliness, but for the Stuart party that Sunday in 1853 was a very expensive wash day.

3

It is a curious irony that the two principal figures in the world's most famous gold discovery, James Marshall and Johann Sutter, were ruined by it.

On the momentous day when Marshall arrived at Sutter's Fort with the bright-colored particles he had found in the mill race, it took some time for the two men to determine that they were beyond doubt pure gold. While the rain beat down on the redwood shakes above, Sutter made some tests and looked up an article in the encyclopedia which gave a formula for determining the specific gravity of old metals and rules for finding the quantity of each in a given bulk. It took a hunt over the whole fort to turn up three and a half dollars in silver, which they borrowed to use in the computation that proved Marshall's find to be gold. "We weighed it in water by balancing the gold dust against the silver on a pair of scales in the air," he later reported. "Then we let the scales down and when it came in contact with the water the gold went down and the silver went up, and that told the story. It was pure stuff."

Returning to Coloma, Sutter and Marshall talked to the workmen there, and they agreed that the best policy was to keep the news quiet until the sawmill was finished; then all could try their luck at digging. But news of such a nature shared by a number of men could hardly be kept a secret. When Sutter came back to the fort, having himself found flakes of gold in the tailrace, he went about hinting that something had happened at Coloma which, if known, would start a revolution. Naturally this focused attention on the activity at the sawmill.

Several discharged members of the Mormon Battalion hung around the fort, and about two weeks after Marshall's first discovery Sutter's head teamster, who freighted supplies to Coloma, told the Mormons that gold had been found at the mill and they were picking it up by the quart. When quizzed, the teamster finally allowed as how he had exaggerated a mite, but he did produce a rag with enough gold in it to prove that his story was no hoax. At the blacksmith shop, after the yellow flakes were tested out in the fire and on the anvil, an exultant shout arose that all would be rich. Hearing the cry, men in the courtyard came running, and the revolution that Sutter had predicted was on. He wanted the men to stay by until the crops were in and the various commodities made at the fort were at a stage of manufacture where the process could be halted without damage. But everybody from the clerk to the cook deserted him to hunt gold. The hides and half-tanned leather in the tannery were left to spoil, and the livestock went untended.

Men began to appear at the scene of the find with pans, shovels, hoes, and picks, and it was all Marshall could do to prevent them from falling to and digging up the mill. But as fast as one party left another arrived. To get rid of them he adopted the expedient of telling them to go to such-and-such a spot where he felt sure there was gold. He sent parties out to all the points of the compass, never dreaming that he was giving accurate information and that he would have done well to follow his own directions. As for the mill on which he had pinned his hopes for the future, although he finally got it into operation, it closed down before the year was out—all the timber had been cut.

After President Polk, in his annual message to Congress on December 5, 1848, confirmed the discovery at Sutter's Mill, adventurers from all over the world made tracks for the Coloma River. Sutter's sheep and cattle were stolen; squatters, whom he never was able to dislodge, took over his land; and by 1852 the man who had once reigned over 140,000 acres was bankrupt.

The news "Gold! Gold in California!" whisked around the world before the end of 1848. Sixty ships left eastern seaports by early January, 1849, and notices of ship departures for California were posted in all the principal ports of Europe, China, and Australia. In America a mighty army converged on Independence, Missouri, the main embarkation point for the long journey to the gold fields. "Oh, Susanna," they sang, "don't you cry for me; I'm off to California with my washbowl on my knee." Ill-prepared though most of them were for the great trials facing them on the road to Eldorado, nonetheless 80,000 immigrants made it across the plains in 1849 and 1850.

The Forty-Niners

DURING THE WINTER of 1848–1849 the eastern states literally seethed with excitement at the news from California, and man after man announced to his neighbors that he had decided to go West. Frequently a number of men in a neighborhood would organize a company, all contributing a certain sum for equipment and pledging themselves to stand by one another and render mutual aid on the journey. Unfortunately, the overwhelming majority had little or no idea of the conditions of travel on the overland trails and no appreciation of the nature of the dangers they would face. No doubt the younger men and the more romantically minded had visions of laying down their lives heroically while a band of whooping redskins circled the wagon, but death seldom came to immigrants in so dramatic a guise.

Sickness, which had been rampant in 1848, was worse in 1849, when the Asiatic cholera, apparently brought to New Orleans by overseas ships and carried up the Missouri River, followed the travelers out onto the prairies. From forty to fifty per cent of the victims died, young people usually within a few hours. Older folk might live several days. But cholera was by no means the only killer. Many deaths resulted from ignorance or carelessness. The food was often bad. Cooking utensils were dirty. Streams on the prairie which ran muddy were by-passed as a source of drinking water in favor of pools which became breeding grounds for disease. Cold rains soaked the travelers to the skin and they stayed wet until fair skies dried out their clothes. In view of such vicissitudes, small wonder that they were beset by diarrhea, dysentery, colds, pneumonia, and various agues and fevers. Doctors were scarce, and the remedies and nostrums sold by unscrupulous profiteers at Independence and St. Joseph were of little avail. Nearly 5,000 immigrants died on the trail in 1849.

1

In the fall of 1848 a group of twenty-five men who proposed to travel to the gold fields had organized a company called the Boston and Newton Joint Stock Association. The members each contributed $300, which was used to pay their passage by rail and steamer to Independence and to secure equipment for the overland journey. Among the group was twenty-six-year-old George Winslow of Newton, who left a young wife and three-year-old son in Massachusetts. Also in the company were two of George's brothers-in-law, Brackett Lord and David Staples, and an uncle, Jesse Winslow.

Leaving Boston on April 16, 1849, they arrived at Independence on May 3. Here they spent nine days, camping on the prairie while they bought teams and wagons, broke the mules, and made other final preparations. During their stopover in Independence, George wrote his wife Eliza suggesting that they number their letters to each other, so that they would know if any were lost. His letter number three, written just before they started on May 12, bore the instruction: "Direct your letters to Sutter's Fort, California."

In reply to Eliza's inquiry as to how he was getting along, George wrote: "My health was never better than now. . . . I see by your letter that you have the blues a little in your anxiety for my welfare. I think we had better not indulge in such feelings. I confess I set the example. I do not worry about myself—then why should you for me—I do not discover in your letter any anxiety on your own account—then let us for the future look on the bright side of the subject and indulge no more in useless anxiety. . . . The reports from the gold regions here are as encouraging as they were at Massachusetts. Just imagine to yourself seeing me return with from $10,000 to $100,000."

As they traveled up the south side of the Kansas River, rain descended frequently and the mud was hub-deep in places, resulting in broken wagon tongues and other difficulties for the drivers, one of whom was George. After ten days of this, the party crossed the river on an Indian-operated ferry, turned northwest over a firm dry prairie, and made good progress until the twenty-ninth when George became violently ill with the cholera. Two others suffered its symptoms also. The company remained in camp three days. Then they went on; they were anxious to proceed and felt that the patients had sufficiently recovered to resume the journey.

They made a bed for George in their largest wagon. His brothers-in-law and his Uncle Jesse gave him every care. He seemed to improve. On the afternoon of June 6 they reached the point where the trail crossed the present Kansas-Nebraska line. The day was pleasant and George was in good spirits. At about five o'clock there occurred one of the electrical storms for which the plains are famous. Never before had the awe-struck Massachusetts folk seen such violence.

Describing the storm and the events of the next few hours, Brackett Lord noted in his diary: "There is nothing on the plains to break the wind and it sweeps on furiously. The lightning is truly terrific and when accompanied with wind, hail, and rain as in this case it is truly sublime. . . . I guarded [George] as thoroughly as possible with our rubber blankets from all dampness that might come through our covered wagons. George did not appear worse. *Wednesday morning.* George remains about the same—traveled most of the day. *3 o'clock.* George appeared worse. I sent immediately for the Doctor who was behind. Camped as soon as we could get to water. . . . Uncle Jesse watched the first part of the night but George growing worse. Uncle Jesse called Staples and myself. . . . *Thursday morning.* [George] continues to sink fast. *9 o'clock.* George is dead.——Our company feel deeply this solemn providence. I never attended so solemn a funeral— here we were on these plains hundreds of miles from any civilized being—and to leave one of our number was most trying."

For George Winslow this was the end of the trail. Letter number three was his last. He was never to look upon the face of the son who, unknown to him, was born on the very day they left Independence. The company, faithful to its trust, put up a rough stone on the grave with his name plainly marked. Then the wagons rolled on toward the gold fields.

Sixty-three years later Winslow's two sons replaced the crude marker in a Nebraska meadow with a suitable memorial.

2

About 40,000 immigrants went over the trail in 1849. Disregarding good advice, which was available but scarce, most of the Forty-Niners seriously overloaded their wagons with household goods. But far more serious than overloading was the disregard of the time required to cross the plains and mountains to the gold fields. In the early fall of 1849 hundreds of wagons were halted in Salt Lake City while the drivers debated whether they should risk the snow in the Sierras or winter-over among the Mormons. Some did neither, choosing to take the longer and drier but snow-free route to San Bernardino, near present-day Los Angeles, a route vaguely known since 1826 when it was traveled by Jedediah Smith.

One wagon train which elected this southern route left Salt Lake City early in October, guided by Captain Jefferson Hunt, a Mormon elder and an experienced mountain man. Known as the Sand Walking Company, it was made up of a hundred and seven wagons and a large number of horses, cattle, and mules. Eighty of the wagons arrived safely in San Bernardino early the following year; the other twenty-seven split off from the main train on November 3, at the headwaters of the Virgin River in southeastern Nevada, in order to take a short cut.

Within a few days the seceding train, later to be directed by William L. Manley, a young man from Wisconsin, had reached a point where it was impossible to find a road for the wagons. Accordingly, some of the seceders turned back to follow Captain Hunt's trail, but the others persevered, found a route, and drove ahead. Manley, however, became convinced that the way they were taking ran too far to the north since it was heading directly into rugged mountains. Again they changed their route, this time taking a course due west.

Day by day the going became more difficult. Water and food for the stock were not to be found, and to ease their load the travelers began to discard all surplus supplies and equipment. Every camp site was strewn with abandoned property. After weary weeks of travel they found their way through the range of mountains they had been flanking on the south [a spur of the front range of the Sierras, now called the Armagosas]. Ahead was a vast valley floor of salt rocks, alkali, and sparse vegetation, beyond which lay another barren, rocky range of mountains [the Panamints]. Fortunately, water was found, flowing from a spring on the eastern edge of the valley.

After laboring across the desert, they failed in their attempt to get the wagons through the mountains, and finally were forced to return to the spring [later named Bennett's Wells, for a member of their party]. At a council held on Christmas day, it was decided as a last desperate measure to send Manley and John Rogers, a strong, young Tennessee farm boy, to try and locate a route out of the death-trap and bring them back help. Oxen were slaughtered, and the dried meat was packed into knapsacks made for Manley and Rogers by the women of the party, who made them moccasins as well. All the immigrants' money—a little over thirty dollars—also was turned over to them. Eleven adults and four children were left in camp when the two young men started away.

During the next two weeks they managed to cross the Panamints and make their way across a narrow stretch of Mojave Desert, and on the fourteenth day reached a ranch not far from the Mission San Fernando. Although worn out from their hard journey and from the terrible mental strain, their whole concern was to get relief back to their comrades. At the ranch they spent their thirty dollars for supplies, two horses, and a pack mule; then they faced the desert once more. On the way to civilization they had kept track of watering places, and this enabled them to proceed confidently. During the forced march, the horses, which could find almost no provender, failed fast and had to be abandoned, but the little mule proved equal to any test. After twelve days on the trail, as they were nearing the stricken camp, they found one of the party dead, face up, in the sand of the valley.

About noon [Manley wrote later] we came in sight of the wagons, still a long way off, but in the clear air we could make them out and tell what they were, without being able to see anything more. Not until we were within a half mile of the camp could we see them very plainly. No signs of life were anywhere about, and the thought of our hard struggles between life and death to go out and return, with the fruitless result that now seemed apparent, was almost more than we could bear.

We kept low and out of sight as much as possible, trusting very much to the little mule that went ahead, for we felt sure she would detect danger in the air sooner than we, and we watched her very closely to see how she acted. One hundred yards now to the wagons and still no sign of life, no positive sign of death. . . . We feared that perhaps there were Indians in ambush, and with nervous irregular breathing we counseled what to do. Finally Rogers suggested that he had two charges in his shotgun and I seven in the Colt's rifle, and that I should fire one of mine and await results before we ventured any nearer; if any of the red devils were there we could kill some of them before they got us. And now, both closely watching the wagons, I fired the shot.

Still as death and not a move for a moment and then a man came out from under the wagon and stood up, looking all around, for he did not see us. Then he threw up his arms and shouted: "The boys have come! The boys have come!" The great suspense was over and our hearts were first in our mouths, and then the blood all went away leaving us almost fainting as we stood.

The group that greeted Manley and Rogers was much smaller than the one which had sent them on their way. Only two families remained; the others, despairing of rescue, had left the camp in an attempt to find their own way to safety. The man whose body they had seen was one of these unfortunates.

As soon as possible, preparations were begun for the two-hundred-and-fifty-mile trip to the coast. Since there was no chance of taking the wagons, they made saddles of the wagon covers and put them on the oxen for the women and children to ride. Their route took them over the Panamint range. When they reached the summit and looked across the Mojave Desert, Manley pointed out the path before them. Then they turned, took off their hats, and stood gazing back at the barren salt and rock waste which had been the scene of trial, suffering, and death. Breaking the silence, one of the survivors spoke for them all—"Goodbye, Death Valley!"

After a weary trip over the Mojave Desert, the party arrived safely at San Francisco ranch on March 7, 1850, four months out from Salt Lake City.

3

As 1849 began in the mother lode country of California, the excitement of 1848 paled in contrast. On February 28 the steamship *California,* with a rated capacity of one hundred, unloaded four hundred gold seekers at San Francisco. By the end of June more than six hundred ships from all parts of the world cast anchor in San Francisco Bay. Most of the Forty-Niners, however, came in wagons, on foot, or on horseback on the overland trails.

A traveler, Frank Marryat, visiting one of the mining camps, described it this way: "Immediately beneath us the swift river glided tranquilly, though foaming still from the great battle which a few yards higher up it had fought with a mass of black obstructing rocks. Over the banks was a village of canvas that the winter rains had bleached to perfection and round it the miners were at work at every point. Many were waist deep in the water, toiling in bands to construct a race and dam to turn the river's course; others were entrenched in holes, like grave diggers, working down to the bed rock. Some were on the brink of the stream washing out prospects from the pans or wooden batteaus, and others worked in company with the long tom, by means of water sluices artfully conveyed from the river. Many were coyote-ing subterranean holes, from which from time to time their heads popped out, like those of squirrels to take a look at the world; and a few with drills, dissatisfied with nature's work, were preparing to remove large rocks with gun-powder. All was life, merriment, vigor and determination, as this part of the earth was being turned inside out to see what it was made of. Small patches of garden surrounded the village which bore so palpably the stamp of cheerfulness and happy industry, that I was disappointed on learning that its name was Murderer's Bar."

One chronicler records that no liquor was too costly for the men of forty-nine and adds that there was more drinking in California during the gold days than in any other time or section. At the end of a stretch of hard labor the average miner felt that he was entitled to recreation of an especially exhilarating sort, and so for the saloon keeper Sundays and holidays were rich harvest times. Each Sunday was a day of rest throughout the gold region. The morning was generally devoted to washing and cleaning, to reading and letter writing, and to an occasional religious service, but for all except a few temperate and frugal ones the afternoon brought another and different order of things. William Taylor, the pioneer preacher, relates that on a Sunday morning in one of the camps a goodly number assembled to hear him preach, and he looked forward to a larger congregation in the afternoon—only to find himself with not a single listener. The men to whom he had preached in the morning were already far gone in their cups.

Gold is where you find it. A miner died and his fellows arranged to give him fitting burial. At the funeral party, having assembled and taken drinks all around, they bore the body to the grave which had been dug a short distance from the camp. The remains lowered, the crowd knelt about the grave and the minister began a prayer. His supplication was a lengthy as well as earnest one, and finally some of the congregation began, in an abstracted way, to finger the loose earth that had been thrown up from the grave. Yellow particles proved it to be rich in gold, and on the instant a common impulse swayed the kneeling crowd. Whereupon the preacher halted his prayer, and asked, "Boys, what's the trouble?" Then, having taken a look at the ground for himself, he shouted, "Gold! gold!—and the richest kind of diggings. The congregation is dismissed!" The dead man was lifted from his grave to be buried elsewhere, while the funeral party, with the minister at its head, made haste to prospect and stake out the new diggings.

In the summer of 1850 Buck Ramsey and his partners were unsuccessfully prospecting on a stream southwest of Placerville, California. One evening while they were sitting about their camp-fire, eating supper and cracking jokes, they heard a crash in the bushes and lo and behold! there was a huge grizzly bear peeking through the forest at them. Buck, by good fortune and quick thinking, got his hands on his rifle and shot the bear between the eyes. Luckily the furry monster, although a very difficult animal to kill, fell dead at the first shot. After a thorough discussion of the whole subject of grizzlies, the miners curled up in their blankets to dream of bears and nuggets.

As they were moving out of the locality the next morning, they met Billy Knox and two companions heading toward the gravel bar they had abandoned. When asked how things were, Billy replied that they hadn't had any luck finding pay diggin's but that they had killed the biggest grizzly they had ever seen in the Sierras. Out of curiosity, the newcomers went down to see the bear for themselves. They agreed that Billy had been dead right about the size of the bear but mistaken about the lack of pay dirt, for they promptly struck the glittering metal in quantity. Their sightseeing trip turned into a prospector's dream. It was late in the fall and they dared not linger too long for fear of being caught by a snowstorm, but they washed out all that they could and staked out the best claims before going to the low land to winter.

Needless to state, the news of their strike leaked out, and when spring came there was a stampede for Grizzly Flats, as the area was named. Soon the whole country was alive with men swinging picks, swirling pans, and joggling rockers. This whole-sale exploitation called for more water. At a miners' meeting, a company was organized which dug ditches and built flumes carrying the water diverted from smaller streams to run through the sluice boxes at the various claims along the river. The pay dirt, having been dug out with pick and shovel, was thrown into the sluice boxes, where the water dissolved the lumps and carried the mud away. The gold and black sand sank to the bottom and were caught and retained by the "riffle"—a series of cleats nailed across the floor of the box. On Saturday afternoon came the "clean-up," when the other work stopped and the gold dust was extracted from the sand with mercury.

As in other early-day mining camps, the miner's code obtained at Grizzly Flats. A man could put his dust into a sack and keep it under his bed or on a shelf, with never a worry that anyone would touch it. But then it began to appear that someone was robbing the sluice boxes. Time after time there was less gold in the clean-up than there should have been; the men could tell because they had seen the color of the pay dirt as they shoveled it into the boxes. For a time they tried cleaning up every day to avoid night losses, but this slowed down the work considerably.

Suspicion pervaded the camp. Every man looked at his neighbor with uneasiness, and certain miners were openly named as possible thieves. A meeting was held and a night patrol organized, but apparently the robber was a ghost, for the gold continued to disappear although no one was ever seen at a box. Finally, a respected miner named Johnny Martin decided to hire a private guard to watch his box; he had one of the richest claims and had been one of the heaviest losers. The man he engaged for the job was a lanky, talkative Missourian named Sam Pritcher. It was Sam's custom to work his claim until he had accumulated a pound of gold dust, then down tools and drink it up or gamble it away. His claim was beginning to peter out, and since Johnny had offered a thousand-dollar reward for catching the thief, Sam was glad to sign on as a watchman. Moreover, he insisted that the other guards be relieved so that he could have the whole reward for himself. Sam was quite vocal about what he was going to do to the thief when he caught him.

About three o'clock one morning Grizzly Flats was awakened by a volley of shots in the vicinity of Johnny's sluice box. When the miners rushed to find out what was happening, they met Sam prodding a Mexican along with the muzzle of his gun. When he had caught him working over the box, Sam said, the rascally greaser had offered him $5,000 to let him escape. Sam was all for lynching the Mexican then and there, but Johnny insisted that law and order should prevail. A saloon was opened to serve as a courtroom, a jury empaneled, and a judge appointed to try the case.

In broken English, the Mexican explained that he had been on his way from the fandango* where he had been cleaned out gambling; the first thing he knew Sam Pritcher jumped out in front of him, fired his gun several times, and then had taken him in custody. Some of the crowd had been at the fandango, and could verify that he had lost all his money. Johnny knew Mexicans, and was more than half-convinced that the man was telling the truth, but when, at Sam's suggestion, the suspect's pockets were searched they were found to contain forty dollars in gold nuggets. To the minds of the jury this was conclusive evidence, since he had said he left the fandango with nothing.

Johnny, however, was still not satisfied that the Mexican was guilty. He stated that it was his claim that had been robbed, and he could not see a man hanged on the evidence that had been brought out. He had known a lot of Mexicans, and invariably if they were guilty they would begin to make excuses. The prisoner had not done so; moreover, he was clearly amazed when the gold was discovered in his pocket. Sam's indignation that anyone would take a greaser's word over his, and even hint that he had planted the nuggets, was something to behold, but Johnny reaffirmed that he did not want any innocent blood on his hands. The sentence was commuted from hanging to fifty lashes, and Sam volunteered to carry it out. When the prisoner fainted at the thirty-fourth stroke, Johnny insisted that the punishment stop.

Nursed back to health by his friends, the Mexican got a job in a neighboring camp. Sam collected his thousand dollars, and

*A Mexican dancing party, usually held in a saloon.

went on a drunken spree which lasted until the reward money had been spent. Then once more the robberies began, with the big loser Johnny Martin as before. "It's your own fault," Sam told him. "I said we should have hung that greaser." He was all for getting up a necktie party and many in camp were inclined to agree with him, but the Mexican was warned that trouble was brewing and hid out.

The whole affair troubled Johnny a great deal. There was a newcomer who had a claim on the flats, a shrewd man, older than most of the other miners; and Johnny heard he had been a policeman back East. Now Johnny looked up this man on the q.t., and it turned out that he had been a detective on the police force, assigned to the robbery detail. After he had heard Johnny's story, he agreed to investigate the matter. At his suggestion, Sam Pritcher was again hired as watchman.

Two weeks passed by during which the sluice boxes were robbed regularly. Many miners were losers, and though, as usual, they gathered at the gambling house on Saturday night following the clean-up, the celebration was far from being as hilarious as usual. Toward the middle of the evening there was a loud hallooing from the hill, and the miners piled outside to see two figures marching tandem down the trail among the trees. The one in the lead with his hands held high over his head was Sam Pritcher, but the man behind him was a stranger to all but Johnny Martin.

Johnny stepped up on the gambling-house porch and introduced the stranger as a New York detective whose aid had been enlisted to apprehend the phantom robber of Grizzly Flats. With many whining pleas for mercy, Sam now confessed that he had made the Mexican the scapegoat for all the robberies he had committed. In less than ten minutes the miners had reached a unanimous decision as to his fate—even Johnny Martin voted with the crowd—but the execution of the sentence had to wait until morning.

The news spread to the adjoining camp, and a jubilant delegation of Mexicans arrived, bringing with them the man whom Pritcher had victimized. By popular consent he was appointed to drop the noose over Sam's head at the hanging. While they waited for sunrise, Sam was allowed to get drunk, and the Mexican was tendered so many drinks by the remorseful miners that by sun-up he was equally under the influence of "tanglefoot." In fact, so great was the general relief that the serpent in their Eden had at last been scotched that before the necktie party was over practically the whole camp was *hors de combat*. The Mexicans joined with the gringoes, and the livelong day was spent in the grandest celebration ever held on Grizzly Flats.

> *Of all the wild animals of the North American conti-* ⸙
> *nent, the grizzly bear was considered the most formidable, even though he usually did not attack unless wounded or surprised at close quarters. While ponderous and ungainly, he was not afraid of a man and was amazingly hard to kill. A bullet, unless it struck in a vital spot, only enraged him without slowing him up.*
> *In the 1840's and 1850's grizzlies were very numerous on the west coast, especially in the lower valleys in berry time and along the Sacramento River in the fall, being attracted there by the abundance of wild grapes. As a rule, the big fellows were given a wide berth by both professional hunters and miners, but now and then someone new to the country, or more brave than wise—or just plain unlucky—had an encounter with a grizzly which would be a topic of conversation around the campfire for weeks.*

Let Her Go, If She Will

IN THE FALL of 1849 there occurred a historic battle between a pack of grizzlies and two prospectors, L. K. Wood and Isaac Wilson. The party to which they belonged had ranged far west of the mother-lode country in their search for gold, discovering Humboldt Bay during the course of their wanderings. As was not uncommon on the frontier, a disagreement had arisen among the members of the party and the group had split up. Worn out by a summer of unsuccessful prospecting, Wood and Wilson started back to Sutter's Fort. By the time they reached the mountains south of Eel River, their provisions were gone and their ammunition exhausted.

As the disheartened pair trudged wearily along, they happened on a pack of eight grizzly bears sunning themselves in a clearing in the woods. Being newcomers to the country and unfamiliar with the ways of grizzlies, Wood and Wilson, instead of backtracking, decided this was their chance to procure a supply of bear steaks. They advanced slowly into the clearing, and when they were about fifty steps from their prey, Wood leveled his rifle and shot the bear nearest to him. The clumsy animal tumbled over, biting and tearing the earth as though in the throes of the death-agony. At the same time Wilson dropped a second bear, which also seemed to be kicking its last. Five of the pack now began a lumbering retreat up the mountain; the sixth sat down on its haunches and seemed to be debating what course of action to take.

Since they were armed with the one-shot muzzle-loading rifles of the period, the men were at the mercy of the beast until they could reload. Seeking a safe place to perform this operation, Wilson took off for the nearest tree. The bear rushed at Wood, who was closer to him, but Wood succeeded in reaching a small tree, and temporarily beat off the grizzly with his clubbed rifle. But then, to his utter astonishment and dismay, the bear he had shot, and which he thought he had killed, came charging toward him. The first lunge of the enraged animal snapped the sapling in which Wood had taken refuge. Closely pursued by the bear, he raced for another small tree, but was traveling so fast that when he grabbed for it with one hand he swung completely around it. Luckily for him, the bear's momentum also carried it past the tree and on down the mountainside about twenty steps. With all the energy of desperation, Wood started to scale the tree, but he had not ascended more than a few feet before the second bear seized him by the ankle and brought him to the ground. The wounded bear now returned and grabbed him by the shoulder, and the two grizzlies proceeded to engage in a tug-of-war in which it seemed Wood would be pulled limb from limb.

In Wood's own words, "My clothes and the bears' grip giving away occasionally, saved me. They continued in this way until they had stripped me of my clothes, except a part of my coat and shirt, dislocated my hip, and inflicted many flesh wounds—none of the latter, however, very serious. They seemed to be unwilling to take hold of my flesh; for, after they had torn the clothes off me, they both left me. The one went entirely away, and the other [the wounded she-bear] walked slowly up the hill, about a hundred yards from me, then deliberately seated herself and fastened her gaze upon me as I lay upon the ground perfectly still."

But the first sign of life from Wood brought the bear back to him, roaring at every jump. After poking her nose violently against his side, she "raised her head and gave vent to two of the most frightful, hideous, and unearthly yells ever heard by mortal man." Wood kept perfectly still, and after a few minutes the bear again left him, and once more took up her station about a hundred yards away, where she sat on her haunches and continued to glare at him. Presently, however, Wood began to inch himself stealthily along the ground and finally made it to a buckeye tree. Despite the pain from his dislocated hip, he managed to climb to a limb about eight feet above the ground.

Wilson, who apparently did not see the sentry bear, now ventured toward his friend, gun in hand. As soon as he came within her field of vision, the watchful grizzly made another ferocious charge, and Wilson barely saved himself by springing up a tree adjacent to the one occupied by Wood. The bear now seated herself midway between her two enemies, growling savagely whenever either one made a move.

Wilson had long since reloaded his gun, but though he drew bead on the grizzly he did not fire. "Shoot her, man, hurry up, shoot her!" Wood entreated him. "She is the one that caused all my trouble." But Wilson, who had had enough bear hunting to last him for a long time, replied, "No, sir; let her go—let her go, if she will." And pretty soon she did disappear for good.

Since Wood was too badly disabled to travel the rest of the way to Sutter's Fort, the first plan was that he should be cared for by a band of Indians in the neighborhood, and Wilson would go for help. The chief agreed to the arrangement, but asked for payment in advance. Then, after collecting all the loose change, trinkets, and spare equipment that the men had on them, he calmly announced that the band was moving on and could not accommodate the injured man.

The situation was resolved by the arrival of three other members of the original prospecting party, also on the homeward trail. They had a pack mule, and Wood was carried to the nearest settlement, strapped to its back. By the time he received medical care, however, his dislocated leg had healed out of joint, and his encounter with the grizzlies left him a cripple for the rest of his life.

She Prayed for the Ravens

GEORGE BROOKS of St. Joseph County, Michigan, was one of the thousands whose heart quickened at the news of the great gold strike in 1849. The father of six children, he could make good use of the riches to be picked up in the land of gold. Furthermore, his health was poor and it was confidently reported that health as well as wealth was to be found in the Golden West. But how would it be possible for him to take his big family thousands of miles overland? How could he expose them to the perils from savage Indians and the hardships of the journey across the endless plains and over two mountain ranges?

All winter the gold fever raged, and in the end Brooks succumbed to it. When spring came he determined to leave his family and go West to seek the fortune which would give his children the chance their parents had never had. Upon his wife Eliza Ann would devolve the sole responsibility for looking after the children and for maintaining the household. But she cheerfully undertook to shoulder the burden because of her hope that in California her husband would regain his health.

It was a great day when at last word came that Mr. Brooks had arrived safely in California and was prospering. By the spring of 1852 he was able to write Eliza Ann the good news that he had recovered his health and was doing so well that he would stay in California if only his family were there. Eliza Ann's reaction to this letter was: *Well, why not? Why shouldn't our home be in California?* Nothing daunted by the prospect of the journey before her, she determined to take the family and go to him. Having disposed of their property and hired a man to drive for her, she loaded the children and the supplies into a wagon and started for the land of good health.

The family joined a Michigan company. But even traveling in a large group did little to mitigate the many hardships of life on the trail. Writing of the experience more than a half century later, her son Elisha said that "a picture lingers in my memory of us children all lying in a row on the ground in our tent, somewhere in Iowa, stricken with the measles, while six inches of snow covered all the ground and the trees were brilliant with icicles. A delay of a week to enjoy the measles put us on our feet again, and we drove on."

At the Missouri River the spring floods prevented an immediate crossing. As the human flood engulfed the Iowa side of the Missouri Valley, tales of Indian massacres, starvation, and the deadly cholera spread among the immigrants, and the Michigan train, which had started out pledged to stick together, began to disintegrate. Among those who refused to go any farther was the teamster Eliza Ann had hired to drive her oxen. But the valiant woman was determined to carry on. All their wealth was in the wagon, all their hopes.

Crossing the Missouri, they made their first camp near a Pawnee village, where the city of Omaha now stands.

Here [wrote Elisha] in the sight of these wild men of the plains, realizing her utter helplessness, even our mother's resolution wavered, and she seemed to be catching at straws for support. For a moment she appeared to lean on her children. She asked us if we wanted to go on, and if we thought we could drive the team, and if we were afraid of the Indians. Of course we could drive the team, and we had just lost our fear of Indians; besides, were we not almost there? Then in the loneliness of that night, we saw her—her form revealed by fitful flashes of our fire—kneeling beside a log, pleading earnestly for a vision of the guiding hand to point her destined way. . . . With the coming of morning, the astral glow in her eyes told us we were going on, so, casting a farewell glance at Council Bluffs and the Missouri River we cut loose . . . from the East.

In the land of the Shoshoni Indians their oxen were stampeded one night by Indians or outlaws, and there was a long discouraging hunt before they found the animals and could proceed. Because of this delay and others, they dropped behind, and now when they arrived at a camping site, they found the grazing grounds eaten bare. As a result, the oxen became gaunt and weak. One by one they dropped by the trail until only two of the eight were left. The human beings had fared almost as badly. It had been necessary to discard such a large portion of their supplies that they were reduced to a starvation diet. But nonetheless Eliza Ann and her little flock carried on, painfully making their way across the salt flats of Utah and Nevada.

Elisha recalled vividly the journey over the sands of Nevada:

After some weeks of feeble existence on half-rations, or less, we camped one night not far from the sink of the Humboldt, where we made our last cup of flour into flapjacks and ate our last slice of bacon, then lay down to sleep in a lone and joyless group, while our mother prayed as fervently as mortal ever prayed that the ravens might feed her children in the morning. No ravens came with the dawn. . . . We made our breakfast on a few small fish that we had caught with a grasshopper-baited hook; then we hitched up our single remaining yoke of oxen, Old Brock and Nig, and crept on toward the sunset, conscious of a vague determination to drag our bones as near to the land of promise as we might before despair could shut the gates against us.

That afternoon as we were creeping wearily on, and the children's hungry cry had been silenced from exhaustion, we saw a little way ahead that fabled solitary horseman, or rather a man on a mule approaching us. As he drew near, something familiar about his form riveted our eyes upon him. He rode up, and presently with a joyful cry we were in the arms of our father.

Since it took three or four months for a letter from the east to reach a man in the mines, by the time Brooks got word that his family was coming west they were hunting their stampeded oxen in the Shoshoni country. Immediately upon learning that they had started for California, he mounted his mule and set out to meet them; he knew from his own overland experiences the dangers to which they were exposed. Rifle in hand he had ridden three hundred miles from the Sacramento Valley, depending upon his marksmanship for food and upon the sky for shelter.

Brooks had filled his saddlebags with hardtack and beans to meet the situation which he anticipated. While the provisions he brought were not the kind of food the children had dreamed about in their fitful sleep, they were all he could carry and guaranteed that their bones would not whiten the desert, as had seemed almost certain only a few hours before. Now that the journey was nearly over, it was with cheerful hearts they helped their father hitch the mule to the wagon to reinforce the flagging oxen and drove on westward to the land of health and gold.

Sagebrush Justice

A MAJOR HAZARD on the California Trail was the Great Basin. This vast depression, lying between the Rocky Mountains and the Sierra Nevada range, is distinguished for an almost total lack of rainfall, sagebrush, sand, and, in the summer, extreme heat. Streams originating on its edges ultimately disappear in the basin's sand. Two of these rivers were important: the Humboldt, which flowed westward from the Utah mountains, finally disappearing in a swampy lake bed known as the Humboldt Sink; and the Carson, starting in the Sierras and flowing eastward to the Carson Sink. Along these two waterways passed the California immigrants, and although the water was brackish it was a life saver. After the mid-1850's it was not uncommon for Indians to attack along this stretch of the trail. Sometimes white renegades would join them in a raid on a train, hoping the Indians alone would be blamed for the outrage.

Usually, overland immigrants banded together at Salt Lake City to traverse this hazardous leg of the journey, but occasionally a small party would go it alone. One such group starting westward from Salt Lake in 1857 belonged to an Englishman by the name of Wood. His party consisted of his wife and child and two hired men, and he had three conveyances: two ox-drawn heavy wagons, driven by the hired men, and a light spring wagon which he drove himself and in which his wife and child rode. Along with other valuables, Wood was carrying $1,500 in gold coins—British guineas and sovereigns—which he had concealed in the wagon bed under a false bottom.

Until August, when they came to the lower reaches of the Humboldt River, the journey had been fairly routine. After camping overnight by the river, the little party made its usual morning preparations to continue the journey. First, the ox teams were caught up, yoked, and started on their way, but since the mules traveled faster than the oxen, Mr. Wood took his time about hooking them up. Mrs. Wood had made herself comfortable in the wagon with the baby and they were almost ready to start when about twenty men on horseback—apparently all Indians—came charging down upon them from the hills.

Wood leaped into the wagon and whipped the mules into a run, following the ox wagons which were out of sight around a point ahead. But they had hardly gotten under way when a wheel ran off the axle—probably he had forgotten to replace the nut when he greased it. Pulling his wife and child from the wagon, Wood boosted them onto one of the mules. Then, having un-hooked the teams, he scrambled on another mule and they started off again. The Indians, now almost upon them, began shooting. Mrs. Wood and the child fell from their mule, and at the same moment Wood's mount was killed and he himself severely wounded in the arm. There was nothing for it but to run as fast as he could after the ox wagons, which he finally man-aged to overtake.

Wood and his men made it back to the scene of the attack in time to see the marauders galloping off into the hills, scared off by an approaching wagon train. Mrs. Wood and the baby were dead. One mule had been wounded, a second killed, and the other two were gone. The spring wagon had been looted of its valuables, including the $1,500 in gold.

Before long several wagon trains had gathered. A doctor from one of them dressed Wood's wounds, and other kind strangers helped him bury his loved ones and gather up the remains of his property. Not wishing to loiter longer than necessary in the vicin-ity of the raiders, the several wagon trains soon were rolling west-ward again on the California Trail.

Toward the end of the day they were overtaken by three men driving in a light wagon drawn by conspicuously good-looking horses. Indeed, the whole outfit—team, wagon, and harness—was noticeably more handsome than that of any of the migrants. The most striking-looking of the men was a heavy-set fellow with broad, square shoulders and a full beard clipped short. He was wearing a buckskin jacket, a full ammunition belt, and an outsize stiff-brimmed hat with a low crown.

The men requested permission to join the wagon train. They said that although they had been on friendly terms with the Shoshoni Indians, the tribe was now in an alarmingly hostile mood because of certain acts committed by travelers, and they wanted to get out of that section of the country. Having received permission to do so, the trio made camp by themselves at one side of the wagon circle.

Mr. Wood got his first good look at the trio during the noon stop while the doctor was dressing his wound. He immediately declared his belief to the doctor that the man in the big hat had been with the Indians who killed his wife and child. Soon word had spread throughout the wagon train, and the atmosphere became very tense. It was suggested that Wood be disguised and taken close enough to the man so that he could make a positive identification, but Wood was in too weak a condition to allow this to be undertaken. Later in the day the strangers announced that they had now passed through the country of the savage Shoshonis, and in the morning the strangers hooked up their rig and went on their way.

A day or two later after the wagons had corralled at sundown, the bearded man in the big hat rode into camp on horseback, accompanied by two strangers. Big Hat announced that he was looking for the Englishman who, so he had heard, had accused him of being leagued with the Indians who had killed his wife and child. Wood came forward and Big Hat threatened him with instant death if he dared to repeat the charge. When Wood kept silent Big Hat subjected him to verbal abuse. Feeling it better to bear insults than to risk death in a fight, none of the immigrant company attempted to put an end to the browbeating. Apparently satisfied that he had intimidated them all sufficiently, Big Hat told the assemblage that his name was Tooley and his companions were brothers named Haines. According to his account, they were honest men who came out from California, bought up tired-out stock from the immigrant trains, took the animals to recuperate in a good pasture they knew of, and drove them to California for the market when they were in condition. After a few more threats to Wood about what awaited him if he couldn't control his tongue, the three "honest men" rode off.

A week later the trains reached the Humboldt Sink and went into camp there. Nearby was a crude little establishment known as Black's Trading Post. Since it was the first sign of civilization in hundreds of miles, a group from the train went to look it over. They were surprised to find that one of the customers for its few wares—cheap whiskey and coarse tobacco—was their nemesis, Tooley. He had drunk enough to be feeling happy and talkative.

Failing to recognize that the newcomers belonged to the company
he had traveled with, he began to brag of his exploits. He had
done in a lot of travelers up the creek, Tooley asserted, and he
was going to take care of some more tomorrow.

As soon as they could leave without arousing suspicion, the
immigrants returned to the camp and reported Tooley's incrimi-
nating boasts. The leaders of the company heard them out, and
then decided it was time to mete out justice. An informal court
was organized; then the judge, sheriff, deputies, and a few other
determined men went to Black's Trading Post to hold a session.
In order not to give the game away prematurely, they entered one
or two at a time as if they were just casually dropping in. They
made sociable talk—asked questions about the country thereabouts, how far it was to Sacramento, the price of gold. Tooley
was still monopolizing the conversation and still bragging about
his ability to hoodwink and rob the ignorant immigrants.

The members of the court listened until enough had been
said to justify a trial; then at an order from the judge, the sheriff
flourished his revolver, shouting "Hands up!" Tooley, evidently
thinking it was some kind of a joke, complied without any protest. But the judge's next words set him straight. He had come to
their camp, the judge said, and had insulted an injured man and
those who were befriending him. At the time Tooley had been
given the benefit of the doubt, but now he was to be tried before
a court. The complaining witness would be called and examined,
and the court would hear any other evidence that might have a
bearing on the case. If Tooley was innocent, the court would find
it out; if he was guilty, that fact would be established. The prisoner was warned that resistance would cost him his life. In every
direction Tooley's eyes turned he looked down the muzzles of
rifles and pistols, and this seemed to convince him of the wisdom
of strict obedience. Hands over his head, he was convoyed by the
deputies out of the trading post to a level spot near the Sink,
where there were large stones for seats. Here the court reconvened.

First of all, a jury was selected, made up for the most part of
immigrants from other trains. The complaining witness, Wood,
now came forward and testified to his belief that Tooley was one

of the renegades who had slain his family, and wounded and robbed him. Confronted by Wood, Tooley claimed he had never seen the man before. Since there was still some uncertainty as to Tooley's identity, the judge ordered him to be searched from the skin out. Now for the first time Tooley made a movement as if to attempt a break. This was quickly checked, and the sheriff reminded the guards to keep their eyes on the prisoner and their trigger-fingers at the ready. He then ordered Tooley to stand quiet or he would be in the class of the good Indian.

As the officer assigned to search him set to work, Tooley's face grew pallid—and with good reason. In the money belt next to his body were five hundred dollars in English gold—one-third of the money stolen from Wood. The judge's instructions to the jury were brief and to the point. He reviewed the evidence that they had seen and heard, and asked for their verdict. With one voice they answered "Guilty."

When the judge asked the prisoner if he had anything to say, Tooley stood speechless, sweat beading his face. It being clear he had no explanation to offer which might affect the court's judgment, the judge informed him he could have his choice of being shot or hanged from the end of a raised wagon tongue. At these words Tooley turned and ran. Simultaneously the judge shouted "Stop!" and the sheriff "Shoot, boys!" and the sentence was executed.

The trial was orderly, justice was swift, and the cost to the citizens nothing except a few hours' time.

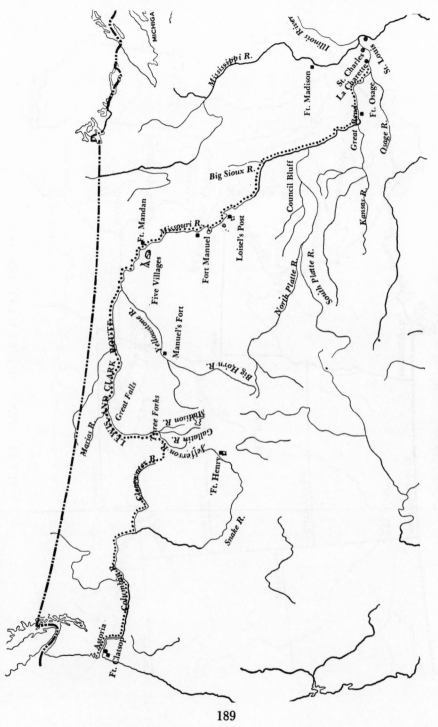

MICHIGA

Mississippi R.

Illinois River

Ft. Madison

St. Charles

La Charette

St. Louis

Ft. Osage

Great Bend

Osage R.

Big Sioux R.

Council Bluff

Kansas R.

Ft. Mandan

Missouri R.

Loisel's Post

Fort Manuel

North Platte R.

South Platte R.

Five Villages

Yellowstone R.

Manuel's Fort

Big Horn R.

LEWIS AND CLARK ROUTE

Marias R.

Great Falls

Three Forks

Madison R.

Gallatin R.

Jefferson R.

Ft. Henry

Clearwater R.

Snake R.

Columbia R.

Astoria

Ft. Clatsop

THE WEST OF LEWIS AND CLARK 1800–1815

189

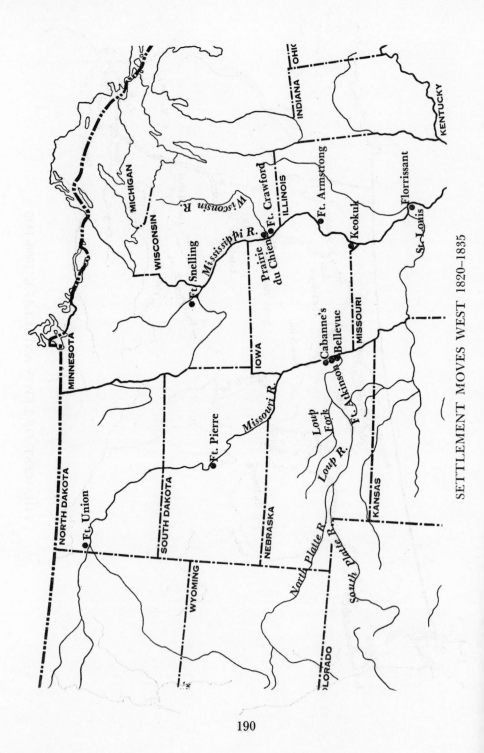

SETTLEMENT MOVES WEST 1820–1835

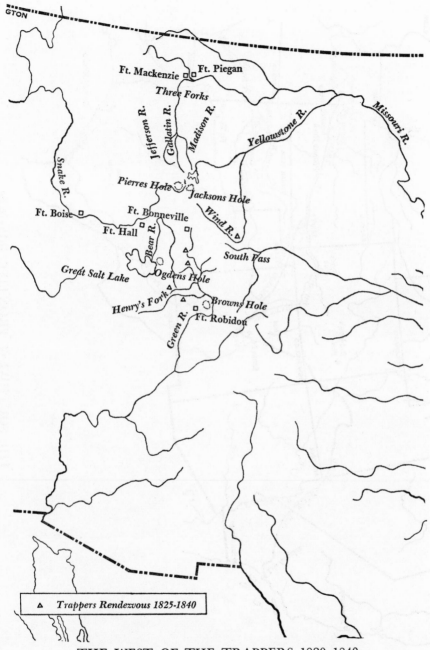

Ft. Mackenzie ☐ ☐ Ft. Piegan

Three Forks

Jefferson R.

Gallatin R.

Madison R.

Yellowstone R.

Missouri R.

Snake R.

Pierres Hole ○ ⟡

Jacksons Hole

Ft. Boise ☐

Ft. Bonneville ☐

Wind R. △

Ft. Hall ☐

Bear R.

South Pass

Great Salt Lake

△
△

Ogdens Hole ○

Henry's Fork △

Browns Hole ○

Green R.

Ft. Robidou

△	*Trappers Rendezvous 1825-1840*

THE WEST OF THE TRAPPERS 1820–1840

191

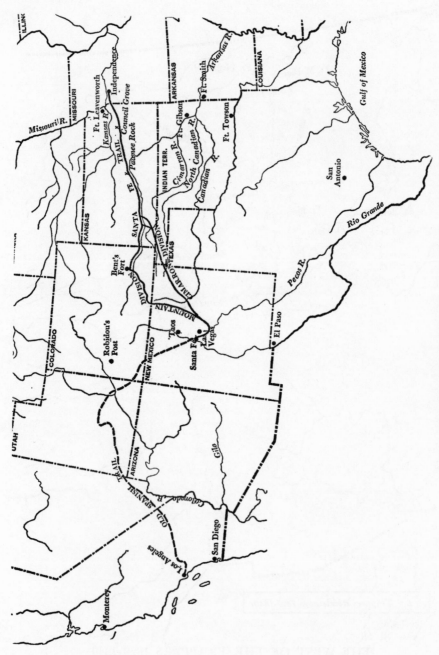

THE SOUTHWEST FRONTIER 1815–1835

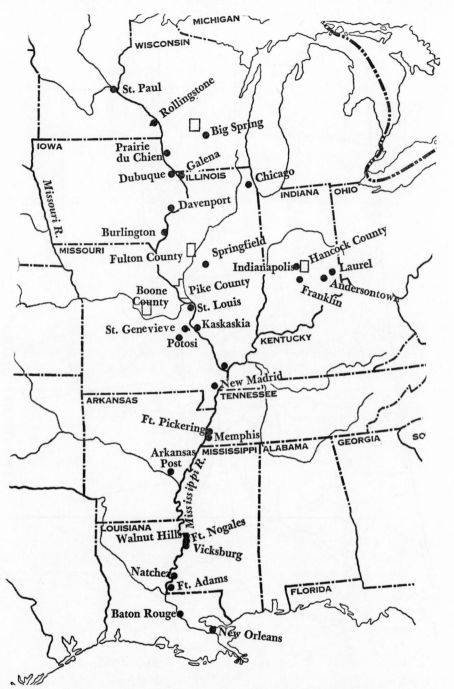

THE MISSISSIPPI VALLEY FRONTIER 1830–1855

THE OVERLAND TRAILS 1835–1860

Map labels (states/territories): MINNESOTA, WISCO, NORTH DAKOTA, SOUTH DAKOTA, NEBRASKA, IOWA, MISSOURI, KANSAS, ARKANSAS, INDIAN TERR., TEXAS, WYOMING, COLORADO, NEW MEXICO, MONTANA, IDAHO, UTAH, ARIZONA, NEVADA, WASHINGTON, OREGON, CALIFORNIA

Rivers: Missouri R., Niobrara R., Blue R., Platte R., North Platte R., South Platte R., Yellowstone R., Milk R., Green R., Snake R., Columbia R., Willamette R., Humboldt R., Carson R., San Joaquin R., Sutter's Fox

Places and forts: Independence, Kanesville, Bellevue, Winter Quarters, Ft. Kearney, Ft. St. Vrain, Ft. Lupton, Ft. Laramie, Independence Rock, South Pass, Ft. Bridger, Ft. Robidou, Salt Lake City, Great Salt Lake, Soda Springs, Ft. Hall, Ft. Boise, Ft. Walla Walla, Ft. Vancouver, Astoria, Champoeg, The Dalles, Carson Sink, San Francisco, Sacramento, Los Angeles

Trails: MORMON TRAIL, OREGON-CALIFORNIA TRAIL, OREGON TRAIL, CALIFORNIA TRAIL, SUBLETTE'S CUTOFF, HASTINGS CUTOFF

194

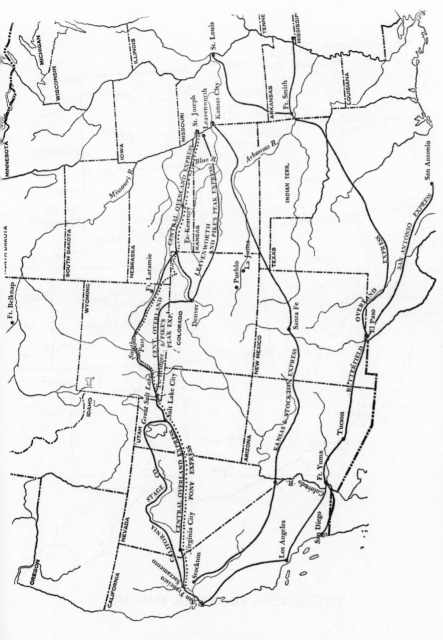

THE OVERLAND TRANSPORTATION FRONTIER 1850–1870

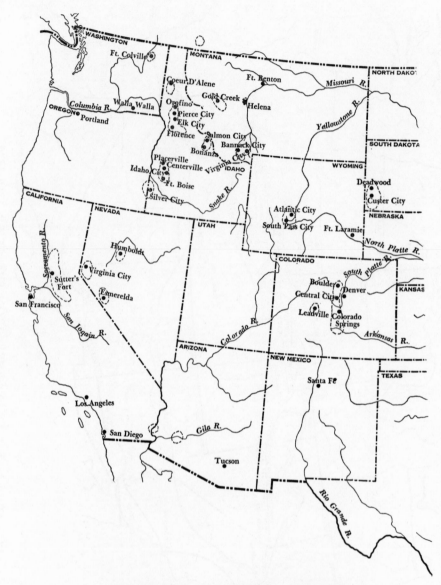

THE MINING FRONTIER 1849–1880

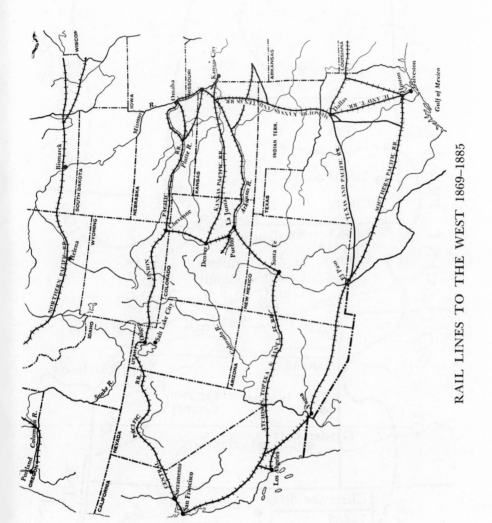

RAIL LINES TO THE WEST 1869–1885

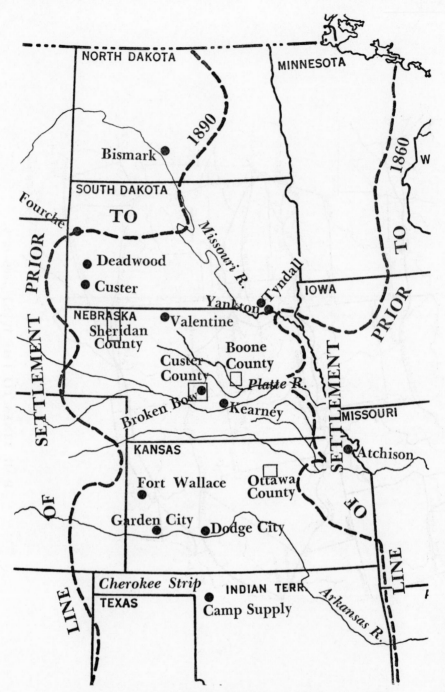

SETTLEMENT OF THE GREAT PLAINS 1860–1890

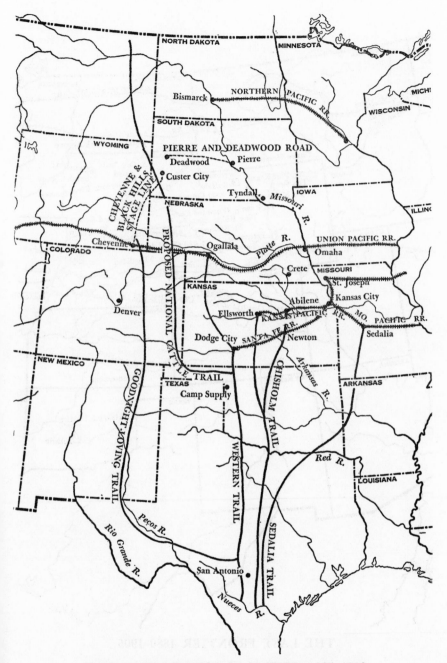

THE CATTLEMEN'S FRONTIER 1865–1880

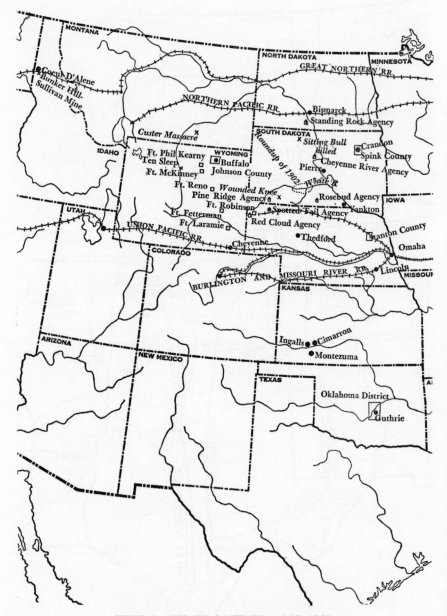

THE LAST FRONTIER 1880–1905

200

IV. The Trans-Missouri Frontier

See the maps on pages 195, 196, and 197.

FIVE YEARS AFTER the gold discovery at Sutter's Mill, the map of the western half of the United States presented a curiously unbalanced picture. In the Far West were the territories of Oregon and Washington and the state of California; in the Southwest were New Mexico Territory and the state of Texas. Except for Utah Territory—an island between the Rockies and California—all the rest of the great domain which began at the banks of the Missouri was unorganized and almost wholly unoccupied.

The 1850's and 1860's were to see a remarkable change in the picture. In 1854 the Kansas-Nebraska Act, confirming the abandonment of the idea that the trans-Missouri country could be used as a dumping ground for displaced Indian tribes, stimulated settlement in Kansas, Nebraska, and the Dakotas. Beginning in 1857, a spectacular series of gold and silver strikes bred a succession of rushes which sent the population spiraling upward in Arizona, Colorado, Nevada, Idaho, Montana, and Wyoming to the point that by 1868 all had achieved territorial status. Meanwhile the pressing necessity to unite east and west with speedier systems of transportation and communication brought into being freight lines, stage lines, the Pony Express, coast-to-coast telegraph service, and finally, after the conclusion of the Civil War, a transcontinental railroad. On the negative side, broken treaties resulted in bloody conflict between the red man and his dispossessor. Although the final settlement of the Indian question was still some years away, by 1870 all but a handful of the nomadic tribes had been subdued and installed on reservations.

Stagecoach drivers, bullwhackers, Pony Express riders, Indian scouts, buffalo hunters, miners, tracklayers, gamblers, dance-hall girls figure in the cast of characters who played out the drama of the '50's and '60's. Life was hard and harried, brutal and brawling during these decades, and yet to later generations the period seems one of the most glamorous in the history of the frontier.

The reports of Pike, Long, and other explorers, describing the Plains as an uninhabitable desert, provided Congress with a seemingly easy solution to the knotty problem of what to do with the Indians standing athwart the early nineteenth-century American advance into the eastern Mississippi Valley: remove them to the Plains, thus opening the land east of the Mississippi to white settlement and at the same time providing a haven for the Indians where they could be free from further white encroachment. . . . Though the line of demarcation was thought of as a "permanent Indian frontier," the process of shifting it westward began almost as soon as it was established.

The shifting frontier and the changing policy presaged what was evident almost from the beginning: the "permanent Indian frontier" was doomed to failure. . . . The American pioneer was not to be stopped at the Mississippi, the Missouri, or any other point short of the Pacific coast. By 1850, the Indian country was not outside the United States; it was right in the middle, a barrier that had to be removed.

—James C. Olson, *History of Nebraska*

A Bushel of Doughnuts

BACK IN 1825, when Secretary of War John C. Calhoun advised President Monroe that the Indians should be moved west of the Missouri River, the best scientific opinion held that while the plains country abounded with game which the Indians were accustomed to use for food, white men would never be able to live in this so-called "Great American Desert." As late as the end of President Jackson's second term, George Catlin, a man who knew

Indians and the West, pronounced the region "almost one entire plain of grass, which is and ever must be, useless to cultivating man."

At first, it appeared that the Indians might be allowed to retain the land between the Missouri and the Rockies, if only because nobody else wanted it. But the Santa Fe trade, the travel to Oregon, and the California gold rush served to threaten the safety of the Indians in their new home. At first the immigrants merely traveled *through* the Indian country, but as the travelers saw fertile spots in the "desert" and began to start "road ranches" with a certain amount of primitive agriculture, ranching, and merchandising, the Indians' permanent home was doomed. Bit by bit the red man was pushed westward by various treaties. He was always near white settlement on the plains and was continually feared by the often panicky settler.

When the first settlers crossed the eastern border of the Indian reserve, the red man, knowing what was their due according to the terms of the Indian Intercourse Act of 1834, demanded payment of each settler for the right to make improvements on land or town lots within the reservation. The settlers were anxious to settle on choice sites and paid the sums without complaint. At Omaha, Nebraska, the sum demanded was ten dollars from each man who built on Indian holdings.

Indian manners and customs were different from those of the whites and often, when the Indian meant no harm but was following the best tribal etiquette, he alarmed the suspicious whites. Like other primitive peoples, Indians were very sociable and hospitable. Their lodges accommodated eight to ten families and property was held more or less in common; moreover, the only white man's habitations they had known in the past were trading posts open to everyone. Habit and usage, therefore, led them to walk right into any dwelling, help themselves to food from the pot that hung over the fire, squat on the floor, smoke, and generally make themselves at home.

These children of the wild moved stealthily, and oftentimes the first warning a pioneer housewife had of her unwelcome company was when she sensed the presence of someone else in the room. With the possibility of an Indian attack seldom out of her thoughts, naturally she was frightened nearly to death when she looked up from her work to see a burly bronzed warrior. Because the ways of the white man were strange and interesting to the Indian, once inside he would pick up every cooking utensil and examine every article of wearing apparel, sometimes even trying on women's clothing. Paying a friendly call on a settlement, an Indian entered every house he could get into and ate everything he could lay his hands on. His password was "Eat! Eat!" or, if he could speak a little more English, "Me heap hungry!" If a woman should happen to see the redskin approach and fasten the door, the would-be caller sought a window, flattened his nose against the glass, and patiently watched the family doings until the frantic mother was glad to feed him to get rid of him.

On one occasion, an Indian's taste for white man's cooking led him to attempt to acquire the cook. In the 1850's John Peterson, a shoemaker, and his bride Mathilda settled in the eastern part of the new territory of Nebraska. Mr. Peterson began to put up a frame building for a hotel. Since there were no lumberyards, he took his axe and adze and daily wrought lumber from the trees of the nearby grove.

Among the inhabitants of the community was an Indian named No-Flesh who bore the reputation of being no good. One day while Mr. Peterson was in the woods, his wife was busy frying doughnuts. No-Flesh and his companions sauntered around the log cabin, entered the room, and squatted on the floor. Although terrified, the young wife tried not to show it and continued with her doughnuts. In her nervousness, however, she dropped one of the boiling hot morsels of baked dough, which rolled across the floor to the feet of No-Flesh. He needed no invitation to reach out and pick up the sizzling circle, but immediately dropped it with a howl of dismay and thrust his burnt fingers into his mouth. The flavor caused him to forget the pain; picking up the cooling doughnut, he devoured it and called for more. For more than an hour the young matron stood over the fire baking the tasty morsels for the hungry redskins. Mr. Peterson arrived home just in time to see the last of the supply disappearing down their throats. The young husband drove the unwelcome visitors away and the young bride collapsed from the strain.

No-Flesh did not forget the doughnuts and later visited Mr. Peterson and proposed that they trade wives. The shoemaker, thinking it a joke, consented. No-Flesh was to bring three Indian women in return for the young wife who could fry doughnuts.

One day while Mr. Peterson was away on an errand, his wife, busy at her work, looked out of the window and saw No-Flesh approaching, accompanied by three squaws. Not having been told of the joke and frightened beyond measure, the young woman darted from the house and sped to the home of a neighbor a quarter of a mile away. No-Flesh, seeing the cherished prize dash away, gave pursuit. She reached the cabin a few steps ahead of the Indian, calling out to her neighbor to save her. No-Flesh was stopped with the muzzle of a rifle and explanations were demanded. It took a council of war and a bushel of doughnuts to heal the breach.

The stagecoach and the Pony Express were developed to supply "fast" transportation in the 1850's and 1860's, but even more exigent than the western demand for better mail and passenger service was the demand for freighted goods. As James C. Olson has written, "The heavy emigration to California, Oregon, and Utah in the Forties and Fifties, the Colorado gold rush of 1859, and the opening of the Montana diggings in the Sixties created an almost insatiable demand for goods of all kinds. Adding heavily to the demand were the military posts established throughout the West to protect trails and settlements from the Indians. California and Oregon could be supplied by ship, but the most feasible way to get goods to Colorado, Utah, and Montana was through the Platte Valley, the route of the emigrants. . . . By its very nature, the freighting business tended to concentrate itself in a relatively few large firms. Costs were high; profits, though occasionally large, were speculative; and in order to bid on government contracts, the most dependable source of income, the freighter needed hundreds of wagons and thousands of oxen. . . . The heavy wagons carried an amazing variety of goods: food, grain, clothing, whiskey, mining machinery, lumber, arms, ammunition—anything for which there was a demand or for which a demand might be created."

Linking Old and New Frontiers

IN THE EARLY 1850's, when the government was supplying seven army posts in the West, overland freighting became big business. The first government contracts had been given in 1848 to the Independence, Missouri, firm of James Brown and William H. Russell, and they were renewed in 1849 and 1850. When Brown died in the latter year, Russell formed a partnership with William B. Waddell; three years later, in 1854, he persuaded their chief rival, Alexander Majors, to join forces with them. Thus came into being the famous firm of Russell, Majors and Waddell, the largest of all the overland freighting companies.

Russell was the visionary, reckless promoter. Waddell was the penny-pinching treasurer. Majors was the field chief—the plainsman who recruited teamsters, bought or built wagons, and supervised operations. Operating out of their headquarters at Fort Leavenworth, Russell, Majors and Waddell virtually monopolized freighting to the West from the mid-1850's to the beginning of the Civil War.

1

If it is hard to think of freighting by wagon train as big business, a few figures may suggest the scale on which Russell, Majors and Waddell operated. In 1857, when the firm secured the contract to supply the Army of Utah in addition to the western military posts, Alexander Majors advertised for sixteen thousand yoke of oxen and fifteen hundred men. In that same year they established a second terminal upriver from Fort Leavenworth at Nebraska City, and ultimately spent more than $300,000 developing it. Although the salaries they paid their men seem chicken-feed by today's standards—a wagon boss received about $75 a month, a teamster about $25—every wagon train that started westward represented an investment of from eighteen to twenty thousand dollars. At one time, they employed six thousand teamsters, owned forty thousand oxen, and had wagon parks covering acres of ground.

The organization of a full-fledged train for crossing the plains [according to an account written by Alexander Majors himself] consisted of twenty-five to twenty-six large wagons that would carry from three to three and one-half tons each, the merchandise or contents of each wagon being protected by three sheets of thin ducking, such as is used for army tents.

The number of cattle necessary to draw each wagon was twelve, making six yokes or pairs, and a prudent freighter would always have from twenty to thirty head of extra oxen, in case of accident to or lameness of some of the animals. In camping or stopping to allow the cattle to graze, a corral or pen of oblong shape is formed by the wagons, the tongues being turned out, and a log chain extended from the hind wheel of each wagon to the fore wheel of the next behind, etc., thus making a solid pen except for a wide gap at each end, through which the cattle are driven when they are to be yoked and made ready for travel, the gaps then being filled by the wagonmaster, his assistant, and the extra men, to prevent the cattle from getting out. When the cattle are driven into this corral or pen, each driver yokes his oxen, drives them out to his wagon, and gets ready to start. The entire train of cattle, including extras, generally numbered from 320 to 330 head and usually from four to five mules for riding and herding.

The force of men for each train consisted of a wagon-master, his assistant, the teamsters, a man to look after the extra cattle, and two or three extra men as a reserve to take the places of any men who might be disabled or sick, the latter case being the rare exception, for as a rule there was no sickness. I think perhaps there was never a set of laboring men in the world who enjoyed more uninterrupted good health than the teamsters on the plains. They walked by the side of their teams, as it was impossible for them to ride and keep them moving with regularity. The average distance traveled with loaded wagons was from twelve to fifteen miles per day, although in some instances, when roads were fine and there was a necessity for rapid movement, I have known them to travel twenty miles. But this was faster traveling than they could keep up for any length of time. Returning with empty wagons they could average twenty miles a day without injury to the animals.

Oxen proved to be the cheapest and most reliable teams for long trips, where they had to live upon the grass. This was invariably the case. They did good work, gathered their own living, and if properly driven would travel 2,000 miles in a season, or during the months from April to November; traveling from 1,000 to 1,200 miles with loaded wagons, and with plenty of good grass and water, they would make the return trip with the empty wagons in the same season.

Now, the distance traveled depended upon the skill of the wagonmasters who had them in charge. . . . If the master was not skilled in handling the animals and men, they could not make anything like good headway and success. To make everything work expeditiously, thorough discipline was required, each man performing his duty and being in the place assigned him without confusion or delay. I remember once of timing my teamsters when they commenced to yoke their teams after the cattle had been driven into their corral and allowed to stand long enough to become quiet. I gave the word to the men to commence yoking, and held my watch in hand while they did so, and in sixteen minutes from the time they commenced, each man had yoked six pairs of oxen and had them hitched to their wagons ready to move. Men who are thoroughly disciplined are ready to "pop the whip" and move out, when unskilled men were often more than an hour doing the same work.

The discipline and rules by which my trains were governed were perfect, and as quick as the men learned each one his place and duty, it became a very pleasant and easy thing for him to do. Good moral conduct was required of them, and no offense from man to man was allowed, thus keeping them good natured and working together harmoniously. They were formed into what they called "messes," there being from six to eight men in a mess, each mess selecting the man best fitted to serve as cook, and the others carrying the water, fuel, and standing guard, so that the cook's sole business when in camp was to get his utensils ready and cook the meals.

We never left the cattle day or night without guard of two men, the teamsters taking turns, and arranging it so that each man was on guard two hours out of twenty-four, and sometimes they were only obliged to go on guard two hours every other night, this matter they arranged among themselves and with the wagonmaster.

The duty of the wagonmaster was about the same as that of a captain of a steamboat or ship, his commands being implicitly obeyed, for in the early stages of travel upon the plains men were at all times liable to be attacked by the Indians; therefore the necessity for a perfect harmony of action throughout the entire band. The assistant wagonmaster's duty was to carry out the wagonmaster's instructions, and he would often be at one end of the train while the master was at the other, as the train was moving. It was arranged, when possible, that no two trains should ever camp together, as there was not grass and water enough for the animals of both, and thus all confusion was avoided. The average salary paid the men was $1.00 a day and expenses.

While it was true that employees of the Russell, Majors and Waddell company were required to take an oath that they would observe certain rules of good conduct, according to the British author and explorer Sir Richard Burton, who met Alexander Majors in 1860, Majors' "meritorious efforts to reform the morals of the land have not yet put forth even the bud of promise. He forbad his drivers and employees to drink, gamble, curse, and travel on Sundays; he desired them to peruse Bibles distributed to them gratis; and though he refrained from a lengthy proclamation commanding them to be good boys and girls, he did not the less expect it of them. Result: I scarcely ever saw a sober driver; as for profanity—the Western equivalent for hard swearing—they would make the blush of shame crimson the cheek of [a] bargee; and, rare exceptions to the rule of the United States, they are not to be deterred from evil talking by the dread presence of a 'lady.' "

In fact, bullwhackers and mule skinners were generally believed to be able to out-cuss anybody on the frontier at a time when cussing was something of a fine art. Their conviction that oxen and mules could not be managed efficiently without considerable profanity and their pride in their dexterity with the long whip were celebrated by a versifier of the day:

> I pop my whip, I bring the blood,
> I make my leaders take the mud,
> We grab the wheel and turn them round,
> One long, long pull, we're on hard ground . . .

> When I got there the hills were steep,
> 'Twould make any tender-hearted person weep
> To hear me cuss and pop my whip,
> To see my oxen pull and slip.

Large-scale freighting by firms such as Russell, Majors and Waddell and Wells, Fargo and Company was to play no small part in the settlement of the West. The road ranches, established at intervals along the trail to provide feed for the oxen and provisions and entertainment for the teamsters, were the nuclei from which grew towns and the great cattle ranches of the 1880's and 1890's.

2

Unquestionably, William H. Russell's most spectacular achievement was the establishment of the Pony Express. Short-lived though it was, it captured the imagination of the entire country and brought home in a dramatic fashion the importance of binding west to east with speedy, efficient modes of transportation and communication.

Almost from the beginning of the "great migration," the government was besieged with requests for improved mail service to the west coast. Congress finally responded in March, 1857, by authorizing twice-weekly service between Missouri and California, and that same year the Butterfield Overland Mail Company began carrying the mail from St. Louis to San Francisco via Arkansas, El Paso, and Fort Yuma on the Gila River. The choice of this route awakened much ill-feeling. It was a foregone conclusion that sooner or later the nation would be linked by a transcontinental rail system, and the route to be taken west from the Missouri River already was a national issue. As a possible precursor of the way the railroad would go, the inauguration of mail service over the southern rather than the central route was greatly disturbing to proponents of the latter; and in 1858 Senator William H. Gwinn of California persuaded Russell to launch a pony express between St. Joseph and Sacramento, with a view to demonstrating the superiority of the central route.

Although Russell had some difficulty in convincing his partners that their firm should undertake the project, in the end he talked them into it. By the spring of 1860, way stations had been built at ten- or twelve-mile intervals along the nineteen-hundred-mile route, riders and station keepers engaged, and five hundred horses purchased. Riders and horses were the pick of the frontier. The men—who had to be small, or at least light—were chosen for their horsemanship, courage, and strength; their mounts for their stamina and speed. Service began on April 3, 1860, with riders leaving simultaneously from Sacramento and St. Joseph. Functioning like clockwork, the Pony Express tore across desert, mountain, and plain to bring the first mail through both ways in the scheduled ten days—half the time taken by stagecoach. In winter this schedule was extended to fifteen days, but it was still better than the time made by the Butterfield Line over the southern route. The fastest run was made in March, 1861, at the time of

Abraham Lincoln's first inaugural address, when the mail went through in seven days and seventeen hours.

Mark Twain, who traveled west in a stagecoach in 1861, included the following description of the Pony Express rider in his book, *Roughing It:*

> The pony-rider was usually a little bit of a man, brimful of spirit and endurance. No matter what time of the day or night his watch came on, and no matter whether it was winter or summer, raining, snowing, hailing, or sleeting, or whether his "beat" was a level straight road or a crazy trail over mountain crags and precipices, or whether it led through peaceful regions or regions that swarmed with hostile Indians, he must always be ready to leap into the saddle and be off like the wind! There was no idling-time for a pony-rider on duty. He rode fifty miles without stopping, by daylight, moonlight, starlight, or through the blackness of darkness—just as it happened. He rode a splendid horse that was born for a racer and fed and lodged like a gentleman; kept him at his utmost speed for ten miles, and then, as he came crashing up to the station where stood two men holding fast a fresh, impatient steed, the transfer of rider and mail-bag was made in the twinkling of an eye, and away flew the eager pair and were out of sight before the spectator could get hardly the ghost of a look. Both rider and horse went "flying light." The rider's dress was thin, and fitted close; he wore a "roundabout," and a skull-cap, and tucked his pantaloons into his boot-tops like a race-rider. He carried no arms—he carried nothing that was not absolutely necessary, for even the postage on his literary freight was worth *five dollars a letter*. He got but little frivolous correspondence to carry—his bag had business letters in it, mostly.
>
> We had had a consuming desire, from the beginning, to see a pony-rider, but somehow or other all that passed us and all that met us managed to streak by in the night, and so we heard only a whiz and a hail, and the swift phantom of the desert was gone before we could get our heads out of the windows. But now we were expecting one along every moment, and would see him in broad daylight. Presently the driver exclaims:
>
> "HERE HE COMES!"

Every neck is stretched further, and every eye strained wider. Away across the endless dead level of the prairie a black speck appears against the sky, and it is plain that it moves. Well, I should think so! In a second or two it becomes a horse and rider, rising and falling, rising and falling—sweeping toward us nearer and still nearer, and the flutter of the hoofs comes faintly to the ear—another instant a whoop and a hurrah from our upper deck, a wave of the rider's hand but no reply, and man and horse burst past our excited faces, and go winging away like a belated fragment of a storm!

So sudden is it all, and so like a flash of unreal fancy, that but for the flake of white foam left quivering and perishing on a mail-sack after the vision had flashed by and disappeared, we might have doubted whether we had seen any actual horse and man at all, maybe.

The Pony Express was in operation less than nineteen months; it discontinued service when the transcontinental telegraph lines were joined at Salt Lake City on October 24, 1861. Although it was a losing venture, contributing to the ultimate financial ruin of Russell, Majors and Waddell, the nation was immeasurably the gainer, for the Pony Express not only demonstrated that the central route was practicable at all seasons of the year, thus blazing the trail for the Iron Horse, but it also helped bind California to the Union during the first crucial months of the Civil War. Moreover, the performance of the riders—the skill, pluck, and endurance they displayed in the discharge of their responsibilities —epitomized the finest qualities of the American frontiersman.

3

The heroes of the Pony Express were the riders. However, successful maintenance of the schedule depended in no small part on the loyal and efficient labors of the corps of station keepers. Each station was in the charge of a relay agent, assisted by a stock tender whose duty it was to care for a considerable band of horses, herding them in summer and stabling them in winter. About once a month a wagon train visited the stations along the line, distributing food for the men and grain for the horses.

During the Paiute War in 1860, Egan's Station, a lonely stop west of Salt Lake City, was attacked one October morning by a large party of Indians. Mike Holt, the station keeper, and a rider named Wilson were at breakfast when the redskins swarmed up around the station. The men grabbed their guns and attempted to make a stand, but they were hopelessly outnumbered. Breaking through the door, a horde of Indians quickly overpowered them.

After the chief had inspected the two captives, he uttered a one-word command: "Bread!" Hoping they might escape death by giving the Indians what they asked, Holt and Wilson piled all the bread in the house upon the table. This, however, was merely an appetizer. When they had licked up the last crumb, the Indians pointed to a number of sacks of flour piled in the corner, and by signs ordered the men to revive the fire and bake bread. All day they baked bread for the ravenous guests.

William Dennis, the rider from the west, was due late in the afternoon. When he did not arrive on schedule, the conscripted bakers suspected the Indians had killed him. Actually, while he was still some distance from the station his keen eyes had spotted the yard full of Indians before they were aware of his approach. Wheeling his horse about, Dennis raced back down the trail. Earlier he had passed a troop of sixty United States Dragoons, commanded by Lieutenant Weed, jogging along eastward. With good luck, they might be able to arrive in time . . .

Meanwhile, back at the station Holt and Wilson were baking for dear life. About sunset the flour was exhausted, and the Indians decided on a new game. Out in the yard was a wagon tongue which had been set in the ground to serve as a hitching post. At the chief's order, the two white men were tied on opposite sides of the post and the Indians began to gather sagebrush, which they heaped around their victims. When the pyre had been completed, a torch was lighted but, not wanting the fun to be over too quickly, the Indians staged a jubilant dance, yelling like demons and shouting insults at the white men.

The arrival of the dragoons put an end to their sport. The soldiers' charge caught the redskins completely by surprise; when the melee was over, the Utes had lost eighteen braves and sixty horses. The Indians' love of playing cat-and-mouse with their victims had saved Holt and Wilson from being roasted alive.

4

William F. Fisher's run was from Salt Lake City to Rush Valley and return. On January 22, 1861, shortly after leaving Rush Valley, he was overtaken by a snowstorm—the bane of the pony riders. With a howling wind blowing and the snow coming down in a blinding curtain, it was with the greatest difficulty that he could find the next station, Camp Floyd. The station agent and stock tender advised him to wait there until the storm was over. But Fisher was a Pony Express rider, and a Pony Express rider did not let the weather boss him around. Changing horses, he rode into the storm.

A few miles out he barely avoided a collision with a freight train belonging to Russell, Majors and Waddell. Like the station agent, the wagonmaster urged Fisher to stop and camp with them until the weather moderated, but he too might as well have saved his breath.

An hour later, Fisher realized he was off the trail, but he kept moving on. Presently he was threading his way among cedar trees, somewhere in the hills; the wind seemed to be blowing even more strongly and his horse could make little progress against the blast. Dismounting, Fisher turned the animal with its tail to the wind, and sat down to rest a moment on the sheltered side of a cedar tree, stretching out his cramped legs. He soon began to feel drowsy, and though he knew what his fate would be if he should fall asleep, his will seemed paralyzed. Fortunately, just as he dozed off, a jackrabbit bounding through the snow came down squarely on his outstretched legs, startling him into broad wakefulness. He instantly jumped up and began stamping his feet and thrashing his arms to stimulate circulation. Although he was able to remount, his hands were too nearly frozen to handle the reins; he tied a knot in them and took a grip on the saddle horn, giving the horse his head.

After what seemed an interminable time—actually, it was an hour—they came out on the bank of the Jordan River, and Fisher was now able to orient himself. Following the stream to the village of Lehi, he soon was sitting down to a hot meal and a steaming mug of coffee. In a half-hour he was sufficiently recuperated to resume his struggle toward Salt Lake City, about thirty miles to the north.

Three hours later night had fallen, and he was lost again. While floundering through a snow-filled coulee, he caught a glimpse of a light shining from a settler's cabin across the valley. Dismounting, he removed the mochila—the leather saddle blanket with pockets for mail—from his horse, and turned him loose. Guided by the friendly gleam of light, he made his way through waist-deep drifts to the cabin. While he thawed out, one of the men there went out and succeeded in locating his horse.

Once more the weary pony-rider remounted and pushed on to Rockwell's Station, where a fresh horse awaited him. From there he proceeded without incident to Salt Lake City, arriving at four in the morning, and saw the mail started on the next leg of the relay east.

●

In the decade following the strike at Sutter's Mill, it is estimated that the California gold yield was approximately half a billion dollars. Although by 1855 mining in California had become a corporate business, the lone hands who had panned gold and made the riffle found it hard to settle down to earn their bread at an everyday occupation. For many of the Forty-Niners, gold fever proved to be a chronic disease. Leading pack mules with their picks and pans, they moved on into the Northwest's "inland Empire." Some drifted eastward into the Rockies. Most of them washed out scarcely enough gold dust to replenish their grubstakes.

In 1857 the tide turned. Prospectors found gold in the sand bars of the Fraser River near Fort Langley in

British Columbia, and by June, 1858, thirty thousand United States miners had invaded Canada. Most of them, however, were soon on their way back home: the Hudson's Bay Company maintained tight control over the diggings and, in any case, the results did not live up to expectations. But the Fraser River strike was only a portent of things to come. Bonanza years were ahead. Gold was discovered at Pikes Peak in 1858, and from then until 1865 there was at least a gold rush a year to some part of the West.

Pikes Peak or Bust

RUMORS OF GOLD in the Pikes Peak area had been rife for years, and gold actually was discovered there as early as 1850, but the strike that sparked the Colorado gold rush did not occur until July 6, 1858. On that date William Green Russell, an experienced miner from Georgia, found gold on Dry Creek, near its mouth. He and his twelve companions worked the find until mid-August, when it played out.

After prospecting elsewhere without success, Russell came up with what seemed to him a better idea. He returned to the scene of the strike and platted the townsite of St. Charles. William Larimer of Leavenworth, Kansas, arriving a little later, platted the Denver City townsite at Cherry Creek. A number of shanties and log buildings were hastily put up on the two sites, and then both gentlemen sat back and awaited the anticipated rush of gold seekers the following spring.

Russell and Larimer had figured correctly. The rather modest findings of the prospectors were played up in wildly exaggerated accounts by newspapers along the Missouri River in Nebraska, Kansas, and Missouri, and word of the strike spread like wildfire. Merchants in the river towns, still feeling the pinch of the Panic of 1857 but trusting that history would repeat itself, stocked their shelves in readiness for the Fifty-Niners. Guidebooks, mainly those of Byers and Oakes, were at a premium all winter, and when spring came a full-fledged gold rush was on. In April, William Tecumseh Sherman wrote from Leavenworth that steamboats were arriving by twos and threes every day, and it was estimated that twenty-five thousand persons already had left for the diggings.

All spring and summer, wagons flaunting the slogan "Pikes Peak or Bust!" streamed westward to the new Golconda, where many of them promptly turned around and rolled back east, their signs now reading "Busted!" These disappointed gold seekers felt strongly that they had been misled for profit by the newspapers and business men of the Missouri River communities, and the chanted doggerel,

> Hang Byers and Oakes
> For starting the Pikes Peak hoax,

was one of the more innocuous expressions of their indignation. The threats of the returning Pikes Peakers so frightened the inhabitants of Omaha that weapons from the territorial arsenal were issued to the citizenry for their protection.

In sober fact, however, there *was* gold at Pikes Peak—and in quantity. This was demonstrated on June 6, 1859, by a wandering prospector named John H. Gregory, who found a rich lode on the North Branch of Clear Creek. By the end of summer, nearly five thousand miners were working the area, and the nearby town of Central City came into being. Gregory, having sold his claim for $21,000, sent a substantial portion of it home to his wife and children, and then walked around Gregory Gulch in a happy daze, watching the proceedings.

The nation had been informed that perhaps the Colorado strike would equal California's. To see for himself, Horace Greeley of the *New York Herald-Tribune* sped west. After examining Gregory Gulch he issued a statement on June 9, 1859, listing the worth of ore already extracted from the diggings. He then added:

We cannot conclude this statement without protesting

most earnestly against a renewal of the infatuation which impelled thousands to rush to this region a month or two since, only to turn back before reaching it, or to hurry away immediately after, more hastily than they came.

Gold mining is a business which eminently requires of its votaries capital, experience, energy, endurance and in which the highest qualities do not always command success. There may be hundreds of ravines in these mountains as rich in gold as that in which we write, and there are probably many; but up to this hour, we do not know that any such have been discovered.

There are said to be 5,000 people already in this ravine, and hundreds more pouring into it daily. Tens of thousands more have been passed by us on our rapid journey to this place, or heard of on their way hither by other routes. For all these, nearly every pound of supplies of every kind must be hauled by teams from the Missouri river, some 700 miles distant, over roads which are mere trails, crossing countless unbridged water courses, always steep-banked and often mirey, and at times so swollen by rains as to be utterly impassable by wagons.

Part of this distance is a desert, yielding grass, wood, and water only at intervals of several miles, and then very scantily. To attempt to cross this desert on foot is madness—suicide—murder. A few months hence—probably by the middle of October—this whole Alpine region will be snowed under and frozen up, so as to put a stop to the working of sluices if not mining altogether. There then, for a period of six months, will be neither employment, food, nor shelter within five hundred miles for the thousands pressing hither under the delusion that gold may be picked up here like pebbles on the sea shore, and that when they arrive here, even though without provisions or money, their fortunes are made. Great disappointment, great suffering are inevitable.

Of the hundred thousand people who set out for Colorado in 1859, only about twenty-five thousand remained to mine the gold and lay the foundations of the territory. But Greeley's assertion that "probably" there were many rich gulches in the mountains far outweighed his cautionary remarks on the inevitability of suf-

fering and disappointment. In 1860 there was a second rush, this
one composed of persons described as more orderly and more
determined than the slap-happy "tourists" of the previous year.

Among the 1860 immigrants was a spirited twenty-one-year-old
girl named Mollie Dorsey Sanford. Born in Indianapolis, she had
come out west in 1857 with her parents and her seven brothers
and sisters. The Dorsey family had settled on a claim on the
Little Nemaha in eastern Nebraska. The log cabin built by Mr.
Dorsey nestled among the trees skirting the sparkling waters of
the little stream, and was christened Hazel Dell. Here Mollie was
wooed and won by Byron Sanford, a personable young blacksmith
from New York State. Shortly after their marriage at "sweet
Hazel Dell," an event occurred which was to change the direction
of their lives. On March 20, 1860, Mollie wrote in her journal:

> Last night we had two strangers, gentlemen from "Pikes
> Peak" or Denver, stop for the night. Mr. George West, editor
> of a paper in the small town of Golden near Denver, was one
> of them, or *the* one, rather, that has given me the Pikes Peak
> fever. He says, "Don't think of going anywhere else but to
> Denver. There are openings there for young beginners. There
> are thousands now crossing the plains. There are good gold
> diggings out there." . . . Mr. West says By can make $8 or $10
> per day at his trade.

On April she wrote that " 'the die is cast' and we go to
Denver. By has laid in 6 months' supplies, bought a small cook
stove, a few housekeeping articles, and some clothing. . . . The
trip probably will take many weeks as we are to travel with oxen."
On April 12, goodbyes were said. The family tried to send Mollie
off in good spirits, but this was difficult for all realized that it
probably would be years before they met again and that the sepa-
ration might be forever. Finally, at two o'clock By hitched their
team of ponies to their wagon, and they started off to join the
friends with whom they were traveling westward. After they had
gone a few hundred yards, Mollie, turning for a last look at the
family group, saw her little brother Charlie running after them,
screaming "Sister! Sister!" Jumping down out of the wagon, she

ran back to meet him, kissed him again and again, and watched him trudge dejectedly back to the cabin.

Mollie's mother had given her a half-dozen fine hens and a rooster which had been placed in a coop on the back of the wagon. When they forded the Big Blue River, the water came up into the coop and drowned the rooster. This was a disaster, for they knew a chicken was worth three or four days' work in Denver. On Sunday the train lay over, but it did not seem much like a day of rest since they had to wash, roast, bake, and do the jobs which could not be done while traveling the other six days.

By April 20 the little party had swung into the main stream of immigration. Mollie wrote in her diary that night: "The road is full of teams. Tonight the camps are thick around us. The dust is dreadful!" They had now reached the Atchison-Denver stagecoach line and thereafter went by a station every ten or fifteen miles. The occasional passing of a coach or a Pony Express rider gave variety to the day's travel. At Fort Kearney they saw many soldiers, and were told that seventy thousand persons had already passed over that route going west.

On June 3 they reached Cottonwood Springs, a well-known point on the trail near the forks of the Platte. During the day Mollie had driven alone in the wagon pulled by the pony team, and now had a real adventure to confide to her journal.

[The ponies] are so full of life early in the mornings that we generally drive ahead a mile or so to cool them down, then drive back and take our line of march in the rear of the "caravan." This morning they were unusually frisky. I gave them the reins, and we cantered ahead at a lively rate. The air was bracing, the roads smooth and hard, and I was enjoying it hugely. Coming down into a ravine where the road curved, what was my horror to come upon a squad of Indian warriors! They immediately surrounded me, and began their gibberish of "Wano Squaw," "Wano White Squaw" (good Squaw), evidently amused at my consternation. For a wonder the ponies were quiet, perhaps as paralyzed as myself. I wear my hair in two long braids for comfort and convenience. An Indian seized hold of each one, took their hunting knives and made every demonstration of cutting them off, *or* scalping, I did not know which. But after almost scaring me to death, they released their hold, and began peeking and poking around in the wagon.

I knew they were fond of sugar. Our box had been filled before starting, so I opened it, gasping, "Help yourselves, gentlemen"—which they did—entirely emptying it, eating all they could and tying the remainder in their dirty blankets. Appreciating my generosity, they began then a howl of "Beeskit, Beeskit." Immediately the bread box was thrown open, and the noon-day lunch that we always carry in our wagon went the way of the sugar. What might have happened next no one knows, but the distant echo of the welcome "Whoa. Haw. Gee" came over the hill, and brandishing their whips and knives, the pesky redskins gave a war whoop, and galloped away. I turned my ponies, now thoroughly frightened, and sped back to the wagon, almost frantic with excitement. . . . Hereafter I shall meekly follow in the rear.

On June 16 Mollie noted that they had "met at least a hundred teams today on the homeward track, mostly Missourians. They denounce the country as a 'fraud' because they could not pick up gold on the streets. The gold excitement takes thousand there. But *we* are not expecting much." On June 21, seventy miles from Denver, for the first time she saw "far away to the west . . . the blue ridge of the mountains, a view of the 'promised land.' Their silver-capped peaks rise above like clouds of glory. . . . Five days later she wrote, "The Promised Land is gained."

Gold Is Where You Find It

THE SAME YEAR as the Pikes Peak strike of 1858, gold and silver were found in Arizona; the year after it, gold discoveries in Nevada, climaxed by the tapping of the king of lodes, the Comstock, touched off a population boom that enabled Nevada to achieve territorial status in 1861. (Similarly, the Pikes Peak rush resulted in the creation of Colorado Territory, also in 1861.) In 1860 gold-hungry men swarmed to Idaho's Clearwater and Salmon River diggings, and three years later Idaho was organized as a territory. In 1862 what began as a minor rush following a strike on Benetsee Creek in Montana turned into a stampede in 1863; then came discoveries at Last Chance Gulch and the founding of Helena, and in 1864, Montana Territory was born. A strike in the Wind River range of Wyoming, near South Pass, in 1867 kept the excitement going but did not produce much gold.

1

The Arizona gold and silver strikes were disappointing, but what they lacked in ore they made up in color. The center of the mining country was the miserable little town of Tucson, once described as the Sodom and Gomorrah of the Far West. Its population of five hundred was made up of escaped convicts from Australia, Mexican outlaws from Sonora, and refugees from the San Francisco Vigilance Committee. Among the latter was Ned McGowan who enjoyed respect in Tucson because, although he had a dozen notches on his gun, he had never killed a man save when acting in behalf of a friend who had taken on more than he could handle. Tucson's reputation as a headquarters for dissipation, vice, and crime was borne out by its graveyard: Of the forty-seven white men buried there, only two had died a natural death.

Tucson came as a bit of a shock to tenderfeet from the East. Phocion R. Way, a native of Ohio who, in 1858, took over as an agent for the Santa Rita Mining Company, wrote his first impressions of the town in his diary entry for June 12:

> Arrived at Tucson about 6 o'clock last evening. We had heard bad reports of this town all along the route and we were fully prepared to see a miserable place—and we were not the least disappointed. . . . There is no hotel or other accommodation here for travelers and I was obliged to roll myself in my blankets and sleep either in the street or the corral, as the station house has no windows or floors and was too close and warm.

The corral is where they keep their horses and mules, but I slept very comfortably as the ground was made soft by manure. I would rather have slept in the street as a great many do, but it is hardly safe for a stranger. Someone might suppose that he had money about his person and quietly stick a knife into him in the night and no one would be the wiser. . . . There is no law here, or if there is it is not enforced—might makes right. Yesterday a dispute occurred between two men about something when one of them shot the other dead on the spot. The man is running at large and no particular notice is taken of it. . . . I guess King Alcohol was at the bottom of the trouble.

2

James Finny—everyone knew him as Old Virginny—enjoyed the reputation of being the steadiest drinker at Gold Canyon, a meager diggings in the Washoe Indian country on the Nevada side of the Sierras. But Old Virginny had an eye for gold. In January, 1859, he found traces of dust in some heavy dark soil on a hill at the head of the canyon. Naming the site Gold Hill, he filed claims. Miners thereabout who came up to look were unimpressed.

The following June two prospectors, Peter O'Riley and Patrick McLaughlin, began digging nearby in Six Mile Canyon. To secure water they moved up to a spring, and while digging a reservoir they came upon the same dark soil found at Old Virginny's diggings. On an impulse they panned it and found a thick layer of gold dust and flakes. They posted claims and got down to business with pick and shovel.

About this moment Henry T. P. Comstock, originally from Ontario, Canada, appeared on the scene. He examined the dust and flakes and announced that the site belonged to him, Old Virginny, and Emanuel "Manny" Penrod. The bluff didn't work, but Comstock kept talking. Since many discoveries played out, O'Riley and McLaughlin ended by making them partners. A few days later Comstock bought out Old Virginny for a bottle of whiskey, and after some more discussion another partner, Joseph D. Winters, was added. Ownership problems settled, four of the partners went to work at the diggings. The fifth, Comstock, watched or talked about his mine to anyone who would listen. Pretty soon everyone began calling it "Comstock's Lode." During this opening phase of the operation, the mine was yielding $300 in gold for every cradle washed.

Soon they encountered a heavy bluish quartz. On a hunch each man filed a claim of six hundred feet, in addition to the forty feet they held for gold. The blue stuff was assayed and the report came back on June 27 that it was worth $1,595 in gold and $4,791 in silver! They had tapped the great Comstock Lode, the world's richest vein of ore. Overanxious to cash in, Comstock sold his claim for a small amount.

Like Sutter's Mill and Pikes Peak before it, Washoe was now the magic word. More than four thousand miners made their way to the district before winter snows clogged the passes. In the next year ten thousand arrived. From the new town of Virginia City, miners fanned out all over the Nevada mountains and other important strikes were made. But the Comstock—over four miles long and of varying depths of hundreds of feet—continued as the center of mining interest.

A journalist, J. Ross Browne, titillated readers of *Harper's Magazine*, with this account of Virginia City in 1860:

> On a slope of mountains speckled with snow, sage brushes, and mounds of upturned earth, without any apparent beginning or end, congruity or regard for the eternal fitness of things, lay outspread the wondrous city of Virginia. Frame shanties, pitched together as if by accident; tents of canvas, of blankets, of brush, of potato sacks and old shirts; smokey hovels of mud and stone; coyote holes in the mountain side forcibly seized and held by men; pits and shafts with smoke issuing from every crevice; piles of goods and rubbish on craggy points, in the hollows, on the rocks, in the mud, in the snow, everywhere, scattered broadcast in pell-mell confusion, as if the clouds had suddenly burst overhead and rained down the dregs of all the flimsy, rickety, filthy little hovels and rubbish of merchandise that had ever undergone the process of evaporation from the earth since the days of Noah.
>
> The intervals of space, which may or may not have been

streets, were dotted with human beings of such sort, variety, and numbers that the famous ant hills of Africa were as nothing in comparison. To say that they were rough, muddy, unkempt, and unwashed, would be but faintly expressive of their actual appearance; they were all this by reason of exposure to the weather; but they seemed to have caught the very diabolical tint and grime of the whole place. Here and there, to be sure, a San Francisco dandy of the "boiled shirt" and "stove-pipe hat" pattern loomed up in proud consciousness of the triumphs of art under adverse circumstances; but they were merely peacocks in the barn yard. . . .

All this time the wind blew in terrific gusts from the four quarters of the compass, tearing away signs, capsizing tents, scattering the grit from the gravel banks with blinding force in everybody's eyes, and sweeping furiously around every crook and corner in search of some sinner to smite. . . . Yet in the midst of the general wreck and crash of matter, the business of trading in claims went on as if the zephyrs of Virginia were as soft and balmy as those of San Francisco. . . . Nobody seemed to own the lots except by right of possession; yet there was trading in lots to an unlimited extent. Nobody had any money; yet everybody was a millionaire in silver claims. Nobody had any credit, yet everybody bought thousands of feet of glittering ore. Sales were made at the most astounding figures—but not a dime passed hands. All was silver underground, and deeds and mortgages on top; silver, silver everywhere, but scarce a dollar in coin. The small change had somehow gotten out of the hands of the public into the gambling saloons.

3

Each mining camp looked the same as the next one, but from their names it was sometimes possible to deduce the richness—or lack of it—of the diggings or the physical characteristics of the site. More frequently, a camp's name reflected the miners' avocations and geographical origins or commemorated some spectacular occurrence in the neighborhood. Back in California there were Rough and Ready, Lousy Level, Gouge Eye, You Bet, Red Dog, Shirt Tail Canyon, Flapjack Canyon, Murderer's Bar, Hell's Half Acre, Devil's Retreat, Humbug Creek, and Whiskey Bar. In

Nevada there were Challenge, Bullion, Imperial, Branch Mint, Rock Island, Baltimore, Kentuck, Yellow Jacket, Let-Her-Rip, Root-Hog-or-Die, and Justice.

In 1860, following a strike near Pierce, on the Clearwater, the miners' frontier was extended north and eastward to Idaho, and in 1862 prospecting parties crossed the Continental Divide into Montana. When it was reported that they had found gold on the Beaverhead River, the original discoverers were soon joined by "yonders"—miners from other areas of the mountains—and "greenhorns"—men making their first try at digging gold. More than four hundred wintered in what was called Bannock City, after the Indian tribe of that region.

The next year prospectors found gold on Alder Creek, west of the Beaverhead. As their provisions were running low, one of the men in the discovery party was sent back to Bannock for supplies, first being sworn to secrecy. But a close-mouthed miner in town on such an errand was watched closely, and two hundred hunch-players dogged his footsteps back to Alder Creek. They had cause to congratulate themselves: the site proved to be the richest in gold ore of any in the West. More than $30,000,000 worth of gold was taken from the diggings in the first three years.

Toward the end of July in 1863, thirteen miners, carrying $25,000 worth of Montana gold dust in buckskin pouches, arrived at Fort Benton, the northwestern terminus for Missouri River steamboats. They were anxious to return to civilization with their loot, and since no steamboat was scheduled to sail, they decided to build a boat and float downriver to some point where they could secure more stylish transportation. Although warned that they would face hostile Sioux for many miles of their passage, the miners went ahead with their boat-building and confidently started on their way home. They were never heard from again.

The mystery was solved in 1871, when William Keyes, a trader wintering on the Missouri near Rocky Point, married an Indian girl. Keyes' buckskin pouch of gold dust reminded her that she had seen just such a pouch in the possession of a squaw. Questioned by Keyes, his wife related the following story:

Eight years before, a hundred-lodge band of Sioux were encamped on the river. One day they had sighted a boatload of
white men on their way downstream and immediately had begun
firing on them. The whites retaliated by loading and firing a
cannon, but the net effect was to do more damage to the boat
than to the Indians. The heavy recoil ripped a plank loose from
the hull and water began to pour in. The men had nothing
aboard to caulk the hole, but they managed to guide the craft to
a sand bar before it could sink. But this was only to exchange one
death for another. On that unsheltered spot in broad daylight,
within easy range of the Sioux arrows, one by one the men were
picked off. When none remained alive, the Sioux crossed over in
their canoes and plundered the boat. They found the buckskin
bags of gold dust, but not knowing what the yellow stuff was they
emptied it out, keeping only the bags. One of them came into the
possession of the squaw whom Keyes' wife had known; she had
preserved it as a trophy of the occasion.

Subsequently, Keyes and his wife got the squaw to show them
her keepsake and the spot on the river where the men had died.
In the spring they traveled to Fort Benton and interested a
rancher in returning with them to hunt for the gold dust. But in
eight years the sand bar had shifted, and though a minute amount
of the gold was recovered, no trace of the missing thirteen men
was ever found.

The Big Thaw

WHILE POPULAR INTEREST was centered on overland travel, steamboats on the upper Missouri played an important role in supplying miners and traders in Montana. Between 1863 and 1870 about
85,000 tons of cargo were carried to and from Fort Benton. In
two years alone—1867 and 1868—$25,000,000 worth of minerals
were transported to St. Louis from the gold fields. Hazards were

not confined to navigating the treacherous Missouri. The men stationed at the isolated forts along the river faced the dangers of severe weather and hostile Indians while gathering wood to fuel the ships and furs to send down river to St. Louis.

The ice was three feet thick on the upper Missouri in the winter of 1865–1866, and the snow was so deep that the trails around Fort Union were impassable. As a result, Ben Arnold Connor, who usually spent the winter hauling in the furs from outlying trading posts, was out of a job. Needing to make a little money, Ben and a few others at the fort decided to go out trapping and hunting on their own account until work was again available in the spring.

They made their headquarters at a small deserted trading post located between the confluence of the Yellowstone and Missouri rivers. The post consisted of two houses about thirty yards apart, with a stockade connecting their ends to form a courtyard in between. Connor, Henry Nelson, and two other men occupied one cabin, some Mexicans and Frenchmen with their Indian women lived in the other. From time to time someone would walk the few miles up the frozen Missouri to Fort Union and tote back coffee, flour, sugar, and other supplies. The partners busied themselves hunting and, when the weather permitted, cutting wood to sell to the steamboats for fuel the following summer.

As the long hard winter dragged to its weary end, an unseasonably warm period caused the deep snow to melt with excessive rapidity. An Indian relative of one of the camp women came to warn the hunters to leave the lowlands before the river rose, but one of them airily replied that if the water got high they would move. However, it was not to be so simple as all that, as Ben Connor's account testifies.

> One night [Connor wrote] I was aroused from a half slumber by the sound of water splashing against the house and running under the door. I yelled, "Here's the water now," and stepped out into ice-cold water up to my ankles. I lit a candle and we got dressed as well as we could. There was no time to plan anything. Henry Nelson proposed that we try to wade

out and I immediately agreed. . . . I took nothing with me
except a blanket, even leaving my gun behind. . . . Henry
carried a five-shooter pistol.

In the darkness we felt and splashed our way out the gate,
taking, as we thought, the direction toward the nearest high
land. Not until we had gone some distance in the timber did
we recall that there were several low channel beds [ahead of
us]. It would be impossible to reach high land, almost two
miles away without passing through swimming-depth water.
In addition to the darkness there was a heavy fog. Neither of
us could remember the direction of the stockade we had left a
few minutes before. The water was rising; the large cakes of
ice striking the trees, breaking off dead trunks and grinding
against each other, gave anything but a pleasant sensation.
Smaller trees were torn up by the roots as if they were frail
garden weeds.

By this time water was up to our waists and as cold as ice
could make it. While there was not much current, we had to
keep our hands before us to ward off small chunks of ice and
driftwood floating down stream. . . . Not knowing where we
were going, any step might plunge us into the channel of the
river beyond our depth. Notwithstanding our exertions our
legs and hands were becoming numb. . . . Henry and I were
but a few yards apart, struggling with every step but saying
nothing. Finally I spoke up, "Henry, we are lost." "I'll fire my
gun," he said. "There's a chance." He fired his pistol into the
air with stiffened fingers. No sooner had he done this than I
asked him, "Save one of those shells for me. I don't want to
freeze to death. If we've got to go, I want to go instantly."

Then suddenly a distant light flared up. We floundered
over to it, and found that our two companions had clambered
up to the dirt roof of our cabin and had started a fire when
they heard our shot. They helped us to the roof, where we
found bedding, an ax, some nails and rope, which they had
shoved through the chimney hole. We wrapped ourselves in
dry blankets and sat by the fire, with limbs numb and teeth
chattering. . . .

Across the courtyard we could see the occupants of the
other cabin, consisting of two Mexicans, two Indian women,
Dutch John, and a Frenchman named La France, also build-

ing a fire. . . . The distance between our roof retreats was not great, yet we had to yell at the top of our voices to be heard above the roar of the river. . . . The whole night long swirling waters swept just under the roof of the house, which would have floated off except for its mooring to the stockade posts set deep in the frozen ground.

Daylight revealed a picture of desolation which left the partners heartsick. The flood extended for two miles on every side of their refuge. The products of all their winter labor had been swept away. The great ricks of cordwood, the packs of skins, and the ice house filled with slaughtered game were all on their way downstream. When the fog lifted, over on the other house, they could see Dutch John prying out the roof logs, which he bound together into a raft. This makeshift lifeboat was tied to a corner of the cabin. Connor and Henry Nelson followed Dutch John's prudent example, planning to use the raft only if the house was swept away.

That night the crash of great chunks of ice hurtling through the trees and the crunch of the floes as they were borne along the swollen stream filled the rooftop refugees with terror. Smaller chunks struck the house, sending tremors through the uncertain structure, and threatening to destroy it. Just before daybreak they heard the roar of a cannon at Fort Union, which they interpreted to mean that a rescue would be attempted. Before they had much chance to rejoice at this prospect, a great chunk of ice came butting its way through the trees and careened into the house Dutch John's party was on, pushing it off its foundations. Transferring to their raft, the group tried to pole it out of the current, but succeeded only in drifting it among the big cottonwood trees, where at least they were protected from the floating ice. Having taken no provisions aboard the raft, they were delighted to find that a porcupine had taken refuge in one of the cottonwood trees. Shot and roasted, it provided a meager meal.

Another long, anxious day went by. Although they saw many forest animals—elk, deer, rabbits—floating by on the ice cakes, there was no point in shooting them for food, since they had no means of retrieving them. Connor was especially struck by the sight of four buffaloes, drifting along as serenely as though they were safe on the prairie grasses.

On the fourth day the immense cakes of ice had largely disappeared, leaving the flood water open. Now it was possible for a boat to navigate the stream without the risk of being ground to splinters. About noon a shout went up that the mackinaw boat was coming down from Fort Union. It first took aboard the people on the raft, then lowered Connor's party down from the cabin and ferried them to the north bank of the river. From there it was an easy walk back to the fort.

Feeling that they had seen enough of the upper Missouri for awhile, Connor and two of his companions jumped at the chance to go downriver on the first mackinaw boat to leave for St. Louis with a cargo of furs.

For a twenty-year period ending in 1869, the brilliant red and green Concord stages jounced across the prairies, mountains, and deserts, carrying mail and passengers to and from points in the trans-Missouri country and the Far West. In 1850, United States mail service began between Independence and Salt Lake City, and the next year from Salt Lake City to Sacramento. The through service inaugurated in 1857 by the Butterfield Line proved inadequate, and in 1859, William Russell, to meet the demand of the burgeoning Rocky Mountain mining communities, established the Leavenworth and Pikes Peak Express, which ran along the Republican and Solomon rivers to Denver. A financial failure from the beginning, it was eventually transferred to the Platte Valley route and combined with the Russell, Majors and Waddell service to Salt Lake. But the losses sustained in organizing the "L. & P. P." and, subsequently, the Pony Express were too great for the firm to bear, and it went under.

After the outbreak of the Civil War, the Butterfield

Overland Mail was transferred from the southern to the central route, and given an annual million-dollar government contract to run a daily mail service to California. Letter mail was supposed to go through in twenty days, but Butterfield could not maintain the schedule and, according to James C. Olson, "the whole operation was denounced as a fraud and a humbug. Ben Holladay purchased the line in 1862 and, despite Indian difficulties in 1864, greatly improved and extended the service. Wells, Fargo purchased the lines in 1866 and continued to operate them until the completion of the transcontinental railroad."

Aboard the Overland Stage

"YOU MAY START by stage to the gold regions about Denver City or Pikes Peak," wrote Sir Richard Burton in 1860, "and thence, if not accidentally or purposely shot, you may proceed by an uncertain ox-train to Great Salt Lake City, which latter part cannot take less than thirty-five days. On the other hand there is 'the great emigration route' from Missouri to California and Oregon, over which so many thousands have travelled within the past few years. I quote from a useful little volume, *The Prairie Traveller*, by Randolph B. Marcy, Captain U. S. Army. 'The track is broad, well worn, and cannot be mistaken . . . .' "

Equally unmistakable were the outlines of the stagecoach universally used, the Concord, made at the city of that name in New Hampshire. It had an arching roof with a railing around the outer edge. In front was the boot where the driver sat with his feet braced against the footboard. Behind his feet were the treasure box, a set of tools, a buffalo robe, a water bucket, and mail pouches. On the back of the coach was the rear boot, a sort of projecting platform covered with a leather curtain. This carried baggage, express, and mail; excess mail and packages were tied on top. Inside the coach were two benches facing each other, furnished with leather cushions and hinged padded backs; each accommodated three. Between them was a broad strap running crosswise of the vehicle to be used as a spare seat; another strap served as a backrest. It could accommodate three, but any passenger who had to ride the spare seat for the nineteen days and nights it took to get from Missouri to California never forgot the experience—assuming he recovered from it.

There were three divisions on the famous daily Overland Stage Line: Atchison, Kansas, to Denver; Denver to Salt Lake City; Salt Lake City to Placerville. These grand divisions were subdivided into runs of from two hundred to two hundred and fifty miles. Bossing the whole operation was the general superintendent; under him were the three division superintendents who bossed the agents in charge of the subdivisions. These latter distributed hay and grain to the stations on their run, and saw to it that the coaches were kept greased and in repair, the horses shod, and the harness mended. The stations, which were from ten to twelve miles apart, were of two types: swing stations, in the charge of a stock tender, at which the horses were changed; and home stations, which were larger and were where the driver was changed and meals were served. The blacksmith and repair shops were at division points, which also were replacement centers for men and animals.

Samuel Bowles, a Massachusetts editor, who traveled on the line in 1865, described the facilities in this way: "The barns and houses are of logs or prairie turf, piled up layer on layer, and smeared over or between with clayey mud. The turf and mud make the best houses, and are used for military forts and for fences around the cattle and horse yards. Their roofs, where covered, are a foot thickness of turfs, sand, clay, and logs or twigs, with an occasional inside lining of skins or thick cloth. Floors are oftenest such as nature offers only. . . . Our meals at the stage station continued very good throughout the ride; the staples were bacon, eggs, hot biscuit, green tea and coffee, dried peaches and

apples, and pies were as uniform. Each meal was the same; breakfast, dinner and supper were undistinguishable save by the hour;
and the price was $1 or $1.50 each. The devastations of the
Indians last summer and fall, and the fear of their repetition,
form the occasion and excuse for enormous prices for everything
now upon the Plains. . . ."

Though prices had gone up, the food at the stage stations
apparently had improved since Burton, in 1860, complained of
"doughnuts, green and poisonous with saleratus, suspicious eggs
in a massive greasy fritter, and rusty bacon, intolerably fat; we
thought 50 cents a dear price to pay." Another traveler, a year or
two after Burton, remarked that "the usual meal is fat ham and
eggs, or boiled pork, potatoes, and bread that looks as if it were
baked in black ashes, while the coffee is the very vilest stuff. . . .
The fact is that they never expect to see passengers again, so they
give them as little as they can and charge as much as possible."
In fact, prices increased steadily during the Civil War, and by
1867 it cost $175 to go from the Missouri to Denver—nearly
twenty-seven cents a mile.

1

▪ During the 1850's, as a rule, the Indians did not bother the
coaches, but after the Civil War had drained troops from the
military posts in the plains and mountains, there were frequent
and violent displays of Indian hostility. For years they had chafed
under the constant pressure of expanding settlement; with growing apprehension they had seen the procession of wagons rolling
westward and the destruction and driving away of the game. The
stringing of the "talking wires" through their domain, the increasing activity on the trails, and the punitive measures taken by the
military after the uprising of the Santee Sioux in Minnesota
added to their fears and hatred, and when the withdrawal of
troops gave them an opportunity for reprisal they took it. In
1862, their repeated attacks on stagecoaches and stations west of
Fort Laramie forced Ben Holladay to move the stage route from
the Oregon Trail south to the Overland Trail.

Eighteen sixty-four was a bloody year on the plains. On

August 7, the Cheyenne, Arapaho and Brule Sioux, after a series of isolated raids, "launched a concerted attack upon stagecoaches, immigrant trains, stations and ranches all along the central and western stretches of the Platte Valley. That day and the next they struck every station and ranch between Julesburg and Fort Kearney. . . . The attack spread to the valley of the Little Blue; here there was no telegraph to warn the settlers and station keepers, and the loss of life was considerably greater. The entire Nebraska frontier was thrown into a state of panic."

At such a time it took a courageous man to drive his stint. On August 8 the rumor came to Atchison that Liberty Farm Station on the Blue River near the Platte had been burned and the station keeper and his family massacred. In the face of this report, none of the drivers—with one exception—was very eager to take the stage out that day. The exception, a young man noted for his skill with a team, was Robert Emery. His brother was the station keeper at Liberty Farm.

Leaving Atchison with nine passengers—two women and seven men—Emery arrived the next day at Big Sandy Station, forty-four miles from Liberty Farm. After a halt while the passengers breakfasted and the horses were changed, the stage started up the divide which separates the Big Blue and the Little Blue. It was a beautiful morning, and they rolled along peacefully till about eleven o'clock. A few miles past Kiowa Station, a rough road of spurs and gulleys ran up a valley whose width gradually dwindled until it reached a point called The Narrows, with hills on one side and the river on the other. Just as they were approaching The Narrows, Emery saw ahead a band of Cheyennes in full war-paint, the sunlight glinting on their lances.

In a moment the quick-thinking driver whirled the horses about and, laying whip to their backs, started back down the road at a dead run. The terrified passengers jumped to their feet, but Emery called to them: "If you value your lives, for God's sake keep your seats or we are lost."

The Indians riders gained on the stage horses, cumbered as they were by the heavy coach. Closer and closer they came, in spite of the desperate efforts of the driver and the horses. Inside the coach the passengers shrieked and groaned. Only young Emery remained cool. At two points abrupt turns compelled him to slow the horses almost to a halt, to the intense consternation of the passengers. But an attempt to make the sharp turns at the speed they had been going would have resulted in an overturned coach and massacre of the whole party. The savages now came within range, and showers of arrows were fired. So many of them struck the coach and stuck in its sides that it looked like a porcupine. Emery was grazed in several places, and one arrow cut the rosette off the bridle of the off-side wheel horse.

George Constable, who was taking a train of twenty-five wagons to Denver, saw the coach and its pursuers coming along the road while they were still a mile away. At once he gave the order to corral and by the time Emery came rattling up the circle was made, except for a space wide enough for him to drive the coach through. Protected by the guns of the tough freighters, the wobbly-legged passengers emerged one by one from the coach. When they had somewhat recovered, they expressed their gratitude to their driver, and thanked God both that Robert Emery had been handling the reins and that they inside the coach, who had succumbed to panic, had not been in a position to interfere.

2

In the fall of 1865, a wagon train of ninety soldiers convalescing from wounds and illness set out from Fort Laramie for Fort Leavenworth, where they would be hospitalized. Sergeant Stewart, a veteran Indian fighter, was placed in charge of the party, each member of which had been issued a Spencer rifle and plenty of ammunition. At Julesburg, Colorado, a large freight train of Pikes Peakers returning from the gold fields joined the hospital train, providing added protection from Indian attack.

When the double train reached the first stage station west of Alkali, Nebraska, the division agent rushed out to greet them with the news that the stage due in from the east was, at that very moment, being attacked by the red men. The wagonmaster, Finn Burnett, quickly corralled the train and posted the teamsters under the wagons. At the same time, a party of the least infirm soldiers and some of the teamsters mounted horses and followed Sergeant Stewart down the trail toward the cloud of dust which indicated the approach of the stagecoach.

At a distance of about a mile, they could make out the coach rolling and swaying behind its three pairs of horses, with the driver high above them, plying his whip and urging them on. Indians on their alert little ponies flanked the flying vehicle, keeping up a veritable tattoo on its sides with arrows, hurled lances, and tomahawk strikes. Sergeant Stewart quickly noted that the stagecoach road passed through a coulee which would provide a perfect place for an ambush. He ordered his men to take cover on each side of the road. By the time they were in position, the hoofbeats of the horses, the yells of the driver, and the whoops of the Indians were plainly heard.

Into the draw bumped the coach, the whirling wheels throwing sand into the air. Hard after it came the horde of Indians, stripped to the waist and waving war clubs and knives as they closed in for the kill. Just as they drew abreast of Stewart he gave the command to fire; the volley crashed out and almost half of the attackers fell. A second volley thinned their ranks still more, and the remaining warriors whirled about and fled in panic and confusion.

The stage driver, who had eyes only for the road ahead, was unaware of his deliverance; he kept going all-out right up to the station. Stewart and his men followed at a leisurely gallop. When they pulled up beside the coach and its panting horses, the passengers were still trying to assimilate the news that the hated redskins had been routed.

After the double train moved out from Alkali on the road over which the stage had come, lances, war clubs, and arrows scattered for miles along the way testified to the ordeal the travelers had gone through in their race for life. Only the fact that the Indians coveted the excellent stage horses, and were unwilling to kill them, had prevented a massacre long before help could have arrived.

The dispossession of the Indian proceeded inexorably in every area of white penetration. The Forty-Niners, in their quest for gold, brooked no interference from the hundred thousand Indians living in California. The miners used every pretext to exterminate the "Diggers"—the contemptuous term they applied indiscriminately to all Indians—and nearly succeeded in doing so before the Paiutes and other tribes of the region were placed on reservations. But in the mountains of the Southwest it was another story. For more than twelve years the Apaches and the Navahos bitterly resisted the white man, and their submission was obtained only after a major military campaign (1863–1864) during which a hundred and forty-three battles were fought, nearly seven hundred Indians killed, and nine thousand captured.

But even more troublesome than the Indians of the Southwest were the Plains tribes—Sioux, Crow, Cheyenne, Arapaho, Comanche, and Kiowa—who, for more than two decades, fought to preserve their hunting grounds from the encroachment of white hunters, emigrants, and settlers. This is not to say that warfare was continuous throughout this period. The Plains Indian Wars, as Donald F. Danker has written, "were not massive sustained hostilities between two armies; they were, rather, a series of skirmishes, punitive campaigns, scouting and patrolling expeditions conducted by the United States Army against tribesmen who might one month be peaceably receiving annuities at their agency and the next raiding traffic and installations along the overland trails or hunting in areas to which they were prohibited entry by treaty agreement."

The Princess of Fort Laramie

ALTHOUGH THE CONCEPT of a permanent "Indian country" closed to white settlement was not finally and officially repudiated until 1854, a new policy calling for a concentration of tribes within fixed boundaries had been put into effect three years earlier. At a council called at Fort Laramie—an American Fur Company trading post purchased and garrisoned by the government in 1849—chiefs of the Sioux, Mandan, Gros Ventres, Assiniboin, Crow, Blackfeet, Cheyenne, and Arapaho pledged themselves to keep the peace and agreed, in exchange for gifts and annuities, to the establishment of tribal boundaries and to allow the government to build roads and military posts.

Except for General William S. Harney's 1855 expedition against the Teton Sioux—a consequence of the "Mormon cow incident" the preceding year*—and Sumner's expedition against the Cheyenne in the summer of 1857—the decade following the Great Fort Laramie Treaty Council was a relatively peaceful one. But it was an uneasy peace at best. The Commissioner of Indian Affairs reported as early as 1852 that the tribes suffered "from the vast number of immigrants who pass through their country, destroying their means of support, and scattering disease and death among them," and the Indian agents protested strongly against General Harney's harsh measures, which instilled fear and distrust in Indian hearts.

*On August 17, 1854, a cow belonging to a party of Mormon immigrants strayed into a Sioux camp and was killed and eaten. When the Mormons protested, a squad of troops was sent out from Fort Laramie under the command of a brash, ignorant, and inexperienced officer, Lieutenant John Grattan. The Bear, chief of the Brule Sioux, did his best to be cooperative, but Grattan, too contemptuous of Indians to parley with them, opened fire on the camp, killing The Bear. There followed a fight in which Grattan and all his men were killed. The Battle of Ash Hollow (September 3, 1855), in which Harney's troops slaughtered more than a hundred Brules, including women and children, was the white man's brutal reprisal.

According to the terms of the Fort Laramie Treaty, the Indian lands ranged roughly from the central Plains to the western slopes of the Rockies, bounded to the north and south by Canada and Mexico. By the late fifties, however, the government, by means of threats and bribes, had moved the boundary westward to clear Kansas and Nebraska territories for settlement. All the while resentment was mounting among the Indians, and when the "fifty-niners" invaded the Cheyenne and Arapaho lands in Colorado it was the last straw.

There began a series of raids and reprisals which reached a peak in the summer and fall of 1864. The First Nebraska Cavalry, on furlough from the fighting in the South, was ordered to Fort Kearny, and this put an end to the concerted attacks along the Platte. Peace negotiations were under way when, on November 22, at Sand Creek, Colorado, Colonel J. M. Chivington led the Third Colorado Cavalry in a massacre of five hundred Cheyennes who had voluntarily surrendered to await the negotiations. This ended any hope of peace for the time being, but it did have the effect of rousing public sentiment against the military's approach to the Indian problem. In 1866 Congress appointed a Peace Commission to go among the tribes and try to discover under what terms the Indians would lay down their arms and agree to accept reservation status.

The commission was expected to arrive at Fort Laramie in June, and on March 9, Colonel Henry E. Maynadier, the commanding officer, reported to the Commissioner of Indian Affairs an event which, it seemed to him, augured well for the future efforts of the Peace Commission. On the previous day, Shan-ta-ga-lisk, or Spotted Tail, head chief of the Brule Sioux, had come to the fort to request that his daughter might be buried in the white graveyard. The officers and men at the fort had known the Indian princess well. Her name was Ah-ho-ap-pa, the Sioux word for wheat flour, which was the whitest thing they knew. Her story was written down by a young cavalry officer, Lieutenant (later) Captain Eugene F. Ware, then stationed at the fort. It is told here as he told it, in somewhat condensed form.

In August of 1864, half-breed runners were sent to bring in Chief Spotted Tail and the leading men of his tribe for a peace conference at Fort Laramie. The fort was not surrounded by walls or barricades; it was a large, rambling collection of one-story adobe buildings, some whitewashed and used for soldiers' quarters, others for stables and storehouses; with a dusty parade ground and a bleak landscape. It had a vast sutler store presided over by an elegant old-school Virginia gentleman; and there we met in the evening and discussed the best way to obtain and keep up friendly relations with the Indians, or keep them off.

On consultation at the sutler's store we deemed it best that the Indians should bring their wives and families to the council, and that we should have a feast and try to accomplish something of value, and if possible make a peace of a permanent character. Another runner was sent out, and after a while in came Shan-ta-ga-lisk and many of his warriors with their families and horses.

A pow-wow was had at which it seemed to be definite and understood that emigration was to be let alone, travelers were not to be molested, nor the overland telegraph wires disturbed. The consideration was principally something to eat, something to drink, and something to wear. The Indian women were presented with red blankets, bright calicoes, looking glasses, etc. Every evening the writer, as adjutant of the post, supervised a distribution of provisions. All of the Indian women sat down in a circle on the parade ground, into the middle of which were rolled barrels and boxes of flour, crackers, bacon, and coffee. Then from the Indian men two or three were selected who entered the ring and made the division with great solemnity, going around the large circle repeatedly. My instructions were to see that everything was fairly done, and the supplies properly divided.

As I came up to the ring on the day of the first division, an Indian girl was standing outside of the ring looking on. She was tall and well dressed, and about eighteen years of age. As the distribution was about to begin I went to her and told her to get in the ring, and motioned her where to go. She gave no sign of heed, looked at me as impassively as if she were a statue, and never moved a muscle. A few teamsters, soldiers, and idlers were standing around and looking on from a respectful distance. I shouted to Smith, the interpreter, to come over, and said to him: "Tell this squaw to get into the ring or she will lose her share."

Smith addressed her. When she replied, he looked puzzled and sort of smiled. "What does she say?" I asked.

"Oh, she says she is the daughter of Shan-ta-ga-lisk."

"I don't care whose daughter she is," I said. "Tell her to get into the ring, and get in quick."

Again Smith addressed and impatiently gestured. She made a reply. "What did she say?" I asked .

"Oh, she says that she don't go into the ring," said Smith.

"Then tell her that if she don't go into the ring she won't get anything to eat."

Back from her, through Smith, came the answer: "I have plenty to eat. I am the daughter of Shan-ta-ga-lisk."

So I let her alone, and she stood and saw the division, and then went off into the Indian camp. Every evening food was distributed and she came and stood outside of the ring alone, acting as before. During the day she came to the sutler's store, and sat by the door watching, as if she was feeding from the sights she saw.

She was particularly fond of watching guard mount in the morning and dress parade in the evening. As I officiated principally on these occasions I put on a few extra touches for her special benefit, at the suggestion of Major Wood. I always appeared in an eighteen-dollar red silk sash, ostrich plume, shoulder straps, and about $200 worth of astonishing raiment, such as in the field we boys used to look on with loathing and contempt. It was a week or ten days that Ah-ho-ap-pa was around Laramie. We all knew her by sight, but she never spoke. At last she went away with her father's band up to Powder River. Her manner was known to us all, and she was frequently referred to as an Indian girl of great style and dignity. She saw everything, but asked no questions and expressed no surprise, nor a particle of emotion.

One evening in the sutler's store the officers of several regiments were hanging around when Elston, a Virginian who had become a trader and lived forty years among the Sioux with a Cheyenne wife, was asked if he knew Ah-ho-ap-pa. "Very well indeed," he said. "I have known her since she was a baby. She is very much stuck up, especially in the last four or five years; she won't marry an Indian; she always said that. Her father has been offered two hundred ponies for her, but won't sell her. She says she won't marry anybody but a 'capitán,' and that idea sort of pleases her father for more reasons than one. Among the Indians every officer, big or little, is a 'capitán.' She always carries a knife, and is as strong as a mule. One day a Blackfoot soldier running with her father's band tried to carry her off, but she fought and cut him almost to pieces—like to have killed him; tickled her father nearly to death. The young bucks seem to think a good deal of her, but all are afraid to tackle her. The squaws all know about her idea of marrying a 'capitán'; they think her head is level, but don't believe she will ever make it. She tried to learn to read and speak English once of a captured boy, but the boy escaped before she got it. She carries around with her a little bit of a red book, with a gold cross printed on it, that General Harney gave her mother many years ago. She's got it wrapped up in a parfleche [piece of dressed rawhide]. You ought to hear her talk when she is mad. She is a holy terror. She tells the Indians they are all fools for not living in houses and making peace with the whites."

Here for a time we leave the daughter of Shan-ta-ga-lisk. She had gone to Powder River with her father's band, and thirty days later the writer was started for the [Civil War] front. . . .

The war finally ended and peace was proffered to the Indian tribes. Commissioners were selected to make treaties for the western tribes. The disbanding armies poured to the West for homes and settlements, and hostile Indians were not again seen in the valley of the Platte. Early in 1866 General Grenville M. Dodge, commanding the Department of the Missouri [which included much of the region between the river and the Rockies], appointed Colonel H. E. Maynadier in charge of the sub-district at Laramie. Though the Indian troubles had slacked up, there was a force of about six hundred men at the post.

Let us now visit the Powder River, far north of Fort Laramie.

It was a cold and dismal day late in February, 1866. Ah-ho-ap-pa was dying of consumption. She had not seen a white person since her visit to Fort Laramie in 1864—during this time there had been a continued state of war. The camp of Shan-ta-ga-lisk had been moved backward and forward all over the Big Horn, Rosebud, and Tongue river country. Ah-ho-ap-pa's heart was broken. She could not stand up against her surroundings; in vain her father had urged her to accept the condition of things as they were and not worry over things out of reach.

Shortly before her death a runner from Laramie announced that commissioners would come with the grass, bringing the words of the Great Father to his Indian children. Shan-ta-ga-lisk was urged to send runners to all the bands south and west of the Missouri River to meet at Laramie as soon as their ponies could live on grass. Ah-ho-ap-pa heard the news, but it came too late. She told her father that she wanted to go, but she would be dead; that it was her wish to be buried in the cemetery at Fort Laramie where the soldiers were buried. This her father solemnly promised her.

When her death took place, after great lamentation among the band, the skin of a freshly killed deer was held over the fire and thoroughly permeated and creosoted with smoke, and Ah-ho-ap-pa was wrapped in it and the skin was tightly bound around her with thongs, so that she was temporarily embalmed. Shan-ta-ga-lisk sent a runner to announce that he was coming in advance of the commissioners to bury his daughter at Laramie.

The landscape was bleak, the streams were ice-covered, and the hills were speckled with snow. The two-hundred-and-sixty-mile trail was rough and mountainous. The two white ponies belonging to Ah-ho-ap-pa were tied together and the body carried upon them. Shan-ta-ga-lisk, with his principal warriors and a number of women, accompanied the dead princess on the sad journey. When within fifteen miles of Fort Laramie a runner was sent to announce the approach of the procession to Colonel Maynadier. The Colonel was a natural prince, a good soldier, and a good judge of Indian character. After conferring with his second in command, Major O'Brien, he dispatched an ambulance guarded by a company of cavalry in full uniform and followed by two twelve-pound howitzers, with postillions in red chevrons. The body was placed in the ambulance, and behind it were led the girl's two white ponies.

When the cavalcade had reached the river a couple of miles from the post, the garrison turned out, and with Colonel Maynadier at the head, met and escorted it into the post. The next day a burial scaffold was erected: it was made of tent poles embedded in the ground and fastened with thongs, over which a buffalo robe was placed. To the poles of the scaffold were nailed the heads and tails of the two white ponies, so that Ah-ho-ap-pa could ride through the hunting grounds of the sky.

A large, lavishly decorated coffin was made, and the body was placed in it, wrapped in a bright red blanket. Just before sunset the coffin was taken to the cemetery, mounted on the wheels of an artillery caisson. After it came a twelve-pound howitzer and the entire garrison in full uniform. The post chaplain suggested an elaborate burial service. "If I consent," asked Shan-ta-ga-lisk, "will she go to where the white men and women go?" Colonel Maynadier answered with a prompt and hearty "Yes." Shan-ta-ga-lisk was silent a long while, but finally assented. He then gave the chaplain the parfleche that contained the little book which General Harney had given Ah-ho-ap-pa's mother. The chaplain deposited it in the coffin. Then Colonel Maynadier stepped forward and deposited a pair of white kid cavalry gauntlets to keep her hands warm while she traveled to the sky, and Major O'Brien put in a crisp greenback to buy what she wanted on the journey.

The soldiers formed a hollow square, within which the Indians stood in a large ring around the coffin. During the reading of the burial service, Shan-ta-ga-lisk stood looking into the coffin, the personification of blank grief. Then each of the Indian women came up and spoke in turn to Ah-ho-ap-pa; when this was done one of them placed a little looking glass in the coffin, and the lid was fastened on. Then the women raised the coffin and placed it on the scaffold. A fresh buffalo robe was laid over it and bound down to the sides of the scaffold with thongs. At the word of command, the soldiers faced forward and fired three volleys in rapid succession. Then they and their visitors marched back to the post. The howitzer squad remained and built a large fire of pine wood, and fired the gun every half-hour all night, until daybreak.

In the morning a council was held at post headquarters; speeches were made, and the evil and misfortunes of the last five years were gone over. Colonel Maynadier told of the expected coming of the commissioners. "There is room enough for all of us in this broad country," he declared. Pointing to the silk flag hanging from the wall, he said to Shan-ta-ga-lisk, "My Indian brother, look at those stripes. Some of them are red, and some of them are white. They remain peacefully side by side—the red and the white—for there is room for each."

After this there was a brief interval of peace.

*

The Indian Wars of the '60's and '70's were waged over a vast area comprising western Kansas and Nebraska, eastern Colorado, Wyoming, Montana, and the Dakotas. In these prairie lands were the pastures of the great buffalo herds, and the buffalo was essential to the Indian way of life. If they lost their hunting grounds to the white men, the Indians knew that they were doomed.

The first major outbreak of the 1860's began on August 18, 1862, among the Santee Sioux on the reserve set aside for them along the Minnesota River. When troops were brought in to stamp out the rebellion, many Santees fled across the prairie toward the Missouri, carrying the war into Dakota Territory. "The uprising," writes Herbert S. Schell, "initiated a series of events that ultimately affected the entire Northern Plains region. [The war] spread to the northern subtribes of Teton Sioux. The wild Hunkpapas,

who roved from the Missouri to the Powder River Val-
ley under Sitting Bull's leadership, were bound to be-
come involved when hostile Santees fled to the rugged
badland region of the Little Missouri. . . . At the same
time, other hostiles, including bands of Oglalas and
Brules, as well as Cheyennes and Arapahos, were mov-
ing into the Powder River country from the region of
the Platte, rendering travel across the Northern Plains
to the Montana gold fields extremely hazardous.

"For the purpose of stabilizing the northern fron-
tier and keeping the traffic lanes open, the military
authorities undertook a campaign to bring the Teton
Sioux and other hostile tribes into subjection. They
also sought to maintain a line of forts along the Boze-
man Trail"—a wagon road they planned to build from
Fort Laramie to the gold fields.

War on the Plains

MINING CAMPS IN MONTANA had long protested the roundabout
routes of getting supplies. One way was up the Missouri River by
boat to Fort Benton and then over the Mullan Road; the other
was via the Oregon Trail to Fort Hall and then on to Virginia
City. The announcement of the federal government in 1865 that
it would build a road from Fort Laramie northwesterly to Bozeman, Montana, infuriated the Sioux, for the projected road
would pass through the heart of their hunting grounds. Peace
gestures failed. The Army was ordered to garrison Fort Reno and
to build Forts Phil Kearny and C. F. Smith to protect road construction crews. The Sioux savagely attacked every detachment
leaving the forts.

1

In December of 1866, Fort Phil Kearny, midway on the road, had been under siege by the Indians for days. It was difficult for the garrison even to secure firewood to keep themselves warm. On December 21 a woodcutting detail was attacked, and eighty men, commanded by Captain W. J. Fetterman, were sent to their rescue. In one brief hour the entire party was wiped out, leaving the fort in a perilous situation. Only a hundred and nineteen men remained within its walls, surrounded by more than three thousand exultant Sioux.

The temperature dropped to twenty-five degrees below zero, and the snow swirled about the fort drifting so high around the stockade that the men had to be kept shoveling snow away from its walls, for fear the Indians would be able to walk right over the stockade and storm the fort. Lights burned in all the quarters that night in anticipation of an attack at any moment.

Shortly before midnight two men walked toward the gate, their heads close together in earnest conversation. One of them was leading a horse. As they approached the gate, they were challenged by the sentry. When the countersign was given, he recognized the shorter of the men as Colonel Henry B. Carrington, the commander of the fort. After a moment or two of further talk, the other man mounted the horse and the Colonel, reaching up, took him by the hand, uttering the fervent words, "May God help you!" The horseman wheeled, passed through the gate, and started off at a trot on one of the famous rides in American history.

Earlier on that fearful night, Colonel Carrington had told the assembled men of the fort the desperate nature of their situation and the urgent need for someone to attempt to ride through the Sioux cordon and get word to Fort Laramie to send reinforcements. A civilian employee at the fort, John "Portugee" Phillips, volunteered to carry the message to the nearest telegraph operator, at Horseshoe Station. Colonel Carrington gave Phillips his own thoroughbred horse for the perilous ride, which would take three days.

After saddling up, Phillips went to the quarters of Lieutenant Grummond, one of the men killed that day in the massacre out in the forest. Grummond's grief-stricken young widow was a stranger to him, but Phillips handed to her a very fine buffalo robe, one of his most cherished belongings. Phillips told her he was going to try to summon help, and if he failed to get through the Indian lines, he wanted her to keep that robe in remembrance of him.

Once he was outside the fort, Phillips avoided the trail, riding parallel to it some distance away, for he knew well that the Indians would be watching for a messenger. He made no attempt to travel by day when he would surely be spotted by the keen-eyed savages. Before daybreak he would ride into a clump of brush and spend the day there, setting out as soon as darkness fell.

On the evening of the second day, he was chased by a number of Indians mounted on ponies, but his big thoroughbred outdistanced them and he rode up on top of a hill where he stood them off with his rifle and revolver. He stayed on the hill all night long, keeping vigil against surprise, but his pursuers did not attack him again. In the morning he made a run for it, made it through the Indian lines safely, and shortly afterward reached the telegraph station where he left the message with John C. Friend, the operator. Fearful that the lines might be down, Phillips pressed on the final fifty miles to Fort Laramie, arriving about eleven o'clock on Christmas night.

When he rode into the parade ground, his horse dropped dead under him. The great-hearted thoroughbred had carried him two hundred and thirty-six miles in four days, or fifty-nine miles each twelve hours, in deep snow and subzero weather, sustained only by the small amount of fodder Phillips had been able to carry in his light pack.

A brilliant Christmas party was in full swing at "Bedlam," the large building at the post used as the officers' clubhouse, where all festivities were held.

Phillips created a sensation when he staggered into the clubhouse—a swaying, gigantic figure swathed in a buffalo-skin overcoat, with buffalo boots, gauntlets, and cap; he was covered from head to foot with frozen snow, and his beard trailed icicles. He managed to gasp out that he was a courier from Fort Phil Kearny, with important dispatches from the commanding officer; then fatigue, privation, and exposure took their toll, and he dropped senseless to the floor.

Later, when he had been revived and given food and drink, he heard the good news that the telegraph message had gotten through and troops were already marching to the relief of Fort Phil Kearny.

2

Army posts along the upper Missouri were not near the telegraph; the only way they could send messages in winter was by couriers traveling on foot or on horseback. The hazardous work of carrying dispatches through territory occupied by hostiles often devolved on hired civilians—frontiersmen familiar with the terrain who could survive in the wilderness when soldiers from other parts of the country, and with little experience frontiering, would quickly have perished.

During the winter of 1868 the weather was so unusually severe and the Indians so frequently on the rampage that even extra large bonuses could not induce the regular mail carriers to travel the route above Fort Stevenson, an army post located about fifty miles from present Bismarck, North Dakota. However, the commander at Fort Buford, a hundred and twenty-five miles upriver, near the Montana border, was determined to open overland communication with the forts below him. He inquired among the guides and trappers, and finally Joseph L'Espagnol—"Joe the Spaniard," although he was actually a Mexican—volunteered to make the trip to Fort Stevenson on foot with a dog travois. The travois consisted of light wooden shafts, one end of which was fastened to the dog, the other ends dragging in the snow. A net suspended between them carried the mail and food for dog and man.

On February 13, 1868, Joe started on his way. He followed the river where possible, but avoided three Indian camps by leaving the stream's wooded protection and following the coulees in the prairie, thus keeping out of sight of the savages, who usually did not wander far out on the plains in the dead of winter. Joe got along so well his success made him over-confident. When he arrived at the mouth of Little Knife River he yielded to the temptation to stop at an abandoned cabin to rest and get warm even at the risk of being caught. The smoke of his breakfast fire was seen the next morning by a party of thirteen Indians who were hunting in the vicinity. They surrounded the cabin and three entered. One took his knife and cut the mail sack which was fastened to the travois. Joe, thinking there were only three Indians, tried to scare off the redskins by putting his hand to his revolver. They pounced upon him, jerked the gun out of his hand, beat him, and threw him on the ground. In the struggle he attempted to draw his knife but they seized it, and in wresting it from his hand cut deep gashes on the inside of his fingers. Then a blow on the head with the pistol knocked him senseless.

Terrible pains in his face brought him back to consciousness. The savages were amusing themselves by yanking out his whiskers and mustache in an effort to bring him to; his face was torn and bleeding. Next the redskins forced Joe to use every scrap of his provisions to cook them a meal; when he faltered they beat him unmercifully. They killed his dog, broke up the travois, and burned the mail. Then they stripped off all his clothes, leaving him nothing but an old pair of trousers and a shirt made of antelope hide. Rather than be left to freeze to death, Joe begged them to shoot him. One warrior promptly placed an arrow in his bow, but the leader stretched out his arm and forbade him to shoot. It was afterward supposed that since Joe had black hair and a very dark complexion his captors took him to be a half-breed Indian and spared his life on that account.

When he was finally left alone, the instinct of self-preservation asserted itself. Although he was weak from loss of blood and the beatings, Joe decided to try and reach Fort Berthold, the nearest army post. All night he walked and ran barefoot in the snow. The next day brought snow and wind which finally turned into a blizzard. In his half-conscious state Joe lost his sense of direction and started back toward the cabin, but at last his strength gave out and he lay down in the snow to die. At this juncture, a party of friendly Indians found him. Wrapping him in a buffalo robe, they fed him, dressed his wounds, and treated his frozen feet before carrying him on horseback to their village. A short time later they took him to Fort Berthold where he completely recovered. Outfitted by the post commander with fur moccasins and warm clothes, Joe went on to Fort Stevenson and made his report some three weeks after he had started from Fort Buford.

Was Joe discouraged about carrying the mail? Not a bit of it. He was anxious to leave the next day on the hundred-and-twenty-five-mile return trip to Fort Buford. He offered to take all the mail if he was furnished a horse; if no horse was available, he would sew the principal dispatches in the lining of his overcoat and make the trip on foot. He had contracted to make two trips for $200 and he was determined to have his $200 or die trying. Impressed by this display of courage, the officers at the fort supplied Joe with a horse, blankets, and ample provisions, and sent him on his way with their blessing.

3

The 1866 Peace Commission, for which such high hopes had been held, did not get very far. Although Brule and Oglala Sioux leaders came into Fort Laramie for another council, just when peace terms were being outlined Colonel Henry B. Carrington arrived with a large force to open the Bozeman Road and man the forts along it. The principal chief of the Oglalas, Red Cloud, and the other chiefs at once broke off negotiations, and hostilities were resumed.

The next year the Peace Commissioners again came to Fort Laramie and sent runners to the Sioux chiefs inviting them to parley, but the council was sparsely attended. Word came from Red Cloud that he would not meet with the white men again so long as the Bozeman Road remained open, and in April, 1868— to the intense disgust of the men in the Montana gold fields—the white men knuckled under. The Laramie Treaty of 1868 set aside the area in Dakota Territory from the Nebraska line to the 46th parallel between the Missouri River and the 104th degree of longitude as the Great Sioux Reservation. The area north of the North Platte in Nebraska and between the 104th meridian and the Big Horn Mountains remained Indian country; the military posts within it were removed, and the Bozeman Road leading to the mines was closed. This meant that the entire Powder River region had been abandoned to the red man. In return, the Indians agreed not to harass immigrant trains or the construction crews of the Union Pacific railroad, which had started laying track west of Omaha after the close of the Civil War. At the same time, they reserved the right to hunt on their old buffalo ranges in the region above the North Platte and along the Republican and Smoky Hill rivers "so long as the buffalo may range thereon, in such numbers as to justify the chase."

The treaty also called for a central agency for the Brules, the Oglalas, and other Sioux bands who had participated in the recent hostilities, to be located on Whetstone Creek, near Fort Randall in eastern Dakota Territory. But this site was unsatisfactory to the Sioux, and after a trip to Washington by Red Cloud, Spotted Tail (Shan-ta-ga-lisk), and other chiefs, the Spotted Tail agency was established on the White River two hundred and twenty-five miles west of the Missouri, while Red Cloud and the Oglalas were placed on the North Platte thirty miles below Fort Laramie.

However, these arrangements were not completed until 1871, and the summer of 1869 saw many troops in the field. One of several punitive expeditions was directed against the "Renegades," a corps of Indians from various tribes—mostly Sioux, Arapaho, and Cheyenne—which raided the settlers in the Saline and Solomon valleys of Nebraska and Kansas, killing a number of them, carrying away captives, and destroying property. General Philip Sheridan called for volunteers to form a company of mounted scouts which would hunt down and punish these Indians. Among the settlers who responded to the call there were many Civil War veterans as well as buffalo hunters and old-time frontiersmen.

On September 10, 1869, a company of fifty men led by Major George A. Forsythe, with Lieutenant Fred Beecher as second in command, set out from Fort Wallace, Kansas, in pursuit of an Indian band believed to number no more than two hundred and fifty. The Indians' trail led into Nebraska and westward along the Republican River. After following the trail for a few days, it was the opinion of the old hands that they were following a much larger number of Indians than had at first been estimated. Forsythe, far from being intimidated, ordered the men to press forward with all possible speed.

On the afternoon of September 16, Indian signs were fresh, and Forsythe ordered camp made early so that the men could prepare for action next day. The camp was situated on the bank of the Arickaree, a branch of the Republican near the Kansas-Colorado boundary line. A sandy island in the middle of the dry river bed was selected as a place to make a stand in case of an attack.

Just at daybreak on September 17, the redmen attacked, expecting to stampede the horses and throw the troops into a panic. Hard on the heels of the pickets, they descended on the camp like a mighty cloudburst, shouting and waving their blankets. Forsythe's men retreated with all haste to the island in the river, preparing as best they could to withstand the coming assault.

The Indians quickly formed for a charge, confident that they would overwhelm the scouts in short order. They were mightily disconcerted, however, when the new seven-shot repeating rifles poured volley after volley into their ranks, emptying scores of saddles. But they kept coming in the face of the fire, and soon the remnants of the charge swept over the defenders, friend and foe and riderless horses mingling in wild confusion. Beaten off, the Indians rode back to the hills skirting the river, picking up some of their dead and wounded as they went.

As opportunity offered, Forsythe's men dug into the sand with knives, scooping out shallow pits—foxholes—which afforded them some protection. Indians began crawling toward the trenches through the tall grass, and whenever a scout raised his head it became a target; similarly, whenever the grass moved, a bullet sped from the island. During the first hour of the assault every one of the defenders' horses was killed.

About ten o'clock, Roman Nose, a courageous Cheyenne chief who was said to bear a charmed life, rallied his men on the bank. Several scouts centered their fire on the chief as, lance in hand, he led the attack. Struck by a dozen bullets, the chief reeled in his saddle, but saved himself from falling by grasping his horse's mane. His warriors gathered around him and bore him from the field, mortally wounded. Thus the second charge was turned back.

About two-thirty in the afternoon, a scout keeping watch with field glasses reported that the celebrated Cheyenne chieftain, Dull Knife, was preparing to lead a charge. Famous as a prophet and wise man, Dull Knife was one of the signatories of the treaty made at Fort Laramie in 1868. He now appeared in full ceremonial dress, wearing a gorgeous war bonnet reaching from the crown of his head to the ground. After haranguing the braves, he took his place in the lead, and swung his rifle over his head as a signal that the charge was to begin. Major Forsythe, lying wounded in his foxhole, ordered the men not to fire until the enemy was in close range. As the charge swept toward them, rifle fire crackled from the island, and one of those who fell was Dull Knife. His horse turned and fled to the hills, followed by the warriors. Here they were met by the squaws, with poles and clubs, threatening them and urging them to return for the chief. Recalled to their manhood, they marched back on foot and rescued their wounded leader amid a hail of bullets.

The Indians now settled down to starve out the defenders. Half of the scouts were wounded, and among the dead was Lieutenant Beecher, for whom the island was later named. The doctor also died during the day, so the wounded men had no medical care. Neither food nor water was available until darkness came; then they dug a hole six feet deep and secured enough muddy water to fill their canteens.

A council was held, and it was decided to send a request for help to Fort Wallace, eighty-five miles away. Jack Stillwell and Pete Trudell, able scouts, volunteered to make the attempt to slip through the Indian lines. Starting at midnight, they were only three miles from the island by daybreak. They lay hidden until nightfall under a hollow bank overhung with grass and sunflowers. The second day they hid in a swamp, in uncomfortable proximity to an Indian village. On the third morning they felt that they were now far enough away from the battlefield to travel in the daylight hours, but got a nasty shock when they sighted a group of Cheyennes. Luck was with them, for lying on the prairie was an old buffalo carcass with enough hide still hanging from its bones to screen them. The two scouts crawled into this inelegant shelter and remained in it until the foe was out of sight. Later on they met two messengers en route to the camp of a Negro cavalry company commanded by Colonel Carpenter, and passed the word of Forsythe's situation to them before hurrying on to Fort Wallace.

In the meantime, the Indians continued to besiege the island. On the night of the third day no help having arrived, it was concluded that Stillwell and Trudell had been killed. Two more men were sent out, but now no one had any hope of leaving the island alive. The wounded, without drugs to help ease the pain of their wounds, suffered greatly. The only food was tainted horse meat, which was sprinkled with gun powder to disguise the taste.

On the morning of the ninth day after the battle, the worn and weary men were roused by cries of "Indians! Indians!" from the sentinels. With ammunition low and spirits lower, every man felt that the end had come, but they crawled into position determined to make the Indians pay a fearful price for victory.

On the distant hill could be seen a line of men riding at great speed. As they drew nearer, the glitter of sabers and carbines in the sunlight told the powder-stained veterans that this was not another Indian charge; Colonel Carpenter's cavalry had arrived. Men embraced each other, tears rolling down their cheeks, and cheer upon cheer went up for their Negro rescuers. Thus ended the famous Battle of the Arickaree in which fifty volunteer scouts stood off nearly a thousand seasoned warriors. In this clash, one of the most disastrous for the red men in the Plains Wars, the Indians lost between seven and eight hundred braves.

A Battle with Plains Bandits

IN THE 60's before the completion of the railroad from Kansas City to Denver, Colorado-bound immigrants had to cross a stretch of western Kansas infested by bands of hostile Indians. Even after the government had established a chain of forts in the area, the route remained hazardous, for the Indian menace was not the only one. During the period immediately after the Civil War, swarms of border ruffians, bushwhackers, and army deserters from both sides roamed the country, preying on travelers and settlers. Sometimes a group of these renegades would join forces with a band of hostiles; others, even more to be feared, would form their own gangs and operate disguised as redskins. So great was the danger from these badmen that a post commander would routinely hold travelers at the fort until they had gathered in sufficient strength either to be able to defend themselves or to forestall the threat of an attack by virtue of their numbers. For most of the migrants this arrangement was a satisfactory one, but there were some who chafed at the delay and looked for opportunities to give the military the slip.

John Royer and Ed Schammel were two of these impatient spirits. When they arrived at Fort Wallace late in October, 1867, the post commander was detaining all travelers until the jaded oxen belonging to some of the trains were rested up; then all could move on together in safety. Royer and Schammel, eager to press on to the wonderful new town of Denver, decided to be on their way in spite of the soldiers. Both men were entirely unacquainted with the West, but they had a good outfit for a quick trip across the plains: a team of excellent young mules, a strong, light wagon with bows and a canvas top, a superior assortment of camping equipment and cooking utensils, and a plentiful supply of ammunition. Worth in all several hundred dollars, the outfit was a prize to arouse the cupidity of any bandits who might be hanging around the fort.

Travelers were allowed outside the fort to secure fuel or to look after stray stock, and Royer and Schammel put forward such reasons as these as pretexts for several trips outside, each time taking part of their baggage which they concealed in a ravine. They had hired an old Indian fighter, Long Texas, as a guide, and when an opportune moment came the three men drove their wagon past the unsuspecting sentry and out of the fort. At the ravine they loaded up their supplies and were soon well on their way, thanking their lucky stars that military red tape was no longer holding them up—and totally unaware that their every move had been watched by a gang of bloodthirsty desperadoes.

At midday, many miles from the protection of the fort, they made their camp on a dry creek. They had finished eating dinner and were hitching up when Long Texas noticed that the mules were uneasy. Reading the danger signal, he announced that they could expect an attack at any moment.

Royer, a good shot, was posted at the back opening of the wagon sheet and Schammel, a good hand with the reins, did the driving; Texas kept watch. For a couple of hours nothing happened, but the mules and the old plainsman were not fooled. As they were driving up a little draw, they saw three men ahead. Texas told his companions not to fire until he did. There was no reason to get rattled, he said, for likely they would be the victors.

The three horsemen closed in swiftly, blocking the way of the team. When their leader shouted to halt, the old guide responded with a shot that killed him, and Royer's fire killed the horse of another man. Schammel, unused to such affrays, whipped the team into a run, spoiling the aim of the marksmen, or that might have been the end of the battle. But as it was, in a few minutes about twenty Indians led by the two surviving bandits rode up from the rear, split into two groups, and streamed past each side of the wagon, firing as they went by. In the resultant hail of bullets the canvas wagon cover was punctured but no one was hit. The attackers, now more cautious, kept up their fire from a distance. After an hour of intermittent sniping their tactics paid off: a bullet struck Schammel and he tumbled out of the wagon, dead.

When Royer and Texas got down to pick up his body, the marauders charged them but were dispersed by a few bullets.

Since it would soon be night Texas now headed the team back toward Fort Wallace, hoping to escape in the darkness; however, constant pressure from the bandits caused him to drift northward. The running battle continued until night blotted out the scene, by which time two more of the attackers had lost their horses. Under cover of darkness, Royer and Long Texas buried their companion. During the dark hours they rested themselves and their tired team.

The respite ended at daybreak when the bandits again rushed upon the wagon, whooping and cursing. Yells and threats in English made it evident that many were either whites or half-breeds. Two of their number fell in this fresh assault and the attackers, burning for revenge, determined on a fight to the finish with the plucky travelers. On the preceding day the mules had not been targets, for they were part of the booty which had inspired the attack. Now, one was wounded in the shoulder and unable to walk without limping. The weather turned bitterly cold with a biting wind from the north. Long Texas and Royer were both wounded, but there was nothing for it but to keep going. The country was rugged and wild and there was no sign of help. As the hours dragged on, the team was tiring fast and to lighten the load the men threw away everything except the ammunition.

Late in the afternoon, being momentarily out of sight of their pursuers, they stopped the wagon by a stream. Royer, whose breath was coming at shorter and shorter intervals, asked Texas to give him a drink of water and let him die there by the little stream. They were his last words. Not daring to let the enemy know he was now alone, the old plainsman propped the body up in the driver's place. Thus even in death Royer aided his companion; the marauders had a healthy respect for the rifles in the wagon and did not press the attack.

The team was exhausted and the wounded mule fell several times, but Tex kept urging them on. His experience in border warfare made his chances for escape good if he could only prolong the fight until dark. The pursuers were no longer following so closely, taking it for granted their prey was in their grasp.

When night came, Tex pulled into a little ravine and buried Royer in a shallow grave. This was nearly his undoing. The bandits, hearing the sound of the shovel, poured in a volley of bullets, killing one of the mules and breaking Tex's left wrist. But crippled though he was, and exhausted from the two-day fight, he nonetheless carried on with his plan for escape. Having removed his store of ammunition, he set fire to the wagon, and, as he had anticipated, the bandits made a rush to take him alive. This was Tex's cue to slide away into the shadows. He had almost made it outside the encircling and tightening human noose when one of the pursuers, mistaking Tex for a fellow bandit, called out in broken English that he must hurry to be in at the kill. Tex ran with him a little way, but as soon as possible veered off and dove into the stormy night.

Now the blowing sand and spiteful snow flurries were his friends. Pausing presently to take breath, he looked back at the blaze which lighted up the ravine and outlined the figures closing in on their supposed victim. He heard their shouts of triumph change suddenly to howls of rage as they realized their quarry had escaped.

Protected by the foul weather and darkness, Tex headed straight east and, as he thought, toward Fort Wallace. But in fact he was due north of the fort, so every step took him farther from safety. All night he staggered along in a half-crazed delirium, the awful scenes of the past hours alternating in his overwrought mind with visions of demons descending on him. At daybreak, he lay down in a little hollow and rested his weary body.

The pain of his wound wakened him in time to see a long train of prairie schooners winding across the prairie. Because of his weakened condition there was little chance of his overtaking it, but he started out anyway. His luck was in. Some of the travelers were combing the countryside for game. They spotted Tex and took him to Fort Wallace.

After the wagon train arrived, a strong force was sent out to hunt down the renegades. They found the burned wagon and other signs of the battle, but the gang's trail led into the sandhills of Nebraska and the soldiers gave up the chase. In all the annals of Kansas history there is no more heroic example of a man winning out against hopeless odds than Tex's battle for survival against the vultures of the plains.

The nation's dream of a transcontinental railroad began to crystallize into reality on May 1, 1862, when Congress passed a bill "to aid in the construction of a railroad and telegraph line from the Missouri River to the Pacific Ocean and to secure to the Government the use of the same for Postal, Military and other purposes." The Pacific Railroad Act authorized the Union Pacific Railroad Company to build a line from Omaha, Nebraska, to Utah, where it was to meet the company directed by Collis P. Huntington and Leland Stanford, the Central Pacific, building east from California.

The inducement offered these companies to undertake the gigantic project was generous. In addition to being accorded a 400-foot right-of-way and the free use of building materials from the public lands, they received a subsidy of $16,000 a mile on the plains and from $32,000 to $48,000 in the mountains, and every alternate section of public land to the amount of five (later raised to ten) sections a mile on each side of the track for the entire distance.

Construction began in California in 1863 and in Nebraska in 1864, but not much track was laid until the close of the Civil War. Once construction really got under way, however, it proceeded with incredible speed. On May 10, 1869, the rails met at Promontory Point in Utah, and when the telegraph flashed the news that the last spike had been driven, whistles were blown, bells rung, and guns fired all over the country.

Frontier Railroading

SECURING AN ADEQUATE FORCE of laborers was a problem at both the eastern and western ends of the railroad. For the Union Pacific, it was largely settled by the demobilization of the armies and the increased immigration at the end of the Civil War. The high wages offered by the company drew discharged soldiers and immigrants, mainly Irish, to the plains of Nebraska. But in the Far West, where it seemed every able-bodied man was more interested in using a pick and shovel in the gold fields than on the railroad right-of-way, the problem was not resolved until it occurred to someone to import Chinese coolies. In all, some twenty-five thousand men were employed in the building of the lines.

In May, 1866, General Grenville M. Dodge resigned from the Army to take over as chief engineer of the Union Pacific, and under his direction work proceeded with military precision. "Track laying on the Union Pacific is a science," wrote an Eastern newspaper correspondent. "A light car, drawn by a single horse, gallops up to the front on the ties with its load of rails. Two men seize the end of a rail and start forward, the rest of the gang taking hold by twos, until it is clear of the car. They come forward at a run. At the command 'Down!' the rail is dropped into its place, right side up, with care, while the same process is going on at the other side of the car. Less than thirty seconds to a rail for each gang, and so four rails go down to the minute. . . . Close behind the first gang come the gaugers, spikers, and bolters, and a lively time they make of it. It is a grand anvil chorus that these sturdy sledges are playing across the plains."

Although Council Bluffs, Iowa, was the eastern terminus of the Union Pacific, there was no bridge across the Missouri at this time and Omaha, therefore, became the construction terminus. For five years, building materials needed from the East were brought up the Missouri by steamboat or across Iowa by wagon. A seventy-ton stationary engine had to be hauled across western Iowa by ox team and then ferried over the river. Locomotives came from St. Louis by boat. After the Chicago and Northwestern was completed to Omaha in 1867, supplies were hauled to that point by rail, but it was still necessary to use a fleet of wagons to take much of this material to the scene of construction.

According to Robert E. Riegel in *The Story of the Western Railroads,* "Construction was carried on in hundred mile stretches. . . . The whole stretch was graded and the bridge work completed before any of the rails were laid. This method of procedure made it necessary for the grading crews to be considerably in advance of the rest of the construction work. Ties were taken from the surrounding country as much as possible. Great difficulty was experienced in securing wood on the treeless plains, and the expense was excessive. In the absence of hard wood, cottonwood was 'Burnetized,' that is, dipped into a solution of zinc chloride."

As the rails thrust westward in hundred-mile leaps, colonies of tents and frame buildings marked the farthest forward point of construction, and although the lines went through uninhabited country, these end-of-track towns often housed during their brief existence a population larger than that of cities in settled areas. Grading crews which might number as many as ten thousand men requiring three hundred freighters to carry supplies, four hundred to five hundred tracklayers, and a floating population of saloonkeepers, prostitutes, gamblers, and sharpers of all kinds moved along with rail construction. One of the most notorious of these ephemeral end-of-track towns was Benton, in the alkali and sagebrush desert of central Wyoming. According to the newspaper correspondent previously cited:

> Here had sprung up in two weeks, as if by the touch of Aladdin's lamp, a city of three thousand people; there were regular squares arranged in five wards, a city government of mayor and alderman, a daily paper, and a volume of ordinances for the public health. It was the end of freight and passenger and the beginning of the construction division:

twice every day immense trains arrived and departed, and stages left for Utah, Montana, and Idaho; all the goods formerly hauled across the plains came here by rail and were reshipped, and for ten hours daily the streets were thronged with motley crowds of railroad men, Mexicans, Indians, gamblers, "cappers," saloon-keepers, merchants, miners, and mule-whackers. The streets were eight inches deep in white dust as I entered the city of canvas tents and pole houses, and a new arrival with black clothes looked like nothing so much as a cockroach struggling through a flour barrel. . . . It was sundown, and the lively notes of the violin and guitar were calling the citizens to evening diversions. Twenty-three saloons and five dance houses amused our elegant leisure. . . . Ten months afterward I visited the site. There was not a house or tent to be seen; a few rock piles and half destroyed chimneys barely sufficed to mark the ruins; the white dust had covered everything else, and desolation reigned supreme.

During the three months of its heyday, Benton reveled in its reputation as "Hell's Tent Town, where the rails and trail begin," and before it faded out of existence bullets furnished the entrance tickets into the local Boot Hill for more than one hundred men. Some towns, of course, did not disappear. For example, Cheyenne, the end of track in 1867–1868, was revivified, after its population started to dwindle, by the South Pass gold strike.

As for construction on the Central Pacific at the western end of the road, according to Riegel, "climactic and engineering difficulties were seemingly insuperable at the outset of the work. The Sierras had to be crossed immediately whereas the Union Pacific was able to build two-thirds of its road before encountering any appreciable engineering difficulties. . . . Initiative, courage, and indomitable perseverance [were called for, and] in spite of all difficulties the work on the Central Pacific was pushed forward energetically after 1865. As it began nearing completion a strong spirit of hostility grew up between the two companies, and in their competition to build more line and thus secure a larger subsidy the construction crews began to parallel each other. . . . The meeting point of the lines had not been settled by Congress in its legislation; it had been assumed that the two roads would merely build until their tracks joined." Since they could not agree on a meeting point, the two companies might have gone on building indefinitely if Congress had not ruled that the junction was to be at Promontory Point.

1

Not mountains, but men—the Indians of the Plains—provided the extra headaches during the building of the Union Pacific across the Platte Valley. Because of Indian hostilities the construction crews frequently had to work under the protection of armed guards. Since many of the men were Civil War veterans, General Dodge issued weapons to them, and if no regular army troops were available, half of a crew would do guard duty while the other half worked. In March, 1867, two hundred of the famous Pawnee Scouts were mustered, and under the command of Major Frank North served to escort Union Pacific engineers and commissioners as well as to protect grading and working parties from the hostiles.

Work and supply trains were forts on wheels. General Dodge spoke of his private car as a "traveling arsenal," and cabooses were double walled and carried racks of rifles. When they took a train out, engineers and firemen kept their rifles handy, and the trainmen wore revolvers. Indian attacks were not confined just to the area under construction, but extended over the entire communication line between end of track and Omaha.

The first train wreck chalked up by the Indians is generally credited to Chief Turkey Leg, although some authorities say that Spotted Wolf actually led the party of Cheyenne saboteurs. At any rate, the place was four miles from Plum Creek Station (present-day Lexington, Nebraska) and the date was August 7, 1867.

About 9 P.M. that evening the station agent at Plum Creek discovered that the telegraph from the west was dead, and sent out William Thompson, the head telegraph linesman, with a crew on a handcar to locate the trouble. As they were pumping along, they saw fire on the north side of the line, and a moment later their handcar crashed into an obstruction which threw it off the track, scattering the men along the grade. While they were still picking themselves up, forty Cheyennes burst from their places of concealment in the tall grass along the right-of-way, and began circling around them firing and whooping. The telegraph crew was well armed and returned their fire, but they were in an exposed position and one by one their guns were silenced.

A bullet hit Thompson in the arm, and a Cheyenne, seeing him drop his rifle, rode in, clubbed him, jumped off his horse, and scalped him. Thompson was fully conscious all during this procedure—"it felt," he said later, "as if the whole top of my head was taken right off"—but dared not make a sound. The job finished, the Indian tucked the scalp under his belt, remounted, and rode away.

From subsequent investigations, it was learned that section hands had been working along that stretch of track during the day, the Indians watching them all the while from the islands in the Platte. When the whites knocked off and returned to Plum Creek, they left their tools at the work site, and this came in very handy for the Indians who used them to pry up the rails. They then blocked them up to the height of three or four feet, tying blocks to each rail with wire obtained from cutting the telegraph lines.

After the telegraph crew fell into their trap, bigger game came along in the form of a westbound freight. When it hit the torn-up patch traveling at about twenty miles an hour, the engine jumped the tracks carrying with it the tender and five boxcars. Two of the latter piled up on the engine and caught fire. Another freight was following close behind, and the conductor sent one of the brakemen hustling back down the track to flag it down. He succeeded in doing so, and the second train backed up to Plum Creek, where it was boarded by the entire population of the town except the telegraph operator. It then returned to Elm Creek, eighteen miles farther east.

Meanwhile the Indians were working their will on the wrecked train and its crew. By the light of the flaming boxcars, Thompson saw some of the savages looting the undamaged cars while others killed and scalped the injured engineer and firemen and the other members of the crew. The flames also revealed to Thompson his own scalp, apparently dropped by the Indian when he got on his horse. Hoping that it might grow back on—and also that he would survive to try the experiment—Thompson retrieved it. When the Indians finally rode off, leaving, as they thought, only dead bodies, Thompson got up and staggered down the track to Willow Island.

The next morning a crew was sent to the scene of the wreck and massacre. According to Michael Delahunty, a section foreman:

> When we got back to Plum Creek we could see a black smoke where the wreck was, so the conductor hooked a flat car on the front of the engine and we all got aboard with our guns and ammunition and started toward the wreck. About a mile from the wreck we stopped as there were Indians around and we were afraid of being surrounded. After the train stopped we saw the Indians riding around in circles with bolts of calico tied to their horses' tails and a bunch of them around two barrels of whiskey. Brother Patrick being a crack rifle shot and having a long range rifle, 50-70 caliber, they delegated him to pick off the leader, which he did with the first shot. This caused them to scatter and leave for the islands in the river. We then moved to the wreck and hooked onto the caboose and pulled it away from the burning cars. We found coffee, sugar, dry goods, and other provisions scattered about; boots with the tops cut off—the Indians cut the tops off and put them on their legs but wouldn't wear the bottom part— in fact we picked up about three car loads of merchandise that was left on the ground.

As for Thompson, he was sent on to Omaha, where he could have medical attention, reaching there thirty-six hours after the scalping. His wound soon healed, but his scalp, which he had brought along in a pail of water, was firmly ignored by the attending physician. After his recovery, Thompson had it framed and took it back with him to his home in England. Some twenty-five years later, he presented this unique souvenir to the Omaha Public Library, where it is still on display.

2

After regular through-service had been established, the weather sometimes played hob with the train schedules. When railroading was new on the plains, the crews had not yet learned how to cope with such regional phenomena as blizzards. Bred in the tradition of bringing through mail and passengers on time, they had still to learn that when it comes to bucking a blizzard, discretion is sometimes the better part of valor.

On January 7, 1875, the snow was swirling in the yards at Kansas City, when the conductor called "All aboard" and the Denver Express, a crack train of the Kansas Pacific Railroad, pulled out on its 600-mile jaunt to Colorado. First chartered in 1855 as the Leavenworth, Pawnee and Western, the line had been renamed in 1869 and had run trains to Denver since 1870.

Before long the Express was heading into the teeth of a Plains blizzard. As the snow increased, visibility was cut almost to zero and the wind whipped the ravines full of drifts, slowing down the train considerably from its normal speed of forty-five miles an hour. It took nearly twenty-four hours to reach Salina, Kansas, where the train was halted to wait until the storm should abate. During the next two days, two more trains came in from the east; but there was no traffic at all from Denver. On Sunday, after a three-day wait, the three westbound trains were combined into one and that night pulled out for the west.

On this new train were two of the Pullman Company's ultra-modern Palace cars—"Atlas" and "Dexter"—which were the last word in travel comfort. It was these sleeping cars, according to Robert G. Athearn, which attracted the greatest admiration from British travelers. Describing their wonders, a gentleman who signed himself "A London Parson" wrote: "I had a sofa to myself, with a table and a lamp. The sofas are widened and made into beds at night. My berth was three feet three inches wide, and six feet three inches long. It had two windows looking out of the train, a handsome mirror, and was well furnished with bedding and curtains."

However, even the Palace cars proved—literally—cold comfort

on this particular run. After going only sixty miles the train was compelled to stop at Russell until morning. The mercury dropped to twenty-two degrees below zero and the wind blew a perfect gale, licking the heat out of the Pullmans. The coal stoves at the end of the car could not begin to warm the sleeping chamber, which became a veritable icebox. The gale continued day after day without a let-up, driving the snow in sheets and filling the cuts with hard drifts. For three days the train sat there in Russell. Water tanks froze up—with thirty-six inches of ice over the surface—and the engineers had to keep their engines alive with melted snow.

On Friday afternoon the train started out again and that day met the snow brigade from Denver, which consisted of a snow plow, five engines, and a crew of shovelers. They had cleared the way on the Denver division. But two miles after passing the snow crew, the train ran into a newly formed snow bank and returned to Park's Fort. Since there was nothing to eat at the station, the general passenger agent authorized the conductor to allow the passengers to eat whatever they could find in the express car, assuring him that the railroad would pay for the goods. It happened that in addition to an abundance of staple goods they were carrying a shipment of canned oysters. A hundred and thirty cans were opened, and the passengers were treated to a luxury intended for the society people of Denver.

In the meantime the snow brigade started ahead to clear the track. They found drifts every few miles, but made eighty miles before they got stuck again within five miles of Wallace. It was then six o'clock. The thermometer reading had been going down all day, and that night the men refused to work. They hung around the stoves in the train or kept warm by the locomotive furnaces during the night. The next morning they were at it again and by noon had cleared the track the five miles to Wallace, where they met two trains which had left Denver on January 11 and 12.

Pulled and pushed through the drifts by five engines, the Denver Express finally arrived in Denver at one o'clock on January 18. A large crowd was down at the station to meet the incoming train. Omnibuses were waiting and whisked the passengers away to warm hotel rooms and good beds. The train brought to the news-hungry city of Denver six tons of mail, an immense amount of Wells, Fargo and Company express, and eighty-five passengers. The next day Denver and the surrounding towns luxuriated in 52,000 letters and an avalanche of newspapers.

The work of the railroad employees was nothing less than heroic from division officials down to section hands. For eleven days the engineers and firemen never left their posts. On the Smoky Hill division in central Kansas there were twenty-two engines in service, of which seven were bounced off the rails by the snow during those days. In a statement drawn up by the passengers thanking the railroad officials for their efforts, one of them commented that the grandest sight he had ever seen was five engines pushing a snow plow through a hundred-foot-long drift. The engines took a half-mile running start, and from the time they struck the drift until they emerged from it, as from a tunnel, they were invisible to onlookers.

Perhaps no wild animal excited more interest among overland travelers on the trans-Missouri frontier than the buffalo. The buffalo bull weighed two thousand pounds; his height at the hump was six feet or more; and in length he was over ten feet. When Sir Richard Burton crossed the plains by stage in 1860, he noted that thirty years earlier the herds had grazed on the banks of the Missouri and that they had been receding westward on an average of ten miles a year. "The annual destruction is variously computed at 200,000 to 300,000 head—the American Fur Company receive per annum about 70,000 robes, which are all cows—and of these not more than 5,000 fall by the hand of white man. At present there are three well-known herds, which split up, at certain seasons, into herds of 2,000 and 3,000 each. The first family is on the headwaters of the Mississippi; the second haunts the vast crescent-shaped valley of the Yellowstone; whilst the third occupies the prairie country between the Platte and the Arkansas. A fourth band, westward of the Rocky Mountains, is quite extinct. . . .

"The Dakotas [Sioux] and other prairie tribes will degenerate, if not disappear, when the buffalo is 'rubbed out.' No part of it is allowed to go to waste. The horns and hoofs make glue for various purposes, especially for feathering arrows; the brains and part of the bowels are used for curing skins; the hide clothes the tribes from head to foot; the calf-skins form their saddle blankets; the sinews make their bowstrings, thread, and finer cord; every part of the flesh . . . is used for food."

Less than a quarter of a century later—at the beginning of the hunting season in 1883—the seven million buffalo that were roaming the plains when Burton wrote his account had dwindled to one herd of ten thousand. White hunters and Indians joined in a final orgy of slaying, and by October the "Monarch of the Prairies" was extinct.

The Monarch of the Prairies

IN THE 1860's, when work began on the Union Pacific, the buffalo was hunted to supply construction gangs with food. Professional hunters, such as William F. Cody, were placed under contract to kill a certain number of bulls—Cody's contract called for him to kill an average of twelve daily—to oversee the cutting and dressing of the meat, and to look after its transportation. For their labors, they received five hundred dollars a month. (The pay was high because killing buffaloes frequently involved killing Indians, too.) In eighteen months as a hunter for the Kansas Pacific Railroad, Cody accounted for 4,280—and was henceforth to be known as "Buffalo Bill."

1

In the late sixties and early seventies, the buffalo became a tourist attraction. Several railroads offered buffalo-hunt excursions. In October, 1868, for the sum of ten dollars, anyone so inclined could make a four-day excursion from Leavenworth, Kansas, to Sheridan, Wyoming, and, so the advertisements assured him, bag a buffalo without leaving his seat in the train. ("Buffaloes are so numerous along the road that they are shot from the cars nearly every day. On our last excursion our party killed twenty buffaloes in a hunt of six hours.") For wealthy visitors from overseas, de luxe hunting tours were arranged, "with servants . . . and everything generally found in a first-class hotel, and [provision] for the conveyance of any trophies of the chase, such as Buffalo skins, Elk Horns and Antlers in limited quantity." The fare for the round trip from England, which included everything "except Wines, Liquors, Cigars, Guns, Rifles, and Ammunition" was ninety guineas—about $475—"but the charge for Ladies will be 100 Guineas each."

One of the most publicized hunting trips was that of Grand Duke Alexis of Russia to the Republican Valley of Western Nebraska early in 1872. The imperial junket was arranged by General Philip Sheridan, who obtained the services of Buffalo Bill Cody as guide, chief huntsman, and master of ceremonies. The Grand Duke, Bill was informed, also wished "to see a body of American Indians and observe the manner in which they killed buffaloes," and Bill's duties included rounding up the performers for that part of the entertainment. Spotted Tail and his Sioux band had permission from the government to hunt the buffalo in the Republican Valley that winter, so when Bill went out to select a suitable site for the distinguished visitor's camp, he stopped off at Spotted Tail's camp and told him of the Grand Duke's request. The old chief said that he would be glad to cooperate; he would call his people together and select a hundred of his leading warriors to hunt with the Grand Duke. By the morning of January 7, 1872, when the special train pulled in with the imperial party, all arrangements were complete. What happened thereafter is told here, somewhat abridged, as Bill Cody told it in his autobiography.

Captain Hays and myself, with five or six ambulances, fifteen or twenty extra saddle horses and a company of cavalry under Captain Egan, were at the depot in time to meet the special train. Presently General Sheridan and a large, fine-looking young man came out of the cars and approached us. General Sheridan at once introduced me to the Grand Duke as Buffalo Bill, and said that I was to take charge of him and show him how to kill buffalo.

In less than half an hour the whole party were dashing away towards the south, and after a halt for lunch at Medicine Creek reached Camp Alexis in the afternoon. Spotted Tail and his Indians were objects of great curiosity to the Grand Duke, who spent considerable time looking at them and watching their exhibitions of horsemanship, sham fights, etc. That evening the Indians gave the grand war dance in his honor, which I had arranged for. The Duke asked me a great many questions as to how we shot buffaloes, and what kind of a gun or pistol we used, and if he was going to have a good horse. I told him that he was going to have my celebrated buffalo horse, Buckskin Joe, and when we went into a buffalo herd all he would have to do was to sit on the horse's back and fire away.

At nine o'clock next morning we were all in our saddles and in a few minutes were galloping over the prairies in search of a buffalo herd. We had not gone far before we observed a herd some distance ahead of us crossing our way; after that we proceeded cautiously, so as to keep out of sight until we were ready to make a charge. The Duke became very much excited and anxious to charge directly toward the buffaloes, but I restrained him for a time, until getting around to windward and keeping behind the sand hills the herd was gradually approached.

"Now," said I, "is your time; you must ride as fast as your horse will go, and don't shoot until you get a good opportunity."

Away we went, tearing down the hill and throwing up a sand-storm in the rear, leaving the Duke's retinue far behind. When within a hundred yards of the fleeing buffaloes the Duke fired, but unfortunately missed, being unused to shooting from a running horse. I now rode up close beside him and advised him not to fire until he could ride directly upon the flank of a buffalo, as the sport was most in the case. We dashed off together and ran our horses on either flank of a large bull, against the side of which the Duke thrust his gun and fired a fatal shot. He was very much elated at his success, taking off his cap and waving it vehemently, at the same time shouting to those who were fully a mile in the rear. When his retinue came up there were congratulations and every one drank to his good health with overflowing glasses of champagne. The hide of the dead buffalo was carefully removed and dressed, and the royal traveler in his journeyings over the world has no doubt often rested himself upon this trophy of his skill (?) on the plains of America.

On the following day, by request of Spotted Tail, the Grand Duke hunted for a while beside "Two Lance," a celebrated chief, who claimed he could send an arrow entirely through the body of the largest buffalo. This feat seemed so incredible that there was a general denial of his ability to perform it; nevertheless, the Grand Duke and several others witnessed, with profound astonishment, an accomplishment of the feat, and the arrow that passed through the buffalo was given to the Duke as a memento of Two Lance's skill and power. On the same day of this performance the Grand Duke killed a buffalo at a distance of one hundred paces with a heavy navy revolver. The shot was a marvelous —scratch. [A miss; Bill, firing simultaneously, made the kill.]

When the Grand Duke was satisfied with the sport, orders were given for the return to the railroad. The conveyance provided for the Grand Duke and General Sheridan was a heavy double-seated open carriage, and it was drawn by six spirited cavalry horses which were not much used to the harness. The driver was Bill Reed, an old overland stage driver and wagonmaster; on our way in, the Grand Duke frequently expressed his admiration of the skillful manner in which Reed handled the reins. General Sheridan informed the Duke that I also had been a stage driver in the Rocky Mountains, and thereupon His Royal Highness expressed a desire to see me drive.

I gave the horses a crack or two of the whip, and they started off at a very rapid gait. They had a light load to pull, and I found it difficult to hold them. They fairly flew over the ground, and at last we reached a steep hill which led down into the valley of the Medicine. There was no brake on the wagon, and the horses were not much on the hold back. I saw that it would be impossible to stop them. All I could do was to keep them straight in the track and let them go it down the hill, for three miles, which distance, I believe, was made in about six minutes. Every once in a while the hind wheels would strike a rut and take a bound, and not touch the ground again for fifteen or twenty feet. The Duke and the General were kept rather busy in holding their positions on the seats, and when they saw that I was keeping the horses straight in the road, they seemed to enjoy the dash which we were making. I was unable to stop the team until they ran into the camp where we were to obtain a fresh relay, and there I succeeded in checking them.

On arriving at the railroad, the Duke invited me into his car, and gave me a valuable scarf pin and a purse of money, at the same time giving me a cordial invitation to visit him, if ever I should come to his country.

2

Buffalo hunting became a business in the early 1870's after a Pennsylvania tannery discovered that buffalo hide could be used in the manufacture of commercial leather goods—harness, shoes, belts, and so on. Soon other tanners, English as well as American, entered the market, one English tannery contracting for ten thousand hides on its first order. According to Douglas Branch, in *The Hunting of the Buffalo*, "Unless one owned a ranch, the quickest way to make money on the frontier was to turn buffalo hunter. In 1870 bull hides brought two dollars each, and cowhides and calf hides twenty-five cents less. The tongues, salted and packed in barrels, brought good side money; and the 'mop,' the bunch of long hair that fell over the buffalo's horns and eyes, was worth seventy-five cents a pound."

The old hunters and scouts who had killed buffalo to feed railroad construction crews and the army jumped at the chance to fatten their purses and enhance their reputations. Among the most prominent were the two Buffalo Bills—Bill Cody and Billy Comstock, chief of scouts at Fort Wallace. Other famed hunters were Billy Dixon and John Cook. Armed with the Sharp's rifle, these men could bring down a buffalo in one shot.

To send a bullet to a buffalo's heart, the hunter aimed just behind the shoulder blade, and about two-thirds of the way down from the top of the hump. Contrary to popular belief, the professional hunter—who was out for hides, not for sport—operated on foot rather than on horseback. Once he had located a herd, he would get as close to it as he could—usually he could approach to within two or three hundred yards—crawling on all fours as he neared the herd, and stopping when the sentinel buffaloes became uneasy. Lying prone on the ground, the hunter then took aim at the most suspicious of the watching buffaloes or, if the herd already was moving, at the one in the lead. As soon as he had fired, the hunter jumped up and pursued the herd, which usually ran fifty to a hundred feet at the sound of the shot. The hunter, who had probably covered half that distance, stopped when the herd did, dropped to the ground, fired again, jumped up, and ran after them. This time, however, they would not run quite so fast or so far, and after a few repetitions of this maneuver the hunter could keep up with them.

After he had brought down several buffaloes, the skinners would move in and remove the hides and stake them on the ground to dry; the meat was left to rot. A capable man could skin fifty buffaloes a day. At the end of the day, a horse- or mule-drawn wagon went around to collect the skins and bring them back to camp. A professional hunter's outfit usually consisted of one or two skinners and one man to cook.

The trick to getting a large number of hides in one day

depended on the hunter's skill in bringing down a large number of buffalo in a small area. If the herd was at rest, the hunter might be lucky enough to make a "stand"—the situation which came about when the leader was the first to be shot down and the rest of the herd, instead of running away, simply stood and allowed themselves to be picked off. Making a stand happened but seldom and was every hunter's dream. The one time that John Cook brought off the maneuver—in June of 1875—he made the biggest killing in all his years of hunting.

It was about midday, and blazing hot even for the southwest plains in summer. Other hunters had been working the area to the north of Cook's camp, popping away at a herd of several hundred which had come to cool off at Beaver Creek. Driven away by their fire, the hot and thirsty animals raced southward to Wolf Creek. After drinking, they came out and stopped to rest on the prairie, not far from the creek. Some of them were lying down when Cook, coming from his camp on the creek above the herd, arrived within range. He was not more than eighty steps away when he fired his first shot, taking for his target a tremendously large bull whom he judged to be the leader. Less than half of the buffaloes who were lying down got to their feet at the report of the gun; but after Cook had dropped three more in as many shots, some of the herd moved off toward the creek. Getting a good shot at the leader, Cook brought him down and the rest went no farther.

Now Cook realized that he had what he so often had heard talked about but never seen—a stand. From past conversations, he remembered three pointers on the management of a stand: not to shoot so fast that the gun barrel is heated to overexpansion; always try to hit the outside buffaloes; to shoot any that started to move off.

When he had killed twenty-five, shooting unhurriedly, the pall of gunsmoke overhanging him enabled him to crawl even closer to the herd. After he had shot a few more times, he heard someone whistle behind him, and his partner, Charlie Cook, came creeping up on all fours. Charlie brought him a canteen of water, an extra sack of ammunition, and another gun. Cook exchanged his rifle for the cool one and commenced firing again.

In the meantime Charlie poured water from the canteen into the hot rifle barrel and cooled it. Then he ran a rag into the eye of the ramrod, swabbed out the dirty rifle, and had it ready to hand over when the other gun was hot. When that time came, Cook said, "You take over. Finish the job, Charlie." But Charlie wasn't going to horn in. "No, you go ahead," he told his partner. "It is the grandest sight I ever saw."

Between shots, the two hunters marveled at the stupidity of the great beasts. Some would start away from the herd and then walk back and cluster beside the fallen ones. Others would come up and hook a dead animal with their horns. Still others would simply stare and sniff.

In the next hour and a quarter Cook changed guns twice. Finally, a shot shattered the leg of a big bull which was standing on the outside of the herd about ninety yards from the hunter. He began to struggle, striking the others as he lashed about, his injured leg flopping. Breaking through the herd, he moved away and the others followed him. The stand was over.

All four men in the crew now started skinning, keeping at it until it was too dark to see. At noon the next day, when they finally finished, eighty-eight hides had been stretched on the prairie and pegged down to dry.

3

One day in the early 1870's a stranger blew into Dodge City, and proceeded to inform everyone who would listen that his name was Fairchild and that he was there to hunt buffalo and shoot Indians. Even if he had not arrived aboard a horse with a "muley" saddle—which immediately made him conspicuous in a country where a hornless saddle was about as useful as a cut-glass hitching post—his plug hat, broadcloth suit, flowered vest, and necktie resembling a prairie sunset would have been a cinch to stop traffic on Main Street.

Now if there was anything the hunters and scouts and other old-timers on the frontier found more obnoxious than a duded-up tenderfoot, it was a blowhard, and when both came wrapped in the same package it was a foregone conclusion that something had to be done about it. The day that Fairchild blossomed out in "native" dress—a plentifully fringed brown twill suit, high-heeled boots, enormous spurs, and a snow-white ten-gallon hat—it was apparent that a small start had been made, for in the arsenal loading down his belt there was a butcher knife as well as cartridges and a pair of six-shooters. Fascinated onlookers at the store where he made his purchases had persuaded him that there was nothing like a butcher knife for lifting the scalp of a pesky redskin.

Being now rigged out for the wilds, Fairchild approached two of Dodge's more prominent citizens, the veteran hunter Billy Dixon and Marshal Bat Masterson, and announced his availability for a buffalo-hunting outfit which they were organizing. At first Bat and Billy did not exactly cotton to the idea of his joining them, but after they had listened to another member of the party, a card named Myers whose forte was practical jokes and who specialized, as he said, in taking the romance out of tenderfeet, they assured Fairchild that they'd be mighty proud to have him along.

After a few days of Fairchild's company, however, they allowed as how Myers had better come up with something pretty good. Since Fairchild had been lucky enough to bag several antelope, he was wearing out their ears with his self-praises, and they also had heard enough about what he was going to do to the first Indian that crossed his path. After thinking it over, Myers decided that maybe what was needed was a turkey hunt. Not far from their camp was a wooded area along a stream, where hundreds of wild turkeys roosted nightly. Myers saw no reason why something else—maybe even wild Injuns—couldn't roost there too, and he issued instructions accordingly. He and Bat would accompany Fairchild on the turkey hunt; Billy Dixon was placed in charge of the other preparations.

Fairchild was flattered to be asked to partner with Masterson and Myers that night, and, bent on impressing them, was even more loquacious than usual about his achievements—past and future—as a rip-snorting, ring-tailed, he-man, Indian-killin' buffalo hunter. He kept right on sounding off until they entered the wooded area, and Bat warned him that they had to be very quiet or they'd scare away the turkeys.

Following a natural trail through the woods, they presently rounded a bend and saw a campfire gleaming through the trees. At once Masterson and Myers dropped noiselessly to the ground and made signs to the surprised Fairchild to do the same.

"Injuns," whispered Myers. "I heered tell Bad Medicine and a war party was over on the Stinking Water. Likely this is them."

"Let's get outta here," said Bat, beginning to wriggle backwards.

"Marshal, we cain't do that!" protested Myers. "We cain't run away from these here varmints—leastways not till we've seen how many of 'em there are."

"Too many," said Bat. "I seen."

The two men kept up the whispered debate, snaking backwards down the trail all the while, with Fairchild doing his best to imitate them. "You keep forgettin', Marshal," Myers said finally. "It ain't just you an' me. We got Fairchild here. Ain't often a man gets a chance to tangle with a chief like Bad Medicine fust time he runs up agin Injuns."

"Who's tellin' Fairchild what to do?" said Masterson before the tenderfoot could get a word in. "Man wants to get along without a scalp, that's his privilege. *I'm* gettin' outta here."

As Masterson started to rise—bang! bang! whir! whir! spat! spat!—a half-dozen shots rang out, clipping the leaves and thudding into tree trunks all around them. Myers let out a howl, jumped like a startled deer, and tore away toward the camp, yelling at the top of his lungs. To make it look good he was really traveling, but Fairchild went past him as though he were glued to the ground. Last of all came Bat, firing a fusillade of pistol shots and taking great pains to crash through the underbrush, so that it must have sounded to the tenderfoot as if the entire Sioux nation were after them.

When the wild-eyed Fairchild came streaking into camp yelling "Injuns! Injuns! Grab your guns, boys, we're surrounded!," the other hunters seemed more solicitous than alarmed. "Why, he's wounded, poor feller," said one. "Fetch the bandages, Joe—

I'll get his shirt off." Which he proceeded to do by taking a hunting knife and ripping Fairchild's fancy shirt from neck to tail.
Next the good Samaritan called for water and was handed a
coffee-pot whose contents he emptied on the tenderfoot's bare
back.

"Is it serious?" quavered Fairchild, who by now actually
believed he was wounded.

"Ain't no more 'n a flea-bite. I reckon you'll live. But where's
Bat? Where's Myers?"

Fairchild gulped a couple of times and finally said, "Killed, I
guess."

Before the camp had a chance to go into mourning, however,
Masterson and Myers showed up, loudly recriminating Fairchild
for abandoning them to the mercy of Bad Medicine and his
braves. On hearing the name of Bad Medicine, the other hunters
at once registered great concern; and when Billy Dixon and
another turkey hunter came rushing into camp with the news
that the whole country was swarming with hostiles, some of the
men were for gathering up their gear and starting back to Dodge
City. Fairchild was among those who strongly urged that this was
the only sensible course of action, but the majority favored stay-
ing and fighting it out.

As a precaution against surprise attack, pickets were posted
around the camp; and in view of Fairchild's wish, so frequently
and ardently expressed, to embark on a career as an Indian-killer,
he was assigned a dangerously exposed position by the river.
"They can sneak up on you by land or by water," he was told by
Billy Dixon, who escorted him to the post, "so keep your eyes
peeled. You'll be relieved in two hours—happen you're still alive."

However, it was a good deal longer than two hours that Fairchild sweated it out on the riverbank, jumping at every sound
and seeing Injuns in every tree shadow. But at long last an insidi-
ous suspicion began to stir in his mind; the more he thought
about it, the stronger it became; and finally he left his post and
slipped back to camp. When he heard the men guffawing around
the fire, and realized the trick that had been played on him, Fairchild became so furious that for a few moments he really was a

rip-snorting, ring-tailed roarer, ready and eager to fight the entire
camp either individually or en masse. It took a respectable number of the boys to hold him down until he had cooled off.

For quite awhile after that they were all careful not to mention Injuns—and in particular Bad Medicine—if Fairchild was
within earshot, but by the time the outfit returned to Dodge it
was the consensus of the old-timers that the tenderfoot had
become a man you could get along with—and even a fair-to-
middlin' shot.

The Indians' Gift

ABOUT THE SAME TIME that Lewis and Clark set out to find the
way to the Western Ocean, an Indian was born who was destined
to be the best friend among Indian chiefs the white man ever
had. His name, translated as Shoots Buffalo Running, was Washakie. Of mixed Umatilla and Shoshoni blood, he was reared among
the Umatilla but joined his mother's people while still a youth,
and by virtue of his prowess on the battlefield and his wisdom in
council he early became chief of the Eastern Band of the Shoshoni, also known as Washakie's Band. He owed his great popularity among his people to his exploits as a warrior. When he
reached the age of seventy, however, a group of ambitious young
braves declared he was too old and feeble to be their chief, and
called a council to consider deposing him. Washakie disappeared
from camp until the night the council was held; then he stalked
into the medicine lodge bearing six scalps which he had taken
alone on the warpath. Although he lived to be ninety-five, no one
ever again questioned his fitness to guide the destinies of his
people.

In his relationships with the whites, no matter what the provo-
cation—white trappers on his hunting grounds, white man's trails
and talking wires across his country, white man battling red man
in his mountains—Washakie always honored the promises he had

made to the Great Father and always kept the peace. Among his proudest possessions was a paper signed by nine thousand immigrants thanking his tribe for their friendly and helpful treatment. During the 1850's when immigrants overflowed the trails, Washakie's Band followed to the letter the injunctions of the government agents to aid overland travelers in recovering strayed or lost cattle, to help parties across dangerous fords, and to refrain from acts of reprisal when their grazing grounds were destroyed by the whites' livestock.

Washakie's dark hour of trial came in 1863 when some of the Shoshonis, refusing to heed his words, joined with the Bannocks in hostilities against the whites. They were defeated in the Battle of Bear River by General P. E. Connor, but because Washakie, faithful to his word, had led the greater portion of his people to asylum at Fort Bridger before the battle, no punitive measures were taken against them and many lives were saved. In 1869, when Fort Brown was established near present Lander, Wyoming, he met the white soldiers with renewed pledges of friendship and frequently served as an army scout in campaigns against tribes hostile to the Shoshoni.

When the time came for the Shoshoni to go on the Wind River reservation, the Indian agent tried to ease the transition to reservation life by expounding its many advantages. For one thing, he said, they would gain much by learning white men's ways. Because the white man looked to the future and knew how to provide for it, he always had a full kettle on his hearth-fire; but since the Indian was content to let tomorrow take care of itself, he was dependent on the whims of nature and his life alternated between feast and famine. But now, said the agent, the Great Father was sending them a teacher who would show them how to make the earth yield crops in such abundance that there would always be plenty to store away for a lean season. Thus in times to come, even when the hunting and fishing were poor, the Shoshoni would never go hungry.

The man engaged as "Boss Farmer" was a courageous and resourceful frontiersman of Irish descent, Finn Burnett, who as a lad had come west to make his fortune. At the age of twenty-six, having worked as a wagon boss, in the Army's Quartermaster Department, and on a grading crew during the construction of the Union Pacific, he had married and settled down in Atlantic City, Wyoming, which at that time was enjoying a brief boom as a mining town. As Boss Farmer on the reservation, Finn's first duties would be to supervise the digging of irrigation ditches, breaking the sod, and preparing the land for farming.

Harness, plows, and other equipment were to be furnished by the government, but when Finn arrived on the reservation, eager to get started, none of the promised items had been delivered. Although there were a few Shoshonis who were not wholly convinced that what was good for the white man was necessarily good for the red man, for the most part, the Indians too were eager to get started, and curiosity about the precise nature of the lessons mounted during the enforced delay.

When the long-awaited implements at last arrived, Finn sent word for the future farmers to come to the agency with their horses. As soon as all were assembled, he proceeded with the first lesson: how to hitch a horse to a plow. While the Indians watched expectantly, he gave a demonstration, using one of the agency horses; then directed a number of the Shoshonis to bring their horses forward and do likewise. But to Finn's utter astonishment the Indians found the whole performance simply hilarious. Since all they knew of "white man's ways" had been derived from their contacts with soldiers, freighters, and herders along the overland trail, they had no conception of farming devices and no notion what to expect. The idea of a horse dragging a knife over the earth struck them as comic beyond belief; and furthermore their horses had never been broken to harness. It took quite a while for Finn to convince them that he was serious.

After a good deal of cajolery, however, they agreed to humor him, and with his help finally got their ponies hitched to the plows. Giggling and chuckling, and followed by every Indian at the agency, they drove out to the acreage where they were to receive a lesson in plowing. According to Finn's instructions, they formed a long line at one side of the field, and when he gave the word took off for the opposite side as if he had signaled the start of a race. The result was a shambles. Horses balked; plows bit too deeply and stalled their teams; three or four teams surged together and got entangled. The frantic horses began to kick, and after a few seconds of explosive action—featuring broken harness and flying lines—a half-dozen snorting ponies were running amok. The panic spread to the other horses. In less time than it takes to tell it, a dozen teams were bolting, their plows bouncing behind them. The Shoshoni spectators loved it, and only stopped laughing long enough to bet on which team would be the first across the dust-enveloped field.

But after this weird and discouraging beginning, Finn's pupils settled down, and some of them, under his patient and sympathetic tutelage, became quite proficient in farming operations. After a few months of working with the Indians and living among them, a warm bond grew up between the Boss Farmer and the tribe. He became their friend and companion, and at their invitation accompanied them on their hunts. When other tribes attacked the Shoshoni, he stood by their side; together they fought Arapaho, Cheyenne, Sioux, and Ute. The Shoshonis found Finn always as honest and trustworthy as he was brave and helpful, and they came to think of him as one of themselves.

After some years, because of the politics which periodically disrupted the Indian Service, Finn resigned and became a rancher. He had just gotten nicely settled on his little parcel of land and was getting it stocked, when one morning Chief Washakie came riding up to the corral leading a cavalcade of ten of his chiefs. The dress of the delegation reflected the change that had come over the Shoshoni: many were buttoned into frock coats and trousers, though they still wore their ornate feathered headdresses and some had robes over their white man's garments.

Since Indian callers were fairly common, neither Finn nor his wife attached any particular importance to this visit. Mrs. Burnett outdid herself in the kitchen and at noon Washakie and his chiefs sat down to a grand dinner. Little was said until the last platter had been licked clean. Then Finn inquired where they were traveling to, so early in the spring. The answer came, "We travel here." Finn asked if they had ridden seventy-five miles just to get their dinner and visit with him. Their answer was "No." Then he asked if they wanted him to do something for them, and now their answer was a positive "Yes!"

When he wanted to know what they had in mind for him to do, all looked to Chief Washakie as their spokesman. The old chief asked Finn, somewhat hesitantly, why he had left them. Because, Finn explained, he could no longer live on the agency as he was not employed there. Washakie waved this aside as of no importance. The Shoshoni wanted him back, the chief said, and the tribe would give him land for a ranch if he would return and be one of them again. In eloquent words, Washakie recalled how Finn had been with them in the early days of the reservation, had taught them how to grow and husband their crops, and had risked his life fighting with them against the hostile tribes. Then, rising, Washakie drew a paper from his robe and handed it to Finn. It was a document drawn up in legal form, signed by the marks of Washakie and the subchiefs and sealed by the Indian agent, deeding land for a ranch in perpetuity to Finn Burnett, at a site to be selected.

When Washakie suggested that he return with them and pick out his land, Finn needed little urging. He saddled up and rode with Washakie to a point west of the Lander road where there was a little valley of about seven hundred acres which could be irrigated. He'd be pleased to have it, Finn said, if that was agreeable. Washakie assented; and then asked him to ride on and pick out the rest of the land. Finn's protest that this spread would do him fine brought an impatient gesture from the chief. Did he think the Shoshonis were unaware he was a man with a family? Their intention was not only to give *him* a ranch, but also to give ranches to his wife and five children. Washakie then offered four thousand acres in the area surrounding the land Finn had chosen, and the deed was duly completed before the Indian agent.

Not long afterward the cattle drives from Texas opened up a great ranching bonanza on the Northern Plains. With his family around him and his Shoshoni friends close by, Finn Burnett settled down to enjoy a busy and prosperous life on the land that the Indians had given back to the white man.

V. The Last Frontiers

See the maps on pages 198, 199, and 200.

IN THE 1870's, after the passage of the Homestead Act and the completion of the transcontinental railroad combined to make land cheap (less than 25 cents an acre) and accessible, large-scale settlement of the Great Plains at last got under way. But claiming the land was one thing; taming it another. Whereas in the East, as Walter Prescott Webb has written, civilization stood on three legs—land, water, and wood—when it reached the Great Plains "not one but two of these legs—water and timber—were withdrawn." Small wonder that for a time the forward progress of the frontier was halted. In the homesteaders' struggle to master this unfamiliar, semiarid environment, the experience gained pioneering in the humid, woodland regions of the East counted for exactly nothing; they had to throw away the book—evolve a whole new set of pioneering techniques.

But once the problems were comprehended, eastern manufacturers—always on the lookout for new, profitable markets—applied their inventive genius and production skills to making the tools which would enable the settlers to conquer the plains. They succeeded so well that by the mid-1880's the farmers' frontier pushed halfway to the Rockies. At the ninety-eighth meridian it abutted the range lands of the cattleman's domain, which had been spreading northward ever since 1865 when Texas herds were first driven north for shipment to eastern markets. The Black Hills gold rush of 1876 created another market for beef, and after the discovery that herds could be successfully wintered on the Northern Plains, there began an era of bonanza ranching which saw the cattle kingdom expand from Texas to the Canadian border.

During the two decades since the Civil War, as homesteaders and waves of European immigrants continued to pour in, millions of acres of the public lands had been gobbled up. Now, in the middle years of the 1880's, an advance guard of farmers—nesters, the cattlemen called them—were beginning to nibble at the unfenced range where the cattle companies ran their herds. At the same time, nesters and ranchers alike cast hungry eyes at the lands reserved for the red man. . . . With the country's last great unoccupied region fast filling up, the stage was set for the final act in the drama of the western American frontier.

"For the first two centuries of American history,"
wrote Walter Prescott Webb, "the log cabin and the
rail fence constituted the chief shield of the American
pioneer against the outside world. . . . On the plains,
the sod and adobe houses and dugouts took the place
of the log cabin, but there was nothing to take the
place of the rail fence. Without fences there would
be no farms; without farms the agricultural frontier
would cease to advance. Words fail to describe the con-
fusion among the farmers when they emerged from the
timber into the plain, where neither rails nor rock
could be obtained for fencing." Except for small groves
along creeks and streams, there were virtually no trees,
and the cost of shipping lumber in was prohibitively
expensive. Although the settlers hunted and experi-
mented for several years, they never did find indigenous
materials which would solve the fence question, and it
remained for a farmer back in DeKalb, Illinois, Joseph
F. Glidden, to save the situation by inventing barbed
wire, first put on the market in 1874. When it came to
material for home-building, however, the pioneers
needed to look no farther than the earth beneath their
feet. The tough prairie sod of the Dakotas, Nebraska,
and Kansas was substituted for timber, and the sod-
house frontier came into being.

The Sod-House Frontier

A TYPICAL HOMESTEADER brought his family and his possessions
to the Plains in a covered wagon; if he came in the '70's, after
the railroad was in service, he might have some of the heavier,
bulkier belongings shipped to the station nearest his claim. Usu-

ally, he would have along with him a few pieces of light furniture, a stove, a barrel or two of kitchen utensils, dishes, clothes, and treasured personal belongings, and, of course, farm implements. He might also be lucky enough to own a few head of livestock, including a cow to provide milk for the younger children.

As soon as his wagon rolled onto the claim, the homesteader would start looking for the best place to build his home. Until he had put up a sod house or made a dugout, the family would live in the wagon or perhaps in a tent. If he spotted a conveniently located ravine, the settler might decide on a dugout; and he would set to work scooping out his dwelling from the side of one of its banks. Preferably the ravine would be situated so that the dugout would face east. After he had excavated to a depth of six or eight feet, he used planks to make a door frame and possibly a window. Once these were put in place, all he had to do— assuming the dugout was wholly underground—was fill in around the door, using layers of square-cut sod, and cut a hole for the stove pipe out through the top of the bank.

When the ravine was too shallow to afford a natural roof, one could be made by covering poles with brush, a thatching of prairie grass, and a layer of dirt. However, such a roof was far from ideal, for after a prolonged rain it would leak or even collapse. There was also the danger that stray livestock might wander on to it and plunge through on to the family underneath.

Sod houses were much more satisfactory; indeed, when a family moved out of a dark little dugout into an eighteen by twenty-four foot soddy—a common size—it seemed to them that the White House could hardly be any grander. But even sod houses, except the most pretentious, were by no means light and airy. One man reported that when his family moved to a frame house after five years in the darkness of a soddy, they could not sleep on account of the light.

When the site for the sod house had been chosen, the homesteader next looked for a low spot in the prairie, where the sod would be thick and strong. With his breaking plow, he turned over furrows on about half an acre of ground, taking pains to make the furrows of even width and thickness so that the sod bricks could be cut in a uniform size and the home walls would rise evenly. A spade was used in cutting the furrowed sod into these bricks, which were about three feet long. They were transported to the building site either in a float made of planks or in the wagon.

The first layer in the wall was made by placing the three-foot bricks side by side around the foundation except where the door would be. When the first row had been placed, the cracks were filled with fine dirt and two more layers were placed on top, the homesteader being careful to break joints as a bricklayer does—that is, staggering the bricks so that the crack between two would be covered by the brick above. Every third course was laid crosswise of the others to bind them together. When the walls were high enough, a door frame was set on the ground and built around with sods, and two window frames put in place, one by the door, the other in the opposite wall.

If the settler could afford it, he had a framed roof, with a ridge peak in the middle. Sheeting was nailed to the rafters, and covered with tar paper and a layer of sod, somewhat thinner than that used in the walls. The gable ends were then either boarded up or sodded over. In most cases, however, the homesteader made his roof of crooked limbs, brush, coarse prairie hay, and a thick covering of sod and dirt. To support this load, a ridge pole, held up by a forked post at each end of the house, ran from one end of the roof to the other. A board floor might eventually be laid, but most floors were dirt. The walls were plastered with a gray-colored clay, dug from underneath the layer of black top soil; when finished with a coat of whitewash it made a very presentable wall.

Thanks to their three-foot-thick walls, the soddies were warm in winter and cool in summer. Like the dugouts, they had their drawbacks—one of them being that they were often infested with fleas—but they were habitable and they served their purpose until such time as the family could afford a frame dwelling.

In the summer of 1871, John Turner, an immigrant from England, settled on the Nebraska prairie. Following the customary practice, he made a dugout as a temporary dwelling for his family while he was building his sod house. The dugout, which was situated in a rather steep slope facing a little stream, was too small to accommodate the furniture and belongings the family had brought from England—bedsteads, tables, chairs, stove, cooking utensils and furniture; and this "plunder," as such a collection was called on the frontier, was piled on the bank between the dugout and the stream. Over it Turner spread a felt carpet, which he fastened down with a rope.

One afternoon while Turner and his twelve-year-old son were at work on the soddy, black clouds of a thunderstorm blotted out the sun. Rain—which he described as like countless gray threads stretching from sky to earth—soon soaked them to the skin, but thinking the storm would soon let up, he sent his son back to the dugout to see how his wife and younger child were getting along.

The boy had not been gone long when Turner heard a shrill whistle—the signal they used to summon one another—and he dashed toward the dugout through the hard-beating rain. His son was standing on the bank of the ravine shouting and waving his hands, and when Turner reached him he saw that the little slough at the bottom of the ravine, usually narrow enough to step across, was now an angry flood, threatening the family and their possessions. Only with the greatest difficulty was he able to ford the swollen stream to the dugout on the opposite side.

He found that when the storm broke, his wife had improvised rafts out of two wooden doors which they had bought for the new house. She had placed them on the floor, piling on them their bed and the supplies in the dugout. At first the idea had simply been to keep their groceries and belongings from getting muddy, but as the cloudburst continued, and water from the stream poured in, she had seated herself on one of the doors, with their younger boy in her lap, and by the time Turner reached there the doors were afloat, the mother's head nearly touching the leaky roof.

Seizing his little boy, Turner carried him across the torrent, left him on the bank with his brother, and then went back for his wife. Carrying her in his arms, he started back but stepped into a hole and went under. In his flounderings to secure a foot-hold, he dropped the poor woman but managed to keep hold of her dress. At last he regained his feet and carried her to the bank.

Helplessly, the family stood in the pouring rain watching the swift floodwater sweep their possessions downstream. Everything that would float was washed away and the boxes of provisions outside the dugout were half inundated. The older boy grabbed a rake and, with his father steadying him, tried to hook out a few things. Once Turner plunged into the swirling flood in a vain effort to rescue a new hat his wife had brought from London.

Seeing that nothing more could be done to save their prop-erty, the family started out for the home of their nearest neigh-bor. The lowlands were impassable, and the wet, shivering little group had to travel through the dark by a roundabout route. Their neighbors' house was small, but the hearts of the family there were large, and soon the Turners were clad in dry clothes and sitting down to a piping hot supper.

On their return to the flooded dugout the next morning, they were astonished and delighted to find that the clothes in some of the boxes were only slightly damaged; they had been so tightly packed that the water had not soaked in very far. Exploring the wreckage-strewn ravine, they found here a shotgun sticking up like a post, there a jug of molasses with the cork still securely in place, over there a keg of pork too heavy to float away.

Having salvaged what they could of their possessions, they carried them to the house of their kind neighbors who had offered them a home until their own was ready. Then, putting the disaster out of his mind, Turner and his son got back to work on their sod house.

The Homestead Act of 1862 extended to the same class of persons included in the Pre-emption Act of 1841* the right to a homestead, not exceeding 160 acres, on the surveyed public domain. The homesteader paid a

*See page 112.

*filing fee of ten dollars and the land became his after
he had "resided or cultivated the same for the term of
five years immediately succeeding the time of filing"
and on payment of a fee for the final patent—twenty-
six dollars except on the Pacific coast where it was
thirty-four. With his application for a claim, the homesteader presented an affidavit that the land was "for his
or her exclusive use and benefit" and that his purpose
was "actual settlement and cultivation."*

*Under the terms of the earlier Pre-emption Act he
could claim another quarter section of 160 acres, and
buy it in at the minimum appraised price, usually $1.25
per acre. After the passage of the Timber Culture Act
in 1873, settlers on the Great Plains could file on an
additional 160 acres and buy it at the $1.25 price pro-
vided that they planted and maintained forty acres of
trees for eight years.*

The Phantom Piccolo Player

IN THE POST-CIVIL WAR YEARS, the government land offices were
lively places, crowded with men studying the diagrams prepared
by the surveyors to show the location of unappropriated public
lands, and with those who already had selected their land and
had come to enter their claims. The crush was particularly great
when a new area was opened to settlement; land seekers would
begin to gather outside the office the night before; and by the
time the doors opened, a deputy sheriff or two would be needed
to preserve order. In fact, the expression "doing a land-office business" came to be generally used to describe any kind of fast and
furious commercial activity.

While many homesteaders stayed to cultivate their claims and
settle up the country, many more did not. Some held the land

only long enough to take title and then sell it to newcomers at a higher price. Speculators were the bane of impoverished home-steaders' existence. If a man had a choice location, all kinds of tempting offers were dangled before him. On occasion he was threatened with harm if he did not relinquish his claim, and sometimes ruses were tried to scare him off. Perhaps the most unusual of these tricks was the one which figured in what a detective-story writer might call "The Case of the Phantom Piccolo Player."

In the 1880's Chris De Laney came out to the Dakota Plains from Kents' Corners, Vermont, with a tubercular cough and a little money to invest. He stopped at Tyndall, in present-day South Dakota, and soon was feeling better. This determined him to claim some Dakota land and cast in his fortune with that of the country. He purchased a team and a farm wagon, loaded it with household goods and farming implements, and drove about eighty miles up into the Red Lake region. Accompanying him was an old-timer, Joe Basford, to help him select the three quarter sections to which he was entitled—homestead, and pre-emption and tree claims—and to stay with him while he was getting established.

By the time Chris got his well dug and his sod barn and shack built, the loneliness of the vast prairie was getting to him and his enthusiasm for pioneering was on the wane. One night as Chris and Joe sat in front of the shack smoking, there came floating to them through the darkness the strains of "Silver Threads Among the Gold" played on a flute or piccolo. Some other numbers were played too but this seemed to be the theme song. The music sounded soft and spooky. Then a light began to burn out on the prairie from whence the music came, perhaps a quarter of a mile away. No one would have thought anything about this back where Chris came from—where the farms were small and the houses close together—but here in the solitude of the wilds it was eerie enough to send the chills up and down a man's spine. Chris and Joe had not seen a person since they left Tyndall and not even a coyote had made an appearance in several days.

As suddenly as it had appeared, the light vanished, but the music continued for a time. Chris felt shaky but Joe strapped on his six-shooter and allowed he'd crawl out through the grass and see who that was out there playing weird music eighty miles from civilization. In about an hour he returned considerably shaken. He had not seen a thing. Away off in another direction there were a few toots on the piccolo as if it were giving them the ha-ha. Then it played "Silver Threads" again.

A few evenings later the music again came floating through the prairie air, and once again Joe grabbed his revolver, saying he would rush that ghost player and find out what was what. Chris begged him not to go, but the old frontiersman already was heading toward that music on the run. The light went out as quick as a wink, and soon bullets were whirring and hissing past Joe's ears, close enough so that he did not feel too comfortable in that vicinity. Since he was a good sprinter, he put his talent to use and soon flopped down at the shack. The rest of the night Joe and Chris lay out in the grass ready to shoot at the first flash of a gun, but the gunfire and music had stopped and they lay there on the ground all night for nothing. Neither a hoof mark nor an empty shell did they find the next day when they searched the whole area again.

At nightfall a week later the weird player again piped away with "Silver Threads," but this time, before Joe could get into action, the bullets began popping and tearing through the shack in a dozen places and kept on as though a platoon were firing at will. Hugging the ground, Joe and Chris snaked out of the shack to the sod stable where the protection was better. With the barn window for a gun port, they blazed away at the flashes, although they were difficult to spot since the shots came from different directions. Seeking a better position from which to locate the assailant, Joe crawled out in the grass and fired in the direction of the flashes, but did no better. The shack was riddled and the barn was well pock-marked with bullets.

When morning came, Chris was completely worn out. He said he was sick and tired of such serenades and figured he had had his fill of the country. For his part, Joe said he wasn't afraid to

stand up and shoot it out with a visible enemy, as he was not altogether unfamiliar with such exchanges of courtesies in the West,
but he asked to be excused when it came to fighting ghost musi-
cians and being shot at in the dark from all angles.

The next morning they loaded up all that was worth carrying
away, put a torch to the tar-paper shack, and pulled out for town.
During the three-day drive with their heavy load they were not
bothered any more by their musical ghost and saw nothing
unusual on the way. Chris sold his belongings and went back to
Kents' Corners where he could hear real music from nearby neighbors, unaccompanied by shots in the dark.

After his adventure in the Red Lake country Joe teamed
awhile at Sioux Falls, and then became a land hunter. The country had settled up a great deal in the two or three years since he
and Chris had their bout with spirit music. One day he took a
party of land buyers out to the Red Lake neighborhood. A railroad had been built through that area and the tracks went right
past the land Chris had abandoned. In fact, a station had been
located there and a little town had sprung up, some of it on the
tract that Chris had claimed. Joe and the land lookers stopped at
the town for a few days. Shacks and houses were going up everywhere and breaking teams were turning the sod on hundreds of
acres.

At dusk one evening as Joe strolled about town he heard a
familiar sound. Following it up he found a fellow sitting on the
porch playing "Silver Threads" on a piccolo. Joe stopped short
and gave the fellow a look that would have killed a more decent
person. Seeing Joe's hand on his belt near his Colt's, the musician
decamped and kept out of sight while Joe was in town. On
inquiry Joe learned that this man with the musical ability was
the first settler in town; in fact, he had been there before the
railroad came.

Joe figured that the musician had heard that the railroad was
coming through that area. Somehow or other—perhaps from the
railroad surveyors—he had been tipped off about the direction
the road would take and the location of the new town. Checking
the Government survey, he found that Chris had claimed the very

land he wanted. Nothing daunted, he improvised his weird music
act to stampede the Eastern tenderfoot. Then he had jumped the
abandoned claim in readiness to cut it into town lots and sell out
at a profit when the railroad located the town there. It was literally a case of getting land for a song—"Silver Threads Among
the Gold."

Look Out Below!

THE FIRST SETTLERS on the Great Plains located their land claims
on rivers or streams, or near springs and water holes which
yielded water the year around. The latecomers were obliged to
locate in areas far removed from surface water. To survive they
had to improvise: cisterns were installed in ravines; draws were
dammed up to catch run-off from rain and melting snow; water
barrels were daily hauled long distances to rivers or streams.

For these less fortunate persons a well was the surest answer
to the problem of water supply. In some parts of the plains, good
supplies were found at depths of fifteen to twenty feet; but in
many areas shafts went down a hundred feet and more. The task
of drawing water from wells of this depth was quite different
from drawing or pumping it fifteen or twenty feet, and in times
of drought when water had to be drawn for thirsty livestock the
task became insuperable, as many on old-timer could testify. The
answer was found in windmills, which were revamped and improved by a Connecticut mechanic, Daniel Halliday, to meet the
special conditions obtaining on the Plains. Since the winds there
were free and constant and of high velocity, Halliday built his
windmills with stronger and smaller blades, better fins, and self-
regulating speed controls.

The new windmills brought a boom in well digging, and
skilled well diggers were much in demand. Once a well got below
shoveling depth, the digger would spade the earth into a rein-

forced half-barrel, called a bucket, which was then hauled by a pulley to the surface and emptied. As the well deepened, its walls were lined with board curbing to prevent cave-ins. The work was dangerous for the digger: sometimes gases were encountered which could be fatal; the rope on the bucket might break and crash down on the digger; or the board lining might give way, releasing an avalanche of earth and burying him alive.

In western Nebraska, for miles around the town of Valentine, Joseph Grewe, a German immigrant known as Dutch Joe, was the undisputed king of the well diggers. In seven years during the 1880's and 1890's, he dug more than six thousand feet of wells, ranging in depth from one hundred to two hundred and sixty feet. A short, stout man of great courage and skill, he took enormous pride in his calling. He would point to a windmill and say, "There's a Joe Grewe well!" And then add, "Straight as a gun barrel!" In a single day he could dig as much as thirty-five feet. Those who watched him in action said there was never a man who could strike his spade into topsoil and sink out of sight in such an astonishingly short space of time.

One day in 1894 Joe was called back to a well he had dug to clear out some obstruction. Standing in the shallow water at the bottom, he gave the signal to hoist a bucket full of loose rock. When it was almost at the top, the bucket slipped from the steel catch holding it to the rope and plummeted to the bottom, killing Joe instantly. He himself had devised the steel catch, which was designed to save time by quickly releasing the bucket from the rope for unloading. Many years' service had worn the catch unnoticed, and his own invention became the instrument of Dutch Joe's death.

Wells on abandoned land claims were often left uncovered, and when hidden by weeds were a hazard to travelers. In the 1870's, F. W. Carlin, traveling through Custer County, Nebraska, about fifteen miles north of Broken Bow, took the wrong road and drove up to some old sod buildings one evening at twilight. He turned his team around in the farmyard and started down what appeared to be a good road. When one of his horses faltered and seemed to step into a low spot, Carlin, sensing that something was wrong, got out of his rig and walked up beside the team.

The next thing he knew he stepped into empty space and began to hurtle downward. Even as he was falling, Carlin realized that he must have stepped into an abandoned well. He lit with a great splash, and went totally under. Though momentarily stunned by the fall, he instinctively raised his head above the water, and after freeing his feet from the mire at the bottom, stood up in the cold water, which fortunately was only arm-deep. Feeling about with his hands, he ascertained that the well was curbed with wood. He managed to break off a board at the bottom, and by wedging it between two cracks in the curbing, he contrived a seat. Here he perched, a hundred and forty-three feet beneath the surface of the earth, until morning.

His team ran away, and with them went his best hope of rescue. If the horses had remained, someone would have noticed them and come to investigate. As it was, no one was likely to venture on the abandoned property, and the nearest house was a mile away. As the night wore on, Carlin became aware that his ankle was badly sprained and one of his ribs was broken.

When morning came and he had light to inspect his prison, he saw that the well was lined with a wooden curbing about three feet square, the boards tight together and covered with slimy mud. However, at intervals there were breaks in the curbing— stretches of uncurbed wall between curbed sections ranging from six to sixteen feet in depth. It occurred to Carlin that he could use his jackknife to whittle handholds in the curbing and scale the well in somewhat the same fashion as a mountaineer scaling a precipice. At once he set to work at the difficult business of carving out the handholds. When he got to the top board of a curbing, he would take off a board, wedge it across the corner, and use it for a seat.

In this manner he got up about fifty feet by late afternoon. Then he came to a sixteen-foot-deep curb, made of the hardest native timber; it was tightly fitted together, and he found it almost impossible to carve. As it was nearly dark, he made a good seat and sat there through the night and until noon the next day, every now and then calling for help.

For a time, he gave up all hope and resigned himself to die. But thoughts of his wife and his little son spurred him on to try again. His knife was now so dull that it would not cut the hard wood, but he scraped some sand from an unlined section of the wall, put it on a board, and used it as a whetstone. With his knife resharpened, he was able to make footholds again in the curb. Higher and higher he climbed until finally he reached the end of the sixteen-foot section.

Above him was a round curb four feet high and absolutely smooth inside. The dirt had washed out behind it until he could see daylight between it and the wall. The curb was held up by just one peg driven into the earth, and he knew that if he tried to climb up inside it, as he had been doing, his weight would tear the curb loose, and he would fall with it to the bottom. His only chance was to burrow between the curb and the earth wall. Using the utmost care he gradually wriggled his way upward, and finally crawled out on the ground at the top. For some time he just lay there, too exhausted to move. Then he knelt and thanked God.

Hobbling and crawling, Carlin made the half-mile to the road, where he waited hopefully for someone with a team to come along. But neither man nor beast appeared, and finally he started on his hands and knees to the house a mile down the road. Night overtook him and he fell into a deep sleep. Toward morning he felt better and started on. Just at daybreak he dragged into the house, where he was hospitably received.

Not the "three r's" but the "three w's"—wood, water, and weather—stood for the three major subject-matter fields in the elementary education of a Great Plains pioneer. But whereas in the case of wood and water the problems arose from there not being enough, when it came to weather there was, if anything, too much— and whether hot or cold, wet or dry, it was more capri-

*cious and more extreme than anything in the pioneers'
previous experience. Blizzards marooned settlers and
brought death to travelers. Tornados whirled across
the prairies, sowing devastation and savaging all that
stood in their murderous course. Hailstorms slashed
down out of purple thunderheads battering to bits
promising crops. Drought, intensified by searing south-
erly winds, left the green land parched and blackened.
If a man was to survive in the Great Plains environment, all these phenomena had to be learned about—
and usually by bitter experience. Then, being able to
anticipate their effects, he could to some extent control them.*

All Kinds of Weather

THE SAME PROMOTIONAL METHODS which were used to attract settlers to the Mississippi Valley* were effectively employed by agencies, companies, and individuals with a stake in the settlement of
the Plains. But from the beginning they had to combat the
adverse publicity generated by government reports and newspaper stories on the fearsome Great Plains weather. The myth of
the "Great American Desert," which had taken root early in the
1800's, persisted throughout the century, reviving every time
there was a major drought. Perhaps even more damaging were
the headlines accorded to the blizzards which periodically swept
Montana, Wyoming, the Dakotas, Nebraska, and Kansas, causing
many deaths, heavy losses of livestock, and much hardship and
suffering.

   During the 1860's the word *blizzard* came into common use to

*See page 119.

denote a particularly terrifying winter storm characterized by subzero temperature, heavy snowfall, gale winds, and the shocking
swiftness of its arrival. Even the later settlers, who were far better
briefed on the ways of the weather than the first arrivals, were
often caught unprepared by the suddenness with which a blizzard hit.

Both the "Easter Blizzard" of April 14–16, 1873, and the
"School Children's Storm" of January 12–13, 1888, followed peri-
ods of such warm weather that men had been working in the
fields in their shirt sleeves. The 1888 blizzard, which was probably the most famous in Plains history, covered the entire region
between the Rockies and the Mississippi from Canada to Texas.
Because in some areas the storm struck while children were still
in school or just starting home, there were many youngsters
among those who lost their lives (the total number of deaths has
been variously estimated as anywhere from two hundred to a
thousand). The terrible experiences of teachers and pupils in
poorly built and inadequately heated one-room schoolhouses
shocked many communities into giving more attention to the
comforts and conveniences of their district schools.

Although not so dramatic or the subject of so many and
such highly colored newspaper accounts as blizzards and floods,
droughts were equally destructive and demoralizing. Also, being
more prolonged, they were harder to bear and more frequently
the cause when a homesteader threw in his hand and went "back
East to the Wife's Folks"—as signs on eastbound schooners sometimes proclaimed. Blizzards and floods, calamitous though they
were, usually affected comparatively small areas and spent themselves quickly; drought was all-pervasive and a slow dying. When
it came, first the crops went, then the cattle had to be disposed
of, and finally either the family gave up and moved out or stayed
and starved.

In Kansas in the spring of 1859, prospects were unusually
bright with bumper crops in the making. Then in late June the
rains stopped, and the settlers did not see another good rain or
snow until November, 1860. The merciless heat opened up wide
cracks in the earth; springs and streams dried up; horses and

oxen grew emaciated. Before the drought broke, thirty thousand men and women called it quits and left the region. But more stayed—and before it was too late, help came in the form of money, clothing, grain, and food sent by groups and persons in the East. The heroism of the "stayers" was largely unsung. To hang on, to endure, to hope seem passive, far from stirring activities compared to battling snowdrifts and flood waters, but the qualities these Kansas settlers displayed—grit, perseverance, and indomitable faith—were essential for the conquest of the Plains.

1

Although tornados were not unheard of in the eastern part of the United States, they were outside the experience of all but a few of the pioneers who came to the Great Plains. These huge funnel-shaped whirlwinds, which dipped out of a cloud-blackened sky, almost invariably traveled from the southwest to the northeast, destroying everything in a path perhaps four hundred yards wide. At times they would rise high above the earth, passing over the fields and homes below, only to dip down, twisting and turning like an elephant's trunk, and resume their ruinous work.

On the afternoon of May 30, 1879, Gerhart Krone, a homesteader living near Delphas, Ottawa County, Kansas, came in from his fields when a gentle rain was succeeded by a fusillade of hail. About three o'clock, Krone looked across the plains to the southwest beyond the Solomon River, and saw an angry, greenish-black cloud from which hung a giant, swaying funnel. It was moving toward the northeast, and as it approached, a dark, smoke-like mass of flying debris was plainly visible at its base.

A number of people were gathered at Krone's home, taking shelter from the storm. Now he warned them that they should seek safety elsewhere, that the building would be no protection. He himself was running toward the northeast, with his grown daughter beside him, when the twister struck the house, reducing it to kindling wood. Krone was flung to the ground, then lifted up and dropped down again several times, sustaining severe injuries. His daughter, after being carried a distance of two hundred yards, was hurled against a barbed wire fence and killed instantly. Every shred of clothing was ripped from her body, and she was covered with black mud. Beyond where she was found, the wire from the fence was ripped from the posts and wound up into a roll. Mr. Krone's eldest son was carried past the fence into a wheat field, his clothing also ripped off and his body plastered with mud. Another daughter, Anna, had a piece of board driven nearly through one thigh; then the wind itself extracted the board, leaving a seven-inch gash. The doctor later found nails, straw, and splinters of wood driven into the ghastly wound.

Other members of the family were tossed about, but none was seriously injured. In every case their clothing was whipped off, their hair so matted with mud that it had to be shaved, and mud filled their eyes and ears, plastering them shut so that they could neither see nor hear.

T. W. Carter, who had stopped at the Krone place for shelter, took refuge in a haystack, burrowing in as deeply as he could. The haystack was overturned by the wind and he was tossed high up in the air—how high he could not say, but he reported later that while airborne he came in contact with a horse and instinctively grabbed at it, clutching either its mane or tail. When he struck ground, he was mother-naked except for his straw hat in one hand and a clump of horse hair in the other.

Chickens were stripped of their feathers and carried great distances, one being found three miles to the northeast. Two lumber wagons were scattered in bits over the prairie, the largest piece left intact being one wheel. A buggy axle was bent double and a cast-iron binder wheel weighing two hundred pounds was carried a half mile.

2

The combination of drought and high wind not infrequently set the stage for a prairie fire. Once kindled, the flames moved across the prairie with appalling speed, buffalo chips and other burning debris being blown far in advance of the main fire and igniting the dry grass, so that a prairie fire literally leaped ahead.

From a purely aesthetic point of view there were few more sublime sights. Albert D. Richardson, describing a prairie fire for the benefit of eastern newspaper readers, wrote of the sky "pierced with tall pyramids of flame, or covered with writhing, leaping, lurid serpents, or transformed into a broad ocean lit up by a blazing sunset. Now a whole avalanche of fire slides off into the prairie, and then opening its great, devouring jaws closes in upon the deadened grass."

The greatest danger of prairie fires came in the fall when a campfire, a bolt of lightning, or sparks from a passing railroad engine would set the dry prairie ablaze. It was impossible to put out a head fire, but side fires, flaring out behind, could be contained by dragging a green animal hide over the flames. Fanned along by high winds prairie fires have been known to leap across streams, but they found it harder to jump a fireguard. This was made by plowing two sets of deep furrows, about fifteeen yards apart around the area to be protected. Then, on a calm day, the grass between the furrows was burned. Seldom did a prairie fire leap across this barrier. The same idea often saved travelers caught in the path of a prairie fire. The traveler would burn off a patch of ground large enough so that when standing in its middle he would not be touched by the advancing flames.

Near Garden City, Kansas, one windy autumn day in 1872, Clinton Gore was driving across country in a light spring wagon drawn by a fast team of horses. He was astonished to see flames erupt from the prairie not far from him. Thinking he could outrun the flames, he applied the lash to his team, and they carried him bouncing across the prairie at breakneck speed. But they were not swift enough to win the race with the devouring flames. Seeing that his relentless pursuer was gaining on him, Gore stopped the team and attempted to kindle a fire, but in the high wind his matches were blown out as fast as he lit them. As the flames drew nearer, the terror-stricken team quivered and snorted, but Gore had no time to waste soothing them. As a last resort, he snatched his buffalo robe from the wagon and put it over him. With this as a windbreak, he at last succeeded in igniting the grass.

Then he hastened to guide his team onto the burned patch, and had them follow on after his backfire as fast as the grass burned. But the wind had now advanced to a gale, and he saw that the wall of flame was only seconds from overtaking him. Jumping out of the wagon, he lay down upon the ground in the burned strip, pulling the buffalo robe over him. He still retained hold of the harness reins, and the plunging and rearing of the team pulled his hands out from under the robe. Fearful that the horses would trample him, he made the mistake of throwing the robe off his face in order to see. He was conscious of an inferno of smoke and flame, and a blast of unimaginable heat, as the prairie fire rolled by on either side at express-train speed.

After the holocaust had passed, the badly burned man crawled out and drove his charred horses sixteen miles to the nearest town, where he put up at the hotel and called a doctor. He hung between life and death for several days, and was not fully recovered for four months. Gore's horses fared worse. Although he had held them on a burnt-off spot fully four yards wide, the intensity of the fire was such that the flesh dropped from the side of their bodies which had been nearest to the flames, and they had to be put to death. It was a miracle that they had lived long enough to pull the wagon to town.

3

Homesteaders entered the Dakotas in fair numbers during the 1860's and early 1870's, but the Panic of 1873 all but stopped the flow of immigration. Anxious to see settlers in the land along its tracks, the bankrupt Northwest Pacific Railroad gave 4,500 acres of Red River Valley land to Oliver Dalrymple, an expert wheat grower from Minnesota. With the backing of the railroad's capital, Dalrymple started a large-scale experiment. The wheat yield was twenty-five bushels per acre and the profits more than a hundred per cent. This electrifying news sparked a Dakota land boom. Between 1877 and 1888 thousands of settlers claimed more than thirty million acres of homestead, plus several more millions sold by the railroad.

The territory's population increased four hundred per cent between 1880 and 1885. Among the newcomers were O. D. Towne and his family. Optimism was in the air and, like everyone else,

Mr. Towne aimed to become a bonanza farmer in the James
River Valley.

It had been a little dry in the early spring of 1883 but in May
and June the rains fell generously. The wheat crop in Spink
County never looked better. By late June it was shoulder-high,
thick as hair, and heavy with grain. With wheat selling for better
than eighty cents a bushel it looked like money in the bank.
Towne and many of his fellow farmers mortgaged their crops to
buy the new-fangled binders and binding twine. The shipment
was delayed several weeks, but one terribly hot day in July Mr.
Towne received word that his machine had arrived at the imple-
ment store in nearby Crandon. That evening the breeze went
down with the sun, and it was so unbearably hot that the family
sat out in the yard until late, giving the house a chance to cool off.

Very early the next morning Mr. Towne was awakened by a
deafening roar accompanied by the sound of breaking window
glass. Rushing to the open window he saw heavy hailstones
pounding the landscape. Running to another window he saw his
cattle humped up, tails to the storm, patiently suffering the pelting. In the adjacent corral the horses were running and neighing
in agony and fear. The icy pellets rattled off the roof in such
profusion that banks of ice accumulated at the base of the house,
and even though the sun came out strongly after the storm, the
ice heaps did not melt until the following day.

None of the livestock was seriously harmed, though many
were bleeding from gashes. But when Mr. Towne walked out to
his fields, the billowy wheat, so nearly ready for the sickle, was
hammered right down to the ground, completely pulverized. On
the battered cornstalks, which had been nearly knee-high, the
glossy leaves were shredded to ribbons; however there was a
chance it would pull through, and the hay would still make a
crop. But wheat, the cash crop, had vanished.

The whole countryside was stricken. Riches so certain one
day that they had been mortgaged were now swept away at a
single stroke. It seemed that half the settlers in Spink County
were pulling out—some to return to their native states, others to
try their luck in the logging camps of Wisconsin and Michigan.

The afternoon after the hailstorm Mr. Towne went into Crandon. In the little trading center he found a crowd of homesteaders, as bewildered and undone as he was at how in a few minutes the elements could undo a season's work and change the future prospects of a whole region. But soon the little gathering turned into a sort of conference. Their spirits rose when it was learned that only an area about fifteen miles wide and forty long had been hailed out. As they talked, their resolution revived and the resilience, the capacity to bounce back, so necessary to a Plains pioneer, began to manifest itself. It was early enough yet for the corn to come out and make a crop; the hay was not damaged, and since there would be no wheat crop to harvest, they could use the time normally consumed by that long, hard job in breaking new acreage. Outside the hail strip, crops were unusually good, and those who had lost their own wheat could hire out to help with the harvest on the farms of the fortunate ones, thus earning cash to tide them over the winter.

While the conference was going on, the agent for the farm machinery company sauntered past the group. "Guess I won't be needing that binder," said Mr. Towne.

The dealer gave him a thump on the shoulder. "Don't worry about that," he said. "This year's wheat is gone, but the land is still here."

Mr. Towne agreed that it would take more than a hailstorm to jar the land loose, but—and he indicated a passing wagon laden with household goods—it seemed to have had an unsettling effect on a good many people.

The agent looked at him for a moment inquiringly, as if wondering whether Towne planned to pull stakes. Apparently he decided Mr. Towne was a "stayer," for he said, "Well—better luck next year. I've got a hunch you'll be needing that binder."

He was correct in both assumptions.

The Kitchen Frontier

THERE WAS A SAYING current during settlement days that "Plains travel and frontier life are hard on women and cattle," and no doubt there were plenty of times when a pioneer wife told her husband that on the whole cattle fared better. Certainly it did seem that the real burden of the adverse conditions which made plains life difficult—the perpetual winds, the absence of trees and water, the temperature extremes, particularly the terrific heat—fell on a wife and mother.

Much of a woman's time was spent alone in surroundings that compared very unfavorably with her old home. The constant wind, blowing day after day, played on her nerves; she stared at the boundless prairie with nothing to halt her gaze over the monotonous expanse, and sometimes the prairie got to staring back. There was nothing to do or see and nowhere to go, and it was the dreary sameness and loneliness of the life that she found hardest of all to bear. One of the greatest trials of the pioneer woman was remaining alone in the isolated sod house for days and even weeks while the husband went to the mill, to town, or worked away from home. The danger of Indian attacks was ever present and every approaching object was looked upon with apprehension. Childbirth also became a terrible dread on the lonely frontier. Miles stretched between the patient and the nearest doctor. Blizzards or floods often made it impossible to secure the help of a doctor. Many times the child was born without medical aid.

The good housekeepers never felt at home in a hole in the ground or in a sod house where sweeping the dirt floor only made it uneven and where a snake's head might suddenly protrude from the sod walls or his slithery length be seen coiled around a rafter.

Simply keeping her family in reasonably clean clothes was a major task for the pioneer mother. Usually, washday was actually "washdays," Monday and Tuesday. Since she had no bar soap, she put soft soap and hot water into a tub or keg, and then dumped in the clothes. After being vigorously prodded with a stick, they were taken out, laid on a block, and pounded with a mallet. When the clothes were as clean as she could get them, she hung them on bushes or fences to dry.

Often the womenfolk had to carry the water long distances from springs or a neighbor's well. Sometimes they supplied themselves with wash water by strewing tubs, dishpans, and other available vessels under the eaves. (A little later the rain barrel, a well-known institution, appeared at the corner of the house to catch the raindrops which dripped from the eaves and were carried to the barrel by means of a trough.) And frequently the women of the family migrated to a little creek or branch on wash day. The ten-gallon iron kettle and the clothes were taken to the bank of the stream, where wood and water were plentiful.

Illumination was usually a problem which involved the woman in a special way. In the homes of the more prosperous, homemade candles were used, and the manufacturing work fell to the lot of the housewife. If there was no candle mold available, the wicks, consisting of twisted string, were dipped into a kettle of hot tallow. When withdrawn, a certain amount of tallow stuck to the wick and hardened quickly in the cool air. After it had solidified it was dipped again, and this process was continued until the wick had accumulated sufficient layers of tallow to form a regular-sized candle. In another method, a candle mold, consisting of a dozen tubes, was called into use. Wicks were drawn in the center of the tubes and hot tallow was poured into them. When the tallow had hardened, the mold was dipped into hot water for a moment and the candles slipped out readily. In the earlier times, the tallow was secured from buffalo and deer, later on from beeves. A lamp popularly known as an "old hussy" was made by filling a bowl or cup half full of sand and placing a stick upright in the center. A wick was then wound around the stick and enough animal oil poured over the sand to fill the cup. Often lard was scarce, and opossums, badgers, coons, and other animals fell a prey to homemade lamps. The wick was lighted at the top and made a fairly good blaze.

In her husband's absence, the pioneer woman had to use her judgment in business transactions as well as in dealing with such minor and major emergencies as cows breaking out of the pasture and lightning starting brushfires. Laura Bower Van Nuys, whose family pioneered in the Black Hills, recalled one occasion on which her mother figured in a horse trade.

> This was when an Indian from the Pine Ridge reservation came to the ranch to see about buying one of our horses. Papa was away, but Mamma knew the asking price was seventy-five dollars. The Indian told Mamma he didn't have that much money with him. He said he would go back to the reservation and get it, and being on foot asked if she would let him take the horse. Mamma consented and the Indian rode off in the general direction of the reservation, which was across the Cheyenne River to the east.
>
> When the men in the family heard what had happened they were somewhat exasperated, to put it mildly. They made it clear to Mamma that three things she could never expect to lay eyes on were the horse, the Indian, and the seventy-five dollars. But all the same she did: the Indian came riding back on the specified date.
>
> There are two possible interpretations of this incident: the distaff side of the family always maintained it merely went to prove Mamma was a good judge of character. But the men-folk never saw it as anything other than an act of divine intervention.

For women as well as men, writes Mrs. Van Nuys, pioneer life was "hard and precarious, a day-to-day affair with disaster always lurking just around the corner. To be sure, not every year was a drought year or a flood year or a grasshopper year, any more than every snowstorm was a blizzard and every high wind a tornado; there were far more friendly Indians than hostiles and far more working cowboys than rustlers. But both nature and man posed threats to existence that had to be reckoned with, and few weeks went by without their quota of emergencies, ranging from small-scale mishaps to genuine catastrophes."

Although the life of women on the plains was rude and hard, with few material compensations, legally, educationally, and socially her position was higher than that of women in the more conservative East. It was in Wyoming that women first gained the right to vote, and the Plains states were the first to enact legislation entitling a married woman to sell her real and personal property, and to engage in any separate trade, business, or employment on her own account free from the control of her husband. Nevertheless, in man's story of the conquest of the plains, woman is given scant credit for her part.

The grasshopper years of the 1870's bulked large and black in the memory of every pioneer who lived through them. In July of 1874, farms on the Great Plains from Canada to Texas were assailed by hordes of grasshoppers (Rocky Mountain locusts) which literally ate them off the face of the earth.

The Hawthorne family, who had taken out a homestead in the Platte Valley, near Grand Island, Nebraska, the preceding year, were just rejoicing over the progress they had made—the garden with potatoes and vegetables almost ready to eat, the sod corn coming up—when the scourge struck. That was an afternoon nine-year-old Monty Hawthorne never forgot, and he later told about it in these words:

> I was standing in the yard looking over the prairie, and I seen a little fire starting way off to the west. I started to run to the house to tell the folks about it, when I seen it wasn't a fire but a storm, because it was off the ground and coming towards us like a big cloud, and I run fast and started yelling that a snowstorm was going to hit us. It was a storm all right. In no time grasshoppers begun raining down on us. The air was so full of them we could hardly see. Mama give me the broom and told me to run for the garden and to beat them off the cabbage plants. Mama worked out there longer than I did, and I never give up until the sharp barbs on their legs had cut me so bad I was bleeding all over and had to go to

the house. Sadie had pulled off her apron and throwed it over her little flower garden before she run out to try to help Mama. When they come back to the house, they seen that the grasshoppers had et clean through her apron and that the plants in underneath was gone. Julia and Father was down by the spring, carrying boards, trying to cover it over and save our water supply, but thousands of grasshoppers drowned in there, and before it was fit to use again Father had to take their bodies out by the bucketful. Aaron had run out to see about the sod corn, but he come in and said that every corn-stalk was as thick as a man's upper arm with them grass-hoppers.

By then we knowed that we was helpless to fight them, and that all we could do was to hole up in our sod house until the wind changed and they moved on some place else. Grass-hoppers is like that. When the wind is blowing from the west, they light, and they don't go on again until the wind changes. Over at Kearney they stopped the railroad train because them mashed grasshopper-bodies made the tracks so slick and oily that they couldn't get no traction. But, of course, we didn't know nothing about that then. We was all in the house, and Mama was using the elm bark salve as sparing as she could because she knowed it would never last to fix all them cuts on our faces and hands and feet and legs where them grass-hoppers dug their sharp barbs into us.

And those of us that wasn't being doctored had to run around killing the ones that had got in the house and was jumping all over the place, and Father was using the broom and a thin board for a dustpan, scooping them up and drop-ping them into the fire where we'd hear them sizzle as the flames licked around that oil in their insides. And for days we had nothing to eat, nothing but some boiled wheat and boiled corn with nothing to put on top.

After the grasshoppers moved on and we opened the door and tried to start living again, we seen long lines of covered wagons coming back. Mama said we couldn't turn back like they was doing. They was still adrift. But we was anchored. We had to stay right there and toughy it out because there wasn't nothing wrong with our sod house—or with the land we'd built her on.

Because the grasshoppers had got so bad they stopped the trains, they was news. Word got out about how folks in Nebraska was starving and was needing most everything, and the government voted money to send help, and all over the country folks started packing relief boxes and shipping them in. The boxes got there first. . . . Father and Mama and our neighbor Porter Brown [were appointed] as a committee to open and divide a big box of clothing for the settlers in our valley, and Porter and the folks went to town and got the box. There was a surplus of buckwheat somewhere else and so the government was sending it to Nebraska, and they was shipping in them old Civil War uniforms too that had been stored in warehouses ever since the soldiers had quit fighting.

When all the folks had gathered at our house, Father took his single-bitted ax and he struck right through the lid. He knocked off the iron bands and Mama stood up by the table and started taking the things out from inside. First, come a man's suit. It was made of black and white checks, real wide ones, and all the fellows let out a yell when she held it up because they'd never seen nothing as sporty as that. A man couldn't of wore it milking; them blamed checks was so loud they'd of scared the cows so bad they wouldn't give down no milk. That one suit was all they'd sent for men. There wasn't a single thing in the box for children. All the rest of the box was packed tight with the fanciest dresses I ever seen. They was made of real heavy silk, with nothing up around the top where a woman's shoulders sunburns bad, and they had all them trailers hanging down in back where she needs her clothes cut off floor length so's to have her legs loose for walking. When Mama got about half done with lifting them dresses out of the box she just quit and set down on a bench and cried like a baby. Porter Brown, trying to cheer her up, grabbed one of them big feathered hats that had been mashed down flat in the packing, and shoved the crown up enough to get his head in and says, "See, Martha, what I've got to wear plowing?"

Blamed if Mama didn't stop crying and start in laughing. Nobody could get her stopped for awhile, neither. But before long she entered into things and was having just as much fun as anybody there. The men and the women and us children got into them fancy dresses and we had a dance. No, sir, we never had so much fun in our lives as we did that night we unpacked the relief box that had come to us straight from New York. We laughed so hard at how folks looked in them dresses, that nobody minded having to go home without no refreshments. Them days, folks was used to cinching up their belts; and having that party done us all a lot of good.

The Traveling Courthouse

THE OPEN-HANDED HOSPITALITY and good neighborliness of families on the Great Plains frontier derived in great part from the conditions of pioneer life. In that big empty country, the opportunity to visit with another human being—friend or stranger—was a welcome break in the monotony, while maintaining friendly relations with the homesteaders on the next claim was very nearly essential—who else was there to turn to in an emergency? As one pioneer woman put it, "We had to get along with each other, and cooperate, to survive." Mutually dependent, and sharing the common experience of battling Indians, drought, devouring insects, and loneliness, the isolated settlers were drawn together in a fellowship that was akin to brotherhood.

But if neighboring families of settlers generally got along well together, the same certainly cannot be said for neighboring towns. For town-dwellers no less than homesteaders, survival was a paramount consideration, and in a sparsely settled area, where the demand for goods and services was small, two towns frequently would be one too many—there just wasn't enough business to go around. Of course local pride eventually entered in, but the bitter enmity which so often developed between two adjacent pioneer communities almost always had its roots in simple economics.

Naturally the founders of a town were anxious to secure any advantage that would promote its growth and development. If, for example, the railroad could be persuaded to build its line that way, the town's prospects were much enhanced and real estate prices rose accordingly. Another solid guarantee for a town's survival was to be chosen as the seat of county government.

In Gray County, Kansas, three towns vied for the honor of becoming the county seat—Cimarron and Ingalls on the Arkansas River, and Montezuma, a few miles to the south of it. A sufficient number of petitions having been sent to the governor, the county was proclaimed organized on July 20, 1887, and Cimarron, the largest of the three towns, was designated as temporary county seat until October 31, when a special election would be held to select the permanent location.

Ingalls, though the smallest of the three towns, had recently acquired an ambitious and well-heeled booster from Rochester, New York—none other than the patent medicine king, A. T. Soule, whose Hop Bitters and kindred products had netted him ten million dollars. Among a welter of other promotional schemes, he was determined to make Ingalls the county seat, and set it on the road to becoming a real city. Forbearing to make campaign speeches in favor of letting his money talk for him, Mr. Soule traveled around the county passing out checks for $100 to $500 in return for the promise of an X opposite Ingalls' name on the ballot.

Apparently, however, he never made contact with a secret organization called the Equalization Society whose sole reason for being was to sell, *en bloc,* the votes of its seventy-two members. The highest bidder turned out to be T. H. Reeves of Cimarron, who, just before the election, agreed to pay the Equalization Society $10,000 to cast its seventy-two votes for his town. As surety, the Society received a bond for the full amount signed by fifteen leading citizens of Cimarron. Came election day—which, appropriately enough, also happened to be Hallowe'en—and the organization duly cast its seventy-two votes, with the result that Cimarron won out by a plurality of forty-three. But when a committee called on Mr. Reeves to collect the $10,000, which was to be divided equally among the membership, they were told that the signatures on the bond were a forgery and they could whistle for their money.

One swallow does not a make a spring, and in those days one election did not make a county seat. Ingalls went to court to challenge the result, and a second election was ordered. This time Ingalls' personal Midas, A. T. Soule, had what seemed to him a sure-fire plan for enlisting the support of the citizenry of Montezuma. Their town, he reminded them, was not on a railroad; very well, then, he would build them one. All he asked in exchange was that they vote for Ingalls to be county seat. This sounded good to the Montezumans, and the bargain was concluded. The patent medicine king, unlike the perfidious Mr. Reeves of Cimarron, was as good as his word. He got busy organizing the Dodge City, Montezuma & Trinidad Railroad, which was helped along by a $60,000 bond issue voted by farmers of two townships on the new line; and for their part the citizens of Montezuma did their duty at the polls, providing the margin of victory.

On February 1, all the county records had been moved from Cimarron to Ingalls, but Cimarron went to court in its turn and right around Valentine's Day came a writ ordering the records returned. By February 21 they had been carted back, and the lights began burning late in lawyers' offices at Ingalls. The result was another writ directing that the records be packed up again and taken back from Cimarron to Ingalls. The Cimarron legal eagles countered with a series of motions for rehearings and other delaying tactics which threatened to prolong judicial proceedings indefinitely.

As matters now stood, Ingalls men held the majority of county offices, but Cimarron had possession of the records and thus remained the official seat of government. After due consideration, the Ingalls partisans started the New Year with a resolution to quit fussing around with the law and take direct action. Early in January, 1889, the sheriff and a couple of friends went over to Dodge City and shopped around for a few gunmen, whom they brought back to Ingalls.

On the morning of January 12, 1889, a wagon carrying ten or twelve men halted in front of the courthouse at Cimarron. Re-

trieving their six-shooters and Winchesters, which had been concealed in the bottom of the wagon bed, one squad stood guard
while a second entered the building and ordered the county clerk
to keep his hands up while they repossessed themselves of the
records.

As word spread that the Ingalls crowd was raiding the courthouse, the men of Cimarron reached for their shooting-irons and
rallied at the courthouse just as the last of the records were being
stowed aboard the wagon. In the running fight that followed
three Cimarron citizens were killed, as was one of the raiders. In
addition, two raiders were wounded and three captured, but the
Ingalls men got home with the records. Before hostilities could be
resumed, the governor sent a company of state troops from Wichita to cool off the rival factions.

On October 5, 1891, after two years of litigation, the Kansas
State Supreme Court finally handed down a decision in favor of
Ingalls. It kept the county seat until the following year when
what was regarded as a fair election restored it for good and all
to Cimarron. But the spoils of victory were not worth the struggle.
In the dry years of the early 1890's, the three little Gray County
towns began to shrivel up.

By 1892 grass was growing in the streets of Montezuma and
its big new hotel stood empty. There was no traffic on the railroad, which had been taken over and then abandoned by the
Rock Island because of the dearth of business. The farmers of the
townships which had voted the $60,000 bond issue vainly sought
redress from the multi-millionaire patent medicine king; he had
recently gone to his reward, and the farmers' temper was such
that his demise must be accounted a timely one. In their rage and
frustration—and also to salvage what they could of their investment—the farmers ripped up the rails and ties and tore down the
station, leaving nothing at all of the nobly named Dodge City,
Montezuma & Trinidad Railroad except the grade. By 1895 not a
soul inhabited Montezuma, and it seemed destined to end as a
ghost town. But some years later a railroad was built over the
same right-of-way, and a new Montezuma rose about a mile from
the original site.

When the Spaniards established settlements in Texas around 1720, they brought with them cattle bred by Moorish herdsmen. These tough animals, the progenitors of the famous Texas Longhorn, thrived under the climate and grazing conditions of their new home. By the time Texas entered the Union there were hundreds of thousands of them running wild in the lush Nueces Valley in addition to those in ranch herds.

Everything was favorable to the development of large-scale ranching in Texas except its distance from the markets. During the 1840's and '50's cattle were driven to New Orleans and other Gulf ports or north to Chicago. One herd of a thousand went as far east as Ohio, and a few were taken west to the Arizona and California gold fields. But the difficulties were great and the profits small. The end of the Civil War, which had temporarily cut off the eastern markets, signaled the beginning of boom days for the range cattle industry. The scarcity of beef in the north, and the increasing demand for it, drove up the price to $40 or $50 a head for steers that sold for $6 and $7 in Texas. With 5,000,000 cattle roaming the state's 152,000,000 acres of unfenced range, the enterprising Texans made the most of a golden opportunity.

In the winter of 1865–1866, several thousand steers were pointed up the trail to the western terminus of the Missouri-Pacific Railroad at Sedalia, Missouri. This initiated the operation which came to be known as "the long drive." The following summer, and for twenty summers thereafter, immense herds of cattle were driven north to railroad shipping points. During these decades the cattlemen, running branded herds over unfenced ranges, ruled over a kingdom which ultimately stretched from Texas to Montana and from the Rockies eastward to the ninety-eighth meridian.

The Long Drive

DURING THE YEARS of the long drive, certain well-defined trails were developed. In 1865 and 1866 the drives went up the Sedalia Trail, delivering 260,000 head of cattle to the railhead there. But the Missourians protested that the herds trampled their farms and infected their cows with tick fever (a disease to which the Texas Longhorns themselves were immune), and in 1867 the route was shifted westward, running from San Antonio, Texas, to Abilene, Kansas, on the Kansas Pacific Railroad. This was the celebrated Chisholm Trail.

The drives usually started north in March. The crew for a herd of 2,500 would consist of a trail boss, a cook, ten or twelve cowboys, and a wrangler or two to look after the string of fifty or more ponies ridden by the cowpunchers. Because of the range cattle industry's Texas origin, there were many Spanish words in cowman's lingo—as, for example, the trail boss and his assistant were also known as the *capitan* and the *segundo,* and the string of ponies was usually called a *remuda.*

Before the drive pulled out, the steers would be "road branded" with the brand of the owner; this usually was done by the crew. Leading the outfit was the chuck wagon, driven by the cook, and next came the horse wrangler and his *remuda.* Following them were the steers, strung out for a mile or more, with two cowboys riding "point" at the head of the herd, and a second pair riding "drag" at the rear to prod along the stragglers. The other cowboys rode along the flanks of the herd, watching to see that none strayed off. Each day's drive started at sun-up, halting for its nooning at a watering place for the cattle and horses. The crew had its noon meal, and the livestock were grazed until about half-past two; then they were driven on again until dark.

The Texas steers were ideally suited for the long trip north. They had the stamina to travel great distances with little food or water, and once "settled down" after a week on the trail, they were generally docile about following the point cowboys. Bedded at night, however, the steers often were nervous. The smell of wolves, a thunderstorm, or any unusual stir among the cowboys or the horses frequently would spook the placid herd into stampeding.

1

In the spring of 1876, J. W. Simpson started north for Abilene with a herd of 2,800. After the usual difficulties and dust-ups—a trail drive was never either orderly or easy—they reached a point on the Solomon River just north of Abilene. They were to hold the herd here until it was sold. Within two or three miles of the Simpson outfit there were perhaps a half-dozen other herds also waiting for instructions from their owners to deliver them.

As the boys unrolled their beds that evening, the sky was clear but the air was warm and humid. At about eleven o'clock one of the night herders rode in to report that a storm was brewing, and at once the order was given: "All hands to the herd." As the boys saddled up, lightning began to play and the cattle were moving about uneasily. Suddenly a flash of lightning directly overhead illuminated the whole landscape in a blaze of blinding light, and the cattle started running even before the thunderclap reached their ears.

It was now the cowboys' job to ride alongside the herd to the leaders, turn them until they were running in a wide circle, and keep closing in on them, narrowing the circle, until the whole herd was moving in a compact body. Riding like Comanches, three or four of the boys finally got ahead of the leaders and turned them into a milling mass of beef on the hoof, the outer steers running and those in the center climbing over one another in panic.

The whole atmosphere was charged with static electricity. Balls of fire played off the ears of the horses and the points of the long horns of the terrified cattle; long, lurid fiery snakes darted down their backs and the horses' manes. Hearing yells and the pounding of hoofs off to the right, the cowboys knew that a neighboring herd was on the run. The frenzied cattle jumped at every thunderclap, and the earth trembled under the impact of twenty thousand hoofs.

As the atmosphere grew even more oppressive, the cowboys, who believed that steel and heat attracted lightning, shed the slickers from their perspiring bodies and shucked off their spurs. Even six-shooters were cast upon the Kansas prairie.

Water began to pour from the heavens in sheets. Those who had their raincoats in hand waved them in an attempt to keep the cattle from breaking through the cordon of riders, but there was no stopping the hysterical animals. They charged through the line and were off on another mad dash. In no time they had run into the neighboring herd and the whole mass was splitting and blending. It was now every man for himself, but the object of all was to hang on and stay with a bunch of cattle. Maybe three riders would wind up herding fifty head, while a single cowboy was trying to handle a thousand. But every man kept with the cattle unless he was hurt or his horse disabled.

At daybreak one of Simpson's cowpunchers, John Young, and a stranger from another outfit found themselves with about eight hundred head of steers, still running. Young raced in front of the bolting herd, flashing his slicker, and finally succeeded in slowing down the leaders. The animals in the rear ranks piled up on them three and four deep, and the run was over.

As the two cowboys drove the cattle back, they saw by the brands that they had parts of four or five herds. Every herd in the whole area around Abilene had stampeded, and from ten to twelve thousand head were all mixed up. It took five days to gather up all the cattle and then cut them out into the original herds. During this period there were a number of thunderstorms and squalls which caused another rash of stampedes, and about half the cutting out had to be done again.

Finally Simpson got orders to deliver his steers to a shipping point on the Platte River, and the weary cowboys gladly headed the herd north again. The animals were spoiled now and ran at every opportunity, but none of the trouble they made could ever begin to compare with the great stampede on the Solomon.

2

Trail routes changed as the various rail lines moved westward, and other Kansas towns supplanted Abilene as railheads—first Ellsworth and Newton, and then, after 1875, the most notorious of them all, Dodge City. By this time, the Union Pacific was making a bid for its share of the profitable cattle trade and was constructing cattle pens and landing chutes at various Platte Valley stations. From 1876 until the middle 1880's, more than 100,000 cattle each year went on up the trail to Nebraska.

"The trail into Ogallala," writes James C. Olson, "was an extension northward from Dodge City of what was known as the Western Trail, which, as settlement moved west in Kansas, replaced the old Chisholm Trail. . . . The Western Trail started at Bandera, Texas, crossed the Red River at a point known as Doan's Store, then pushed on to Dodge City, the Santa Fe's boisterous shipping town on the Arkansas River. Some of the longhorns were left there, but most of the younger animals were driven on to [stock the northern ranges]. From Dodge City the trail angled north and west to Buffalo Station, about sixty miles west of Hays on the Kansas Pacific. The last leg of the journey was the most difficult, principally because of the lack of water. Streams were few and far between at best, and the drovers frequently found that many of the smaller streams on which they were depending had dried up."

Lack of water was undoubtedly the grimmest of all the problems connected with the trail drive. In June of 1882, Jim Flood was trail bossing a herd of 3,100 steers up through Kansas. Before leaving Brownsville on April 1, he and his crew of fourteen had road-branded the herd with the circle-dot hair brand of the owner. The herd was soon well broken to trail driving and moved right along until, south of Dodge City, they hit a drought area. For three days the herd went without water, and the evening of the third day found them still twenty miles from a watering place. The ordeal of the next forty-two hours was described by one of Flood's cowboys, Andy Adams.

Holding the herd this third night required all hands.

What few cattle attempted to rest were prevented by the more restless ones. . . . Good cloudy weather would have saved us, but in its stead was a sultry morning without a breath of air, which bespoke another day of sizzling heat. We had not been on the trail over two hours before the heat became almost unbearable to man and beast. Had it not been for the condition of the herd all might have gone well; but over three days had now elapsed without water for the cattle, and they became feverish and ungovernable. The lead cattle turned back several times, wandering aimlessly in any direction, and it was with considerable difficulty that the herd could be held on the trail. No sooner was the milling stopped than they would surge hither and yon. Six-shooters were discharged so close to the leaders' faces as to singe their hair, yet, under a noonday sun, they disregarded this and every other device to turn them. In a number of instances wild steers deliberately walked against our horses, and then for the first time a fact dawned on us that chilled the marrow in our bones—the herd was going blind. . . .

It was nearly noon the next day before the cattle began to arrive at the water holes in squads of from twenty to fifty. Pitiful objects as they were, it was a novelty to see them reach the water and slake their thirst. Wading out into the lakes until their sides were half covered, they would stand and low in a soft moaning voice, often for half an hour before attempting to drink.

Contrary to our expectations, they drank very little at first, but stood in the water for hours. After coming out, they would lie down and rest for hours longer, and then drink again before attempting to graze, their thirst overpowering hunger. That they were blind there was no question, but with the causes that produced it once removed, it was probable their eyesight would gradually return.

After a few days the herd had recuperated, and were in fair-to-middling shape as they continued on past Dodge City toward Ogallala. As they neared the Republican River they encountered a different kind of trail hazard. But it was not at first recognized as such, and this time the cowhands, not the cattle, were the victims. Jim Flood had ridden on ahead to talk business with the

buyer, leaving his *segundo,* Joe Stallings, to bring the herd on to
the Republican crossing.

Near noon [as Andy Adams tells it] we were overtaken by
an old, long-whiskered man and a boy of possibly fifteen.
They were riding in a light, rickety vehicle, drawn by a small
Spanish mule and a rough but clean-limbed mare. The strangers appealed to our sympathy, for they were guileless in
appearance, and asked many questions indicating that ours
might have been the first herd of trail cattle they had ever
seen. . . . After dinner, when our *remuda* was corralled to
catch fresh mounts, our guest bubbled over with admiration
for our horses, and pointed out several of promising speed
and action. He innocently inquired which was considered the
fastest horse in *remuda,* and Stallings pointed out a brown
gelding belonging to Flood as the best quarter horse in the
band.

It turned out that the old man was from Tennessee on his
way to the Republican to locate a homestead. He was as talkative as he was friendly, and a good story-teller, always using the
form "Says I" in relating some incident involving himself. The
cook loaned him a saddle for his mule, and he rode the rest of
the day with the cowpunchers, leaving his son to drive the rig.
Before supper that evening some of the crew entertained the guest
with a little game of freeze-out for a dollar a corner, and the old
fellow lost. Offered a chance for revenge after supper was over, he
said he was unlucky at cards and couldn't afford to gamble anyway. Finally, however, he was persuaded to sit in, and in a
remarkably short space of time had relieved the boys of twenty
dollars.

As they were about to turn in for the night, the Tennessean
remarked that if the brown horse pointed out to him earlier was
really the fastest they had, hanged if he didn't think his bay harness mare could outrun any animal in their *remuda.*

"You think so, do you?" said Joe Stallings, who was still smart-
ing over the outcome of the card game. "Then you stick with us
tomorrow, and when we meet our foreman at the Republican

crossing, if he'll loan me his horse, I'll race you for any sum you name."

The stranger said he and his boy wanted to get away early in the morning as they still had a long way to go, but he'd think about it. On the chance that the old fellow might take the bet, Stallings and a couple of the boys decided to check out just how fast the harness mare really was. At midnight they stole the bay off the picket line and secretly tried her against Flood's brown gelding. The result convinced them the race would be a shoo-in. "Why, that old bay harness mare can't run fast enough to keep up with a funeral," Joe reported. "I rode her myself, and if she's got any run in her, rowel and quirt won't bring it out. If the old man wasn't bluffing, we'll get our money back—with interest."

The next morning the harness mare was grazing peacefully at the end of her tether, and Stallings went over to have a last word with the homesteader. He said that the herd would be at the river around the middle of the afternoon, and urged him to be sure and stay overnight there. "If you still think that your mare can outrun that brown cowhorse," he said, "you can sure get action on your money." But the venerable visitor would make no promise beyond saying that he would see them again later that day.

About noon Jim Flood rode in, bringing the buyer who had purchased their herd. He readily agreed to lending his horse for the race, assuming it came off, but warned them to steer clear of the whiskey sellers who had set up in business near the Republican ford and were running every sort of skin game ever devised to fleece the unwary.

After they reached the Republican and were watering the herd, the bewhiskered Tennessean ambled up to Stallings, flashed a thick roll of bills, and announced that he had borrowed it from a saloon-keeper, giving as security his harness mare and his Spanish mule. If they were still in the mood for a race, he was prepared to wager the lot on his mare. The bet was soon covered, and the Tennessean hospitably invited the whole crew to come and have a drink on him at the tent saloon. There was already quite a crowd on hand when the Circle Dot outfit pushed up to the bar, and when word got around among them of the race to be held the next evening, there was quite a lot of additional betting. When all the crew's ready money had been wagered, some of the saloon bunch offered to take six-shooters, saddles, and watches. Flood warned his boys not to bet their saddles, but Stallings and one of the others already had bet theirs, and were taking them off the horses to carry to the saloon-keeper who was holding the stakes. By the end of the evening, every watch and six-shooter in the outfit was in the hands of the saloon-keeper, and the saddles would have been there too, had it not been for the boss.

Next evening Stallings and the homesteader measured off the course, laying a rope on the ground to mark the start and another at the finish line. It was getting dark by the time the old man signaled to his boy to bring up the bay mare, who was covered with an army blanket. The keyed-up cowboys waiting at the finish line peered through the gloom, hardly able to tell which horse was which, but loudly cheering their man on. However, when the bay mare crossed the finish line an easy winner a profound silence fell, and they were still speechless when they returned to the wagons and bedded down for the night. The next morning Stallings and the other man who had lost his saddle sheepishly went to Flood, and asked for an advance on wages so that they could redeem this essential gear. They got the money, but after such a talking-to that when the herd pulled out they were riding mighty low in the saddle.

> Such a crestfallen looking lot of men as we were would be hard to conceive [wrote Andy Adams]. But the cruellest exposure of the whole affair occurred when Nat Straw, riding ahead, overtook us one day out from Ogallala, Nebraska.
>
> "I met old 'Says I' Littlefield," said Nat, "back at the ford of the Republican, and he tells me that they won over five hundred dollars off this Circle Dot outfit on a horse race. He showed me a whole basketful of your watches. I used to meet old 'Says I' over on the Chisholm Trail, and he's a foxy old innocent. He knew you fool Texans would bet your last dollar on such a cinch. That's one of his tricks. You see the mare you saw wasn't the one you ran the race against. I've seen them

both, and they are as much alike as two pint bottles. My, but you fellows are easy fish!"

And then Jim Flood lay down on the grass and laughed until the tears came into his eyes, and we understood that there were tricks in other trades than ours.

3

From Ogallala, the Circle Dot outfit headed up the North Platte River, bound for Fort Benton, Montana. There the herd would be turned over to its new owner, and would be held on his grazing grounds to mature and fatten for market. Until a few years before, the North Platte had marked the northern boundary of the cattlemen's domain. Although most of the Sioux had been settled in the Red Cloud and Spotted Tail agencies by 1874, small bands of hostiles were still fairly common in the region. But the campaigns of General Crook and Colonel Miles in 1876 put an end to this menace, and the Northern Plains were thrown open to cattlemen. Since the buffalo herds were fast disappearing, leaving the rich grasses of Plains available for cattle grazing, by the beginning of the 1880's more than five million Texas Longhorns and the new breed of "Kansas Herefords" were roaming the open ranges of western Kansas and Nebraska, Wyoming, Montana, and the Dakotas. Among the scores of new ranches, many were owned by easterners and Europeans who had heard exciting stories of the money to be made in the range cattle industry, and who did not permit their inexperience to interfere with their urge to set themselves up as cattle barons. These haughty tenderfeet were a source of both exasperation and amusement to hardbitten cowhands such as Jim Flood and his men.

By the latter part of July, the Circle Dot outfit had reached the Forty Mile crossing of the North Platte, a few miles above the Nebraska-Wyoming line. Heavy rains in the mountains had raised the water to "big swimming" level, and a herd belonging to the Prairie Cattle Company was already at the ford, waiting for high water to subside.

The trail boss, a Texan named Wade Scholar, was an acquaintance of Flood's, and the two men talked the situation over.

Having had considerable experience with swollen streams, Flood proposed to swim the Circle Dot herd over without wasting time. "When one of these sandy rivers has had a big freshet," he said, "look out for quicksands when it falls. We've swum a half a dozen rivers already, and I'd much rather swim this one than attempt to ford it." But Scholar, who seemed to dread swimming a river, could not make up his mind to do it, though he promised to have his crew on hand to help Flood's men.

With a double crew to handle the crossing, the operation went off smoothly and efficiently. The Prairie Company men fed the cattle slowly into the water, while Flood's riders swam their horses alongside, keeping the chain of cattle unbroken. In less than an hour, the Circle Dot herd was across and had fanned out on the grazing ground beyond.

Encouraged by the smoothness of the Circle Dot operation, Scholar finally decided to take his herd across, too. All went well until the last two or three hundred of the tail-enders were part way across, and the men working in the rear started to swim the channel. There was a good deal of laughing and joking, then suddenly a terrified cry for help. Andy Adams, who was on the opposite bank, at once plunged his gray into the river and swam to the scene of the trouble.

> Horses and men [wrote Adams] were drifting with the current down the channel, and as I appealed to the men I could get no answer but their blanched faces, though it was plain in every countenance that one of our number was under water if not drowned. There were not less than twenty horsemen drifting in the middle channel in the hope that whoever it was would come to the surface, and a hand could be stretched out in succor.
>
> About two hundred yards down the river was an island . . . , and on landing I learned that the unfortunate man was none other than Wade Scholar, the foreman of the herd. . . . A hundred conjectures were offered as to how it occurred; but no one saw either horse or rider after sinking. A free horse would be hard to drown, and on the nonappearance of Scholar's mount it was concluded that he must have become entangled in the reins or that Scholar had clutched them in his

death grip, and horse and man thus met death together. It was believed by his own outfit that Scholar had no intention until the last moment to risk swimming the river, but when he saw all the others plunge into the channel, his better judgment was overcome, and rather than remain behind and cause comment, he had followed and lost his life.

The next day, Sunday, the body of the drowned man was found among the driftwood near an island. Within a few minutes of its recovery, a collection was taken up, and a wagon sent to buy a coffin at nearby Fort Laramie. The night before the tragedy, the cook had been talking with members of an immigrant train which was going to wait over Sunday to observe the day, and it was thought that among such conscientious people there would be a minister. A messenger was sent to the train, and returned with word that a retired minister had promised to conduct the service and bring his two granddaughters to sing.

The funeral, attended by the crews of both outfits and about twenty passengers from the immigrant train, was conducted by the side of the open grave. As Andy Adams remembered him, "The minister was a tall, homely man with a flowing beard, which the frosts of many a winter had whitened, and as he mingled among us in the final preparations he had a kind word for everyone. The two granddaughters of the old man opened the simple service by singing very impressively the first three verses of the Portuguese hymn. . . . We stood with uncovered heads during the service, and when the old minister addressed us he spoke as though he might have been holding family worship and we had been his children." After the concluding prayer, the young ladies sang "Shall We Gather by the River?" and the coffin was lowered into the grave.

The time had come to separate. The Prairie Cattle Company crew had elected a new trail boss, a man named Campbell, and he held his herd on the river while the Circle Dot herd trailed out toward the northwest. On August 26, not quite five months after leaving Brownsville, they reached Fort Benton and the end of their twenty-five-hundred-mile drive.

"*They Went Thataway!*"

ONE COWTOWN looked much like the next—but after months on the trail any town looked good to the cowboys. "Main Street" was perhaps a couple of blocks long; there would be a post office and a jail, some general supply stores, a hotel or two, and a row of saloons and gambling establishments. Every town had its "Cowboy's Rest" and "Last Chance" saloon and "Crystal Palace" —indistinguishable except for their names—in which, as present-day entertainment media continue to make relentlessly clear, "gold flowed freely across the tables, liquor across the bar, and occasionally blood across the floor as a bullet brought some unlucky cowhand to the end of the trail. . . ."

Vice and violence did indeed flourish in these trail towns, and the disreputable and the dissolute were irresistably drawn to them. The doings of such professional badmen as William (Billy the Kid) Antrim, Jesse James, Sam Bass, John Wesley Hardin, "Bone" Wilson, and Charley Bowdre were as much of a conversational staple as the weather in places like El Paso, Abilene, Fort Griffin, Dodge City, Ogallala, and Deadwood.

The life of a peace officer in a trail town might be short but it was seldom merry, and the responsible members of the citizenry frequently decided to hire celebrated "fast guns" like Pat Garrett, Wyatt Earp, Red Hall, and Bill Hickok to keep the hoodlums in line. Down in Texas, where the Rangers were charged with preserving law and order, the list of men wanted for rustling, armed robbery, and murder would run as high as five thousand names—but the Rangers had a special problem because Texas was a refuge for desperate men from every state in the Union. "The Texas trail hands and the ranch cowboys," writes Mari Sandoz, "often included men called G.T.T.'s, meaning Gone to Texas, one jump ahead of the U. S. marshal. When these men got into trouble they might become G.N.'s, Gone Norths, perhaps from the law or to escape an avenger."

There were a half-dozen contenders for the title of wildest, wickedest, most flamboyant cowtown on the trail, but while a good case could be made for several, in our day, at least, Dodge City is remembered as the epitome of the Wild West at its wildest.

Robert Wright, recalling Dodge City in its heyday, tells the story of a devil-may-care cowboy who got on a train about thirty miles from Dodge. "I want to go to Hades," he told the conductor when asked his destination. "All right," said the conductor. "Give me a dollar and get off at Dodge."

At Dodge [Wright continues] people congregated from the east, south, north, and west; people of all sorts, sizes, conditions, and nationalities; people of all colors, good, bad, and indifferent. Some came to Dodge City out of curiosity, others strictly for business. The stockmen came because it was a great cattle market, the cowboy because it was his delight and here he drew wages and spent them. Last but not least the gambler and the crook came because of the wealth and excitement.

Money was plentiful and spent lavishly. There were numbers of people, to my certain knowledge, who would carefully save up as much as a thousand dollars and then come to Dodge City and turn it loose, never letting up until every dollar was gone.

There was "a man for breakfast," to use a common expression, every once in a while, and this was kept up through the winter of 1872. It was a common occurrence. In fact, so numerous were the killings that it is impossible for me to remember them all. . . .

1

Cattle stealing—rustling—was of course a crime on the cattlemen's frontier, but unless the animal was branded it was difficult to prove ownership. In such cases the unwritten law dated back to 1845 when—one story is—Samuel A. Maverick, a San Antonio lawyer, reluctantly accepted 400 head of cattle in payment of a $1,200 debt. He put them in the charge of a shiftless herder. The herd multiplied, but the calves, once weaned, were allowed to

roam the range. Neighbors put their own brands on them, and
when Maverick sold the herd he had fewer than when he began.
But his name was immortalized, for ever after that any unbranded
cattle found on the open range were known as "one of Maverick's"—or simply mavericks. It was a case of finders keepers and
became generally recognized as the law of the Cattle Kingdom.

Horse stealing, in whatever circumstances, was considered
worse than murder. A man who killed another sometimes was not
even arrested. Usually he skipped the country until the matter
had blown over, or if he was taken into custody, more often than
not "took leg bail"—as an escape from an insecure frontier jail
was described. If he was brought to trial, he had a much better-
than-even chance of being acquitted on the ground of self-defense.
Even the rare person who was convicted seldom spent more than
a few years in prison and could look forward to returning home
with an unblemished reputation.

But the horse thief was regarded in no such benevolent light.
The horse was essential to the cattle business, and was the only
means of conveyance generally in use by private individuals in
the West. The man who stole a horse was the mortal enemy of
the whole community, since no one knew when he himself might
be victimized and find himself on foot.

As horses were allowed to run on the range unguarded, the
cattlemen decided that the best insurance against theft would be
to make the punishment for horse stealing certain and prompt.
Either thieves had to be discouraged by fear of violent death or
no one would be able to go to sleep at night with any assurance
that he would have a horse to ride in the morning. In localities
where "the law" was weak, vigilantes stepped in and reversed the
time-honored rule that the accused is presumed innocent until he
is proved guilty. A man accused of horse stealing was judged
guilty unless he could establish his innocence.

In the mid-1870's, a ring of horse-thieves, taking advantage of
lax and inept law enforcement, were preying on the southern
Nebraska counties, stealing horses right and left, running them
across the state line, and marketing the stolen animals in Kansas.
Finally, the Nebraskans who had been robbed got together and

organized a protective association, determined to put an end to their losses, even if it meant stringing up a horse thief on every cottonwood along the Big Blue.

On a pleasant summer day in 1876, J. B. Boswell of Russell, Kansas, a citizen of good reputation, alone, unarmed, and with a conscience void of offense, rode into the little Nebraska town of Crete. Without warning or cause, he was suddenly arrested and charged with stealing horses. At a hearing presided over by the mayor, he was subjected to a grilling which left him confused and nonplussed. After a long session of questioning, his examiners told him of the recent plague of horse thievery, and added that they had just hanged one horse thief who, before the execution, had confessed his accomplice was a Kansas man. Unfortunately for Boswell, he was the only Kansan they had been able to lay their hands on, and it was therefore presumed that he must be the guilty party.

The logical fallacy of this reasoning was perfectly plain to Boswell, but not to the exacerbated Nebraskans, and no amount of vehement denial of any connection with *any* illicit enterprise impressed them in the slightest. In vain he protested that at the time of the theft he was going about his regular business in Kansas, and that it was ridiculous to hold him on the strength of such a vaguely worded confession. His accusers simply repeated that a Kansas man was involved, and it was up to Boswell either to prove that he wasn't that particular Kansas man or else to admit his guilt.

He was taken to jail, but not allowed to languish there long. That night about nine o'clock, some twenty-five men came for him and took him a mile or so out of town to a spot where there was a suitable tree. He begged piteously for his life, but his executioners were in no mood for clemency. Seeing that there was no hope they would spare him, Boswell asked that they do him the favor of hanging him from the railroad bridge over a nearby creek. The fall from that height would probably break his neck, and this would be preferable to slow death from strangulation— the end he could expect if he were drawn up a tree limb.

One of the party quickly vetoed his request on the ground

that strangulation was good enough for a Jayhawker; however, the majority of the crowd did agree that he should have time to make out a will. Boswell then directed how his property should be disposed of, and asked two of the crowd to witness to his last testament. Then he said he was ready.

Something in Boswell's bearing impressed the leader of the mob, and raised in his mind doubts as to Boswell's guilt. He proposed to the others that they take a vote whether or not to hang the captive; if they felt Boswell was guilty, the leader said, then he should swing; otherwise he should go free. There ensued an argument which seemed interminable to poor Boswell, and in the end he was granted a forty-eight hour reprieve to prove that he was innocent.

Although there was little Boswell had an opportunity to do but repeat what he already had told his inquisitors, after a couple of days they let him go. Neither the mayor nor anyone else made him any apology, but at the time Boswell hardly noticed the oversight. He just wanted to get on his horse and take off for home. And when at last he crossed the state line, Boswell thought he had never seen any place so beautiful as Kansas.

2

Toward sundown of an afternoon in early September, 1877, six men leading pack horses rode into Ogallala, Nebraska, and made camp about a hundred yards west of the Rooney Hotel on Railroad Street. After stopping by the Crystal Palace for liquid refreshment, they continued on to the Rooney where they had supper. As they rose to leave, a bunch of cowboys tore past the hotel, shooting "high, wide, and scattering," and scaring the wits out of two women guests who were sitting in the parlor. Noticing their fright, one of the men, a very gentlemanly looking, softspoken fellow, at once came over to the women, tipped his hat, and assured them that they were in no danger—"The boys are just having a little play spell; they don't mean any harm." Then, tipping his hat again, he rejoined his companions and left the hotel.

Much impressed by his appearance and manner, the ladies

asked Miss Gast, the daughter of the hotel proprietor, who the gallant stranger might be.

"Oh, he's a no-account, swindling cowhand from Texas," said Miss Gast. "Goes by the name of Collins—Joel Collins. I don't place the others, except the one in the checked shirt; that's his sidekick, Sam Bass. They're poison, both of them."

"Oh, surely not," said one of the ladies. "Anyway, not Mr. Collins. He has such a *fine* face—so sensitive."

"So is a rattlesnake," said Miss Gast. The ladies smiled politely but were obviously unconvinced.

Having other guests to attend to, Miss Gast did not pursue the argument. But some two weeks later, when the great Union Pacific train robbery was making headlines across the nation and there was a $10,000 reward out for the arrest of the Collins gang, she recalled the conversation and wondered what the ladies thought now of the "sensitive" Mr. Collins.

On his one previous visit to Ogallala, Joel Collins had made his presence felt. He had trailed a herd north from Texas in the summer of 1875, and after a brief but gaudy interlude of high living had skipped town with the proceeds from the sale of his employer's herd. With him went a chap named Sam Bass, who was building a reputation as a cattle rustler. Collins was next heard of as a dance-hall proprietor in Deadwood, which became the new miners' Mecca after the gold strike there in April of 1876. It seemed that neither Collins nor his friend Sam could stay away from the gambling tables, where they were spectacularly unsuccessful, and the grapevine had it that they were compelled to make ends meet by robbing stages.

Perhaps there was too much competition, or perhaps Collins figured that with the spotlight on the Black Hills people might get absent-minded about the gold in transit from other places—notably that from California, which was carried east by rail. At any rate, he and Sam Bass rounded up four kindred spirits and came on down the trail from Deadwood to Ogallala. Eighteen miles east of the cowtown was an isolated water-tank stop called Big Springs, and a little reconnoitering established that the Union

Pacific's eastbound passenger train Number 4, with an express car, passed through there around midnight.

On the evening of September 18, Collins and Sam Bass and the other members of the gang—Bill Hefferidge, John Underwood, Tim Nixon, and Jim Berry—passed a convivial hour at a corner table in Tuck's saloon, and then rode away over the moonlit prairie toward Big Springs. Since Big Springs was not exactly over-populated—there was nothing there but a water tank, some cattle pens, and the wooden shack which served as a freight and passenger depot—the station agent was surprised and curious when he heard approaching hoofbeats. His curiosity was quickly but unpleasantly dispelled when two masked men with drawn revolvers entered the station and ordered him to dismantle the telegraph instruments. After making sure that he had done so, they told him to hang out a red signal light and gave him explicit instructions about what he was to do after the train came in.

When Number 4 chugged in from the west and stopped, obedient to the signal, two of the bandits climbed up in the engine cab, flashed their guns, and compelled the engineer and fireman to extinguish the fire in the fire-box. At the same time, one of the gang ran down the train to cover the conductor; the three others, prodding the station agent along with their revolvers, walked over to the express car. The agent, a gun jammed against his spine, called out to the express messenger to open the door, and a moment later two of the robbers were aboard the car. While one of them backed the expressmen into a corner, the other collared the messenger and told him to get busy and open the safe. When the messenger said that he couldn't oblige because he didn't know the combination, he was savagely beaten, but saved from more serious damage by the arrival of the conductor, escorted by the sixth bandit. Both the conductor and the station agent verified the messenger's statement that the combination to the safe was known only to officials at the east and west terminals.

For a moment it seemed that the would-be train robbers were stymied, but then one of them spotted three heavy wooden boxes stacked at the end of the car. No sooner had he pried up the lid of the top one than he let out a triumphant yell—"Struck it rich!"

—and, dipping up a handful of gold coins, let them cascade back into the box. Now, with one man keeping the railroad personnel covered, the other three really got down to business. Further investigation turned up $300,000 in gold bullion being shipped east from the California gold fields, but this the bandits left in the car. Not that they were choosy, but the gold bars were too heavy for them to carry.

Leaving two of the men to sack up the gold coins, Collins and another of the gang worked their way through the train, collecting money and valuables from the passengers. The doors to the Pullmans were locked, but they reaped a modest harvest in the chair cars. As it happened, one of the coach passengers was a cowhand named Andrew Riley who had become well acquainted with Collins on the trail drive from Texas, and who had, in fact, run into him in Ogallala only a few days before. Although Collins' face was muffled to the eyes in a bandana, Riley recognized him at once—but had sense enough to keep his mouth shut.

Loading up their loot, the gang headed back to Ogallala to collect their gear. Outside of town they left the gold at a previously prepared cache, and then had the nerve to stop at the Crystal Palace for a round of drinks before breaking camp and pulling out. They camped a day on the Republican and divided the gold, then split into groups of two and headed for points south.

The news of the robbery created a furor. It was the first time a Union Pacific train had ever been held up, and the $10,000 reward was enough to send a host of sleuths, amateur and professional, on the outlaws' trail. After Riley had positively identified Collins for the railroad detectives, the "wanted" call went out at once to peace officers.

Meanwhile, M. F. Leech, proprietor of the Ogallala supply store, had been building up his own case against Collins and Bass. At the scene of the robbery he had picked up a piece of red, white, and black cloth which had been used as a mask by one bandit. Leech recognized it as coming from a bolt of goods in his store, and further remembered that he recently had sold a strip of it to one of the gang. Figuring that the $10,000 reward would buy a power of drygoods, harness, and other fixings, he saddled his best horse and started out to hunt down the outlaws.

He soon picked up the trail of Collins and Hefferidge, who had joined a group of drovers convoying some cattle to a Kansas Pacific shipping point. A few nights later Leech caught up with the outfit, spotted Collins and Hefferidge, and tipped off the authorities. On the morning of September 26, the two fugitives rode into the little prairie station of Buffalo, Kansas, and stopped to buy some provisions at the store run by the station agent, who had been alerted that they might be coming that way. Although he did not have their descriptions, he became suspicious when he noted that their pack horses, which seemed to be carrying very small loads, were jaded and sweating freely. As soon as the men started south, he telegraphed Sheriff Beardsley of Hays, who collected ten cavalry troopers and set out in hot pursuit.

When overtaken and questioned, Collins and Hefferidge insisted that it was a case of mistaken identity and offered to return to the station to clear up the matter. After riding a short distance, Collins whistled to his horse and both he and Hefferidge reached for their guns. They were instantly chopped down by the cavalry troopers' fire. Twenty thousand in gold, tied up in sacks made of overall legs, was found on the pack horses of the late bandits.

Somehow or other Leech missed out receiving any part of the reward for this phase of the operation, but the railroad company encouraged him to carry on with the good work. By the following summer he was close on the trail of Jim Berry. Unfortunately, the day before he caught up with him, Berry was killed in Mexico, Missouri. He had carelessly deposited large sums of gold in banks in that area and became so restive when questioned about it that the peace officers were compelled to shoot him.

Sam Bass and Tom Nixon made their getaway safely to Texas, traveling in the guise of land-seeking farmers. Sam Bass had ten more months in which to enhance his reputation as a badman; then he was killed by the Texas Rangers, though his ill-fame lived on in a celebrated cowboy ballad. Nixon escaped to Mexico, and nobody seems to know what became of the sixth bandit, John Underwood.

As for the indefatigable Mr. M. F. Leech, sad to report none of the reward money ever came his way, nor did he ever have the satisfaction of actually "getting his man." Always he would catch up with his quarry just in time to attend the funeral and congratulate the peace officers. But at least he was a hero to the homefolks, who elected him to the office of county sheriff. After three months of trying to cope with drink-crazed, trigger-happy cowhands, however, Mr. Leech "throwed up the job" and thankfully retired behind the counter of his store, with only the pinholes in his vest where the sheriff's star had once blazed to remind him of the days when he was "the law" in that particular part of God's country.

Where the Horse Was King

CATTLE COUNTRY was a man's world—and it called for the kind of man who could stand up against stampedes, "hard cases," and all kinds of weather, who could find his way without a trail, and who could accept the fact that danger always rode at his side without worrying about it. Courage and cheerfulness were essential cowboy traits and—though he might be happy-go-lucky where only he himself was concerned—a sense of responsibility to his employer and his outfit was another.

"The cowboy's hours were from sunrise until his tasks were done," writes Robert Sturgis, "and that was often long after dark. There were horses to be broken and trained and inspection trips to be made about the range—'outridings,' as they were called—to locate and check on the condition of the scattered groups of cattle, and to drive them to better territory if food or water was found to be insufficient. There were strays to be driven back to the herd, and mired stock to be pulled at rope's end from mud bogs. There was the need to keep a constant lookout for thieves and predatory animals, and to set traps for any beasts that might endanger the herds.

"It is a popular fallacy that the cowboy always carried a gun. The truth is he went armed only when absolutely necessary: that is, when expecting a personal attack, when riding in Indian country or near the border, or when riding the range where he might meet injured or diseased cattle which would have to be shot. He also wore a gun when he went on a holiday visit to town or when he called on his girl. At such times the gun was as necessary for correct cowboy dress as a white tie is for formal evening wear.

"The average cowboy looked after the comfort of his horse before he did his own. Literally he lived on his horse. His high-heeled boots made walking difficult, and if there were more than two hundred feet to be traversed the puncher got in his saddle. Most had learned to ride before they had taken their first steps, and they considered it undignified to walk. . . . Living a lonely life when on duty on the range, the puncher became deeply attached to his mount. Men who regarded sentimentality as an unforgivable weakness were not ashamed to pour their troubles into their horse's sympathetic ear."

In fact, it wasn't just the man who made the range cattle business pay—it was man *and* horse. Around the campfire nine-tenths of the talk was of horses—size, color, speed, stamina, and cutting ability. Strong and allegedly silent men could discourse for hours about the qualities and personal characteristics of their "mount"—the string of extra horses furnished them for a trail drive—on which they would bestow such revealing names as Red Dog, Bug Henry, Cannonball, Monkey Face, Few Brains, and Rat Hash.

Probably at some point in these campfire discussions, an old-timer would break in and complain that "there ain't no more good ponies"; and then there would come an unending, impossible-to-settle argument about the merits of great cow ponies, past and present. Feats of endurance and famous races would be cited as evidence, and it was a lead-pipe cinch that sooner or later the talk would get around to Jim Murray's champion horse "Fiddler" and the time he had the Indian sign put on him at White Clay Creek.

In the early 1880's a Frenchman named Joe Larvie, who had married an Indian girl and settled in northwestern Nebraska, heard from the Indians thereabouts of a place in the Black Hills where hot water poured from the ground. Larvie and his partner acquired the tract in which the spring was located and moved their families to the site. Other settlers heard of the tonic and healing quality of the warm, medicinal water and moved to the vicinity. Eventually Larvie and his partner sold their holding (which later became the townsite of Hot Springs, South Dakota) for six hundred dollars and a thoroughbred stallion.

When the grey proved to be unusually fast, Larvie took him to the Red Cloud Agency and matched him against the fleetest ponies the Indians and neighboring ranchers could produce. Not once was he defeated and seldom even forced to extend himself. He became the idol of the agency, and was so admired by the Indians that they were willing to bet their most cherished possessions the grey could beat any horse this side of the happy hunting grounds.

About this time a beautiful bay horse made his appearance in the Black Hills. This was Fiddler, the pride of the Western Trail, who had won match races from the Pecos River to Ogallala. His owner, whose real name was Dahlman, but who was traveling under the name of Jim Murray, drifted into the Red Cloud Agency with two other cowboys going under the names of Nebo and Leneaugh.

It was not long before the Texans let it be known they were spoiling for a horse race and ready to bet everything they had to uphold the honor of the Lone Star state. They found plenty of takers. From Chief American Horse down to the least boy, the Oglalas bet their blankets, guns, money, and horses that Larvie's grey could outrun Fiddler. Many northern cowboys were ready to bet their cash on the Sioux champion. One of these, Big Bat Pourier, a famous frontier scout who lived on the reservation, laid down a thousand dollars to back the grey stallion, who was

being trained by another famous horseman and plainsman, Buckskin Jack Russell.

The Texans declared openly that they would kill any white
man who rode the Indian horse and they personally threatened
Buckskin Jack. He was a brave scout, but being a married man
he decided not to take the chance. Joe Larvie, called Joe Hansha
by the Sioux, had several half-breed girls who were beautiful. A
bantam cowboy named Tom Brady loved one of the girls and,
seeing an opportunity to win the favor of the father of the dark-
eyed beauty, volunteered to ride the big grey. Although small in
stature, he was an excellent horseman and his services were
accepted.

The race was to be run over a 600-yard-straightaway near
Dier's Trading Post at a place later called White Clay Creek.
Thousands of Indians and cowboys lined the race course. So
lively was the betting that, it was said, horses, wagons, and other
property wagered on the race covered about two acres near the
trading post.

Jim Murray came out first on Fiddler. A shout of admiration
went up from the cowboy section as the splendid, shiny bay
tossed his head and pranced before the crowd. Even some Sioux
shook their heads. Suddenly a warrior called Little Horse, clad in
a blanket, stepped out on the side of the track on which the Texas
horse was to run. With every eye watching him, he knelt and put
his hands on the earth. Then he stood up and walked away saying loud enough for those nearby to hear: "Let him run past
here." This done, Little Horse slipped into the crowd.

Presently Tom Brady rode out, his mount eager for the race.
As he passed the Indian maiden he loved, he caused the horse to
rear and saluted her with his quirt. At the starting line, Fiddler
was collected and Murray sat on him quietly, confident of the
outcome. The grey horse was harder to manage. It was some time
before the two horses were lined up side by side.

The gun cracked, and Fiddler was off to a length's lead while
the grey was fidgeting. Then the grey settled down and moved up
until he had drawn even with Fiddler. Fiddler's ears flattened;
his stride lengthened as he turned on the power. He had started

to make his drive for home. Brady leaned far over on the grey horse; he cried shrilly; the quirt rose and fell. For the first time in his life the thoroughbred was under the whip. He drew even with Fiddler, and they came on like the wind, neck and neck. If they had not been running in separate lanes, a single blanket would have covered the horses.

Then came the incident that was to be debated for years, wherever cowmen gathered. When Fiddler reached the spot where the Indian had touched the ground, he broke his rushing stride, swerved, and ran wide. Murray knew every trick of getting the most out of a horse and Fiddler stretched out low and fairly ate up the ground. But it was too late; the grey thoroughbred shot past the finish line the winner by half a length.

Both horses ran far out into the valley of the White Clay before they could be checked. Murray was the first to come back. To the angry questions of the cowboys who gathered around him, he could only say, "I don't know what happened. Fiddler quit running for the first time in his life."

In discussing the race around campfires and in bunkhouses, the cowboys generally concluded that Fiddler must have stepped in a molehole. The Indians' comment was simply that Little Horse's medicine was good that day. What *is* certain is that the Indians made a great haul; the cowboys were stripped of practically everything they owned.

The next year Larvie's great grey was struck by lightning and killed. Although Tom Brady won the race, and later became well known as a rider, he could not win the love of Larvie's daughter, who married the agency blacksmith. After his ranching years were over, Jim Murray moved to Omaha and there, under his "square handle" of Dahlman, was mayor for many years.

To the Sioux the Black Hills, with their jagged granite peaks and pine forests rising above the northern grasslands, were a sacred place and keeping them undefiled had deep spiritual significance. But after gold was

*reported there by General George A. Custer in August,
1874, not even the white man's army could keep the
white man out. A constant and increasing stream of
prospecting parties moved into the region despite the
efforts of patrols assigned to turn back trespassers.
However, in September, 1875, when the Sioux chiefs
refused either to lease or sell the Hills to the United
States, the government withdrew its troops, thus tacitly
sanctioning entry into lands guaranteed to the Indians
by treaty.*

*In December an order sent by the Indian Office
enjoined roving Sioux bands to settle down on their
reservations by January 31. When Crazy Horse, Sitting
Bull, and other chiefs refused to comply, General
Crook initiated what was intended to be a quick
campaign to disarm and dismount the hostiles. Fought
mainly between the Big Horn and Powder rivers in
Montana and Wyoming, the Sioux War of 1876 inevit-
ably ended in the capitulation of the resisting bands,
but not until white complacency had been rudely
shattered when Crook's forces were turned back at the
Rosebud and Custer's command was annihilated at
the Little Big Horn.*

*A commission visited the Teton agencies in the
fall, carrying an agreement made out in advance. Without guns or ponies and threatened with starvation—no
funds would be voted for their support unless they
relinquished the Hills—the chiefs bowed their heads
and signed away their last sacred hunting ground.
When the region was legally opened to white settlement, on February 28, 1877, Deadwood alone already
had a population of 25,000.*

Road Agents

ALTHOUGH LATER ECLIPSED by Deadwood, the first mining town
in the Black Hills was Custer City near French Creek, in whose
sands Custer's men had found traces of gold. The first to arrive
at the site were a party of twenty-six Iowans, including a woman
and a nine-year-old boy. Led by a Sioux City newspaperman,
Charles H. Collins, they sifted through the military patrols and
reached French Creek on December 23, 1874. After constructing
a stockade and some cabins, the group spent the winter profitably taking placer gold out of the creek, where the dirt yielded
"pay in every pan." But in April the army caught up with them.
They were forcibly evicted and removed to Fort Laramie by
troopers of the Second U.S. Cavalry, after being given one day
to pack up. As it happened, their luck was still in, for the notorious Sioux chief, Lame Antelope, and three thousand braves
were hiding nearby, preparing to attack.

More than eight hundred prospectors made their way through
the military cordon during the summer, and on July 29 General
Crook arrived with a cavalry force and instructions to clear out
"miners or other unauthorized persons . . . until some new treaty
arrangements have been made with the Indians." On August 10,
1875, five days before they were required to leave, the prospectors
organized a townsite company and laid out Custer City, in an
attempt to protect the claims which would be held for them forty
days after the Hills were lawfully opened. The first mining district
had been formed just a few months before, on May 29, 1875,
by a company of Dakotans operating on French Creek.

Following the failure of the government's negotiations with
the Sioux, the troops were withdrawn and within three months
Custer had become a community of six thousand. Then in
November gold was discovered in Deadwood Gulch, and a stampede began to the northern areas. The town of Deadwood was

founded in late April, 1876, and by the first of June seventy
saloons and three dance halls were going full blast. The most
notorious of the many acts of violence perpetrated in this
"seething cauldron of restless, reckless humanity" was the murder
of Wild Bill Hickok by Jack McCall in a saloon on August 2,
1876. Another name associated with Deadwood is that of Calamity
Jane Canary. Her usual attire was a man's buckskin suit and
she was an expert shot and horsewoman, but she was revered on
the frontier for her many acts of charity and her skill as a nurse.

Beginning in February, 1876, the Cheyenne and Black Hills
Stage, Mail and Express Line began regular service twice a week
to Custer—a five-day trip. (Three months later the service was
extended to Deadwood.) Part of the stage route ran through
mountainous country with heavily wooded ravines and canyons
which made ideal lurking places for bandits. At first, the loot was
mainly the money and jewelry of the passengers, but as the
flow of gold increased the passengers' valuables became only a
secondary target.

In 1877, when robberies of its treasure coaches began to occur
with monotonous regularity, the stage company replaced the
wooden chests in which the gold had been carried with steel
chests, called "salamanders." These were too heavy to be carried
by a man on horseback and so strongly built that they would
require several hours to force open.

As an added security measure, a new coach—called "The
Monitor" after the Union Army's famous ironclad warship—was
designed and first used in 1878. It was lined with steel plates
which could not be penetrated by a rifle bullet, even when
fired at a distance of less than fifty feet; and there were portholes
in the doors from which the express messengers could snipe at
the bandits. Not surprisingly, there was a marked decline in
treasure-coach holdups after the Monitor began to clank through
the Hills. But soon there was a corresponding rise in the way-
laying of ordinary coaches and, for the first time, the road agents
began to rob the U.S. mails.

When the first mail robbery was reported, the stage line
immediately engaged mounted express messengers, one or two

of whom were assigned to escort each coach. The next coach out was stopped by bandits at Lightning Creek, but they were forced to suspend their activities when the mounted rearguard rode up blazing away with his shotgun. Although his horse was killed, the surprised bandits departed empty-handed. To counter this strategy, the outlaws increased the size of their gangs, and eventually as many as six express messengers would accompany a stagecoach.

The most famous of the Black Hills stage robberies occurred on September 26, 1878, at Canyon Springs Ranch station. The station building, a combination stable and living quarters for the stock tender, was located in a rugged, heavily timbered country, about forty miles south of Deadwood.

For some reason, no escort accompanied the ironclad treasure coach which left Deadwood the morning of the twenty-sixth. While it was being loaded for the trip, a confederate of the road agents noted that a quantity of gold dust and bullion was being taken aboard. He wasted no time in stealing a horse and making tracks for the gang's hide-out in the woods south of Deadwood.

A few minutes before the coach was due in at Canyon Springs, a man rode up on horseback and asked the stock tender, William Miner, for a drink of water. When he returned to Miner after dismounting from his horse, he had a gun in his hand and with this as a persuader marched the stock tender into the stable and locked him in the grain bin. The way being clear, four others of the gang now arrived, stabled their horses, and went on into the living quarters. Here they completed their preparations by pulling the chinking and daubing out from between the logs of the wall fronting on the spot where the coach always stopped to change horses. They then rested their rifles in their improvised loopholes and waited for business.

At four in the afternoon the stage drew up, stopping about ten feet in front of the station. After calling the stock tender and getting no reply, Gale Hill, the messenger riding shotgun, dismounted and picked up a block of wood to chock the hind wheel. Just as he straightened up and started for the barn, a volley of fire met him, one bullet striking his right arm. In spite of this, he pulled his gun with his left hand and wounded one of the robbers before a rifle bullet passed through his body. Even after he fell he continued shooting, wounding another robber; then managed to crawl to the other side of the stable out of the line of fire.

Inside the stage were two guards, Smith and Davis, and an employee of the telegraph company who rode as a special passenger. The roof of the coach was not armored—that was the one flaw in its design—and now a bandit fired through the top, his bullet grazing Smith and stunning him. Seeing him slumped down unconscious, Davis thought he was dead.

After returning the bandits' fire for a time, Davis and the unarmed passenger made a run for some trees across the road from the station. The telegraph company employee was killed, but Davis got behind a tree and continued firing. But he felt his situation was hopeless and since he knew the safe was guaranteed to be crack-proof for twenty-four hours, he slipped away to summon help.

When Smith regained consciousness the robbers disarmed him, put him and the driver into the coach, and drove it into the timber some distance from the station. After tying Smith and the driver to the stage wheels, the robbers took a sledge hammer and chisel and in about two hours broke open the "bandit-proof" safe. The loot totaled $27,000: about $22,500 was in gold dust or gold bars, the rest in money and jewelry. They packed this on their horses and fled.

As soon as William Miner could extricate himself from his prison in the grain bin, he tended the wounded express messenger, making him as comfortable as he could in the station, and then rode to Deadwood for a doctor. Several groups of citizens and peace officers accompanied him back, and the hunt for the outlaws was on.

One posse picked up their trail and succeeded in locating their camp, but delayed in rushing it until daylight, and during the dark hours the robbers one by one slipped away. A member of the posse, a doctor from Rapid City, was riding a horse which could not keep up with the rest, so he decided to give up the chase. He paused to look over the robbers' camping place, and expressed his frustration at the turn of events by giving the dead campfire a kick; seeing a pair of overalls, he kicked them, too, and the next moment was hopping about clasping his toe. The overalls were wrapped around a gold brick worth $3,200. The doctor's fortuitous kick netted him a reward of $1,100.

The search now settled down to painstaking detective work, and there was a general roundup of road agents. During its course a number of confessions of men involved in other robberies were secured. One of the Canyon Springs bandits was traced to his home in Atlantic, Iowa, where his arrest created a sensation since he was the son of the local banker. The young man had placed a gold bar worth $4,300 in the bank safe, saying that he had sold his interest in a mine and had received the bar in payment. When arrested, he had in his possession an assortment of watches, rings, and other jewelry. He was taken into custody by a stage company officer, but while en route to face trial he escaped from the train in Nebraska.

Within a few weeks after the Canyon Springs robbery, the stage company had recovered sixty percent of the plunder. It was the first and last robbery of an ironclad treasure coach. From then until the coming of the railroad, the coaches of the Cheyenne and Black Hills Stage Line made the Deadwood-Cheyenne run unmolested.

Although a few far-seeing men realized that the national resources were being squandered at a ruinous rate, the idea of America as a land of inexhaustible plenty prevailed almost until the passing of the frontier. In 1865 Secretary of the Interior James Harlan vainly opposed legislation which made the mineral lands of the public domain "free and open to exploration and settlement"; for, as he said, only if they were placed under the guardianship of private owners could "the great forests of timber, the growth of centuries,

*and of vast value to the nation be effectually preserved
from waste." Recommendations made in 1877 by
Secretary of the Interior Carl Schurz were aimed at
preserving the western forests, and contained the
essentials of what later became the general forest
policy, but during Schurz's term of office the "indis-
criminate and remediless" stripping of timber lands in
the southern states, the Great Lakes region, and on
the Pacific Coast continued unchecked.*

*The land-reform movement of the 1880's, which
culminated in the Revision Act of 1891, heralded the
later and more important development known as the
conservation movement. While primarily intended to
help out the settler, the placer miner, the hand logger,
and the individual grazer in their losing battle with
monopolistic corporations and moneyed interests on
the last American frontier, the 1891 legislation also
allowed the President to set aside areas of timber lands
as national parks. But in itself this measure was too
little and—it began to seem—too late. In his message
to Congress in 1893, President Cleveland stressed that
the government was "rapidly losing title to immense
tracts ... which should properly be reserved as permanent sources of timber supply." Moreover, the Forestry
Bureau incessantly called attention to the need for
legislation to prevent forest fires which, it insisted,
could be controlled. But still Congress did nothing.*

The Iron Horse to the Rescue

A FOREST FIRE was more destructive and more awe-inspiring than
a prairie fire. It ran faster, burned hotter, and lasted longer.
From 1870 until the end of the century the annual loss from

forest fires averaged fifty million dollars, but there was no federal legislation dealing with fire-prevention measures and no systematic organization set up for fighting these often catastrophic conflagrations. In the absence of any state or federal regulations, early-day logging operations were not only wasteful but created conditions which made large-scale forest fires almost inevitable. When logging crews worked through a forest, they left the branches and tops of trees in piles, where they dried out and became as inflammable as tinder. Similarly, railroad builders left acres of slashings where they cut trees for ties and other construction purposes. In logged-over areas, a lightning bolt or the smoldering embers of a carelessly extinguished campfire could within minutes turn a peaceful woodland scene into a hellish inferno.

As the frontier disappeared and the land became settled up, the cost of forest fires began to be measured in terms of hundreds of human lives as well as millions of dollars. For the inhabitants of communities in logging country, the fall of the year was a particularly anxious time; it was then that the dried-out slashings were at their most combustible, and when hunters roaming the woods created an extra hazard. What could happen may be judged from Stewart H. Holbrook's account (presented here in condensed form) of the holocaust at Hinckley, Minnesota, on September 1, 1894.

There was little of dawn about the morning of September 1, 1894, in the woods of eastern Minnesota. Clocks indicated that the hour was eight, but nothing else did. It was all sort of graylike, neither day nor night. It had been that way around Hinckley for a week. If the sun came out at all, it was a mere circle of sullen red, to be hidden long before noon as a smoky slatecolored haze slowly settled over everything. Occasionally, when the wind had been from the south, stray flecks of burned-out embers floated into town. When picked up and pinched between the fingers they were like black and white powder—ashes. But Hinckley seemed too big a town to be worried about. It had a population of twelve hundred, an Oddfellows hall, a fire department, three churches, five hotels and saloons, eight stores, a restaurant, two railroad stations, and a roundhouse, besides the big sawmill that cut two hundred thousand feet of lumber every day. Both railroads ran north to Duluth, and southwest to St. Paul or Minneapolis.

On the morning of September 1, things took a new turn. The pall of gray seemed to lift for a few minutes, and everything appeared as though in a ghastly light of pale yellow that seemed not to be any doing of the sun. Human beings and objects looked unreal. The strange light passed and again the gray sifted down, deeper and darker this time.

Shortly after noon a stiff wind blew up from the south, and on the wind were riding coals that burned and smoldered where they fell in a street that was more sawdust than dirt. And soon a cloud as big and as dark as night appeared over the timber line, and the Hinckley station agent of the St. Paul & Duluth said he just had word that Pokegama, nine miles south on the line, had been totally destroyed by forest fire and most of its inhabitants burned to death.

Now the volunteer fire department was called to the edge of Hinckley village where half a dozen fires had sprung to life at once. It wasn't long before Father Lawler, the village priest, came running through town shouting for them to flee for their lives. And then, in a seeming instant, hell itself roared into Hinckley, riding the back of a rising hurricane. There was no time to save anything. Mothers snatched babies out of sugar-barrel cradles and fled. The volunteer firemen now numbered hundreds but they quickly saw they could do nothing with *this* fire. They fled, too.

Many folks ran to the Eastern Minnesota Railroad siding where stood a passenger and a freight train, preparatory to passing. The trains were hastily joined, with Ed Barry and William Best at the throttles of the two long locomotives. They held the train until four hundred and seventy-five persons were packed into the coaches and paint on the car sides was bubbling into big blisters. Then they pulled her open. As they steamed out of town Engineer Best saw men and horses stagger in the street, then go down to stay. Fire leaped at the sides of houses and burned them so quickly that Best saw bedroom sets plainly outlined against the flames.

The train ran ten miles north to Sandstone, and stopped a moment while passengers shouted warnings to Sandstone folks. Just as the train pulled off the smoking Kettle River bridge at Sandstone, the structure gave way. And fifteen or twenty minutes later fire belched out of the timber and swept the village, burning forty-five persons and everything else.

Back in blazing Hinckley, ninety people took refuge in a cleared space along the Eastern Minnesota Railroad, and there they burned to black crisps or gray-white ashes. More than a hundred others were saved when they got into the shallow water of a gravel pit. A few others splashed into the water of a creek on the northern edge of Hinckley, where some lived it out and some were swept away to drown.

Heading up the tracks of the St. Paul & Duluth Railroad, fire caught and stopped thirty-three of a party of some two hundred refugees before they met a southbound passenger train. The train was Number Four, on its way from Duluth to St. Paul, with Jim Root, who had run a locomotive for General Sherman in Georgia, in the cab. When he saw men and women running up the track toward his train he stopped it and got out of the cab.

White-faced kids were helped aboard by women whose hair smelled of singeing and by men who had blistered hands but no eyebrows at all. From what they told him, Engineer Root knew that the nearest water was a swamp hole, known as Skunk Lake, six miles back. He climbed into his cab and reversed the lever. Just as he opened the throttle there came a terrific explosion somewhere outside. It shattered a cab window and the flying glass cut deep gashes in Root's neck and forehead. By the time the train got under way flames were racing along both sides of the tracks; the ties were blazing and so were parts of the moving coaches. Root could see that the far end of his train was afire.

Ahead in the train John Blair, colored porter in the chair car, was performing like a hero. A young woman, Mrs. Frank Spriggs, remembers it well. "Our car was afire from end to end," she recalls. "Paint was running down the walls, inside. The lamps were lighted when we left Hinckley, but they were smashed and blown out by several loud explosions which also broke almost every window of the coach. The bits of glass scattered. Many of us were cut and bleeding. The Negro porter was the steadiest man of the lot. He stood calmly by the water cooler, passing out cups of water until it was all gone. He talked to children and adults in a soothing manner; even joked. He acted as if it was all a summer excursion train. Indeed, he was a hero."

Back in the cab the heat was something men don't live through. Root fainted with his hand on the throttle. When he came to, he saw he had only ninety-five pounds of steam, and the train was moving very slowly. He thought that he had instinctively started to shut the throttle when he fainted; it was half-closed. Now he pulled her wide open.

The very coal in the locomotive tender was burning when Number Four clanked slowly across Skunk Lake bridge; they could see the muddy water, red in the glare. Grabbing a pail in the cab the fireman got down. He threw water on the flaming coach doors so the passengers could get out. Engineer Root was down and out on his cab floor.

The entire train broke into fire almost the moment it stopped, and passengers dismounted and looked for a spot where they could live. Mrs. Frank Spriggs had her six-weeks-old baby in her arms. "Throw that kid away," a "big grain man of Duluth" shouted at her. "You can't save it and yourself."

Many tumbled into the water mud of Skunk Lake. Mrs. Spriggs with her child and some other people—she thinks about five or six—made for a large potato patch near the lake. Fire seemed to be everywhere. As Mrs. Spriggs stumbled over the hot ground she saw a tall man running. He was carrying a woman in his arms, and her long hair streamed out behind in a mass of flame. Mrs. Spriggs has often wondered who they were and if the woman with the flaming hair survived.

Engineer Root lived. So did some three hundred others who came to Skunk Lake. But the fire had taken a terrible toll. It had caught loggers in camp and burned them to death, ax in hand, in one savage moment. And it had destroyed the towns of Hinckley, Sandstone, Mission Creek, Pokegama, and Partridge. A list of the dead was not completed until six weeks after the fire. On that day the body of Fred Molander was found deep in a well on his farm. It was number four hundred and thirteen.

In an article written for a popular magazine in 1875, W. B. Hazen declared that the time was fast approaching when "the landless and the homeless" could no longer hope to "acquire both lands and homes merely by settling." Soon, he said, the only unoccupied public domain would be waterless regions incapable of yielding crops, "and the old song that 'Uncle Sam is rich enough to give us all a farm' will no longer be true, unless we take farms incapable of cultivation." But it is doubtful if Mr. Hazen's article reached even a fraction of the international audience that pored over railroad and steamship brochures advertising the land bonanza of the West. "America fever," sedulously cultivated by the companies' immigration agents, reached epidemic proportions in many Old World countries, and during the last three decades of the nineteenth century, twelve million Europeans made the long journey to "dollar land."

In the late 1870's and 1880's Plains settlement pushed on out into the semiarid grasslands west of the ninety-eighth meridian where the rainfall averages less than twenty inches annually. (The theory had been advanced that "rainfall follows the plow." It didn't: farmers had to learn the hard way the truth of the cowmen's saying, "The flats were made for grazin', 'twan't made for no corn raisin'.") But still the westbound tide continued, and by 1890—the year the U.S. Director of Census announced that "there can hardly be said to be a frontier line"—settlers no longer were asking themselves if the Indians really needed all that good reservation land. They were taking it.

The Last Land Rushes

SINCE THE 1830's, when the "Five Civilized Nations" moved westward over the "Trail of Tears," upwards of fifty tribes—or what was left of them—had been placed on reservations in Indian Territory (present-day Oklahoma). In 1880 those white settlers who thought this was a waste of good land found a leader in David Payne, and followed him in several unsuccessful attempts to take the territory by force. After his death in November, 1884, Payne was succeeded by W. L. Crouch, who organized the "Boomers" and carried on the agitation for the land-grab.

In 1887, their way was made easier by the passage of the Dawes Act, which actually was intended to benefit the Indian by making him eligible for citizenship but which instead expedited the process of dispossessing him of his land. The act, according to Roy W. Robbins, "provided means by which the communal organization of the Indian tribes of the West could be dissolved, their reservations broken up, and the individual members admitted as American citizens. Homesteads were granted to individual members of the tribes, 160 acres to heads of families, 80 acres to single adults and orphans, and 40 acres to each dependent child." Surplus lands were held in trust, but could be opened to white settlement if the government would "bestow upon the tribe an adequate payment. Citizenship was conferred upon all Indians who accepted the benefits of the act . . . [and] by 1892 agreements had been negotiated with fourteen Indian tribes restoring to the public domain 26,000,000 acres . . . ."

1

In 1889, the "Boomers'" day came when President Harrison announced that the Oklahoma District, comprising two million acres ceded by the Creeks and Seminoles, would be thrown open to settlement at noon on April 29. Among the hundred thousand land seekers who rimmed the district was Hamilton S. Wicks of

New York City, a correspondent for an Eastern newspaper. Here is how the scene—which sober historians have described as "bedlam"—looked to young Wicks:

> Now the hour of twelve was at hand. All was excitement and expectation. Every nerve was on tension and every muscle strained. The great event was on the verge of transpiring.
>
> Suddenly the air was pierced with the blast of a bugle. Hundreds of throats echoed the sound with shouts of exultation. The quivering limbs of saddled steeds, no longer restrained by the hands that held their bridles, bounded forward simultaneously into the "beautiful land" of Oklahoma; and wagons and carriages and buggies and prairie schooners and a whole congregation of curious equipages joined in this unparalleled race, where every starter was bound to win a prize.
>
> The occupants of our [railroad] train now became absorbed in their own fate. Indeed, our train was one of the participants in this unexampled race, and while watching the scurrying horsemen, we ourselves had been gliding through the picturesque landscape. All that there was of Guthrie on April 29, at 1:30 P.M. when the first train from the north drew up to the station and unloaded its first settlers was a water tank, a small station-house, a shanty for the Wells-Fargo Express, and a Government Land Office. . . .
>
> I remember throwing my blankets out of the car window the instant the train stopped at the station. I remember tumbling after them through the self-same window. Then I joined the wild scramble for a town lot up the sloping hillside . . . . There were several thousand people converging on the same plot of ground, each eager for a town lot which would be acquired without cost or without price. . . .
>
> The race was not over when you reached the particular lot you were content to select for your possession. The contest was still who should drive their stakes first, who would erect little tents soonest, and then, who would be quickest to build the little wooden shanty.
>
> One did not know how far to go before stopping. Everyone appeared dazed. . . . Where the boldest led many others fol-

lowed. It occurred to me that a street would probably run past the depot. I accosted a man and asked him if this was to be a street along here.

"Yes," he replied, "We are laying off four corner lots right here for a lumber yard."

"Is this the corner where I stand?" I inquired.

"Yes," he responded, approaching me.

"Then I claim this corner lot!" I said with decision, as I jammed my location stick in the ground and hammered it severely home with my heel. "I propose to have one lot at all hazards on this town site, and you will have to limit yourself to three, in this location at least."

An angry altercation ensued. I proceeded at once to unstrap a small folding cot I brought with me, and by standing it on its end it made a tolerable center pole for a tent. I then threw a couple of my blankets over the cot, and staked them securely into the ground on either side. Thus I had a claim that was unjumpable because of substantial improvements, and I felt safe. . . .

Ten thousand people "squatted" upon a square mile of virgin prairie that first afternoon, and as the myriad of white tents suddenly appeared upon the face of the country, it was as though a vast flock of white-winged birds had settled down upon the hillsides and valleys. Thousands of campfires sparkled upon the dark bosom of the prairie as far as the eye could reach, and there rose from this huge camp a subdued hum declaring that this multitude had come to stay and work. . . .

The tents were not silent. On the contrary, there were fusillades of shots on all sides from Winchesters, Colts, and Remingtons, disturbing the stillness of the night, mingled with halloos, and shouting, and the rebel yell, and the imitated warwhoop of the savage. I expected on the morrow to see the prairie strewn with gory corpses, but not a single corpse appeared, and I was not slow in making up my mind that nine-tenths of all the shots were fired in a mere wanton spirit of bravado to intimidate a few such nervous tenderfeet as myself.

Within a few hours, 1,920,000 acres had been settled and by

nightfall Oklahoma City had been born with a population of 10,000. But this was only the "Boomers' " first bite—a rehearsal for a still wilder performance four years later.

2

In the same year as the rush on the former Creek and Seminole lands in the Oklahoma District, the government negotiated an agreement for the reduction of the Great Sioux Reservation in South Dakota. By its terms, approximately 9,000,000 acres were made available to the white man, and the 21,000 remaining Sioux were split up and placed on five separate and very much smaller reservations. But when the new lands were officially opened to white settlement in February, 1890, not even townsite boomers could conjure up a land rush. Although drought conditions were partly to blame, undoubtedly the current "ghost-dance" scare—to say nothing of the dread reputation of the Sioux themselves—was largely responsible for the slim turnout.

At the conclusion of the Sioux War of 1876, the Sioux reluctantly accepted reservation status, the Oglalas under Chief Red Cloud and Crazy Horse going to Pine Ridge and the Brules under Spotted Tail to the adjacent Rosebud agency. The Two Kettle, Sans Arc, and Minneconjou tribes were assigned to the Cheyenne River agency farther north, and the Hunkpapas to Standing Rock, near the North Dakota line. Of the great chiefs, Sitting Bull alone refused to surrender and fled to Canada. But in 1881 he asked for peace and returned to his people at the Standing Rock agency.

Fear of the Sioux was too deeply ingrained, however, for it to disappear overnight, and in the late 1880's it was fed by rumors that the tribes were working themselves up to go on the warpath. These rumors were inspired by a new Indian religious movement. It had originated in Nevada with a Paiute named Wovoka (in English, Cutter), who preached that an Indian millennium was to come in the spring of 1891: the white men would be driven from the Plains and the Great Spirit would send the buffaloes forth from caves in the south; then the

Indians would return to their old ways and once again roam freely on the lands that had been theirs.

In view of poor crops, no game, reduced rations, unscrupulous agents, and general loss of faith in the government, it is no wonder that Wovoka's preaching spread through the reservations. An important part of the cult was the ceremonial known as the ghost dance. A delegation of Sioux visited Wovoka in 1890, and on their return in April of that year taught the dance to their tribes. The dancers, men and women together, held hands and moved slowly around in a circle, facing toward the center. They wore sack-like shirts of unbleached muslin, which—so Wovoka preached—could miraculously turn aside white bullets.

The ghost-dance craze was actually nothing more than an expression of wishful thinking on the part of a defeated people, an outlet for their restlessness and dissatisfaction. But unfortunately there was a new agent at Pine Ridge, a political appointee named Royer, who was utterly unexperienced in the ways of Indians. He insisted that the military move in and protect the settlers, and by mid-November nearly half of the infantry and cavalry of the United States Army had been moved to the area. Meanwhile the ghost dance had spread to Standing Rock reservation, being organized there by Chief Kicking Bear at the suggestion of Sitting Bull. Since Sitting Bull was known to be still unreconciled, though he was living on the reservation, there was a demand for his arrest. On December 15, Sergeant Red Tomahawk and a squad of Indian Police attempted to carry out the order. Sitting Bull, his son Crow Foot, and eight other warriors were killed, and six of the police.

The news threw the whole frontier into a state of panic. Some of Sitting Bull's followers fled and joined Chiefs Hump and Big Foot, two of Wovoka's most zealous disciples. Persuaded by a cavalry officer to come into the Cheyenne River agency peaceably, Big Foot and his band of about 340 started south next day for Pine Ridge to seek the protection of Red Cloud. Misconstruing this as a hostile gesture, the Seventh Cavalry intercepted them and demanded unconditional surrender, which was given. On December 28, the Big Foot band, which numbered 106 warriors, the rest being women and children, was escorted to Wounded Knee Creek by a total force of 470 men commanded by Colonel James W. Forsyth—eight cavalry troops, one company of Cheyenne Scouts, and four pieces of light artillery.

At Wounded Knee, about seventeen miles northeast of Pine Ridge agency, Colonel Forsyth decided to disarm the Indians, although the band had shown no inclination to fight and a large white flag flew between two of the Indian tipis. The Indians were reluctant to turn in their weapons—the guns were a means of livelihood and cherished possessions—so a detachment of troops searched the tipis. They found only forty rifles, but were convinced that the Indians had others hidden. At this juncture a medicine man began circling among the braves, allegedly urging resistance and reminding them of their ghosts shirts with the magic power to turn aside bullets. Suddenly the medicine man threw a handful of dust into the air. A young Indian—whether accidentally or deliberately is not known—discharged a rifle. The soldiers opened up fire, and from a nearby elevation the Hotchkiss guns raked the camp, killing warriors, women and children. Big Foot, ill with pneumonia, staggered to the door of his tipi and was shot down. When the smoke cleared, eighty-four Indian warriors were dead, forty-four women, and eighteen children. Many others died later of wounds or exposure. Most of the women and children were slaughtered as they tried to escape. According to Herbert S. Schell, "Their bodies were scattered over a distance of about two miles. Nearly half the Indians were killed by the first volley of the Hotchkiss guns. The survivors of the cannon barrage escaped to a nearby ravine, where the pursuing troops hunted them down like wild prey. Thirty-one soldiers [including one officer] were killed, most of them in fierce hand-to-hand fighting."

Hearing of the incident, four thousand ghost dancers who were on their way to Pine Ridge to surrender, became greatly aroused and threatened to destroy the agency. There were several skirmishes, but the command of the white troops had now passed to General Nelson A. Miles, who brought with him officers experienced in dealing with Indians. Miles chose men from among them to replace the agents at the Rosebud and Pine River reserve, and by January 19 order was restored.

Bitter controversy raged over the Wounded Knee massacre. It has since been agreed that the ghost dancers planned no general uprising against the whites; the press and alarmists among the settlers had played up the disturbances out of all proportion to the actual conditions. While no one denied that an Indian fired the first shot, some witnesses—both whites and red men—held that two soldiers were scuffling with him for possession of the rifle and it was accidentally discharged in the air. Other investigators testified that the Indians had virtually no guns, and that a good many of the white soldiers were killed by the fire of troops behind them, not by Indian bullets. Also, it was widely believed that the Seventh Cavalry was out to avenge the Little Big Horn, and that their conduct was governed by a desire to settle old scores rather than by military necessity. Eighteen soldiers received Congressional Medals of Honor for heroism under fire, but Colonel Forsyth was relieved of his command for "reprehensible action."

The "battle" at Wounded Knee was the last armed resistance of the Plains Indians, ending a tragic and, many feel, disgraceful chapter in American history. Now that the tomahawk was buried forever, only legal formalities barred the white man from the remaining Indian lands he coveted.

3

Under the terms of the 1887 Dawes Act (also known as the Severalty or Indian Allotment Act), new agreements for the reduction of lands reserved to the Indians were concluded with commendable alacrity. After the first "Boomer" rush and the dismemberment of the Great Sioux Reservation in 1890, 900,000 acres belonging to the Sauk, Fox, and Potawatomi in the new territory of Oklahoma were opened to settlement in 1891, and 3,000,000 acres of the Cheyenne–Arapahoe reservation in 1892. Then, on September 16, 1893, came the last and greatest of the major land rushes, the second "Boomer" invasion of the old Indian country. This time the target was a 6,000,000 acre tract known as the Cherokee Strip, now comprising the Oklahoma panhandle.

Hoping to prevent a repetition of the wild and disorderly conditions which had prevailed at the 1889 rush, the government sent troops to patrol the two lines—that to the north at the Kansas border, that to the south at the Oklahoma boundary—from which the run for land would begin. But it was soon obvious that the number of troops was totally inadequate, and it was impossible to see to the enforcement of the order that all rushers should turn in their guns. Only a few hundred were collected.

At twelve o'clock noon the starting signal would be given by discharging a cannon at the east end of the Strip; the soldiers stationed along its length would transmit the signal to the west end, a hundred and sixty-eight miles away, by consecutively firing their rifles. As the morning of September 16 dragged on, there was evidence of considerable tension; it was far from a holiday atmosphere, for no one could be sure he would get anything but exercise for his trouble. In each township four sections—one-ninth of the land—were reserved for the state and schools, and when a man staked out his claim he had no way of knowing whether it was on this reserved land. Thus, one man in every nine who succeeded in—he thought—claiming a quarter section was bound to be disappointed.

Seth K. Humphrey and his brother were ineligible to take homesteads, as they already had claimed their full legal complement of lands, but they decided to "make the run" as sightseers. Because of the problem of finding water for horses, they arrived on bicycles. People in all kinds of equipages were lined up several rows deep, the line stretching like a great snake to the western horizon. A hundred yards out in front and twice that distance apart were the soldiers, holding their rifles easily and keeping a casual eye on the crowd to see that they stayed behind the line. Seth wondered how on earth they would get out of the way of the great onrush when the time came.

Not far from him was a locomotive, its cowcatcher even with the starting line and its tender and ten cattle cars trailing back into Kansas. The cars were jammed with people; scores perched on their roofs or clung to their sides wherever they could find a handhold. So that the train passengers would not have an unfair advantage over the men and women in buggies and wagons and on horseback, the Land Office had ruled that the train's speed should not exceed eight miles an hour. But it was later said that a few bills fluttering around the engineer had such a confusing effect that fifteen miles an hour seemed to him just like eight.

At about ten minutes to twelve someone down the line fired a revolver, and a man who mistook it for the starting gun gave a yell and went galloping away down the line. The crowd roared "Come back!" and the nearest sentinel called "Halt!" but apparently the man did not understand what they were shouting and in all the din, he certainly could not have heard the command to halt. When he did not stop, the soldier obeyed instructions and shot him through the head. It caused no stir.

Finally, there came the cannon's boom and the succeeding rifle shots. A great shout went up; the living wall of humanity shuddered, hesitated, pushed, swayed, and spilled out into the prairie in a ragged line, with a few riders spurting on ahead. The dust and sand rose in dense clouds. Men knocked each other down, wagons collided, horses reared and bucked. Thrown from her horse, Mrs. Charles Barnes of El Dorado, Kansas, was trampled to death under the hoofs of the horses ridden by those behind her. Vehicles of all kinds were smashed, many too badly to continue the race. Some of the rushers had not gone a mile before they saw they were hopelessly outdistanced and turned back. Here and there, men were fighting with knives and pistols to establish priority in staking a claim. Clouds of smoke billowed up from the south where the front-runners had fired the prairie in an effort to discourage those pounding on after them.

By the time the Humphrey brothers had peddled their bicycles to the heart of the Strip, their canteens were empty and their mouths parched. They saw horses nearly dead of thirst being led to the towns along the railroad, where their owners hoped to obtain water from the railroad water tanks.

That night the brothers camped out on the dry prairie grass. A little before midnight they were awakened by a clatter of hoofs, shouting, and shooting. A man's voice called out the section, township, and range number of his claim— "Get off and stay off!" Then crack, crack, crack, more rifle fire. Evidently a mounted gang of ruffians was cleaning up a few quarter sections for their own occupancy. The next morning, however, the Humphreys saw no dead and heard nothing about a murder in their vicinity, so they concluded somebody had been indulging in the form of bluff known as "shooting past the ears."

But not all gunplay was bluffing by any means, and the Humphreys were told of one man who had been found hanging from a tree in a deep ravine. Pinned to his shirt was a note which said simply, "Too soon." He was one of a number of sharp operators who had sneaked out onto the Strip well ahead of the appointed date and had staked out choice claims, then laid low till they saw the legitimate rushers approaching. Unfortunately for the sharpies, just prior to the run the Land Office had sent out an order that each man had to have proof of a new registration or he was not entitled to stake out a claim. When a legitimate rusher asked to see a claimant's papers and he failed to produce the required proof, it was taken as evidence that he was a "Sooner." The homesteaders held no brief for cheats, so if a Sooner succumbed to lead poisoning there were likely to be few complaints.

Later that morning Seth talked with a boy on his way back to Kansas in company with a multitude of disconsolate rushers. After staking out his claim, he had found the markers of a half-dozen other claimants, and, as frequently happened, there was no way of establishing which one was the first. For this boy, however, the question had been pretty well settled when he heard the gunshots and threats the night before. So far as he was concerned, he was not even a poor second and would make no attempt to claim any part of the land which is known today as Oklahoma, the Sooner state.

⚬ *At the peak of the beef bonanza, "big business" bought
its way into ranching. Great stock-raising companies,
backed by eastern and British capital, purchased land
sites, hired expensive ranch managers, and introduced
a new speculative fever into the cattle trade by paying
as much as $30 or $35 a head for mixed range stock
that would have brought $20 or less in 1880. Their
constant demand for young stock kept the herds
moving up from the south despite mounting costs
and the increasing difficulties of trail driving. Under
pressure from the homesteaders, in 1884 the Kansas
legislature pushed the quarantine line west of Dodge
City, and in 1885, after an epidemic of tick fever,
closed the entire state to Texas cattle from March to
December. Some of the drives already had been traveling up to Wyoming by way of New Mexico, and
now a National Cattle Trail through Colorado
was proposed.*

*But in 1885 beef prices plummeted; severe droughts
took their toll on the overstocked northern ranges
that year and the next; and a series of blizzards,
which began early in the fall of 1886 and continued
throughout a winter of subzero temperatures, dealt
even more punishing blows. Though some areas were
less hard hit than others, herd losses on the range
lands of Montana, North Dakota, Wyoming, the
Belle Fourche region of South Dakota, and the Nebraska Sandhills ran from fifty to ninety per cent.
Many small operators were forced out, and even some
of the large outfits like Wyoming's Swan Land and
Cattle Company and the Niobrara Cattle Company of
Nebraska went bankrupt.*

*The cattle kingdom was tottering. It remained for
the coup de grace to be delivered, not by the forces of
nature, but by a haughty, ruthless, acquisitive group
of men—the high-and-mighty cattle barons themselves.*

The End of the Open Range

WHEN THE CATTLE BUSINESS slid into the doldrums, a host of small problems, like a cloud of gnats, harassed the already worried and irritable cattle barons. Homesteaders began to invade their ranges from the east and sheepherders from the west, while right under their proud noses were the peskiest nuisances of them all—cowboys who couldn't find enough work, or who had grown tired of drifting, and had claimed homestead land to start their own small ranches in the heart of the big companies' kingdom.

From the beginning the big ranchers had run their cattle on the public domain without paying either taxes or rent, and though theoretically the range was still open, the rulers of the cattle kingdom had come to regard it as their own personal fief. To the east, where nesters were building soddies and fencing quarter sections, wire-cutters became standard equipment for range riders, and to the west, night raiders attacked camps and slaughtered thousands of "woollies" in an effort to end the sheepherders' encroachments.

Despite continuous sabotage punctuated by outbreaks of shocking violence, the cattlemen's conflicts with the homesteaders and the sheepmen had something of the nature of a cold war, with much of the fighting carried on in courtrooms and legislative halls. But in Wyoming, where the cattle barons' powers verged on the absolute, the battle between the big stock-raising corporations and the small ranches culminated in a genuine shooting war.

1

During the late 1870's and early 1880's, the years when so many new cattle-raising companies came into being, the big operators banded together to form local (later state or regional) stockmen's associations. These organizations defined the limits of each rancher's grazing ground and set rules for the working of the range which had the force of law. They also did considerable effective lobbying in behalf of legislation to protect or advance their members' interests.

In Wyoming, as elsewhere in cow country, mavericking had not been regarded as illegal.* Cattlemen had in effect sanctioned the practice by paying a cowboy a five-dollar bonus for every motherless calf he branded with his employer's brand. Figuring that what is sauce for the goose is sauce for the gander, cowboys who quit riding for the big outfits to set up for themselves regularly indulged—and perhaps over-indulged—in the twilight activity of "swinging a long rope" and carrying a "running iron" (used for on the spot branding—or brand-changing) to augment their herds. Seeing their range dwindling, the cattle barons, in the name of the Wyoming Stock Growers Association, secured passage in 1884 of a law making it a felony to capture mavericks. Henceforth all mavericks became the property of the state, which would then sell them to pay the expenses of registering and inspecting brands and other activities connected with enforcing range law. Nonetheless, the little ranchers continued mavericking. If caught on the range using a running iron, a man always insisted the calf was from his own herd, but undoubtedly some ranchers were not too discriminating.

At the beginning of the 1890's, the number of small ranchers was decidedly on the increase—a homesteader, haled into court for branding a maverick, was found not guilty by a jury well-filled with little ranchers—and the big operators, whose herds had been reduced nearly fifty per cent in the five disastrous years after 1885, were less and less satisfied with half measures, and more and more in the mood for a showdown. During 1891 three more little ranchers were "dry gulched"—taken to a lonely canyon and shot or hanged—and in 1892 the cattle lords decided the time had come for an all-out power play.

*See page 336.

Organizing under the name of the Regulators, they raised $100,000 and recruited twenty-five Texas gunmen to lead the invasion task force. Their target was Johnson County in north-central Wyoming, where the little ranchers were riding high, having elected their man, Pat Angus, sheriff. The primary objective was Buffalo, the county seat, where arms and ammunition were stored in the courthouse for use by the militia. After they had captured the courthouse, the hired gunmen would proceed to eliminate seventy persons designated as "rustlers" on a list which included the sheriff and three county commissioners.

On April 5, 1892, a special train pulled into Cheyenne from Denver, and at once watchmen were posted up and down its length; not even railroad personnel were allowed to approach. There was a baggage car, a flatcar carrying wagons, three stock cars loaded with horses, and a passenger coach behind whose drawn shades were the twenty-five imported gunmen. Before the train moved on north to Casper they were joined by twenty-five Wyoming Regulators and—a stylish touch—a "war correspondent," Sam T. Clover of the *Chicago Herald*.

While the mystery train still stood in the Cheyenne yards, a curious railroad employee managed to ferret out its destination and the mission of its passengers. He telegraphed a warning to Sheriff Angus, but as Buffalo was not on the railroad the message did not reach him for thirty hours, and was ignored by Angus when he did receive it.

In the early morning of April 7, the special pulled into Casper, and there the wagon train—supposedly it belonged to a group of surveyors—was made up, and set out for Buffalo, a hundred and twenty-five miles to the northeast. In an attempt to keep their "surprise party" a secret, the Regulators took captive a sheepherder and three other men whom they met on the road. The prisoners were released after it had been impressed on them that if they breathed a word of what they had seen, they would be the deadest corpses in seven counties.

Word now came to the Regulators that two of the men on their rub-out list, Nate Champion and Nick Ray, were at the KC Ranch, which was on their route. As the principal organizer of little-rancher resistance, Nate Champion, an excellent cowboy and gun handler, was Number One among the twenty-five most wanted rustlers. The big operators had tried and failed to get him the previous November; no time like the present to get the job done.

Arriving at the ranch about daybreak, some of the gunmen hid in the barn and others deployed in the brush along the creek, bottling up the four-room cabin where Champion and Ray were living. As it happened, two trappers who had stayed with them overnight were the first to come out. They were captured and placed under arrest. Questioned, they readily told the invaders that there was no one in the cabin but Ray and Champion, and that the cowboys had no more idea than they did the cabin was surrounded. Shortly afterward, Nick Ray came out to fill a bucket at the well. The Winchesters blazed and he went down. Champion, though realizing his enemies must be present in force, nonetheless came out firing and managed to drag Ray back into the cabin. Ray died of wounds a few hours later.

The shooting now began in earnest, but Champion, rushing from window to window, returned the Regulators' fire so effectively that no one made any move to charge the house. At nine A.M. they drew off for consultation, and decided to keep up the siege, hoping to pick him off or exhaust his ammunition. Meanwhile a neighbor, Terrence Smith, had heard the gunfire and had ridden over to see what was going on. Unseen by the invaders he took in the situation from a vantage point on the bluffs along the Powder River, then rode hard for Buffalo, alerting the countryside en route.

Throughout the day Champion continued to stand off the Regulators single-handed, coolly recording in a pocket memorandum book the circumstances and progress of the attack whenever there was a lull in the firing. Toward the end of the afternoon a neighboring rancher, Jack Flagg, and his seventeen-year-old son happened along the road; they were seen and greeted by a hail of bullets but managed to escape.

Knowing that the alarm would now be raised, the Regulators changed their tactics. They improvised a "fire ship" by loading a wagon with hay and pine knots, ignited it, and sent it rolling down a slope at the rear of the cabin. While this was going on, Champion was writing in his memo book: "Well, they have got through shelling the house like hail. I guess they are going to fire the house tonight. I think I will make a break when night comes, if alive. I think they will fire the house [at] this time. It's not night yet. The house is all fired. Goodbye, boys, if I never see you again." He then put the memo book in his pocket and prepared to attempt a dash for freedom through the clouds of smoke.

The subsequent events at the KC Ranch were reported in breathless prose by the "war correspondent," Sam Clover:

> The roof of the cabin was the first to catch on fire, spreading rapidly downward until the north wall was a sheet of flames. Volumes of smoke poured in at the open window from the burning wagon. . . . Still the doomed man remained doggedly concealed. Fiercer and hotter grew the flames. . . . There was a shout, "There he goes!" and a man clad in his stocking feet, bearing a Winchester in his hands and a revolver in his belt, emerged from a volume of black smoke . . . and started off across the open space surrounding the cabin into a ravine, fifty yards south of the house, but the poor devil jumped square into the arms of two of the best shots in the outfit, who stood with leveled Winchesters around the bend waiting for his appearance. Champion saw them too late, for he overshot his mark just as a bullet struck his rifle arm, causing the gun to fall from his nerveless grasp. Before he could draw his revolver a second shot struck him. . . . Nate Champion, the king of the cattle thieves, and bravest man in Johnson County, was dead.

The Regulators now took off lickety-cut for Buffalo, sixty miles away, which they hoped to reach before dawn. They had nothing to show for a long day's work but two names with lines drawn through them, and they had lost their chance of taking by surprise what they had been calling "the doomed city of the Plains." A few miles outside of Buffalo a spy reported that Sheriff Angus knew of the attack on Champion and had left for Powder River, and that there were two hundred hornet-mad citizens under arms in Buffalo. This intelligence called for another change in plans: the hunters were now the hunted. They pressed on to the TA Ranch, arriving a little before noon, and after fortifying the ranch buildings with breastworks at their exposed points, took refuge behind barricaded doors.

The Buffalo citizenry, in the absence of Sheriff Angus, elected another leader and marched on the TA Ranch. Volunteers continued to pour in until about four hundred were assembled there. During the next two days there was plenty of shooting, but the Regulators' defenses remained unbreached. The besiegers had, however, captured their supply wagons, in one of which were several boxes of dynamite and lengths of fuse. They now got busy constructing a movable fort: two of the captured wagons were fastened together with a log framework and at the business end they built a six-foot-high protective shield, studded with loopholes. This homemade tank, which they called the "Go-Devil" and "Ark of Safety" would carry a forty-man crew, with fifteen men pushing to supply the motive power. The idea was to move the "Go-Devil" close enough so that the attackers could hurl dynamite sticks into the Regulators' blockhouse.

The machine had been completed and was actually being moved up for the attack on the morning of April 13, when Colonel J. J. Van Horn and Sheriff Angus arrived from Fort McKinney with three troops of cavalry. On seeing them ride up, one of the Texans exclaimed, "Jehoshaphat, must we fight the Army too?" But in fact the arrival of the military probably saved their lives. Under a flag of truce, Colonel Van Horn and the sheriff rode forward and demanded their surrender. When it was given, the Regulators were taken under guard to Fort McKinney, and the citizens dispersed to their homes. They had neither suffered nor inflicted a single casualty during the siege, but two of the Texans were killed by the accidental discharge of their own guns.

The use of United States Army troops to intervene reflected the degree to which the big operators controlled state officials: the governor had secured the services of the soldiers by appealing to the President for their help in putting down "an insurrection."

From Fort McKinney, the Regulators were taken to Cheyenne and held in jail until January, 1893, when they were released without ever standing trial.

While they had managed to finagle immunity for their hirelings, the cattle barons had nothing else to show for the $105,000 the invasion ultimately cost them. To the contrary, they had succeeded only in arousing public indignation, inviting reprisals, and shortening their own numbered days. For several years to come, their ranches were subject to raids in which much personal property was destroyed and thousands of cattle killed off.

2

The sheepmen with their woollies moved onto the western range toward the end of the 1870's. Until the Civil War, sheep raising was done mainly in the East. Scarcity of feed sent the sheepmen searching out new grazing grounds, first on the dry ranges of California, New Mexico, and Arizona, then in the plains and mountain valleys of the cowmen's domain.

By 1878 J. D. Hale had located a flock of three thousand as far north as the Bear Butte neighborhood in present-day South Dakota. Cattlemen claimed that a flock of this size grazing across grass range would eat the grass down to its roots, and that the sheep's sharp little hoofs trampling into the grass permanently damaged its roots. Furthermore, they said that the woollies left such a stink behind them the cattle would not graze over the same ground or drink at their water holes. But there was not much factual basis for these charges. The cattlemen's real objection to sheep derived simply from their determination to keep the government lands for their own use.

Sheep first came to Wyoming in 1888. As the number of flocks increased, the ranchers attempted to delimit the invasion by setting up deadlines which the sheepmen were warned not to cross. Those who ignored the warning invited the attention of the "gunny sackers"—cowboys who swooped down on the sheep camp, yanked a gunny sack over the herder's head, and kept him tied up while they hazed his flock over the edge of a cliff. This maneuver was known as "rim rocking." Once a few sheep had been driven over the brink, the rest of the docile creatures would follow, plunging to their death on the rocks below. Those who were not killed by the fall were usually smothered in the pile-up.

There were other, equally cruel practices. Sometimes the cattlemen would stampede a herd of horses or cattle through a flock, leaving many of them crippled. They would beat sheep to death with clubs; or dynamite a tight flock on their bed ground; or immolate them—set fire to the helpless creatures after drenching them with kerosene.

Eventually, the sheepherders themselves became objects of attack. One of the most notorious incidents in the long drawnout war occurred in the Tensleep country in the north central part of Wyoming. Two sheepmen, Joseph Enge and Joe Allemand, had to cross a deadline while trailing their flocks from the railroad to their own sheep reserve. Having reached it, they thought they were safe, but on the night of April 3, 1909, cattlemen attacked their camp. Allemand was killed by a revolver shot, and Enge and his herder, a Frenchman named Jules Lazier, were burned up in their wagon, after which the raiders emptied their guns on the flocks.

Since the telephone wires had been cut, the sheriff did not learn of the raid until the next morning. He was the first to examine the ground, and took particular note of the distinctive tracks left by a man's boot; it had been half-soled and the heel was worn down on one side. The bodies of the victims were taken to a neighboring ranch, where a number of people came to view them. Among those present was a cowboy named Brink, who was wearing a boot which made tracks identical with those spotted by the sheriff at the scene of the crime.

Although the sheriff was warned not to pry into the matter too far, he continued with the investigation. For one thing, the National Wool Growers Association had offered a large reward for the apprehension of the raiders; moreover, the murdered sheepherder, Jules Lazier, was a French citizen, and the French government had interested itself in the case. After a key witness committed suicide leaving letters implicating the killers, two

cowboys turned state's evidence and incriminated five others.
State troops were called out to protect the witnesses, whose lives
had been threatened, and the raiders were brought to trial.
They were found guilty by the jury, but the judge, who was
friendly to the cattle interests, let them off with light sentences.
Before the books were finally closed on the case, however, the
United States paid France a $25,000 indemnity for the life of
Jules Lazier.

Public indignation had been thoroughly aroused by this atro-
cious killing, and a dark night no longer would suffice to cloak
the deeds of the gunny sackers. Though the sheepmen and cattlemen were far from resolving their differences, the reign of terror
on the Wyoming ranges was ended.

3

The lure of big profits during the era of bonanza ranching
had led to overextended operations and overgrazing; drastic reor-
ganization was necessary if the ranch cattle industry was to
survive. The 1890's saw many changes in ranching methods. By
the turn of the century, writes James C. Olson, "blooded stock—
Shorthorns, Herefords, and Angus—replaced the unsatisfactory
Texas longhorn. Fenced land replaced the open range. Supple-
mental feed was added to grass, to produce more and better
beef and to tide herds over the hard winters. Haying became as
much a part of the cowboy's regular activity as riding the range,
and the great flats interspersed among the hills came to be dotted
with stacks of wild hay."

Although a federal law enacted in 1885 made it illegal to
enclose the public domain, the cattle barons took a lot of convincing that this or any other inconvenient law applied to them.
To keep out homesteaders they fenced in hundreds of thousands
of acres of public land, and it was not until the administration
of President Theodore Roosevelt—who had ridden the range
himself and was a dedicated conservationist—that it began to
sink in they couldn't get away with it. In 1905, two of the big
operators pleaded guilty to having illegally fenced 210,000 acres
of government land, and though they were given ridiculously

light sentences and special treatment during their stay in jail, they got the message.

Unfortunately—from the cattlemen's point of view—developments which they had promoted to serve their own interests also worked against them. While the extension of railroad lines into the Dakotas solved the problem of getting their livestock to market, it made the region more accessible to the hated nesters. Similarly, the opening of the Great Sioux Reservation, for which they had so long agitated, provided them with new pasturage but also brought a new influx of settlers into the range country.

Even before the government made any serious effort to enforce the law against illegal fencing, the homesteaders, by sheer force of numbers, already had prevailed in many sectors. It would take more than the hand of man to drive them out. Although in years to come much of the range land occupied by homesteaders would pass back into the hands of the large ranchers, it would be vacated, not at gunpoint, but for the good reason that it had proved unsuitable for general farming.

The prime function of the livestock associations, once so powerful, came to be organizing the open range roundups, usually held twice yearly. During the winter, particularly if it had been a stormy one, cattle drifted miles from their ranges and became hopelessly mixed with the animals from other ranches. At the spring roundup, the cowboys' job was to concentrate the herds in one area, unscramble the branded animals, brand the calves (a calf was given the brand of the cow it followed), and drive the separated herds back to the grazing grounds of their home ranches. At the fall roundup, the matured cattle ready for market were cut out and herded to rail shipping points, their next stop the stockyards.

The last of these large general roundups in South Dakota was held in 1908, but cowpunchers declared that the 1902 spring roundup was the greatest ever staged anywhere in the West. Thirteen outfits, driving before them every "cow brute" that could be found in the western part of the state, met toward the end of May at the forks of the White River. The camp extended from the present site of Murdo to a point twenty-seven miles south, and east and west along the White River for twenty miles. Since there were fifteen riders in each outfit and every man had a dozen horses in his "mount," there were about two hundred men and twenty-four hundred horses to tend to something like fifty thousand head of cattle.

Quickly and efficiently, the riders began the task of cutting out their own stock from the main herd. As soon as a sizeable bunch of cattle had been assembled, the branding team took over and the smell of burning cow hair filled the prairie air. One by one, each calf was roped and dragged near the fire where the irons were heating—not red-hot but gray-hot. The animal was then pinned down, and in less than a minute branded and ear-marked (for quick identification in winter when hair might cover the brand), and sent bawling on its way. Burning a brand is not painful, according to cowmen, and the bawling was mostly from fear.

Except for its size, the most memorable thing about the 1902 roundup was the storm that hit the camp one evening about the time the night herders went on duty. Just before it broke, the 6 L outfit was moving its herd of a thousand head up a hill, hoping to keep it separated from other nearby herds and prevent a mixup if the storm was bad. The animals were strung out for about three-quarters of a mile. George Gunn and Ray Kehiler were riding drag, prodding along the stragglers, when a great gust of wind and hail struck them. The cattle, which had been heading in the direction from which the storm came, now turned tail to run with it, and the two cowboys were caught in the thick of the stampede. Their frightened horses reared and wheeled, throwing their riders in the path of the onrushing cattle. But Gunn held on to his reins and he and Kehiler clung to the flanks of his horse as the living avalanche of beef swerved and thundered on by. Both of them then got aboard the horse and went in search of the 6 L wagon, which had been leading the herd and was near the crest of the ridge when the storm hit. Its team also had wheeled, turning so short that the wagon upset and rolled down a steep incline to the bottom of the canyon, scattering utensils and grub as it went. No one was hurt, but several were left horseless and hatless.

A member of another outfit, Dick Jones, had been sent out to relieve the day herders and hold the cattle during the supper hour until the first relief of night herders mounted guard at eight o'clock. He saw that an angry black cloud was coming up fast, and he wasted no time when the "night hawks" took over. As he reached the bed tent, the storm caught up with him and a tremendous blast of wind whirled the tent up into the air. Racing for the cook tent some twenty-five yards away, Dick saw it go sailing away like an untidy balloon. At the same moment, the saddle horses broke out of the rope corral and exploded past him. It seemed to Dick that there were hoofs coming at him from every direction, but by some miracle he was untouched. Not knowing where to find protection, he drifted across the prairie and by good luck ran into the wagon of one of the other outfits. It was staked down, and he crawled under it and hung onto the coupling-pole to be out of the hail. The wind was lifting the wagon just as high as the stakes would allow it; the whole vehicle was rocking and swaying as if it would take off at any minute. Although the storm was making a great noise, a cowhand in the wagon was praying so strenuously that Dick could hear him over the din of the elements.

When the rainsoaked, weary cowhands came into camp after that interminable night, they found wagons overturned and bed and cook tents down. Cattle of the thirteen outfits—maybe that ill-starred number thirteen had something to do with it—were hopelessly mixed, and riderless horses were scattered all up and down the White River. It took two days to capture and cut out those hundreds of horses, and get crews squared around to start cutting out and separating once more all those acres of mixed-up cattle. There was another two weeks of hard work before the wagons could be packed up and the last "so longs" said. Then the herds were headed toward their home ranges, and the Great Dakota Roundup was history.

Sources

(In some cases, excerpts from primary material have been condensed or abridged, and the punctuation modernized.)

THE SCHOOLMASTER SEES THE DEVIL

W. S. Bryan, "Daniel Boone" and "Peculiarities of Life in Daniel Boone's Missouri Settlement," *Missouri Historical Review*, III, 2 (January 1909), 89–98 and IV, 2 (January 1910), 85–87; Frederick W. Hodge (ed.), *Handbook of American Indians North of Mexico*, Bureau of American Ethnology Bulletin 30 (New York: Pageant Books, 1959), II, 164–166.

NORTHWEST TO EMPIRE

Paul Allen (ed.), *History of the Expedition Under Command of Lewis and Clark* (New York: A. L. Fowle, 1900), pp. 299–330; Bernard DeVoto (ed.), *The Journals of Lewis and Clark* (Boston: Houghton Mifflin Co., 1953), pp. 3, 4, 11, 16–17, 35–36, 42–43, 136, 152, 168–169, 171, 181–182, 185–186, 188–189, 190–191, 201, 202–203, 279; Bernard DeVoto, *The Course of Empire* (Boston: Houghton Mifflin, 1952), pp. 435–438, 448; Herbert S. Schell, *History of South Dakota* (Lincoln: University of Nebraska Press, 1961), pp. 40–42; Frederick W. Hodge (ed.), *Handbook of American Indians North of Mexico*, Bureau of American Ethnology, Bulletin 30 (New York: Pageant Books, 1959), II, 401.

DORANTO

Henry Inman and William F. Cody, *The Great Salt Lake Trail* (Topeka: Crane and Co., 1914), pp. 36–62; Herbert F. Schell, *History of South Dakota* (Lincoln: University of Nebraska Press, 1961), pp. 42–46; Bernard DeVoto (ed.), *The Journals of Lewis and Clark* (Boston: Houghton Mifflin, 1953), p. 457; Frederick W. Hodge (ed.), *Handbook of American Indians North of Mexico*, Bureau of American Ethnology, Bulletin 30 (New York: Pageant Books, 1959).

THE RACE OF DEATH

Eliphalet Price, "A Scene of the Border," *Annals of Iowa*, 1st series, VI (January 1868), 31–36; "Zachary Taylor and Old Fort Snelling," *Minnesota History*, XVIII, 1 (March 1947), 15–19; Moses M. Strong, *History of the Territory of Wisconsin* (Madison, 1885), pp. 124 ff.; Henry R. Schoolcraft, *Personal Memoirs of a Residence of Thirty Years with Indian Tribes, 1812–1842* (Philadelphia: Lippincott, Granbo, 1851), pp. 213–219, 266–267.

MOTHER LOVE

Isaac Galland, "The Indian Tribes of the West," *Annals of Iowa*, 1st series, VII, 3 (July 1869), 266–270.

ADVENTURES OF AN ENGAGÉ
Hiram M. Chittenden, *History of Early Steamboat Navigation on the Missouri River. Life and Adventures of Joseph LaBarge* (New York: Harper, 1903), I, 1–50; William E. Lass, *A History of Steamboating on the Upper Missouri* (Lincoln: University of Nebraska Press, 1962), pp. 5–11; Herbert S. Schell, *History of South Dakota* (Lincoln: University of Nebraska Press, 1961), pp. 50, 52, 68; *Nebraska: A Guide to the Cornhusker State* (New York: Hastings House, 1939), pp. 245, 267.

NICOMI
J. Sterling Morton and Albert Watkins, *Illustrated History of Nebraska* (Lincoln: Jacob North, 1903), II, 149–150; James C. Olson, *History of Nebraska* (Lincoln: University of Nebraska Press, 1954), pp. 44–51; William J. Shallcross, *Romance of a Village: The Story of Bellevue* (Omaha: Roncka Bros., 1954), pp. 35 ff.; Mrs. Harriet S. MacMurphy, "Nikumi," *Nebraska Pioneer Reminiscences* (Cedar Rapids, Iowa: Torch Press, 1916), pp. 307–321.

THE MOUNTAIN MEN
Mrs. Frances Fuller Victor, *The River of the West* (Hartford: Columbian Book Co., 1870), Chapter XII; Stanley Vestal, *Joe Meek, the Merry Mountain Man* (Lincoln: University of Nebraska Press, 1963), pp. 3–5, 28–38, 48–54, 93–96, 120–125, 160–165, 208–210.

FAT MAN'S MISERY
Colonel Prentiss Ingraham (ed.), *Seventy Years on the Frontier: Alexander Majors' Memoirs of a Lifetime on the Border* (Chicago and New York: Rand McNally & Co., 1893), pp. 32–41.

FRIDAY, THE INDIAN WHITE BOY
Rufus B. Sage, *Scenes in the Rocky Mountains* (2nd ed.; Philadelphia: Carey & Hunt, 1847), pp. 294–301; Leroy R. Hafen and W. J. Ghent, *Broken Hand: The Life Story of Thomas Fitzpatrick, Chief of the Mountain Men* (Denver: Old West Publishing Co., 1931), pp. 269–282; Frank E. Root and William E. Connolley, *The Overland Stage to California* (Topeka: privately printed, 1901), pp. 347–348.

BENT'S FORT
George Bird Grinnell, "Bent's Old Fort and Its Builder," *Collections of Kansas State Historical Society, 1919–1922* (Topeka: Kansas State Printing Plant, 1923), XV, 28–88; Henry Inman, *The Old Santa Fe Trail: The Story of a Great Highway* (Topeka: Crane & Co., 1912), pp. 28–44, 142, 278–280, 283–299, 389–393; Leroy R. Hafen and W. J. Ghent, *Broken Hand: The Life Story of Thomas Fitzpatrick, Chief of the Mountain Men* (Denver: Old West Publishing Co., 1931), p. 197.

A CONNETICUT YANKEE IN THE SANTA FE TRADE
James Josiah Webb, *Adventures in the Santa Fe Trade, 1844–1877,* ed. Ralph P. Bieber (Glendale: Arthur H. Clark Co., 1931), pp. 24–28, 128–170.

IN THE POTTER'S FIELD

Seymour Dunbar, *A History of Travel in America* (Indianapolis: Bobbs-Merrill Co., 1915), II, pp. 418–419, 428–429, 625, 651–653, 675–676.

THE SETTLERS' STRATAGEM

William M. Cockrum, *Pioneer History of Indiana* (Oakland City, Calif.: Press of Oakland City *Journal,* 1907), pp. 404–408; Roy M. Robbins, *Our Landed Heritage: The Public Domain, 1776–1936* (Lincoln: University of Nebraska Press, 1962), pp. 4–6, 16–17, 33–34.

TRADERS ON THE MISSISSIPPI

Daniel H. Brush, *Growing Up in Southern Illinois,* ed. Milo M. Quaife (Chicago: Lakeside Press, 1944), pp. 86–95; J. W. Spencer and J. M. D. Burrows, *The Early Days of Rock Island and Davenport,* ed. Milo M. Quaife (Chicago: Lakeside Press, 1942), pp. 154–161.

THE CIRCUIT RIDER AND THE SINNERS

Peter Cartwright, *Autobiography of Peter Cartwright* (New York: Cranston & Stowe, 1856), pp. 321–323, 312–316.

BARRING OUT THE TEACHER

Millard F. Kennedy and A. F. Harlow, *Schoolmaster of Yesterday* (New York: McGraw-Hill Book Co., 1940), Chapter XVIII.

PIONEER HORSE PLAY

Mrs. John H. Kinzie, *Wau-Bun: The Early Day in the North-West,* ed. Milo M. Quaife (Chicago: The Lakeside Press, 1932), pp. 341–345; *History of Grant County, Wisconsin* (Chicago: Western Historical Co., 1881).

THE SETTLERS HOLD THEIR OWN

Rebecca Burlend, *A True Story of Emigration,* ed. Milo M. Quaife (Chicago: Lakeside Press, 1936), pp. 132–139; Landt MSS, Wisconsin State Historical Society, Madison, Wisconsin; Roy M. Robbins, *Our Landed Heritage: The Public Domain 1776–1936* (Lincoln: University of Nebraska Press, 1962), pp. 18–19, 40, 48–50, 85–90.

ROLLINGSTONE

Charles Edward Russell, *A-Rafting on the Mississip'* (New York: Century Co., 1928), pp. 120, 123–128.

FASTEN DOWN THE SAFETY VALVE

Charles Edward Russell, *A-Rafting on the Mississip'* (New York: Century Co., 1928), pp. 116–119, 277–279.

THE OREGON TRAIL

John Bidwell, *Echoes of the Past,* ed. Milo M. Quaife (Chicago: Lakeside Classics, 1928), pp. 20–30, 110–125; Jesse Applegate, "A Day with the Cow Column in 1843," *Quarterly of the Oregon Historical Society,* I, 4 (December 1900), 372–373.

WHEN THE APPLE ORCHARD MOVED
   Iowa Journal of History and Politics, XXVII, 4 (October 1929), 55; *Oregon Quarterly Journal of History*, XIII, 3 (September 1912), 279.

THE MORMON TRAIL
   Thomas L. Kane, *The Mormons* (Philadelphia, 1850), pp. 206–208; Leroy R. Hafen and C. C. Rister, *Western America* (New York: Prentice-Hall, 1941), pp. 362–370; "Journal of Priddy Weeks," *Utah State Historical Quarterly*, X, 4 (October 1942), 163–164.

BY HANDCART TO ZION
   T. B. H. Stenhouse, *The Rocky Mountain Saints* (Salt Lake City: Shepard Book Co., 1904), pp. 325–326; William A. Linn, *The Story of the Mormons* (New York: Macmillan, 1902), pp. 422–423.

THE CALIFORNIA TRAIL
   "Recollections of B. F. Bonney," *Quarterly of the Oregon Historical Society*, XXIV, 1 (March 1923), 40–43; Eliza P. Donner Houghton, *Expedition of the Donner Party and Its Tragic Fate* (Los Angeles: Grafton Publishing Co., 1920), pp. 54–122; Charles F. McGlashan, *History of the Donner Party* (Sacramento: H. S. Croker Co., 1907), pp. 40–190; Ray Allen Billington, *The Far Western Frontier, 1836–1860* (New York: Harper & Row, 1956), pp. 111–115.

GOLD! GOLD!! GOLD!!!
   Evelyn Wells and Harry C. Peterson, *The Forty Niners* (New York: Doubleday, 1949), pp. 4–10; Sam Ward, *Sam Ward in the Gold Rush* (Palo Alto: Stanford University Press, 1949), pp. 86–107; Granville Stuart, *Forty Years on the Frontier*, ed. P. C. Phillips (Cleveland: Arthur H. Clark Co., 1925), II, 73–75; Rufus Rockwell Wilson, *Out of the West* (New York: Wilson-Erickson, 1936), pp. 143–146, 228–230; Lola M. Homsher (ed.), *South Pass, 1868: James Chisholm's Journal of the Wyoming Gold Rush* (Lincoln: University of Nebraska Press, 1960), pp. 211–216.

THE FORTY-NINERS
   George W. Hansen, "A Tragedy on the Oregon Trail" in Albert Watkins (ed.), *Nebraska State Historical Society Collections*, Vol. XVII (Lincoln: Nebraska State Historical Society, 1913), pp. 110–126; William E. Manley, *Death Valley in '49* (New York: Wallace Hebard, 1894), pp. 71–221; Evelyn Wells and Harry C. Peterson, *The Forty-Niners* (New York: Doubleday, 1949), pp. 186–191; Rufus Rockwell Wilson, *Out of the West* (New York: Wilson-Erickson, 1936), pp. 152–168; Leroy R. Hafen and Carl C. Rister, *Western America* (New York: Prentice-Hall, 1941), pp. 358–359.

LET HER GO, IF SHE WILL
   David R. Leeper, *The Argonauts of Forty-Nine* (South Bend, Indiana: J. B. Stoll Co., 1894), Appendix xi–xiv.

SHE PRAYED FOR THE RAVENS
   Elisha Brooks, *A Pioneer Mother of California* (San Francisco: Harr Wagner Publishing Co., 1922), pp. 10–34.

SAGEBRUSH JUSTICE
   William Audley Maxwell, *Crossing the Plains: Days of '57* (San Francisco: Sunset Publishing House, 1915), pp. 116–159.

A BUSHEL OF DOUGHNUTS
   Everett Dick, *The Sod-House Frontier, 1854–1890* (Lincoln: Johnsen Publishing Co., 1954), pp. 164–168.

LINKING OLD AND NEW FRONTIERS
   Colonel Prentiss Ingraham (ed.), *Seventy Years on the Frontier: Alexander Majors' Memoirs of a Lifetime on the Border* (Chicago and New York: Rand McNally Co., 1893), pp. 102–105; Mark Twain, *Roughing It* (New York: Harper & Bros., 1899), pp. 45–46, 53–74; Sir Richard Burton, *The Look of the West, 1860* (Lincoln: University of Nebraska Press, 1963), pp. 3–4; Mary Ann Settle and Raymond W. Settle, *Saddles and Spurs* (Harrisburg, Pennsylvania: The Stackpole Co., 1955), pp. 91–93, 159–160; James C. Olson, *History of Nebraska* (Lincoln: University of Nebraska Press, 1954), pp. 107–114.

PIKES PEAK OR BUST
   Caroline Bancroft, "The Illusive Figure of John H. Gregory," *Colorado Magazine*, XX, 4 (July 1943), 121–135; Horace Greeley, *An Overland Journey from New York to San Francisco* (New York, 1860), pp. 264–266; Donald F. Danker (ed.), *Mollie: The Journal of Mollie Dorsey Sanford in Nebraska and Colorado Territories, 1857–1866* (Lincoln: University of Nebraska Press, 1959), pp. viii–ix, 115–131.

GOLD IS WHERE YOU FIND IT
   W. Clement Eaton, "Frontier Life in Southern Arizona, 1858–1861," *Southwestern Historical Quarterly*, XXXVI, 3 (January 1933), 175–185; Grant H. Smith, *The History of the Comstock Lode, 1850–1920* (Reno: Nevada Bureau of Mines, University of Nevada Press, 1943), pp. 1–98; 292–293; J. Ross Browne, "A Peep at Washoe" *Harper's New Monthly Magazine*, XXII,, 128 (December 1860), 1–17; Ray Allen Billington, *The Far Western Frontier* (New York: Harper & Row, 1956), p. 235.

THE BIG THAW
   Lewis Crawford, *Rekindling Campfires* (Bismarck: Capital Book Co., 1926), pp. 116–127; William E. Lass, *Steamboating on the Upper Missouri* (Lincoln: University of Nebraska Press, 1962), pp. 21–37.

ABOARD THE OVERLAND STAGE
   Frank E. Root and William E. Connelley, *The Overland Stage to California* (Topeka: privately printed, 1901), pp. 363–365; Sir Richard Burton, *The Look of the West, 1860* (Lincoln: University of Nebraska Press, 1963), pp. 6, 15–16;

Stanley Vestal, *The Missouri* (Lincoln: University of Nebraska Press, 1964), p. 132; James C. Olson, *History of Nebraska* (Lincoln: University of Nebraska Press, 1954), pp. 107, 115–116; Robert Beebe David, *Finn Burnett, Frontiersman* (Glendale: Arthur H. Clark Co., 1937), pp. 97–102.

THE PRINCESS OF FORT LARAMIE

Captain Eugene F. Ware, *The Indian War of 1864* (Lincoln: University of Nebraska, 1963), pp. 407–418; Donald F. Danker (ed.), *Man of the Plains: Recollections of Luther North, 1856–1882* (Lincoln: University of Nebraska Press, 1961), pp. xi–xii.

WAR ON THE PLAINS

Grace Raymond Hebard and E. A. Brinistool, *The Bozeman Trail* (Cleveland: Arthur H. Clark Co., 1922), II, 15–18; Milo M. Quaife (ed.), *Selections from the Journal of Philippe de Trobriand* (Chicago: Lakeside Press, 1941), pp. 232–329; Winfield Freeman, "The Battle of the Arickaree" in George W. Martin (ed.), *Transactions of the Kansas State Historical Society*, Vol. VI (Topeka: State Printer, 1900), pp. 346–357; Everett Dick, *The Sod-House Frontier* (Lincoln: Johnsen Publishing Co., 1954), pp. 180–184.

A BATTLE WITH PLAINS BANDITS

Adolph Roenigk, *Pioneer History of Kansas* (Lincoln, Kansas: privately printed, 1933), pp. 51–55.

FRONTIER RAILROADING

Edwin L. Sabin, *Building the Union Pacific Railroad* (Philadelphia: J. B. Lippincott Co., 1919), pp. 244–251; Robert Edgar Riegel, *The Story of the Western Railroads* (Lincoln: University of Nebraska Press, 1964), pp. 82–91; John P. Davis, *The Union Pacific Railway* (Chicago: S. C. Griggs Co., 1894), pp. 142–149; *Denver News*, January 19, 1875, quoted in Winfield, Kansas, *Courier*, January 28, 1875; Robert G. Athearn, *Westward the Briton* (Lincoln: University of Nebraska Press, 1963), p. 17.

THE MONARCH OF THE PRAIRIES

E. Douglas Branch, *The Hunting of the Buffalo* (Lincoln: University of Nebraska Press, 1962), xxxii, 138–142, 152–168, 219–220; William F. Cody, *The Story of the Wild West: Autobiography of Buffalo Bill* (New York: Historical Publishing Co., 1888), pp. 619–628; John R. Cook, *The Border and the Buffalo* (Topeka: Crane & Co., 1907), pp. 164–167; Billy Dixon, *Life of Billy Dixon* (Dallas: P. L. Turner Co., 1927), pp. 113–129.

THE INDIANS' GIFT

Robert Beebe David, *Finn Burnett, Frontiersman* (Glendale: Arthur H. Clark Co., 1937), pp. 363–366; Frederick W. Hodge (ed.), *Handbook of American Indians North of Mexico*, Bureau of American Ethnology, Bulletin 30 (New York: Pageant Books, 1959), II, 19.

THE SOD-HOUSE FRONTIER

Walter Prescott Webb, "The Great Plains and the Industrial Revolution" in James F. Willard and Colin B. Goodykoontz (eds.), *The Trans-Mississippi West* (Boulder: University of Colorado Press, 1930), pp. 5 ff.; Cass G. Barnes, *The Sod House* (Madison, Nebraska: privately printed, 1930), pp. 57–63; John Turner, *Pioneers of the West* (Cincinnati: Jennings & Pye, 1903), pp. 75–86, 145–182.

THE PHANTOM PICCOLO PLAYER

Roy M. Robbins, *Our Landed Heritage: The Public Domain, 1776–1936* (Lincoln: University of Nebraska Press, 1962), pp. 206–216; Arthur E. Towne, *Old Prairie Days* (Otsego, Michigan: Otsego Union Press, 1941), pp. 99–105.

LOOK OUT BELOW!

Homer Croy, *Corn Country* (New York: Duell, Sloan & Pearce, 1947), pp. 113–114; Addison E. Sheldon, "A Hero of the Nebraska Frontier," *Nebraska History and Record of Pioneer Days*, I, 1 (February 1918) 5; *Custer County Beacon*, Broken Bow, Nebraska, September 5, 1895; Arthur Towne, *Old Prairie Days* (Otsego, Michigan: Otsego Union Press, 1941), pp. 306–309.

ALL KINDS OF WEATHER

E. G. Manning, "In at the Birth and Death" in George W. Martin (ed.), *Transactions of the Kansas State Historical Society*, Vol. VII (Topeka: State Printer, 1901), pp. 203–204; Sergeant J. P. Finley, *Report of the Tornados of May 29 and 30, 1879* (Washington, D.C.: Government Printing Office, 1881), pp. 71–74; Albert D. Richardson, *Beyond the Mississippi* (Philadelphia: American Publishing Co., pp. 143–144; Henry Inman, *Buffalo Jones: Forty Years of Adventure* (Topeka: Crane & Co., 1899), Chapter VII; Arthur Towne, *Old Prairie Days* (Otsego, Michigan: Otsego Union Press, 1941), pp. 180–188.

THE KITCHEN FRONTIER

Everett Dick, *The Sod-House Frontier* (Lincoln: Johnsen Publishing Co., 1954), pp. 232–242, 251–252; Laura Bower Van Nuys, *The Family Band: From the Missouri to the Black Hills, 1881–1900* (Lincoln: University of Nebraska Press, 1961), pp. 109, 119–120; Martha Ferguson McKeown, *Them Was the Days* (Lincoln: University of Nebraska Press, 1961), pp. 114–116, 118–119. 463–467.

THE TRAVELING COURTHOUSE

Tom A. McNeal, *When Kansas Was Young* (Topeka: Capper Publications, 1940), pp. 46–48; G. W. Martin (ed.), "Some Lost Towns of Kansas," *Kansas State Historical Society Collections*, Vol. XII (Topeka: State Printer, 1912), pp. 463–467.

THE LONG DRIVE

J. Frank Dobie, *A Vaquero of the Brush Country* (Boston: Little, Brown, 1942), pp. 96–100; Andy Adams, *The Log of a Cowboy* (Boston: Houghton Mifflin, 1903), pp. 62–65, 240–252, 255–257, 288–308.

"THEY WENT THATAWAY!"

Robert M. Wright, *Dodge City, the Cowboy Capital* (Wichita: Wichita Eagle Press, 1913), pp. 166–169; Tom A. McNeal, *When Kansas Was Young* (Topeka: Capper Publications, 1940), pp. 20–21; Norbert R. Mahnken, "Ogallala—Nebraska's Cowboy Capital," *Nebraska History*, XVIII, 2 (April–June 1947), 85–109; James H. Clark, "Early Days in Ogallala," *Nebraska History*, XIV, 2 (April–June 1933), 86–99; Alfred Sorenson, *The Story of Omaha* (Omaha: National Printing Co., 1923), pp. 328–337; Mari Sandoz, *Lovesong to the Plains* (New York: Harper & Row, 1961), p. 251.

WHERE THE HORSE WAS KING

Eddie Herman, "Historic Horse Race," Rapid City *Daily Journal*, May 13, 1951; Robert Sturgis, "The Real Cowboy," *Prairie Schooner*, VI, 1 (Winter 1932), 30–38.

ROAD AGENTS

Agnes Wright Spring, *The Cheyenne and Black Hills Stage and Express Route* (Glendale: Arthur H. Clark, 1949).

THE IRON HORSE TO THE RESCUE

Stewart H. Holbrook, *Holy Old Mackinaw* (New York: Macmillan, 1938), pp. 143–151.

THE LAST LAND RUSHES

Elaine Goodale Eastman, "The Ghost Dance," *Nebraska History*, XXVI, 1 (January–March 1945), 26–42; General L. W. Colby, "The Sioux Indian War of 1890–91," *Transactions and Reports of the Nebraska State Historical Society*, Vol. III (Lincoln: Nebraska State Historical Society, 1892), pp. 144–190; Merrill J. Mattes, "The Enigma of Wounded Knee," *Plains Anthropologist*, V, 9 (May 1960), 1–12; Hamilton S. Wicks, "The Opening of Oklahoma," *Chronicles of Oklahoma*, IV, 2 (June 1926), 134–139; Seth K. Humphrey, *Following the Prairie Frontier* (Minneapolis: University of Minnesota Press, 1931), pp. 229–259.

THE END OF THE OPEN RANGE

Alfred J. Mokler, *History of Natrona County, Wyoming* (Chicago: Lakeside Press, 1923), pp. 344–367; Tacetta B. Walker, *Stories of Early Days in Wyoming* (Casper: Prairie Publishing Co., 1936), pp. 89–90, 103–107; A. S. Walker, *The Banditti of the Plains* (Norman: University of Oklahoma Press, 1954), Chapters III–VII; Bert L. Hall (ed.) *Roundup Years: Old Muddy to the Black Hills* (Pierre: Reminder, Inc., 1954) pp. 285, 367–379, 422, 537; James C. Olson *History of Nebraska* (Lincoln: University of Nebraska Press, 1954), pp. 193–201.

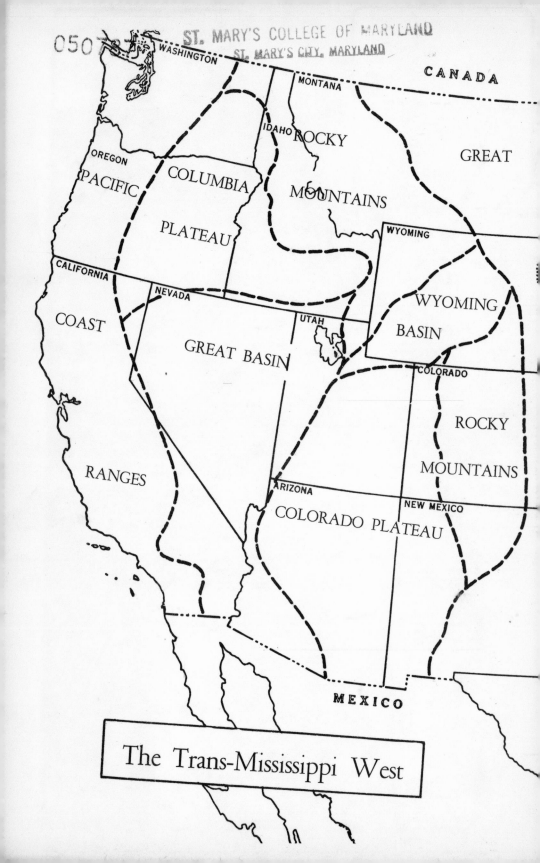

CANADA

WASHINGTON

MONTANA

OREGON

IDAHO

ROCKY

GREAT

PACIFIC

COLUMBIA

MOUNTAINS

PLATEAU

WYOMING

CALIFORNIA

NEVADA

COAST

UTAH

WYOMING

GREAT BASIN

BASIN

COLORADO

RANGES

ROCKY

MOUNTAINS

ARIZONA

NEW MEXICO

COLORADO PLATEAU

MEXICO

The Trans-Mississippi West